ARIS & PHILLIPS CLASSICAL TEXTS

SENECA
Medea

with an Introduction, Translation and Commentary by
H.M. Hine

Aris & Phillips is an imprint of
Oxbow Books

First published 2000. Reprinted 2007.

ISBN 0-85668-692-1
ISBN 978-0-85668-692-4

A CIP record for this book is available from the British Library

Printed in Great Britain
by CPI Antony Rowe, Eastbourne

Contents

Preface

In line with the aims of the series, this edition is directed primarily at students, both those who will read the play in Latin, and those who will read it in translation. At the same time I hope my edition has something to offer more advanced scholars.

In 1974 C. D. N. Costa began the preface to his edition of Seneca's *Medea* by saying 'There is no detailed commentary in English on a Senecan tragedy.' Much has changed since then, for Costa was one of the pioneers in the renewal of serious interest in Seneca's tragedies among English-speaking scholars during the last quarter of the twentieth century. My edition owes much to his, and has also been able to benefit from the scholarly work that has appeared since he wrote. In that period nobody has contributed more to the establishment of the text than O. Zwierlein. I have not looked at any manuscripts myself, but for the manuscript readings in my select apparatus I rely primarily on his Oxford Classical Text (1986), supplemented by the reports of the Michigan fragment in Markus and Schwendner (1997), and occasionally by Chaumartin (1996). I print a different text from Zwierlein at lines 23, 115, 242, 307, 660a, 747, 886 and 905, and I accept the authenticity of 242-3 and 746; I also have a different punctuation at some points. In the colometry of the anapaests I follow Zwierlein.

My translation has no literary pretensions: it tries to compromise between being close enough to the Latin to help those reading the original text, and remaining readable in its own right. It is a prose translation, but it is set out in lines that correspond, as closely as English sentence-structure will allow, to the lines of the Latin. The reasons for this are, first, to facilitate comparison between the Latin and the English; secondly, to help users of the translation to pinpoint a particular passage for which they have the Latin line numbers; thirdly, to give readers of the translation some awareness of the different metrical forms used in the Latin. But it should be emphasised that, because of differences between Latin and English word-order, often there is not complete correspondence between the lines of text and translation. In the commentary the lemmata are keyed to the translation, but the line numbers are those of the Latin.

It is a pleasure to thank various people who have helped me during the long gestation of this book. I was able to start serious work on the *Medea* during a term spent as Visiting Professor at Stanford University in 1994, and enjoyed and benefited from detailed discussions of the play with Brendon Reay. Over the years I have tried out various ideas about Senecan tragedy on students and colleagues at the University of St Andrews, and have learnt from their reactions. Malcolm Campbell has willingly responded to various queries. Adrian Gratwick and Malcolm Willcock, the series editor, both read through drafts of the entire work, and their detailed comments have led to many corrections and improvements. But I have vi

sometimes resisted their good advice, or have had afterthoughts, and all remaining faults are entirely my own responsibility. Malcolm Willcock also helped with the proofs.

Finally my thanks to my family, Rosalind, Catriona and Jonathan, for all their support during the writing of this book.

Harry Hine   St Andrews
                                                                                                          March 2000

Introduction

1 The Author

1.1 Seneca's life and career[1]

The public career of Lucius Annaeus Seneca, the Younger, illustrates the opportunities and the perils that faced a talented and ambitious man in the first century A.D. He was born at Corduba in Spain between 4 B.C. and A.D. 1, and died in Italy in A.D. 65. His father, Seneca the Elder, was of equestrian status, and the son pursued a senatorial career, rising to the suffect consulship in 55 or 56.[2] But the formal magistracies he held were less significant than the informal power he exercised during the reign of Nero.

He came to Rome as a young boy, and was educated for a public career in the law courts and Senate. His progress into public life was delayed, both because in his early years he devoted much of his energy to philosophy, and because serious illness required a period of convalescence in Egypt. Once back in Italy, in around 31, he rapidly rose to prominence as an orator—such prominence that we hear that the emperor Gaius Caligula, out of jealousy, would have had him put to death, had he not been assured that Seneca was in any case dying from illness. Whatever the truth of this anecdote, Gaius was murdered after a brief reign (37-41), and Seneca survived, only to find himself, soon after the start of Claudius' reign, banished to the island of Corsica, where he spent eight years in exile. He had been found guilty of adultery with one of the women of the imperial family, a charge which he firmly denied, and which may have been a pretext for removing him from Rome. Plainly he was moving in high and dangerous circles and had made enemies close to the emperor. He owed his prominence to a combination of factors, including his success as an orator, his powerful family connections, and perhaps, too, the sharp wit that appears some years later in the *Apocolocyntosis*, his satire on the deified Claudius, and occasionally in his philosophical writings.

Eventually in 49 he was recalled from exile, thanks to the influence of Agrippina, Claudius' new wife, who made Seneca tutor to her son Nero. Britannicus was Claudius's son by an earlier marriage, but Agrippina ensured that her own son Nero became Claudius' successor. In 54 Claudius died and Nero was declared emperor. Seneca became one of his closest advisers, along with Burrus, the prefect of the praetorian guard. Seneca wrote speeches for Nero, and advised on public affairs. He shared some of Nero's unpopularity, particularly in 59, when it was widely believed that Nero had ordered the murder of his mother Agrippina, and

---

1   See *OCD³* on 'Annaeus Seneca (2), Lucius'; Griffin in Costa (1974), 1-38; Griffin (1976).
2   From now on all dates in this section are A.D.

that Seneca had been forced to condone this act and even justify it publicly. In 62 Burrus died, and Seneca's power was weakened as Nero turned to other advisers. Seneca effectively withdrew from court life, but this did not save him from being charged with involvement in the Pisonian conspiracy against Nero in 65, for which he was ordered to commit suicide. Tacitus (*Ann.* 15.60-5) was uncertain whether Seneca was really involved, and we should emulate his caution.

1.2   Seneca and philosophy[3]

Seneca maintained his interest in philosophy throughout his lifetime, and wrote many philosophical works, of which a considerable number survive, ranging in date from *To Marcia, on Consolation* (*Dialogue* 6), written probably in 39 or 40, to *Natural Questions* and *Moral Letters* written in the 60s. His primary philosophical allegiance was to the Stoic school, yet he was no doctrinaire Stoic, and was ready to disagree with his Stoic predecessors. He also expressed admiration for philosophers of other schools whom he had heard in his youth, and he had a sympathetic though critical interest in the philosophy of Epicurus.

For Seneca, as for most philosophers of the Roman period, philosophy was a guide to living one's life and not just an intellectual pursuit, though it was that too. Here it is impossible to summarise all his philosophical views, and indeed they resist tidy summary, but some of the ideas that potentially relate to the plays are as follows.

Goodness. The Stoics argued that the terms 'good' and 'bad' should properly be confined to the moral sphere. We, like the Greeks and Romans, apply the terms to all sorts of other things, such as a good meal, a good game, good weather, although we would recognise that these are not moral evaluations. Those examples may be trivial, but the Stoics also insisted that health, wealth, freedom, life, and many other things by which most people set great store, are not really good either, nor are their opposites bad. They argued that these are morally indifferent, since, after all, to learn whether a person is healthy or sick, slave or free, alive or dead, tells us nothing about the person's moral worth. The Stoics agree that, given the choice, we shall indeed prefer health to sickness, wealth to poverty, freedom to slavery, pleasure to pain, but that does not make these things morally good or bad.

Happiness. 'Happiness' is the conventional translation of the Greek *eudaimonia*, Latin *beatitas* or *beatitudo*,[4] or some recent writers use the translation '(human) flourishing'. Ancient philosophers were concerned to help people live the best possible life, but they disagreed about the constituents of such a life, and about the criteria that should guide us in deciding how to live. The Stoics insisted that only

---

3   For general accounts of Stoic philosophy see e.g.: Sandbach (1975); Sharples (1996).
4   Seneca does not use either of these terms, but uses *beata uita*, 'the happy life', or similar expressions.

moral virtue is necessary to happiness; all the other things conventionally called 'good' are not necessary, and indeed do not even increase one's happiness. Other Stoic descriptions of our true goal in life are 'living according to nature', or 'according to reason.'

Emotions. The orthodox Stoic view of the emotions, or passions, as the Greek and Roman words are often translated, was an intellectualist one: that is, the Stoics maintained that emotions are caused by, or consist of, beliefs of certain kinds. Furthermore, the Stoics said that the beliefs that produce emotions are all false, and the emotions themselves are harmful. Therefore emotions ought all to be eradicated by replacing the false beliefs with true ones; in other words, the correct use of reason will free us from all emotions. For example, if I get angry because somebody has slandered me, the Stoic would interpret the anger as caused by beliefs such as the following: 'This slander has harmed me. I ought to correct the falsehoods that have been put about concerning myself. The slanderer ought to be punished, and I should do something about it.' These beliefs are false, in Stoic terms, because slander is not a morally bad thing for me,[5] therefore it does not affect my happiness, and so I do not need to do anything about it. If I hold correct beliefs then I shall not get angry. The intellectualist position adopted by the Stoics was opposed to the Platonic view, which said that our souls have not just a rational part, but also non-rational parts, from which anger and other emotions spring; therefore emotions are not directly amenable to reason. It was also opposed to the Aristotelian view, which held that moderate emotions can be good, but extreme emotions are to be avoided.

The cosmos. Whereas the Epicureans argued that the universe consists of atoms jostling at random in the void, the Stoics argued that the universe is a physical continuum, with no void in it, and with every part connected to, and potentially affected by, every other part. Whereas the Epicureans said that everything is the product of chance movements of the atoms, the Stoics said that everything happens under the guidance of a controlling divine reason, which can also be called nature, or god, or fate.

1.3 The date of composition of Seneca's tragedies
There are ten tragedies in the Senecan corpus.[6] It is generally agreed that one of them, the *Octavia*, is not by Seneca himself, but was written by an imitator after his death. Another play, *Hercules on Oeta*, is of disputed authorship: there are significant differences in style and language from the other genuinely Senecan plays, so that most scholars think it is not by Seneca; but there is also a view that it could

---

5   I.e. it is not morally bad for the target of the slander, although spreading slander may be
     a morally bad act for the agent.
6   For a brief account of the Latin manuscripts in which the tragedies are preserved, see
     Introduction §7.

have been written by Seneca some years later than the other plays. There is precious little evidence to date the genuine plays, and we should not assume that they were all written during the same period of Seneca's life. One piece of external evidence comes from Quintilian (*Inst.* 8.3.31), who, writing at the end of the first century A.D., records that he heard Seneca debate a point of tragic diction with Pomponius Secundus, an event that can be dated to the late 40s or early 50s. If Seneca was indulging in public debate about tragedy it is likely that he had already written some plays. Another piece of evidence is the presence of parallels in phrasing between the *Hercules Furens*[7] and the *Apocolocyntosis*, the satire on the deification of the emperor Claudius written in 54 shortly after Claudius's death. It is normally thought more likely that the *Apocolocyntosis* parodies the tragedy, rather than that the tragedy gives a 'straight' reworking of material from the humorous work. Such arguments are never entirely safe, and if one admits the possibility of a lost common source influencing both works, then the argument is weakened. Nevertheless the more probable inference is that the *Hercules* was written by A.D. 54.

The dating question was given new direction by Fitch (1981), who analysed the relative frequency of several distinct stylistic phenomena in the individual plays, and argued that the plays fall into three groups, representing successive stages in the development of Seneca's dramatic technique: I *Agamemnon, Phaedra, Oedipus*; II *Medea, Troades, Hercules*; III *Thyestes, Phoenissae.* No evidence has yet been offered to contradict this relative dating, and if a pre-Neronian date is accepted for the *Hercules*, that implies that the *Medea* too was written before Nero's reign.

The argument is not absolutely secure, and provides no indication of how much earlier the *Medea* was. One thing is certain, that we must not take it for granted, as some writers have, that the play is of Neronian date. Nisbet (1990), 96-7, has argued on internal grounds that a Neronian date is implausible, and that *Medea* 375-9 fits best in Claudius' reign, as a compliment to his invasion of Britain. But an earlier date cannot be ruled out.

1.4 Seneca and poetry[8]

Seneca's prose works never mention his tragedies. They frequently quote or refer to earlier poetry, and thus reveal something about his knowledge of literature. On the Latin side he most frequently quotes Vergil (chiefly the *Aeneid*), and next most frequently Ovid (chiefly the *Metamorphoses*); there are some misquotations of a kind that suggest he relied on memory, and so was familiar with these writers. A considerable number of other Latin writers are referred to occasionally. On the Greek side Homer is referred to fairly frequently, less often cited, and a large

---

7   Seneca probably called this play just *Hercules*, but it is conventionally called *Hercules Furens* (*Hercules Mad* or *Raging*) to distinguish it from *Hercules on Oeta.*

8   See Mazzoli (1970); Dingel (1974).

number of other writers are occasionally mentioned or quoted, usually in Latin translation.

The prose works provide scant evidence of familiarity with tragedy. The few references to Greek tragedy either are well-known poetic tags, or probably come from earlier philosophical works or poetic anthologies, rather than from personal familiarity with the tragedians (*Clem.* 2.2.2; *Nat.* 4a.2.17; *Epist.* 49.12, 115.14-5). Evidence of familiarity with Roman tragedy is not much greater: he makes clear his distaste for the archaic style of Ennius and other early writers (*Epist.* frag. ap. Gell. 12.2.2-13, cf. *Epist.* 108.33-5). His two quotations from Ennius' tragedies are of lines that were quoted earlier by Cicero, and so could be known via him or another intermediary (*Apoc.* 8.3, *Dial.* 11.11.2, cf. Cic. *Rep.* 1.30, *Diu.* 2.30, *Tusc.* 3.28). He three times quotes a famous phrase from Accius (*Clem.* 1.12.4, 2.2.2, *Dial.* 3.20.4), once a well-known tag from Naevius (*Epist.* 102.16). There is even less evidence of knowledge of Augustan or later tragedy: one of the two anonymous tragic quotations in *Epist.* 80.7-8 may be post-Republican.

In his prose works Seneca makes a number of passing remarks about poetry, which are worth briefly reviewing (see Nussbaum [1993]; Schiesaro [1997]; Burnett [1998], 8-18). He is well aware that poetry can have different effects on different readers, and he thinks that some of the effects are harmful. Following a long philosophical tradition, he says that poetry purveys many falsehoods, which gain plausibility from the vibrancy and attractiveness of poetic language. He singles out false stories about the underworld that encourage people to be afraid of death; false stories about the gods behaving in morally reprehensible ways, which blunt people's moral sensibilities; false stories that encourage people to place an unwarranted value on wealth (see Nussbaum [1993], 124). Such dangers were widely recognised in antiquity, and young people could be taught strategies for reading poetry properly, so that they were both well informed about the literary techniques and conventions that writers use, and well equipped to read literature in an ethically alert fashion. Seneca, by pointing out that poetry can persuade people to believe falsehoods, is implicitly recognising that readers can be taught to recognise those falsehoods.

Seneca also believes that poetry has the ability to give powerful expression to truths, and particularly ethical truths. For instance, he quotes words of Cleanthes to this effect: 'Just as our breath produces a clearer sound when a trumpet draws it through a long, narrow tube and finally emits it through a broader opening, so the narrow constraints of poetry make our ideas clearer' (*Epist.* 108.10). But poetry does not exist just to convey straightforward moral truths. Seneca is aware that works of literature can be appropriated by different philosophical positions: there were Stoic, Epicurean, Platonic and Aristotelian readings of Homer (*Epist.* 88.5). On the other hand he recognises that there is a power in poetry that can arouse strong emotions (*Epist.* 115.12-15). However, closer analysis shows that drama does not produce full-blown emotions, in that what we see on stage does not spur us to action (such as running away or intervening) in the way that what we see in real life may do (*Dial.* 4.2.1-6).

From Seneca's scattered remarks, it is not possible to construct a coherent theory of poetry, nor did he necessarily have a coherent theory at all. Furthermore, his surviving works never discuss the nature of tragedy as such. However, the very diversity of his remarks can be taken to show that he had a firm sense of the complexity of poetry and of our responses to it, and in that case he would not have been surprised if his own tragedies evoked complex responses.

2 The Development of Tragedy

2.1 Tragedy in Greece[9]

Greek tragedy emerged in Greece in the late 6th century B.C., and is known to us mainly through the surviving corpus of over thirty tragedies written in the 5th century B.C. by Aeschylus, Sophocles and Euripides. At first, tragedies were specially written for performance at Athenian religious festivals, principally at the City Dionysia. They were performed in open-air theatres by a chorus and up to three speaking actors, plus other non-speaking actors when necessary. Chorus and actors wore costumes and masks, and the chorus danced as they sang their odes to musical accompaniment. At each festival several poets competed, and a prize was awarded to the best.

Aeschylus died in 456/5 B.C., and Euripides and Sophocles within a few months of each other in 407/6 B.C. Over four hundred years intervened before the birth of Seneca, and from those centuries no tragedy survives complete, save the *Rhesus*, attributed to Euripides, but probably written in the fourth century by an unidentified writer. In the absence of entire plays written between the *Rhesus* and Seneca, our understanding of developments in tragedy during that period relies on the surviving fragments of numerous Greek and Roman playwrights, on second-hand reports about tragedies and their performance, and on discussion of tragedy in ancient works of literary criticism. From such sources we know that as early as the fifth century the practice arose of reviving older tragedies for stage performances, in Athens and elsewhere. At the same time, dramatic competitions with new plays continued in the Greek world for centuries, until well after the death of Seneca.[10] Stone theatres were built throughout the Greek world, and tragedy, like comedy, became not just an Attic, but a Panhellenic phenomenon. Some of the features of later Greek tragedy can be established: thus, for instance, there was a diminution in the dramatic unity of plays, with choral odes tending to become more detached from

---

9   See *OCD³* on 'tragedy, Greek'.
10   See *TGF* Vol. 1, pp. 16, 20-21; Dio Chrys. *Or.* 19; Jones (1993).

the action, dialogue scenes becoming more self-contained, and dramatic time being treated more loosely. Senecan tragedy shares such features (see Tarrant [1978]).

2.2 Writers of tragedy at Rome

In Rome, the first known performance of a tragedy in Latin took place in 240 B.C. Whereas a sizeable corpus of comedies by Plautus and Terence has survived, no early Roman tragedy survives complete. The earliest tragedians were L. Livius Andronicus and Cn. Naevius, both of whom were writing between 240 and about 200 B.C. In the next century the main figures were Q. Ennius (239-169 B.C.), M. Pacuvius (ca. 220-130 B.C.), and L. Accius (170-ca. 86 B.C.). The earliest tragedies were either Latin versions of older Greek tragedies, or entirely new plays whose plots were based on episodes from Roman history, called *praetextae*. The only surviving example of this Roman form of tragedy is the *Octavia*, written much later, after Seneca's death, and included by our manuscripts in the corpus of Senecan tragedy (see §1.3 above). None of the men known to have written tragedy at Rome in the 3rd and earlier 2nd centuries was of equestrian or senatorial status, and some were not Roman citizens by birth. From the quantity of known titles of their plays, and from other biographical evidence, it seems that for most of them writing tragedy (and in some cases other forms of poetry) was their profession.[11] Their plays were usually performed at religious festivals, and were financed by wealthy aristocratic patrons.

When we turn to the first centuries B.C. and A.D., the profile of writers of tragedy changes. For a start, we know the names of more than thirty writers of tragedy in these two centuries, compared with just half a dozen or so in the earlier period. This may reflect the more abundant evidence for the later period, and the way that in the earlier period a few eminent tragedians totally eclipsed lesser contemporaries, but even so it shows that writing tragedy by no means lost its popularity in the late Republic and early empire. A more striking trend is that, although some of these later writers are otherwise unknown, a significant proportion are prominent figures best known for their political, military or other literary activities. Those known in the political sphere include: C. Iulius Caesar Strabo, patrician, aedile in 90 B.C., leading orator; Julius Caesar the dictator, who is said to have written a tragedy in his youth; Cicero's brother Quintus, whose tragedies included four written in sixteen days in 54 B.C. while he was serving with Caesar in

---

11   See Gratwick in *CHCL* 2, 127-37; *OCD³* on: Livius Andronicus, a freedman, i.e. ex-slave; Naevius, background uncertain; Ennius, a Messapian, given Roman citizenship later in life; Pacuvius, from south Italy; Accius, from a municipal freedman's family; Pompilius, whose origins are unknown. There is uncertainty about the date, and nothing is known about the origins, of the Acilius who wrote a version of Sophocles' *Electra*. On the other hand, C. Titius was an *eques* (see *OCD³* on 'Titius (*RE* 7), Gaius'). The earliest playwrights wrote comedy and tragedy (and epic); Pacuvius and Accius were the first to specialise in tragedy.

Britain; C. Asinius Pollio, a prominent military supporter of Caesar, and a historian; Augustus, who began a tragedy but did not complete it; P. Pomponius Secundus, active in the reigns of Tiberius, Gaius and Claudius (see §1.3 above); and the younger Pliny, who wrote a kind of tragedy in Greek at the age of fourteen. Well-known writers in other genres who also turned their hand to tragedy include (besides Julius Caesar, Pollio and Pliny, already mentioned): L. Varius Rufus, a contemporary of Vergil's; Ovid, who wrote a *Medea* that does not survive; Persius, who wrote a tragedy on a Roman theme in his youth; and Lucan, said to have left an uncompleted *Medea*.[12] From the number of military and political figures who turned their hand to tragedy, one may guess that writing a tragedy was a challenge that not infrequently appealed to men with poetic ambitions; for someone who was not content with writing epigrams and other light-weight poetry, writing a tragedy was perhaps a realistic goal for one's leisure time, whereas writing full-scale epic was not. So it is not surprising that a public figure and writer of Seneca's stature should also have turned his hand to writing tragedy.

All these men were amateur tragedians, when compared to an Ennius or an Accius, and one must wonder how much experience they had of the practicalities of stagecraft and of dealing with actors. But their plays did not have to be staged: they could be read to a small audience by the writer, or circulated in book form (see §2.3, §6 below).

---

12   C. Iulius Caesar, *Oedipus*: Suet. *Iul.* 56.7; Q. Tullius Cicero: Cic. *Q. fr.* 3.1.13, 3.5.7; C. Asinius Pollio: Hor. *Carm.* 2.1.9-12, Tac. *Dial.* 21.7; Augustus, *Ajax*: Suet. *Aug.* 85.2, Macr. *Sat.* 2.4.2; P. Pomponius Secundus: Plin. *Epist.* 7.17.10-2, Quint. 8.3.31, 10.1.98, Tac. *Ann.* 11.13, 12.28; Pliny: Plin. *Epist.* 7.4.2; Ovid, *Medea*: Quint. *Inst.* 10.1.98, Tac. *Dial.* 12.6; L. Varius Rufus: Ovid, *Ex P.* 4.16.31, Quint. 10.1.98, Tac. *Dial.* 12.6; Persius: Probus, *Vita Persi*; Lucan, Vacca, *Vita Lucani*. Others reliably attested as having written tragedies include Santra, *Nuntii/Nuptiae Bacchi* (Non. 78, 104 M.); C. Iulius Caesar Strabo, *Adrastus, Teuthras, Tecmesa* (Cic. *Brut.* 177, *De orat.* 3.30, Asc. *Sc.* 22); Gracchus, *Thyestes, Atalante, Peliades* (frr. 1-3 Ribbeck; Ovid, *Ex P.* 4.16.31); L. Cornelius Balbus minor (praetexta about himself; Cic. *Fam.* 10.32.3); 'Lynceus' (Prop. 2.34.41-2); Turranius (Ovid, *Ex P.* 4.16.29); Mamercus Aemilius Scaurus, *Atreus* (Tac. *Ann.* 6.29, Suet. *Tib.* 61.3, Dio 58.24.3); and Curiatius Maternus, *Cato, Thyestes* (Tac. *Dial.* 2.1, 3.3). Less reliable are statements in the ancient commentators on Vergil and Horace that the following wrote tragedies: Alfenus Varus (Serv. *Buc.* 3.20, 6.3), Cassius (Parmensis?) Etruscus, *Thyestes* (Porph. Hor. *Epist.* 1.4.3, *Serm.* 1.10.61-2), Titius (Hor. *Epist.* 1.3.9-14 and schol.). Martial and Juvenal, and their scholia, mention several other writers of tragedy, who may be real writers, or some may be fictions—but even their fictions needed some plausibility, and suggest that writing tragedy was still popular: Memor (Mart. 11.9-10); Canius Rufus (Mart. 3.20.1-7); Ligurinus (?*Thyestes*, Mart. 3.45); Bassus (Mart. 5.53); Varro (Mart. 5.30); Tucca (Mart. 12.94); Cordus (Schol. *Iuu.* 1.2); Faustus (*Iuu.* 7.12); Paccius (*Iuu.* 7.12); Rubrenus Lappa (*Iuu.* 7.71-2).

2.3 The Roman theatre[13]

At Rome, as in Greece, tragedy was originally performed at annual religious festivals, and also on special occasions such as temple dedications or aristocratic funerals. For almost two centuries, performances took place on temporary wooden stages erected for each occasion, for there was no permanent stone theatre in Rome until Pompey dedicated his in 55 B.C. That was followed by the theatres of Balbus in 13 B.C. and of Marcellus in 13 or 11 B.C. The first three centuries A.D. were a great age of theatre building in other cities in Italy and throughout the Roman world. These theatres were used for a variety of popular entertainments, including mime (comic sketches with speaking actors), and pantomime (more like mime in the modern sense: a silent dancer represented scenes that were described in a choral song).[14] But it is uncertain how frequently tragedies were performed in these theatres. In the lifetime of Cicero we hear of tragic performances, but they are mainly revivals of old plays: significantly, Pompey celebrated the opening of his new theatre not with a newly commissioned play but with revivals of plays by Livius Andronicus and Accius (Cic. *Fam.* 7.1.2). On the other hand, in 29 B.C. the *Thyestes* of Varius Rufus was performed at the games celebrating the battle of Actium, and Augustus gave the author a large reward (Ovid, *Ex P.* 4.16.31; Quint. 10.1.98; Tac. *Dial.* 12.6). Tacitus mentions unruly behaviour by a theatre audience when Pomponius Secundus was staging his work in A.D. 47 (*Ann.* 11.13); this is the only direct reference to the staging of tragedy in Italy during Seneca's lifetime. The tiny number of references to conventional performances of tragedy has often been interpreted as an indication that performances were very rare in the early empire; but this is not necessarily the case, for perhaps they were rarely noteworthy in a way that interested our historical sources. Our sources several times refer to Nero's fondness for acting tragic parts on stage, but the context of his performances is unclear. We do not know whether they took place at regular festivals or were special events laid on by the emperor, nor whether they were performances of entire plays or just of selected scenes, nor whether they were Roman tragedies or Greek ones, or both (see Schmidt [1990]; Edwards [1994]). However, performance in large public theatres was not the only possibility: small private theatres are attested (see Suet. *Dom.* 7.1; S. *Nat.* 7.32.3; Jones [1991]).

It is sometimes argued that, for writers such as Seneca, writing for performance on stage had been superseded by writing for recitation in a public hall or at a private gathering. Already in the fourth century B.C. Aristotle had observed that tragedies were being written that could only be fully appreciated by reading them, though that perhaps refers to private reading rather than recitations.[15] There is certainly clear evidence of tragedies being read in public by the author. For instance, in Tacitus'

---

13   See Beacham (1992).
14   See *OCD³* on 'mime' and 'pantomime'; Gratwick in *CHCL* 2, 77-80.
15   Arist. *Rhet.* 1413b12-4; cf. *OCD³* on 'Chaeremon (1)'.

Dialogus, written at the end of the first century A.D., but portraying a fictional conversation set in the early 70s A.D., the poet Curiatius Maternus is described reading his tragedies to a circle of friends.

However, it should not be assumed that such recitation was an end in itself. Maternus's play *Cato* was going to be available in book form for people to read (*Dial.* 3.3). The recitation, whether by chance or design, provided an opportunity for friends to suggest improvements, although in this case Maternus rejects his friends' urgent advice to tone down the political content of the play. We know of other recitations that were occasions for friendly criticism: there was a story of how Accius read his latest play to the elderly Pacuvius (Gell. 13.2), and the younger Pliny tells how the tragedian Pomponius appealed to the crowd over the heads of his friends, when he disagreed with their criticisms (*Epist.* 7.17.10-2; admittedly we have to infer that the context here was a public recitation). Recitation may well have played a role in Seneca's case too, but not, in all likelihood, as an end in itself. The proper question to ask is whether he envisaged his tragedies circulating principally in book form, as it seems Maternus did, or whether he also expected to see his plays performed on stage. A closely related question is to what extent Seneca and his contemporaries knew earlier tragedies from reading them as opposed to seeing them performed. Whatever the answer to these questions—and there is no direct evidence to help us—it seems inherently likely that they regarded all tragedies, including Seneca's, as in principle suitable for stage performance. But it is important to ask how well his plays work on stage in practice (see further §6 below).

3 Seneca and the Myth of Medea

3.1 Summary of the plot of Seneca's *Medea*

Act One: The play is set in Corinth. Medea, in a monologue, complains that Jason is divorcing her so that he can marry king Creon's daughter, Creusa. Medea plans to kill Creusa and her family, and to devise some grim form of vengeance on Jason.

First Choral Ode: The Chorus prays for the wedding of Jason and Creusa.

Act Two: Medea, with her resolve to seek vengeance now strengthened, discusses with her Nurse the best tactics, and then confronts Creon. She is unable to persuade him to revoke the sentence of banishment from Corinth, but she does obtain permission to stay in Corinth for a few hours longer.

Second Choral Ode: The Chorus reflects on the voyage of the Argonauts and the excessive daring of those first sailors. Medea, in their view, is a fitting reward for such a voyage.

Act Three: The Nurse voices her apprehension about what Medea will do. Medea confronts Jason, who tries in vain to defend his actions. During the confrontation he reveals the depth of his love for his children, and that gives Medea the idea of using them to punish him. At the end of the Act she tells the Nurse of her plan to send poisoned gifts to Creusa.

Third Choral Ode: The Chorus reflects on how many of the Argonauts have met untimely deaths, and prays that Jason may be spared a similar fate.

Act Four: The Nurse describes how Medea has begun her magical rituals to poison the wedding gifts. Medea appears on stage and completes the rituals, then summons her children to take the gifts to Creusa.

Fourth Choral Ode: A brief Ode in which the Chorus voices its intense fears about what Medea may do.

Act Five: A Messenger briefly reports that Medea's gifts have caused the death of Creusa and Creon, and have set fire to the royal palace. Medea appears and in a long monologue rejoices at what she has done, but is torn between her love for her sons and her intention to kill them in order to punish Jason. The turning point comes when she sees the Furies approaching with the ghost of her brother Apsyrtus, who seeks vengeance for his own murder. She kills the first of her sons. Jason is heard approaching with armed men, so she goes on the roof of the house with the remaining son, carrying the corpse of the first. From the roof she taunts Jason. She remains deaf to his appeals to spare the other son, whom she kills. At the end of the play she flies off in her serpent-drawn chariot, leaving Jason with the corpses of his sons.

3.2 The myth of Medea

Medea's murder of her own children is one of the most famous stories from Greek mythology, and yet in the earliest versions of the myth she did not murder them. Like all major Greek myths, the story of Medea was told and retold in different forms at different times and places, in literature and in the visual arts. The earliest literary accounts of Medea are brief and usually relate to only one episode in her life, but eventually she acquired a full biography. The action of Seneca's play covers just one day, though a crucial one, in her life. But there are copious allusions to earlier events in her life with which Seneca obviously expects the reader to be familiar. The following is a brief account of her life, largely consistent with the allusions in Seneca's play; but some details on which Seneca is not specific— including, importantly, the events that follow the action of the play—are filled in from other sources, and some variant versions are mentioned.

(a) *Medea and the Argonauts*

When Jason reached manhood, Pelias, the half-brother of Jason's father Aeson, sent him to bring back the golden fleece,[16] which came from the ram which had once carried off Phrixus and Helle to safety. The fleece had ended up in the kingdom of Colchis, at the eastern end of the Black Sea, where king Aeetes had it guarded by a dragon. Pelias was confident that Jason would not return alive from the mission. With the help of Pallas Athena, Jason had the Argo built, the first-ever sea-going ship.[17] He gathered a crew that included most of the great heroes of Greece, such as Orpheus, Hercules, Castor and Pollux. These heroes were known as the Argonauts, which in Greek means 'Argo-sailors'. They set sail and, after a series of adventures, reached Colchis.

Jason explained his mission to Aeetes, who did not refuse outright to give him the golden fleece, but said that first he must yoke two fire-breathing bulls,[18] and use them to plough a field and sow the teeth of a dragon. The task seemed impossible, but Aeetes' daughter Medea, who was skilled in magic, had fallen in love with Jason, and gave him a magic ointment that protected him against the bulls. She also warned him that armed warriors would grow up when he sowed the teeth, but told him that he had only to throw a stone among them, and they would start fighting and kill each other. With her help he completed the task, then by her magic she put to sleep the dragon that was guarding the fleece. Jason set sail for home with the fleece,[19] taking Medea with him to Greece in order to marry her, as he had promised to do if she helped him.

Aeetes had earlier tried to kill Jason and his men after he yoked the bulls and sowed the teeth, and he now set off in pursuit of the Argonauts. But Medea had brought her young brother Apsyrtus with her, and she killed him, dismembered his corpse, and scattered the pieces, so that Aeetes' pursuit was held up while he searched for the remnants of his son.[20] The Argo thus escaped, and with Medea's help survived further dangers before returning to Iolcus.[21]

(b) *Medea at Iolcus*

When Jason and Medea returned to Iolcus, it might have been expected that he would recover his throne and the two of them would settle down to a happy life

---

16   See comm. on 133-4 for the varied accounts of the legality or illegality of Pelias' position in Iolcus, and of his motives for sending Jason to get the golden fleece.
17   See comm. on 366 for different accounts of the building of the Argo; and introductory comm. on the second choral ode, 301-79, for other claimants to the first ship.
18   See on 241 on the number of bulls.
19   For other accounts of how he obtained the fleece, see on 472-3.
20   See on 452-3 for the different accounts of Apsyrtus' death.
21   This account skips over the variants in the descriptions of the routes taken to and from Colchis, and the adventures encountered on the way; for discussion of points of immediate relevance to Seneca see comm. on 342-6, 618, 622, 652-3, 654-5.

together. But that did not happen, because of the vengeance that Medea devised against Pelias, the usurper of the throne. She managed to convince his daughters that, with her knowledge of herbs, she could help them to rejuvenate their ageing father, but she did not give them the right herbs, and so they unwittingly killed him (see comm. on 133-4). As a consequence Pelias's son, Acastus, drove Jason and Medea out of Iolcus, and pursued them, seeking vengeance.

(c) Medea at Corinth

Medea had a close connection with Corinth, where there was a cult of her children in historical times (Burnett [1998], 219 and n. 106). In one version she was credited with rescuing Corinth from plague or famine. According to another early version, her father Aeetes was originally from Corinth, but had emigrated to Colchis, and when the throne of Corinth fell vacant, the people invited his daughter Medea and Jason back to be their rulers.[22] But according to what became the standard version, which is followed by Seneca, Jason and Medea came to Corinth when they escaped from Iolcus. At Corinth Creon was king, and Jason divorced Medea and married his daughter, variously called Glauce or Creusa. In revenge Medea killed Creon and the daughter.

At Corinth, too, there occurred the deaths of Medea's children—but there were several accounts of how this came about. One story said that the Corinthians killed them in revenge after Medea had killed Creon (Schol. Eur. *Med.* 264). Another said that Medea tried to protect her children, or to make them immortal, but inadvertently caused their death (Schol. Pi. *Ol.* 13.74g, Eumelus fr. 3; Paus. 2.3.10-1); and, some added, the Corinthians spread a false rumour that she had murdered them. Finally, there was the version that Medea killed the children deliberately in order to avenge herself on Jason—in extant literature this story is first found in Euripides, but it is disputed whether the innovation was his, or occurred earlier in a *Medea* by the tragedian Neophron. An ancient source says that Neophron's play was earlier than Euripides', though some modern scholars have challenged that statement and argued for the priority of Euripides (see *OCD³* on 'Neophron', with bibliography). As a result of the murders, Medea had to leave Corinth.

(d) Medea at Athens

Seneca's play does not refer to Medea's experiences after she left Corinth. Aegeus was king of Athens, and suffered from sterility. Medea promised to cure his sterility if he married her, which he did. He appears in Euripides' play as he passes through Corinth, and promises to give Medea refuge; with that promise of a safe refuge, she sets about achieving her vengeance. However, Aegeus already had one child, Theseus, though he did not know this, because he had been tricked into fathering

---

22 Eumelus fr. 3, probably an invention by Eumelus to support Corinthian claims in the Black Sea area; Simonides fr. 545.

him during a visit to Troezen. Theseus grew up in Troezen, and later went to Athens. There Medea, wanting to protect her own children, tried to kill him before Aegeus discovered who he was. But her plan was thwarted, and she was forced to leave Athens.

(e) *Medea and the Medes*

There were various stories linking Medea to the Medes, the inhabitants of Media, a region to the south-west of the Caspian sea. In the late pseudo-Hesiodic ending of the *Theogony* (1001) Medea has a son Medeius by Jason. Later this son, Medeius or Medus, was said to have been fathered by Aegeus, and born after Medea fled from Athens; subsequently he became the ancestor of the Medes. In other versions Medus was a king whom Medea married when she fled from Athens. Sometimes it was said that Medea eventually returned home to Colchis and was reconciled with her family.[23]

3.3 The main surviving versions of the Medea story

The variety of ancient portrayals of Medea may be conveyed by briefly looking at four of the most significant surviving literary accounts, and highlighting the major differences from Seneca's account. The most important, though not the earliest, is Euripides' *Medea*, written in 431 B.C., in Greek. This play covers the same events as Seneca's. At the level of plot and dramatic structure, differences between the two plays include the following:

- In Euripides, Jason's marriage has taken place before the play begins; in Seneca it is taking place in the background during the first part of the play (see comm. on 1-55).

- Euripides' Chorus is sympathetic to Medea, and shares her distress at the way in which women are treated, whereas Seneca's Chorus is hostile to her and sympathetic to Jason (though this sympathy is qualified to some extent in the second and third odes).

- Euripides' Jason is a more prominent and vigorous character than Seneca's, but also arguably less sympathetic (see below §4.1).

- There is no mention of Acastus in Euripides. In Seneca, Acastus' pursuit provides a main motive for Jason's repudiation of Medea and marriage to Creusa.

- In Euripides the magical powers of Medea are not prominent until the end of the play, and for most of the play she is presented as an ordinary woman, whereas

---

23   For fuller discussions of the myths of Medea see *OCD³* on 'Medea'; Clauss & Johnston (1997), chapters 1-4; Gantz (1993), index s.v. 'Medeia'; Moreau (1994).

Seneca makes her appeal to the deities of magic in her opening speech, and he devotes a whole act to her magical rituals.

- Euripides' Medea can take her children into exile, whereas Seneca's must leave them behind in Corinth.

- In Euripides, Aegeus unexpectedly comes upon the scene and Medea persuades him to give her refuge in Athens; with this guarantee of safety Medea is willing to carry out her plans for vengeance. In Seneca there is no mention of Aegeus, Medea has no apprehensions for the future, and there is never any allusion to her future life.

- Euripides has a long messenger scene to describe the deaths of Creon and his daughter, Seneca an extremely short one.

- In Seneca, when Medea is deliberating whether to kill her children, the turning point comes when she sees the Furies and the ghost of her dead brother Apsyrtus. There is nothing corresponding to this in Euripides.

- Euripides' Medea kills the children off-stage, Seneca's kills them on-stage.[24]

The relationship between the two plays will be further discussed below, and in the commentary.

There are two important accounts of the earlier stages of Medea's career. First, Pindar's *Fourth Pythian Ode*, written in Greek in 462/1 B.C., is the earliest surviving account of Medea's encounter with the Argonauts. The ode begins with a prophecy given by Medea on Thera, during the homeward voyage of the Argonauts (9-58). Later there is a lengthy narrative of Jason's arrival in Iolcus to claim the throne from Pelias, and of the voyage of the Argo, but the poet breaks off after the killing of the dragon that guarded the fleece, and briefly mentions just a few events of the return journey, including the fact that Medea murdered Pelias (70-254). Thus Pindar narrates at length episodes that Seneca alludes to only briefly. One difference is worth attention: in Pindar, Aphrodite shows Jason how to win Medea's love with a magic wheel, a form of love-charm. Later writers, too, stress the role of Aphrodite (the Roman Venus), but she is never mentioned in Seneca. He presents a more independent Medea who is not subject to the power of any god (see comm. on 219-20).

The *Argonautica* of Apollonius of Rhodes, written in Greek in the 3rd century B.C., is an epic in four books. The first two describe the outward voyage of the Argo, the third and the beginning of the fourth cover events in Colchis, as Medea falls in love with Jason and helps him to win the golden fleece. The rest of book four describes the return voyage of the Argo to Iolcus. There is no reference to the

---

24 For further comparison between Euripides and Seneca see e.g. Henry and Walker (1967).

events on which Seneca's play is based, and Apollonius' narrative is far more detailed than Seneca's brief references to the voyage of the Argo. Major elements of Apollonius' story, such as the stop on Lemnos, or the role of Chalciope (daughter of Aeetes, wife of Phrixus) and her children, are never alluded to by Seneca. As in Pindar, the gods have an important role in Apollonius, where Hera protects Jason because of her desire to punish Pelias, and persuades Aphrodite to send Eros to make Medea fall in love with Jason. Juno (the Roman counterpart of Hera) has no such role in Seneca, nor, as we have seen, does he assign any such role to Venus, or to Cupid. In view of the importance of the death of Apsyrtus in Seneca's play, it should be pointed out that in Apollonius, Jason does the killing, and later the murder is expiated by Circe; in Seneca, Medea is held responsible, and there is no mention of expiation.

From the Roman world, there are two extended treatments of Medea in Ovid's surviving works, written in the Augustan period, the first in *Heroides* 12.[25] The *Heroides* are letters from mythological heroines to absent husbands or lovers, and letter 12 is written by Medea to Jason when she has just been divorced and he is about to marry Creusa; in fact she hears the wedding procession as she is writing the letter. The situation in which Ovid's Medea is writing her letter is very close to the situation of Seneca's Medea at the start of the play, and there are various close parallels that are noted in the commentary.

Secondly, *Metamorphoses* book 7 tells the story of Medea in detail, but the treatment is uneven, in the manner of Ovid's poem. Thus the outward voyage of the Argo receives only six lines (1-6), the return voyage only three lines (156-8), and the events in Corinth, the subject of Seneca's play, are dealt with in just four lines (394-7). But there is much fuller treatment of events in Colchis (7-156); of the rejuvenation of Jason's father Aeson and the killing of Pelias (159-356); of Medea's flight from Iolcus (357-93); and of her arrival in Athens and the near-death of Theseus (398-452). Although there is little overlap between Ovid and the action of S.'s play, nevertheless there are various similarities of phrasing, and Ovid provides a precedent (179-293, on the rejuvenation of Aeson) for the extended description of Medea's magical rituals in Seneca's fourth act.

We have to remember that Ovid also wrote a tragedy *Medea*, which does not survive (see §2.2).

3.4 Seneca and his literary predecessors

For us today, Pindar, Euripides, Apollonius and Ovid are the major earlier writers on Medea; it is natural and helpful to compare Seneca's play with them, and particularly with Euripides' play. But it is important to realise that these four writers were probably not the most important predecessors from the point of view of Seneca

---

25   *Heroides* means 'Heroines'. The full title was perhaps *Epistulae heroidum*, 'Letters from heroines', and so in the commentary *Epist.* is the abbreviation used.

himself or of his original audience, nor was Euripides' the only earlier *Medea* play that they knew. As has already been said, the death of Euripides was separated from the birth of Seneca by four centuries (see § 2.1), during which many tragedies and much other literature that no longer survives was written. Some of these lost works would probably have been influential on Seneca, but precise speculation on the matter is hazardous.

We have seen already that Seneca was closely familiar with Vergil and Ovid in a way that he was not with other poetry, Greek or Latin. That is not to say he had no acquaintance with earlier tragedy, but the evidence suggests he did not have anything like the same degree of familiarity. From his dislike of early Latin poetry and fondness for Ovid, it seems likely that he was acquainted with Ovid's lost tragedy *Medea*, and indeed the two lines of that play that survive have parallels in Seneca's play (see comm. on 123-4, 228-9, 862). But we do not know how many other plays about *Medea* had been written in the first century B.C. or in Seneca's own lifetime. If we can trust Lucan's biographer, he began writing a *Medea*, apparently undeterred by the play that Seneca, his uncle, had written.[26] Going back in time, there was the fifth-century *Medea* by Neophron (see §3.2(c) on the question of priority between Neophron and Euripides); in the fourth century Carcinus wrote a *Medea* in which she did not kill her sons (*OCD³* s.v. 'Carcinus (2)'); we may doubt whether Seneca was familiar with these plays, but they may have been known to writers with whom he was familiar. Ennius wrote a Latin version of Euripides' play.[27] At *Epist.* 56.6 Seneca quotes a line of Varro of Atax's version of the *Argonautica* of Apollonius (fr. 10 Courtney); this suggests Seneca knew Varro's version of the poem (unless he remembers his father's quotation of it at *Contr.* 7.1.27).

Although the most plausible guess is that Ovid's play was for Seneca his most important predecessor, it would be wrong to assume that Seneca's play was necessarily closer in structure and plot to Ovid's than to Euripides' or any other predecessor. For there is no need to think that Seneca followed one particular model. The Republican dramatists based their Greek tragedies closely on Greek models, so that, for instance, the fragments of Ennius' *Medea* can be matched with the lines of Euripides that they refashion; but there had always been the parallel tradition of tragedies on Roman historical themes, for which there were no Greek models. The *Octavia* shows how a competent poet could take a few historical events and create tragic drama from them. There is every likelihood that Seneca in

---

26 It is conceivable that Seneca's play was the later of the two, but see §1.3. Compare Seneca's encouragement to Lucilius to write on Etna and not to be deterred by all the distinguished poets who have done so already (*Epist.* 79.5).

27 In fact Ennius probably wrote two plays on Medea, one set in Athens. Other early Roman tragedians wrote plays on different episodes in Medea's life: Pacuvius, *Medus*; Accius, *Medea* or *Argonautae*.

his mythological tragedies did the same, starting from the framework of the story itself, not from any one predecessor (for none of his plays stands in the same relationship to any extant Greek play as Ennius' *Medea* did to Euripides'). That is not to say that Ovid's *Medea* would not have been influential on Seneca, but the influence may not have been very different in kind from the influence of his *Heroides* or *Metamorphoses*.

4 Seneca's Medea

Medea dominates Seneca's play, appearing on stage in every act, and speaking more than half the lines of the play.[28] She speaks nine times as many lines as Jason, who appears on stage in only two of the five acts. Nevertheless he is the focus of her thoughts and words in other parts of the play, and the desire to punish him is her chief motive for murdering her sons; furthermore, he is prominent in three of the four choral odes. So let us begin by looking at him, then briefly at the other characters, before turning to Medea.

4.1 The character of Jason

When Jason first appears on stage, he says that he is faced with a cruel dilemma (431-46): if he remains loyal to Medea, then he must die; in order to save his life, he must break faith with her.[29] In deciding for the latter course, he is influenced by his love for his sons: if he dies, so will his sons, and love for them overrides loyalty to Medea. As we have seen, the threat to his life comes from Acastus, who is seeking vengeance for the death of his father Pelias. Creon offers Jason protection, on condition that he marries his daughter Creusa; Acastus will then be content to pursue Medea alone. Seneca's Jason is thus in Creon's power, and has less independence than Euripides' Jason.[30] If one concentrates on these elements in Jason's presentation, it can be argued that he is essentially an honourable man, and the tragedy is really his (so Zwierlein [1978a]). He is faced by an inescapable dilemma, and he acts according to his strongest feelings, his love for his children, but as a result Medea punishes him by killing those very children.

But the portrayal of Jason is more complex than that. Admittedly, Medea herself sometimes seems to accept Jason's innocence (see 137-49 and 417). But that

---

28   The exact figures in the present edition are: Medea 540; Chorus 262; Nurse 107½; Jason 60; Creon 47½; Messenger 10. The play is 1027 lines long; in this edition, two lines are regarded as interpolated (477, 666), and two lines are divided into two (660a-b, 801a-b). The figures will vary marginally if different views are taken about interpolations and line-divisions.

29   Compare his later claim (at 1003) that it is not his disloyalty that has betrayed her.

30   See also 538-9 and comm. The chorus describes him as 'under orders' at 669. This refers to Pelias ordering him to bring back the golden fleece; but it adds to the impression of a Jason who has to obey other people.

is not her attitude in the opening act, nor, when Jason confronts her in the third act, is she persuaded by his self-defence. In the first place, she maintains that he is not limited to the two options he recognises, either death for himself and his sons at Acastus' hands, or else life on Creon's terms: in her view, he should escape with her and trust in her ability to overcome their enemies by her supernatural powers, just as he did when they escaped from Colchis. Jason might respond (as does Zwierlein [1978a]) that at present both Medea and he are relying for safety on Creon's political and military protection, not on her powers, which she has not used up till now to protect them from Acastus.

Not only does Medea offer a way out of Jason's dilemma, but she also doubts that concern for his children is his sole motive. When she says that true love can fear nobody, she implicitly accuses him of not loving her truly (415-6). Later she says he is 'removing a hateful mistress' (495), meaning that, whatever he may say about pressure from Creon, he has really lost his love for herself, and now loves Creusa. Jason's reply is not to deny this, but to say 'So Medea accuses me of love?': i.e. she is in no position to complain, given that she once betrayed her own family for love of Jason. The charge that he has ceased to love her is not really contradicted by his words at 434-44, or by the fact that he pleaded with Creon for her life to be spared (183-6, 490-1), for these lines display gratitude, loyalty and concern, but not necessarily passion. The Chorus at the end of the first choral ode had described his alienation from her in harsh terms (102-6). It must not be taken for granted that the Chorus accurately represents Jason's attitude to Medea, but public opinion of this sort can only reinforce her view that his feelings for her have changed, and that the political pressures are not his only reason for deserting her.

There are further strands to Medea's accusations against Jason. In 529 she insinuates that he is marrying Creusa from desire for kingly power (for he will become heir to Creon's throne). Furthermore, she vehemently rejects his view that she alone is guilty of the death of Pelias and the other crimes she committed for his sake, so that he is morally justified in abandoning her to punishment by Acastus. Her view is that he was the one who benefited from her crimes against her family and his, so he should stand by her (497-505); indeed, she protests to Creon that without her crimes not only Jason but all the Argonauts would have perished (222-45).

For the audience, there are other factors, besides the arguments put forward by Medea, to disturb the view that Jason is an honourable character caught in a tragic dilemma. At lines 7-8 she refers to the gods by whom Jason swore to her. These oaths were a standard feature of the story: he swore by them that, if she helped him gain the golden fleece, he would take her away with him and marry her (see comm. on 7-8). When Jason later refers to keeping faith with Medea (434-7), these oaths are in the background. In the terms of ancient literature, the gods will punish anyone who breaks an oath sworn by the gods, and coercion is no defence. So Jason can expect divine punishment for oath-breaking (which is not to say that he deserves the particular form of punishment that Medea administers, or that she is justified in what she does).[31]

A further disturbing element in the portrayal of Jason is found in the second and third choral odes. Again, one must not assume that the Chorus represents Seneca's own views, nor even that within the world of the play their views are to be taken as more reliable than those of other characters, for they may be naïve or mistaken. That said, the second and, especially, the third choral odes speak of the Argonauts incurring punishment for invading the sea and arousing Neptune's wrath. The third ode ends with a prayer that Jason may be spared. Thus the Chorus implies that Jason too deserves to be punished for leading the voyage. The ending of the ode recalls that he only undertook the voyage on the instructions of Pelias, but again it is no defence that he was acting under orders.

So Medea, though she does not know it, can be seen by the audience as the instrument of divine vengeance for Jason's infringement of Neptune's domain and for his breaking of his oath to her.[32] The third choral ode hints at this link, for it begins with a portrait of Medea as dangerous and angry, and she is compared to the powerful destructive forces of nature; but the Chorus's prayer at 595-8 is not that Jason may be protected from Medea, but that he may be pardoned for his role in the Argonauts' expedition.

4.2 Other characters

Creon appears in the second act (179-300) to order Medea into exile, and is persuaded by Medea to let her remain in Corinth one day longer. In broad outline the scene is similar to the corresponding one in Euripides (271-356), but Seneca's Creon is a weaker figure. In Euripides Creon immediately confronts Medea with the sentence of banishment, whereas in Seneca he at first tries to avoid speaking to her, telling his servants to keep her away. In Seneca the confrontation takes on the aspect of a trial, and is dominated by a long speech of Medea (see comm. on 203-51). One main issue is Jason's responsibility for the death of Pelias. Creon says that the fault lies solely with Medea; she protests that this and all her crimes were committed for his sake, and so morally he shares responsibility. For a moment Creon seems to behave in a high-handed way, impervious to Medea's arguments (192-8), but he does allow her to present her side of the case, and is anxious to rebut the charge of violence or harshness (252-7). Thus he is not a wilful tyrant like

---

31   There is a parallel to Dido in the *Aeneid*. She also swore oaths—an oath that she would not remarry but live in lifelong faithfulness to her dead husband Sychaeus, an oath she renews in 4.24-7; when she breaks her oath she brings punishment upon herself, in the terms of the religious world of the epic.

32   Seneca does not use the idea that Medea is being punished by Venus because she is a descendant of the Sun; cf. Cleo Curiensis, *Suppl. Hell.* 339-339A, which apparently has Aphrodite punishing Pasiphae, Phaedra, Ariadne and Medea. Seneca does refer to the tradition concerning Phaedra in *Phae.* 124-8.

Atreus in *Thyestes* or Lycus in *Hercules Furens*, and from his point of view he is adopting the best means of ensuring his country's safety in the face of threats from Acastus and from Medea.

The Nurse appears in every act except the first. In the second and third acts she urges Medea to be cautious in dialogues that are interrupted by Creon and Jason respectively (150-78, 380-430). In the fourth act she gives an extended description of Medea's magical preparations (670-739), until Medea herself appears on stage. In the final act she just has two lines urging Medea to flee (see comm. on 891-2). Where she argues with Medea her arguments are entirely prudential, concerned with what is safe or practical, rather than what is right or wrong. Indeed at the start of her opening dialogue with Medea she appears to be advising Medea on how best to achieve vengeance, although later she counsels against vengeance (see comm. on 150-76). There are no references to the Nurse's relationship with Medea in the past, and she has little individual character.

The Messenger scene is one of the shortest in ancient drama (879-890), giving no hint of the individuality of the Messenger.

The members of the Chorus are more clearly characterised than in some other Senecan plays, though less clearly than in Attic tragedy. In the opening ode they are plainly citizens of Corinth, though whether male or female, young or old, is not specified.[33] They pray for the wedding and the bride and groom, clearly showing their hatred of Medea and their support for Jason and Creusa (whereas Euripides' chorus is sympathetic to Medea). Concern for Jason, and fear of what Medea may do, recur in subsequent odes, where the Chorus also develops the theme of divine punishment being visited on the Argonauts. The Chorus only once engages in dialogue with another character, for it responds to the Messenger in the brief messenger scene.

4.3 The character of Medea

At all periods the figure of Medea was complex and contradictory. In the earliest accounts she is clearly divine, the granddaughter of the Sun, yet she dies and marries the shade of Achilles in the underworld (see comm. on 218-9). In Euripides' play her vulnerable, human side is prominent, but as she flies away in her chariot at the end of the play we see her supernatural aspect. She can be the innocent young princess overwhelmed by Aphrodite; she can be a benefactress of humankind, rescuing from plagues with her knowledge of herbs; but she is also the evil witch, with supernatural magical powers, and the woman who can kill her own children to avenge herself on her husband. Any presentation of Medea has to negotiate such contradictions.

Seneca's Medea may appear more straightforward, but she still has her complexities. Already in her opening speech she is enraged, and speaks of killing

---

33   On the possibility that there is a double chorus, see introductory comm. on 56-115.

Creon and Creusa and punishing Jason with something worse than death, so it may seem that after such a beginning there is not much scope for her intentions or her character to develop. On the other hand, it takes her some time to formulate consciously the plan to kill her children, and it costs her much inner turmoil to bring herself to the point of carrying out the plan. For the audience, her deliberations regularly contain implicit pointers to what she will subsequently do, a form of dramatic irony that is common in Seneca (see comm. on 25-6, 39, 40, 549-50). She also has discussions with her Nurse, dramatic confrontations with Creon and Jason, and she delivers a series of monologues that reveal her inner conflicts. At times, too, we see the complexity of her character, or at least her self-presentation: she started life as a princess from a flourishing royal family with excellent prospects (203-19), but gave all that up, betrayed her father and her country, and murdered her brother, for love of Jason. Now she finds that Jason has renounced that love, divorced her, and is marrying another bride.

It is no ordinary divorce, for Medea has nowhere to go (see comm. on 52-3): she is banished from Corinth; she cannot return to her father and her homeland, Colchis, since she betrayed her father and murdered her brother in order to help Jason and the Argonauts; she cannot return to Iolcus, Jason's home city, from which they both had to flee after the death of Pelias. Her isolation, then, is absolute, and strengthens her thirst for revenge. It is no ordinary divorce for another reason: marriage in the ancient world was not usually founded on passionate love (though it might lead to passionate love), but the passion of Jason and Medea was one of the most famous love-stories in antiquity. The play explores the closeness of love, once it is rejected, to anger and hatred. Her affection for Jason briefly flares up again at 139-42, but, as we have seen, she believes that Jason has found a new love.

In achieving her revenge, Medea can employ all her magical powers; quite literally, she can move heaven and earth to get what she wants. In the long magical ritual of the fourth act, where she prepares the poisoned gifts to send to Creusa, she gathers her ingredients from the stars, from the monsters imprisoned in the underworld, from many regions of the earth. And yet the consequences of all these grandiose magical histrionics are described with arresting brevity in the messenger scene at the start of the fifth act. Furthermore, within the structure of the play, and in Medea's mind, they are but a prelude to the climax of her revenge, the killing of her sons, something that requires none of her supernatural powers.[34]

Any writer presenting the story of Medea at Corinth has to explore the reasons why a woman is driven to kill her own children. In Seneca her motivation is complex. Psychologically she is prepared by the fact that she is sentenced to exile without her children, who are to stay with Jason (unlike in Euripides). After he

---

34 Hence it can be argued that the play is more concerned with Medea's interior world, her words and her self-image, than with her objective power; e.g. Henry and Walker (1965); Nussbaum (1994), 474-5.

declares how strong is his love for the children, the idea of using them to punish him first begins to take shape in her mind. A further component of Medea's motivation in Seneca is her desire to equal and surpass her past misdeeds: she has a reputation for crime and must live up to it, or even enhance it (see §5.5). Her striving for vengeance thus becomes also a striving for supremacy in evil (see 49-50, 116-36, 893-977 passim). Evildoing and revenge give her pleasure, and she strives to maximise this pleasure with the ultimate evil (see comm. on 896).

In the last act, she veers between her own love for her children and the impulse to kill them. The decisive turning point comes when she sees the Furies, the goddesses of vengeance, and the ghost of her brother Apsyrtus, demanding revenge for his murder at her hands. She kills the first son as a sacrifice to appease them (958-71). If we imagine the play being performed on stage, there is room for debate whether the Furies and the ghost would be played by non-speaking actors, or would simply be described by Medea's words. There is also a separate, though related, debate whether the Furies and ghost are to be regarded as projections or symbols of her guilty conscience, or as external realities. One should probably not be too ready to take for granted the reductionist, psychologising approach that says they are just projections of her own feelings. Nevertheless, whichever view one takes, Medea plainly does acknowledge a degree of guilt for the murder of Apsyrtus. The audience may therefore wonder whether the murder of her sons may in turn lead to guilty feelings and to divine retribution. But nothing of that sort is said in the play, nor do any ancient accounts of her later life include retribution for the murder of the children.

4.4 The triumph of evil

What is tragic about Senecan tragedy? If Seneca had any views on the nature of tragedy, his prose works do not reveal them straightforwardly. In one of his letters he tells the following story (*Epist.* 115.14-6). At a performance of a tragedy by Euripides, when one character spoke some lines in praise of money, the entire audience was so appalled that they tried to stop the performance; but Euripides rushed on stage to beg them to watch the rest of the play and see what happened in the end to the eulogist of money. Seneca tells this anecdote as part of a warning about the allurements of money, and not to make a statement about the nature of tragic drama. Perhaps the Medea story had become so familiar that by Seneca's day it had lost some of its power to shock, but nevertheless, it is worth reflecting that, if the original audience of Seneca's *Medea* had been similarly appalled at what Medea said or did, Seneca could not have offered such a straightforward defence, for, on the face of it, right does not prevail at the end of the play.

By the end of the play Medea has achieved her revenge against Creon, Creusa and Jason, and achieved it triumphantly. She has certainly been wronged by them, but achieving revenge is not in itself normally held to be tragic, unless there is some significant cost to the avenger. To be sure, Medea has achieved it at the cost of murdering her own children, and that may be viewed as the essence of her tragedy. However, this cost is less prominent in Seneca's play than in Euripides', for several reasons: in Seneca, Medea is not allowed to take the children with her into exile, so she is going to lose them anyway; in Euripides much of her long soliloquy is addressed to the children, whereas in Seneca she directly addresses them only very briefly (see comm. on 893-977), and as a consequence much of the soliloquy leading up the murders seems rather detached;[35] at the end of her soliloquy, when the ghost of her murdered brother appears, the need to atone for his murder eclipses her love for the children and any remorse she has for killing them. After Jason arrives she does waver for a moment, feeling a pang of remorse (988-91), but that soon passes, and as she kills the second child, the pleasure of punishing Jason, and of leaving him nothing but the corpses of his sons, eclipses any sense that she is causing suffering for herself. The horror of a mother killing her own children is intensified by the contrast with Jason's readiness, at the end, to be killed himself in order to save his second son (1005). At the end Medea escapes on her serpent-drawn chariot, and this gives her the status like that of a god, as at the end of Euripides' play.[36] Whereas Seneca's Atreus says, metaphorically, *aequalis astris gradior*, 'I walk on a level with the stars' (*Thy.* 885), Medea does so literally.

Since the Renaissance, the triumph of Medea's wickedness has troubled many critics and writers. There have been retellings of the story with Medeas who die in the fire that consumes the palace, or commit suicide after killing their sons, or do not kill the sons at all.[37] We shall look shortly at some moral readings of Seneca's play, but we naturally need to recognise that moral reactions are not the only ones possible, for people will react in diverse and often complex ways to this or any play. It may well be that most people feel at the end of the play that what Medea has done is wrong and abhorrent, but that is not likely to be their only feeling, and will not necessarily be the strongest. For some readers the sheer brute triumph of Medea's evildoing is the most prominent feature of the play, and perhaps one of the hallmarks of much of Senecan tragedy. Even while condemning what Medea does, we may feel strong sympathy for the sufferings and the unjust treatment that have driven her to her crimes. We may admire her ambition, energy and ruthlessness. We may gain vicarious enjoyment from a character who, unhindered by social and

---

35 We should also remember that, in accordance with the conventions that operate both in Euripides and Seneca, the children are non-speaking characters. This can limit the audience's engagement with them, and if Seneca's plays were read or recited rather than acted the engagement is limited still further.

36 For the adventurous alternative view that Medea should be imagined falling from the roof onto the stage, because the chariot only exists in her deranged imagination, see Johnson (1988).

37 Already in the fourth century B.C. Carcinus (*OCD*[3] s.v. Carcinus (2)) wrote a *Medea* in which she did not kill her sons, but we do not know the context. On versions of Medea since the Renaissance see Kerrigan (1996), 88-110; McDonald (1997); Corti (1998).

moral conventions, can do evil and achieve revenge without limit or restraint. We may get a frisson of enjoyment from the violence and murders themselves, or from the long magic scene. We may simultaneously be disturbed and guilty that we enjoy the play at such a level. Or our main reaction to the play may be disgust.

This list does not exhaust the possibilities, and we have not yet started to look at moral responses. When faced with such a variety of reactions, it is natural to ask whether Seneca expected, maybe even encouraged, his audience to react in certain ways rather than others. Of course, even if he did expect or encourage certain reactions, there was no guarantee that his expectations would be fulfilled or his encouragement heeded (see Schiesaro [1997]); but nevertheless we may pose the question. Is it possible that Seneca did not expect any strong moral reaction to his plays, but rather, say, a purely aesthetic response, or an amoral admiration for Medea? It seems unlikely that Seneca expected no moral response, first, because so much of the dialogue of the play, and so much of the choral odes, is taken up with moral comment and moral debate, and the audience can scarcely avoid being drawn into that debate. It is unlikely secondly because in the ancient world it was often assumed that literature should be read to learn moral lessons, an assumption illustrated, for example, by Horace, when he says he has been re-reading Homer's *Iliad*, where the poet 'says more clearly and effectively than Chrysippus or Crantor[38] what is fine, what is disgraceful, what is beneficial, what is not' (*Epist.* 1.2.1-4). The modern reader may agree that one important element in the process of reading literature of any sort is grappling with the ethical issues that are raised in it, indeed that literature (and today television and film) provides an important source of knowledge and experience of how to handle moral problems.[39]

4.5 Moral readings of *Medea*

If we grant that Seneca expected a moral response from his audience (which is not to say he expected a *purely* moral response), there is then an important question whether he expected this response to be based on conventional moral values, or on Stoic values, which differed significantly (see §1.2). Let us first look at a number of responses that appeal to conventional values. The responses, on the whole, are not mutually exclusive.

First, as was said in §4.3, we may argue that Medea will eventually be punished for murdering her children, just as the ghost of Apsyrtus is seeking

---

38   Two Hellenistic philosophers, respectively Stoic and Academic.

39   Indeed some would claim that the study of literature has an important, even essential, role in moral philosophy. See Nussbaum (1990) and McGinn (1997) for two stimulating and contrasting approaches.

vengeance for his murder. But there is little within or outside the text to support this view, and that is not how either Medea or Jason sees it at the end.[40]

Secondly, it can be argued that we should look elsewhere for the cost to Medea of what she has done. We can detect the disintegration of Medea's personality, her descent into madness.[41] Or we can focus on the play's bleak silence about the future that faces Medea, and the hollowness of her victory, as she flies off into the heavens with no apparent destination, heavens that, according to Jason's last words, are not even populated by gods (see §4.10); she has had to destroy all those she has been close to and to deny all her most human feelings of love for her children in order to achieve her vengeance.

Thirdly, we may argue that, although Medea does indeed triumph, and there is no visible prospect of retribution, nevertheless the play clearly implies that her actions are wrong, and provides a strong warning against such actions. But the terms in which her wrongdoing is described are varied. Traditionally the play is often treated as a warning about anger, showing the lengths to which uninhibited anger may go. Anger is a broad category, and the play may be seen, more specifically, as concerned with the dangers of vengeful anger. Then again, we may, with Nussbaum (1994), (1997), sharpens the focus more, and see the play principally as an exploration of the nature of sexual love and the vengeful anger that it can generate: Medea has previously submitted to a powerful erotic passion for Jason, and when later Jason betrays her, the passion turns to anger, hatred and violence. For Nussbaum the play shows how the person who accepts passionate love can never guarantee that he or she will be immune to angry jealousy or impulses to violent revenge. On the other hand one can broaden the focus, and see warning not just about anger, but about the passions in general (e.g. Pratt [1983], 81-91). Such interpretations often have a Stoic colouring (see §4.6).

Fourthly, we may argue that the play is concerned not so much with the behaviour and psychology of Medea the individual, as with the structures and behavioural codes of the society in which she lives. Some, depending particularly on the second and third choral odes, argue that the play shows how civilisation contains the seeds of its own downfall: when the Argonauts conquer the seas, when Creon tries to create peace and stability in his country, they are unable to master the forces of nature, and their efforts end in death and destruction (cf. Lawall [1979]; Fyfe [1983]). Some think that Medea's crimes are an index of the violence done to women in a patriarchal system such as the play exemplifies, or of the violence done to children both in patriarchal and in other social systems (cf. Corti [1998]).

These approaches illustrate how from this (or any) play one can abstract moral lessons at different levels of generality or specificity—lessons about society as a

---

40   By contrast, see the comm. on 963-4 for Jason's prayer to the Erinyes and Justice in Euripides.

41   For the concept of madness in the play, see comm. on 139-40.

whole, about the individual; lessons about the passions in general, or about anger, or vengeful anger, or the vengeful anger caused by erotic love. It may be left to the reader to decide how far each of these interpretations finds support in the text.

4.6 Stoic readings of *Medea*

The previous section has appealed to conventional moral values, but many interpreters argue that the tragedies of Seneca contain some sort of Stoic message, or at least embody Stoic values. The argument can take various forms: different interpreters find different Stoic doctrines in the plays; some argue that the plays contain explicit pointers to a Stoic interpretation, others rather (or also) argue that the original audience would have been predisposed to a Stoic reading of the play; some argue that the Stoic message is the most important function of the tragedies, whereas others see it as only one function. Others, however, would argue that the plays are neutral as far as Stoic ideas are concerned, others again have argued that the plays are incompatible with Stoicism (e.g. Dingel [1974]).

Let us start from an ancient Stoic's verdict on Medea. Epictetus said in an imaginary address to Medea (he is thinking of the heroine of the traditional story, without reference to any particular work of literature): 'Stop wanting your husband, and you will not fail to get anything you want. Stop wanting him to live with you at all, stop wanting to remain in Corinth; in short, want nothing except what god wants. And who will stop you, who will force you? No one, no more than they will Zeus.' So Medea's problem, on this account, is that she places a false value on love, marriage, home, exile, which to Stoics are morally indifferent (see §1.2). Notice that Epictetus could equally have said to Jason 'Stop wanting to remain alive at all costs, stop being afraid of what people can do to your body, stop valuing political power,' and so on, and similar messages could be delivered to Creon and the other characters.

It may be that Seneca hoped his audience would make such judgements as they experienced his play, but there is not much encouragement in the text itself to make such Stoic evaluations of the situations in which the characters find themselves: nothing said in the play is at all similar to what Epictetus says. Furthermore, some of the key terms of Stoic moral discourse are absent from the *Medea*: 'reason' (*ratio*), 'nature' (*natura*), 'wise' and 'wisdom' (*sapiens, sapientia*), even 'good' (*bonus*[42]) are among the words not found in the play. One may say that this is in itself a trivial indication, because the issues of what is natural, of rational behaviour, wisdom, good and evil, feature in the play, even if the Stoic terms are not used. However, if Stoic analysis was at the forefront of Seneca's mind, the absence of

---

42 The comparative adjective and adverb is found, cf. 12, 139, 555, 930, but not in the context of moral debate. 'Bad', 'mad', and other negative terms are frequent in the play.

such basic terms of Stoicism, terms that were all part of the everyday Roman moral discourse too, *is* surprising.

Furthermore, the moral issues that are given prominence in the play are mostly not those that exercised the Stoics. It is true that the Chorus, in the second and third odes, does imply that there is something unnatural about seafaring, and so one may argue that here the moral preoccupations of the play have a point of contact with Stoicism. But the resemblance to Stoic ideas of nature is rather superficial, because in the Chorus's thinking the transgression of the natural boundaries of sea and land by the Argonauts has incurred divine punishment—a concept remote from Stoicism. Moreover, the principal moral debates in the play are not about what is demanded by nature, nor about the conflict between reason and passion (contrast, for example, the *Phaedra*). Issues that are debated include the question whether Jason shares the responsibility and guilt for Medea's crimes, given that she committed them in order to help him; and whether Jason is justified in breaking his promises to Medea in order to save his sons' lives, or his own. All this is remote from the central, indeed from the more occasional, preoccupations of Seneca's philosophical works. In a few places there may be allusions to specific Stoic doctrines, but the allusions imply the distance between Medea and the Stoic sage—an implication that will escape anybody not already familiar with the doctrine (see comm. on 176, 505, 520). So a general Stoic reading of the play is problematic.

4.7 *Medea* and Stoic psychology

The most recent advocates of a Stoic interpretation focus specifically on the psychology of Medea, and argue that the Stoic doctrine of the passions is illustrated by her behaviour. It is certainly true that, at the level of description, there are strong similarities between the way that Seneca describes the outward manifestations of Medea's anger in the play, and the way he describes angry behaviour in his philosophical works (see comm. on 380-96). That coincidence is hardly surprising, but it does not itself entail that the play exemplifies a Stoic *analysis* of the emotions. However, it is also claimed that we find in the play the Stoic analysis of anger and other passions. This is a stronger claim, and more difficult to prove. The orthodox Stoic analysis of passions was that they were all the result of decisions of the rational faculty (see §1.2). False judgements lead to passions, and in the case of Medea the false judgements in question are precisely those that Epictetus focused on. As was said above, there is nothing in the play that draws attention to these judgements or their falsehood, nor anything in the play that shows that passions can be extirpated by correction of these false judgements. Nor, indeed, is there anything in the play to show that Medea ought to extirpate her passions completely (the Stoic view), rather than moderate and control them (the Aristotelian view).[43] Such views will only be read out of the play by those who already hold them.

A more restricted claim is made by Nussbaum, that the play demonstrates the Stoic doctrine of the unity of soul, the denial that the soul consists of separate, conflicting components. She argues that (a) the identity of emotion with belief is prominent, (b) the unity of the personality is exemplified, and (c) different passions—love, anger, grief—are treated as identical, which accords with the Stoic doctrine that indeed they are identical because they all stem from the same set of false judgements. But Nussbaum's arguments must be examined carefully. In support of (a), she points out, for example, that at 155-6 Medea refers to anguish being capable of deliberation; 'it is not something that stands in a certain relation to thought, it is a form of thought' (Nussbaum [1994], 449-50, [1997], 226); and at 917-8 Medea's angry soul decides. However, 155-6 can be read as showing the opposite: 'Feeble is any anguish that can deliberate / and can conceal itself' could mean that violent anguish is incapable of deliberation, that it is distinct from, and beyond the power of, deliberation or reason. In support of (b), Nussbaum picks, for example, on the line 'the wife in me is driven out, the mother is completely reinstated' (928) as showing the unitary nature of Medea's being. However, one could select lines that prima facie suggest the opposite, that there are distinct and conflicting components in her psyche: 'why does anger now drag me off in one direction, love now in another?' (938-9), 'anger banishes love, love anger—anguish, surrender to love' (943-4).[44] Of course one can give a Stoic reading of these lines, as Nussbaum does ([1994], 450-1, [1997] 226-8), but nothing in the text itself privileges the 'unitary' psychological reading over the 'composite' one. As for (c), it is true that in Medea love and grief and anger are closely entwined, but that may be understood as a product of her situation and her temperament, rather than as evidence of the Stoic theory of the unity of the emotions; there are obviously many other situations where, *prima facie*, one of these three emotions manifests itself independently of the other two.[45]

Inwood (1993) has shown how in Seneca's prose works, when he is explicitly engaged in philosophical discussion, Seneca uses language and imagery which at some points seem to suggest a unitary theory of the soul, and at others a dualist theory. Recently it has been suggested that Galen, who provides our principal evidence that Posidonius abandoned the Stoic view of the soul in favour of a dualist

---

43 Other characters appeal to Medea to restrain her emotions (e.g. 157, 381, 506), but these brief appeals have no specific philosophical colouring.

44 These lines do not, on any reading, indicate a distinction between reason and passion, but rather between different passions; but the point is that they *can* be read as attributing different components to the soul.

45 Nussbaum (1994), 451-2, (1997), 228, questions the translation of *dolor* by 'anger', a translation that weakens her argument; but for that meaning see Zwierlein (1978a), 28 n. 2; *TLL* 5.1.1841.25-1842.39; comm. on 49.

Platonic one, may have misinterpreted or misrepresented what Posidonius said (Gill [1997]). If ancient philosophical texts are open to different interpretations of their stance on Stoic psychology, it is scarcely surprising that the plays do not impose a Stoic psychological reading.

4.8 *Medea* and Stoic physics

Stoic physics undoubtedly contributes richly to the imagery of Seneca's plays, notably, for instance, in the fourth choral ode of *Thyestes*, where the Chorus express their fear that the universe is coming to an end in terms of a Stoic conflagration (see Tarrant on lines 830-5). The doctrine of the interconnectedness of the whole universe (συμπάθεια τῶν ὅλων, the sympathy of everything; see §1.2) functions in various ways in the plays. Orthodox Stoicism accepted the validity of traditional divination, and the belief that events in the heavens, atmosphere or earth could be causally connected to human actions. In this play Medea by her magic powers is able to control the forces of nature, a power traditionally attributed to witches. Belief in magic of this kind had no place in Stoicism, but nevertheless, in poetic terms, such magical powers can be viewed in the light of, or through the metaphor of, Stoic physics, as another instance of the way in which human and cosmic affairs can be intimately and causally interconnected (see comm. on 28). For other possible links between the plays and Stoic physics see especially Rosenmeyer (1989). But although the imagery of the plays is influenced by Stoic physics, there is no sense in which the plays are trying to communicate or support the physical tenets of Stoicism.

4.9 *Medea* and politics

The play is not just concerned with individuals. Medea pits herself against the whole city of Corinth: her words strike at the heart of the city's social structures (see comm. on 56-115, 269-70), and she kills the king and his daughter. The Chorus in the second ode regards the voyage of the Argo as implicated in the decline of the whole of human society from the golden age (see especially 329-34), and in the third ode it traces the suffering and death of the leaders of many parts of Greece to the punishment incurred by the Argonauts. There is a broad resemblance to the ideas of a historical golden age, followed by moral decline, espoused by Seneca in his philosophical works (see comm. on 329-30).

   The precarious political world of the play, and of other Senecan tragedies, in which both rulers and ruled can be overwhelmed by sudden, unpredicted calamity, bears a strong general resemblance to the political climate of Seneca's own lifetime, as evidenced in the ups and downs of his own public career (see §1.1); and unpredictability is also a feature of the vehement debates and verbal agility of the plays (see §5). Some have claimed that Seneca's tragedies contain more specific allusions to, and lessons for, his contemporary Roman society. Certainly some prominent themes in the play, such as exile, divorce, magic, were of concern or interest to Seneca's contemporaries; but there is scarcely a clear message on these topics for the contemporary audience, and indeed the differences from the Roman world are as important as the similarities.[46] Sometimes allusions to contemporary political figures or political events are claimed for the plays. But if critical allusions to the emperor were discerned in a tragedy, that could put the writer at risk, and Seneca presumably took care to avoid that.[47] The debate between Medea and Creon partly concerns good and bad ways of ruling (192-202); it has some relevance to Rome, but is unlikely to have been read as criticism of any emperor, because, as we have seen (§4.2), Creon is no wilful tyrant, but is doing his best to protect the interests of his city. The modern reader may well see in Seneca's portrayal of Medea something of the same mind-set as is found in ancient portrayals of prominent Julio-Claudian women as wielding considerable, though informal, political influence, but also posing a threat to the male-controlled political order. However, Seneca himself would presumably have avoided appearing to criticise living female members of the imperial family.

4.10 The gods in *Medea*

The gods are prominent in the play. Medea's first word is 'gods', as she opens the play with a long prayer; later she prays to Jupiter (531-7); and in the long magic scene she invokes Hecate, and other underworld gods. Jason appeals to the goddess Justice (439-41). In the first choral ode the Chorus prayed to some of the same gods as Medea in the opening act, but in very different vein. Their second and third odes speak of the gods being offended by the voyage of the Argo. In the last ode they pray to Phoebus and Hesperus. The view of the Chorus seems to imply that Medea is achieving the gods' punishment of Jason for the transgression of the Argo's voyage. But that view is never revealed to him, and there is no recognition of that as the cause of his sufferings; indeed to the audience the suffering may seem out of proportion to the crime.

The last word of the play is also 'gods': as Medea rides off, Jason delivers a stunning final judgement on her and the world: 'bear witness that wherever you go there are no gods.' At one level this achieves superb closure; T. S. Eliot said 'I can think of no other play which reserves such a shock for the last word' (Eliot [1951], 73). But at the moral and religious level the line is provocatively open-ended. First, what exactly does Jason mean: that there are no gods at all, anywhere? or that there are no gods wherever Medea goes, for they retreat in horror before her? or that there are no gods in the regions she is escaping to, that is in the heavens, but, by

---

46   For points of contact between the play and contemporary issues, political and otherwise, see comm. on 20-1, 35, 52-3, 196, 364-79, 459-60, 545, 668-9, 670-848.

47   See Tac. *Ann.* 6.29, Dio 58.24.3-5, Suet. *Tib.* 61.3, on Mamercus Aemilius Scaurus; Tac. *Dial.* 2-4 on Curiatius Maternus; Nisbet (1990).

implication, there are indeed gods in the underworld, who have supported Medea's evildoing?

The line is arguably more pointed and forceful if it means '... there are no gods where *you* are', a further attack on Medea personally, rather than 'a mere outburst of atheism' (so Eliot [1951], 73 n. 2; the latter phrase is his). But one cannot entirely rule out the possibility that this is an outburst of atheism. One possible audience response, to either interpretation, is that Jason is simply wrong (e.g. Boyle [1997], 125-6): as the audience knows, the gods are still there, but the gods of marriage, and more especially the gods of the underworld, have sided with Medea, not with Jason and the Corinthians. One might go on to say that the ultimate triumph of Medea's revenge is to rob Jason not just of his new wife and his sons, but also of his metaphysical and religious certainties.

But another response is that Jason's last words really call into question the metaphysical and religious certainties of the other characters in the play, and perhaps of the audience too. The words effectively cast doubt on the Chorus's interpretation of events: is there a divine scheme working out in Medea's revenge, or are the Chorus mistaken, just imagining a pattern of transgression and divine punishment among chance, unconnected events? Certainly the fates of most of the Argonauts, as they narrate them in the third choral ode, have no clear connection with the voyage of the Argo at all; and the Chorus's misgivings about seafaring are vague and redolent of the timidity of the ordinary man or woman. But what of Medea and the gods, one might ask? Can we really think that her gods do not exist? Her prayers in the opening speech of the play have, it seems, been answered, Hecate has heard her prayers in the fourth act, the gods are on her side as she triumphs at the end. But Jason's closing line can be read as questioning that too. After all, the killing of her sons requires no magical powers; the Furies and the ghost of Apsyrtus can be interpreted as a symbol or projection of her guilty conscience; her chariot is traditionally a symbol that she has herself attained quasi-divine status, but is Jason perhaps implying that it should be seen just as a piece of superior technology? But this is pressing Jason's words very hard, perhaps far too hard, in one direction, and in the end we may decide that there is an irreducible divine dimension in the play, within its own terms; or we may indeed decide that here, as in the rest of Senecan tragedy, the traditional gods are unmasked and shown to be unreal (see Lefèvre [1981], [1995]).

But a further interpretation of Jason's words is that he is making a deeper point: of course he knows, or can guess, that Medea has succeeded by appealing to her gods, but he means that the powers that control a world in which a Medea can succeed so abundantly have no moral right to be called gods.

So Jason's final line opens or reopens fundamental questions about the play as a whole. We have seen how various moral and religious questions are raised in the play, but it has been argued that the play leaves us with no clear resolution of any of these problems. Maybe the play represents something of the multifaceted and open-ended complexity of all moral and religious debate, and it is by drawing us into that complex debate, rather than by offering particular solutions, whether Stoic or not, that it can be said to work at a philosophical level.

5 The Medea as literature
In his prose works, as well as acknowledging the didactic function of poetry, Seneca also acknowledges the power of the medium to delight and move (see §1.4). The following are some of the chief characteristics of Seneca's writing:

5.1 Allusiveness and learning
Seneca presupposes that his audience have a good knowledge of the story of Medea and of other classical myths, and expects them to understand allusions that are not explicit. One recurrent feature of his writing is that instead of using a proper name, he uses an epithet or longer description to identify a deity or a character from mythology. This allusiveness is well exemplified in the first 18 lines of the play, where Medea prays to a long series of deities (see comm.): a few are referred to by name, but most are referred to by a description. In addition one must be sufficiently familiar with the story to know that Tiphys (line 2) was the first steersman of the Argo, the 'new wife' of line 17 is Creusa (sometimes called Glauce), and the 'father-in-law' of 18 is Creon; and when in 11-2 Medea invokes 'master of the grim realm, and mistress carried off with greater faithfulness than I', we must realise that this refers to Pluto and his wife Persephone, whom he carried off to the underworld to be his bride, just as Medea was carried off to Greece to be Jason's bride; but Pluto remained faithful to Persephone, whereas Jason has divorced Medea. The choral odes in particular, as the commentary will make clear, are full of this kind of allusiveness. It makes demands on the audience, and flatters them that they are capable of understanding it. It is also one way for the writer to counteract any feeling the audience may have that the story is over-worked and over-familiar. Sometimes, perhaps, Seneca overreaches himself. On geographical matters occasionally he can be vague, even confused (see comm. on 384, 712-3, 720, 891). Sometimes he is accused of confusion on mythological matters, but here, given the degree of variation often found in ancient accounts of the same myth, and given the scope for poetic innovation, one should not be too swift to make the accusation (see comm. on 635-6, 652-3).

5.2 Brevity and epigram
The structure of the Latin language allows many things to be said in fewer words than they can in English; for example, Latin has no definite or indefinite article. Seneca also exploits the potential for brevity of thought. In lines 11-12, just referred to, the Latin actually says just '... and mistress carried off with greater faithfulness';

the words 'than I' are not in the Latin, where the audience is left to realise that Medea means 'than I have been carried off by Jason.' This elliptical style of writing, like the avoidance of proper names, makes the audience work hard. It is a regular feature of rapid dialogue; for instance, in the exchange between the Nurse and Medea at 168-9, the Nurse first says 'You must fear the king', meaning that Medea must fear what Creon can do. Medea replies 'My father was a king', meaning 'I managed to escape from my father, Aeetes, when he was pursuing Jason and myself, so I can escape from Creon too.' The Nurse then says 'Are you not afraid of armed men', meaning she will be pursued by Acastus' troops, and maybe Creon's too, but Medea replies 'Not even if they spring up from the earth', alluding to the armed men who sprang up when Jason sowed the dragon's teeth.

Succinctness of language is a feature of Seneca's prose as well as his tragedies, and in both spheres he is fond of the epigram or, in Latin, the *sententia*, a pithy expression of a general truth. Epigrams often occur in rapid dialogue, for example in the same exchange between the Nurse and Medea, Medea says (159) 'Fortune fears the brave, but she overwhelms the cowardly' (see comm. ad loc.), (163) 'Anyone who has nothing to hope for should despair of nothing.' Epigrams can also round off a speech or a section of a speech, for instance at 559 Jason's parting words are the epigram 'calmness assuages miseries', words whose blandness conveys his lack of understanding of Medea.

Seneca is also fond of terse, rapid dialogue, in which speakers regularly speak only a line or half-line at a time, and pick up each other's words to cap or twist them (see comm. on 155-76).

5.3 Other rhetorical features

The fondness for epigram and brevity is shared with the rhetorical practice of Seneca's day, as can be seen easily from the *Suasoriae* and *Controversiae* of his father, which record extracts from many of the leading orators whom the elder Seneca had listened to. *Suasoriae* and *controversiae* were forms of declamation, the school-room oratory that became immensely popular in the early empire. Figures of speech, often associated with rhetoric, but also typical of other stylistic registers, are frequent in the play, for example (line numbers in brackets refer to discussions in the comm.): alliteration (14); anaphora (117); antithesis (261); asyndeton (20-1); balance (56-7); iteration (13); oxymoron (10, 419); paronomasia (28-9); polyptoton (233).

The striving for novelty and surprise that characterises the declaimers' performances is also found in Seneca's plays. For instance, at 19-20 Medea asks whether she can find a punishment worse than death for Jason, and answers her own question with the paradoxical 'Let him live!' (see comm.; and for other examples of paradox see on 10, 15, 261, 346, 585, 727, 853-4, 874-8, 879). Other features of declamation that are apparent in Seneca's plays include the fondness for moralising and for long set speeches (see comm. on 203-51), and the detailed and macabre descriptions of violence; although in *Medea* it is remarkable how brief is the Messenger's description of the deaths of Creon and Creusa (see comm. on 836-9, 879-90). Ovid was also familiar with the rhetoric of the declaimers, and his poetry was influenced by it (see Sen. *Contr.* 2.2.8-12). Seneca, as we have seen (§1.4, 3.4), was familiar with Ovid, and may even have learnt from him the potential of brevity, for in the *Metamorphoses* he often gives only a very brief description of familiar episodes (cf. §3.3).

'His characters all seem to speak with the same voice, and at the top of it; they recite in turn' (Eliot [1951], 68). Eliot of course exaggerates, knowingly. A modern reciter or actor will not literally speak every line at the top of his or her voice: Medea's reasoned, measured appeal to Creon (203-51) demands a more subdued delivery; some of her angriest lines might be delivered effectively in a hissing whisper. But Eliot puts his finger on the fact that every character can deliver the same telling epigrams, the same concise repartee, the same learned mythological allusions, and other stylistic tricks that have been reviewed above. S. has often been accused of being excessively rhetorical. However there is also variety in his writing: the erratic wanderings of thought in Medea's opening speech are deliberately contrasted with the formal neatness of the first choral ode (see comm. on 56-115); her long speech pleading with Creon and defending her past life (203-51) is more controlled, less passionate, than her soliloquies. And there are surprises in the action and the structure of the play: the arrival of Medea on stage at 740, while the Nurse is describing her actions off stage (see comm. on 670-848); the brevity of the last choral ode, and its unexpected theme (see comm. on 849-78); the startling brevity of the Messenger scene (see comm. on 879-90).

5.4 Imagery

In Seneca's plays, one often finds that identical or related images recur at various points during the play, and thereby create a nexus of ideas that contributes to the unity of the play at the imagistic level. For instance, in this play, whose climax is the murder of Medea's children, the imagery of birth is prominent in Medea's opening speech. At 25-6 she envisages her vengeance being born metaphorically, and literally, for her children will provide it (see comm. ad loc.); at 50 she sees the birth of her children as a crucial step in her life, after which she must be capable of greater wickedness; at 55 the home she has shared with Jason was 'born through wickedness.'

Natural forces provide another prominent range of images in the play. One of the powers traditionally ascribed to witches was the ability to control the normal processes of nature, to make rivers stop or run backwards, to move or eclipse the moon (see on 401-5, 762). Medea possesses such powers in the play, and also she equates herself with the forces of nature (166-7): 'Medea is left: in her you see ocean and land / and steel and fire and gods and thunderbolts!' Her magical song shows her power over fire in particular (817-42), and when her poisoned gifts set the royal palace on fire, water feeds the flames instead of extinguishing them (887-90). But fire has other meanings too. It is also a regular image of anger—the Chorus compares the anger of a betrayed wife to fire and water (579-94)—and it is an image of love (see 591), and present in the torches that symbolise marriage (see on 37-9). Thus fire imagery links the love, anger, and supernatural power of Medea.

For other imagery see comm. on 2-3, 103, 590, 644-6, 811, 939-43 (also e.g. Fyfe [1983]; Boyle [1988], 81-3).

5.5 Metadrama

The words of the play contain pointers to, and implicit comment on, the nature of drama. 'Let the story they tell of your divorce be like the one they tell of your marriage' (52-3): Seneca's Medea is aware that she already has a reputation, and she must live up to it now: 'This day will achieve ... something that no future day will ever stop retelling' (423-4). She must be able to do greater evil than in the past, for then she was a girl, now she is a woman and a mother (49-50, 907-10). This Medea knows that her deeds have been and will be an oft-told story. The audience knows this is the case, that this play is one in a continuing succession of poetic retellings. At the end of the play Medea is up on the palace roof, she wants to be seen, and she calls Jason a spectator (see comm. on 993), as though she is an actor, and the roof her stage. Medea's urge to equal and surpass herself and her earlier deeds runs parallel to the poet's urge to equal and surpass previous tellings of the Medea story (see also comm. on 54), her 'staging' of her final actions runs parallel to the poet's writing of a drama. Her ambition to do 'something that no future day will cease to tell of' echoes the commonplace that poetry gives immortality to human deeds. Just as Medea works her magic by collecting all the snakes and herbs and sinister substances that she can, so the poet proceeds by cataloguing all these things, and by heaping up and mixing together all his poetic magical tricks—magic, the ability to enchant or bewitch, was a regular image of the poet's art (see e.g. Masters [1992], 206-7). Just as Medea chooses to do evil, so the poet chooses to write a play about evil, rather than not write at all; the Stoic philosopher must leave behind his Stoicism and enter into the world of suffering and of un-Stoic evaluation of suffering, without which there is no tragedy.[48]

5.6 Language

At certain periods English poets have used different vocabulary from prose writers. This was true at all periods of classical Latin poetry. Seneca is the only classical Latin author from whose hand we have a substantial body of poetic and prose

---

48   For various approaches to Senecan drama as metadrama, see Segal (1986), 215-20; Boyle (1988), 94-7; Rosenmeyer (1989), 47-56; Schiesaro (1994), (1997). Compare Masters (1992), 205-15, on Lucan.

works.[49] This enables us to see very clearly how his poetic language differs from his prose language. There are words and expressions that he uses in his poetry but not in his prose. For instance, in the plays he uses the word *haud* for 'not' (*Med.* 200, 254; in prose he uses only *non* and *ne*), *ensis* for sword (*Med.* 1013; the usual prose word is *gladius*, which is also found in the plays), *famulus* for slave (*Med.* 188; in prose the normal word is *seruus*), or *carina* (literally 'keel') to mean 'ship' (*Med.* 363, 607, 623, 665; in prose the normal word is *nauis*). One of the commonest forms of distinctively poetic vocabulary is the compound adjective (sometimes a compound noun). These were a standard feature of the Greek language, but much rarer in Latin, and Roman poets imitated the Greek poets' use of compound adjectives by creating similar compounds in Latin. Examples in *Medea* are 'sceptre-bearing', *sceptrifer* (59), 'war-waging', *belliger* (64), or 'heaven-dwellers', *caelicolae* (90).[50]

Seneca's tragic diction resembles the poetic language of the Augustan period in epic and other genres. Only occasionally does he use expressions with an archaic flavour reminiscent of early Republican tragedy (see comm. on 156, 285-8, 434-9, 905), or conversational expressions such as are found in early tragedy or comedy (see comm. on 398-9, 562).

A particular characteristic of Seneca is the use of abstract expressions instead of, or alongside, concrete ones. For instance, at 144-5 after the simple physical expression 'he [Creon] drags a mother away from her children' there follows 'and tears apart faithfulness that was bound with tight pledges', where 'tears apart' is concrete, but 'faithfulness that was bound with tight pledges' is abstract, and its interpretation elusive (see comm. ad loc.; also on 246, 573, 576, 618, 843, 874-8).

5.7 Metre

The metre of Senecan tragedy is significantly different from that of early Republican tragedy, and closer to the metre of Greek tragedy. The main metre used for dialogue is the iambic trimeter, with each line essentially composed of three iambic metra (the iambic metron is $\cup - \cup -$), but variations are allowed, because (a) a long syllable can be substituted for the first short syllable of the metron, and (b) with certain restrictions, two short syllables can be substituted for a long one. The pattern of the Senecan trimeter is as follows (the numbers mark the six feet of the line):

---

49 Though we do have several hundred lines of Cicero's poetry; but none of his poetic works survives complete.

50 Other examples are 110, 111, 467-8 (and 980), 470, 577, 643-4, 685, 687, 714, 724-5, 841-2. The only such compound used in the play which is also at home in prose is 'death-bringing', *mortifer* (see on 688).

1	2	3	4	5	6
⏑ —	⏑ —	⏑ —	⏑ —	⏑ —	⏑ —
— —		— —		— —	⏑ ⏑
⏑⏑⏑	⏑⏑⏑	⏑⏑⏑	⏑⏑⏑		
— ⏑⏑		— ⏑⏑		— ⏑⏑	
⏑⏑ —		⏑⏑ —		⏑⏑ —	
⏑⏑⏑⏑					

An important difference between Seneca's iambic metre and that of the early Roman tragedians is that they can have a long syllable as the first element of the second and fourth foot, but Seneca, following the practice of Greek tragedy, does not allow this. The main difference between Seneca and the metre of Greek tragedy is that he scarcely ever has a single short syllable as the first element of the fifth foot, but nearly always a long syllable (or its resolution into two shorts).

In the choral odes, and in Medea's magic song (740-848), various metres are used. In order of occurrence they are:

First Choral Ode
56-74 Lesser Asclepiad

— — — ⏑ ⏑ —   — ⏑ ⏑ — ⏑ ⏓

75-92 Glyconic

— — — ⏑ ⏑ — ⏑ ⏓

93-109 Lesser Asclepiad (as in 56-74)
110-5 Dactylic hexameter (the metre of epic, used only rarely in the tragedies, see comm. on 110-5)

— ⏑⏑	— ⏑⏑	— ⏑⏑	— ⏑⏑	— ⏑⏑	— —
— —	— —	— —	— —		— ⏑

Second Choral Ode
301-79 Anapaestic dimeters

⏑⏑ —	⏑⏑ —	⏑⏑ —	⏑⏑ —
— ⏑⏑	— ⏑⏑	— ⏑⏑	— ⏑⏑
— —	— —	— —	— —

interspersed with anapaestic monometers

⏑⏑ —	⏑⏑ —
— ⏑⏑	— ⏑⏑
— —	— —

Third Choral Ode
Sapphic metre:
579-606 four line units of three Sapphic hendecasyllables

— ∪ — — — ∪ ∪ — ∪ — ∪̲

followed by an adoneus

— ∪ ∪ — ∪̲

This is the Sapphic stanza found in Catullus 11 and 51 and in many of Horace's odes.
607-69 A variant on the standard Sapphic stanza: nine-line units of eight Sapphic hendecasyllables followed by an adoneus.[51]

Medea's Magical Incantation
740-70 Trochaic tetrameters catalectic ('catalectic' means that one syllable is omitted from the end of the last metron)

— ∪ — ∪ — ∪ — ∪ — ∪ — ∪ — ∪ ∪̲
  — —   — —   — —

771-86 Iambic trimeters (the usual dialogue metre) alternating with iambic dimeters (two metra, or four feet long):

∪ —   ∪ —   ∪ —   ∪ ∪̲

— —   — —

∪ ∪ ∪   ∪ ∪ ∪   ∪ ∪ ∪

∪ ∪ —   ∪ ∪ —

— ∪ ∪   — ∪ ∪

787-842 Anapaestic dimeters interspersed with anapaestic monometers (as in 301-79).
She concludes with iambic trimeters (843-8).

Fourth Choral Ode
849-78 Iambic dimeters catalectic

∪ —   ∪ —   ∪ —   ∪̄

— —

∪ ∪ —

with lines one syllable shorter rounding off each section (at 857, 865, 878):

— —   ∪ —   ∪ —

6 Seneca's Medea and the Question of Staging
It has been suggested above (§2.2) that Seneca and his contemporaries probably regarded any tragedy as in principle capable of being performed on stage. The Latin manuscripts of Seneca's plays contain no stage-directions, though modern

---

51   On the textual problems, which relate to the metrical pattern, see comm. on 657-62.

translators and editors often supply them. We have no external evidence of whether his plays were ever staged in his lifetime, or whether he had strong expectations of them being staged rather than read in book form. Argument therefore has to concentrate on the internal evidence of the plays.

One set of arguments is concerned with stage conventions: on the one hand many people have argued that parts of the plays would be impossible to perform on the ancient stage, or at least would be clumsy or otherwise unsatisfactory in stage performance; such arguments are countered by others who suggest how the same parts could be staged successfully. The arguments are handicapped by the scantiness of surviving evidence for stage conventions in Seneca's day. We know a lot about the conventions of fifth century Athenian tragedy, and something about how conventions changed over the following centuries (see Tarrant [1978]), but Seneca's plays themselves are potentially one of the main sources of evidence for the stage conventions of his day, so that there is a danger of circular argument.

There is another, overlapping, set of arguments about whether the positive strengths of the tragedies would emerge better in stage performance or in reading or recitation.

There is not room here to consider all Seneca's plays, so attention will be confined to *Medea* (and in any case the various plays may differ in regard to their suitability for staging, just as in other respects). In the *Medea*, argument has focused particularly on the action at the end of the play, but there are other issues too, which will briefly be reviewed in order, beginning with two general issues:

The two-building stage-set: The play's action requires that both Creon's palace (177-8) and Medea's house (e.g. 847-8, 973-4, 995-7) open onto the stage. It may seem implausible that Medea can conduct her magic ritual undetected outside her house when Creon's palace is not far from it on the stage, and Zwierlein uses this as part of his argument that Seneca is writing more for the imagination of the hearer than for the viewer of a stage performance. But it can be argued that stage space is sufficiently flexible for this not to be a problem.[52] The Messenger describes Creon's palace being consumed by flames (879-90), but ancient stage conventions did not require realistic representations of such fires (see comm. on 885-7).

Entrances and exits: It is well known that, whereas in Greek tragedy entrances and exits are generally signalled in the text, in Senecan tragedy this is not always so, and there are several uncertainties about actors' movements in *Medea*. See comm. on 1-12; 55; 116-300 (introductory note); 265; 568-78; 893-977 (on the movements of the Nurse and the children).

670-739: The Nurse describes Medea's magic rituals; then at 740 Medea herself appears and continues the rituals on stage. Rosenmeyer (1993), 239-40, argues that the actions described by the Nurse—particularly the summoning of snakes from

---

52   For more detailed discussion see Zwierlein (1966), 40-2; Sutton (1986), 11-2, 68-70.

remote parts of the earth and from the sky—could not have been performed on stage, whereas the actions accompanying Medea's words after she appears are performable, which, he argues, lends support to the view Seneca wrote with staging in mind.

740-848: There is a good deal of stage business during Medea's magic ritual. She makes a series of exotic offerings to Hecate at 771-84, including a garland of serpents, limbs of Typhoeus, and feathers from a Harpy and a Stymphalian bird. Presumably all these things could be represented by stage props of some sort, though to modern taste the impact of the passage may seem to depend more on the literary and mythological resonance of the descriptions than on any visual stage effects. At 785-6 Medea hears a noise from the altar (see comm.). Altars were a regular feature of the ancient stage (but there are problems with the location and nature of the altar in this play, see comm. on 797). The audience need not hear the noise that Medea describes, though conceivably it was possible to make altars shake or flames flare up from them on the Roman stage. At 806-11 she apparently bares her breast, and then slashes her arm and lets the blood drip on the altar. There were stage knives and stage blood that could have been used here (see comm. on 811). At 817-42 she poisons the gifts she is sending to Creusa, and at the end of the scene summons her sons to take the gifts to her (843-8).

970-1: At this point Medea kills one of her two sons, and she kills the other at 1016-7. This contravenes Horace's injunction that Medea should not kill her sons on stage (*Ars Poetica* 185), and in Euripides the killings take place off stage and are reported by a messenger. But this should not be used as an argument against staging. Horace's injuction would presumably be unnecessary if there were no dramatists who portrayed murder on stage; already in the fifth century, in Sophocles' *Ajax*, the hero kills himself on stage.

971-7: Medea hears troops approaching and climbs up on the roof of the palace, carrying the corpse of the dead son, and a sword, and making the other son go with her. It has been objected that it would be very difficult for the actor to do this; and even if the corpse and the sword can be managed, how can the other son be prevented from running away? But the objections are captious. Small actors could be used for the sons. There are paintings showing Medea with a dead son over each shoulder, so there is no difficulty about her carrying one, and her gestures with the sword could terrify the other son into obedience. Other paintings show Medea sword in hand with both sons, still alive, cowering, and with a tutor trying to protect them—plainly nobody thought that the children would run away or the tutor would rescue them.[53] Then it is objected that Medea and son do not have enough time to climb on the roof—they must do so while only four lines are spoken by Jason (978-

---

53   For these paintings see *LIMC* 6.2, 195 nos. 8, 10. The appeal to paintings is not meant to suggest that they necessarily portray scenes from tragedy.

81); but this too can be managed, for the arrival of the troops summoned by Jason will take time (see comm. on 980-1).

996-7: Jason orders his attendants to set fire to the building on whose roof Medea is standing. But this is a desperate, impulsive order that need not be acted upon immediately, indeed Medea goes on to taunt him by pointing out that the fire will engulf his sons as well.

1023: Medea's chariot, drawn by snakes, appears on the roof and carries her away. This would presumably be just as manageable in the Roman theatre as it was in the Greek (see comm.).

1024: This line is sometimes thought to indicate that Medea throws the corpses of her two sons down from the top of the palace to the stage, where Jason is standing. This could be managed if there was some sort of parapet on the roof, and if dummies were substituted for the actors. However, the line need not imply this at all (see comm.).

Other staging questions are discussed in the comm. on 380-96, 553, 670-848, 958-66, 970.

In the debate about staging neither side can deliver a knock-out blow to the other. Besides offering solutions to particular problems, supporters of staging can point to the dramatic energy of the discussions between Medea and her Nurse and the confrontations between Medea and Creon, and Medea and Jason; to the dramatic potential of Medea's magic song; and especially to the violent actions and tense arguments of the last act. On the other hand, those who doubt the plays' suitability for staging will emphasise the number of rather static monologues from Medea that are accompanied by little or no dramatic action, and will argue that, particularly in the case of the magic scene, staging with props might well detract from, rather than enhance, the dense allusiveness and verbal energy that are as effective in private reading or in recitation as in stage performance. Perhaps everyone can agree that some parts of *Medea* would work better in performance than others. If we remember that Seneca was one of the considerable number of political and literary figures who were not professional dramatists, but turned their hand to writing tragedy in the late Republic and early Empire (see § 2.2, 2.3), it is not surprising if he was not totally conversant with the practicalities of the stage. But finally, perhaps any reading or hearing of the play will be enriched by making the effort to imagine it being performed.

7 The manuscript tradition

The mediaeval manuscripts of the tragedies divide into two branches. One branch consists of just one manuscript, now in Florence, denoted by the abbreviation *E* (for details of individual manuscripts see the next page). The other branch contains a number of related manuscripts; the shared readings of the five principal manuscripts of this branch (denoted by abbreviations *CSVPT*) are denoted by the abbreviation *A*. Where the manuscripts divide, β denotes *CSV*, and δ denotes *PT*. Three sections of *Medea* (196-274, 694-708, 722-44) are also preserved in a much earlier, fifth century manuscript, *R*, a palimpsest (that is, a manuscript where the Senecan text has been erased so that another text could be written over it); and a fragment of a recently discovered fourth century manuscript contains lines 663-704 (P.Mich.: see Markus and Schwendner [1997]). Sometimes later manuscripts contain better readings. For further information about the manuscripts, see Zwierlein's OCT edition, and for information about the sources of scholarly conjectures, see his bibliography. The apparatus criticus lists selected major variants of *A*, *E*, *R* and P.Mich., all the conjectures printed in the text, and a small selection of other conjectures.

Abbreviations for manuscripts used in this edition

P.Mich. Michigan inv. no. 4969 fr. 36 (4th cent.)
R   Milan, Biblioteca Ambrosiana G. 82 sup. (early 5th cent.)
E   Florence, Biblioteca Medicea Laurenziana plut. 37.13 (late 11th cent.)
P   Paris, Bibliothèque Nationale lat. 8260 (13th cent., second quarter)
T   Paris, Bibliothèque Nationale lat. 8031 (early 15th cent.)
C   Cambridge, Corpus Christi College 406 (early 13th cent.)
S   El Escorial, Real Biblioteca T. III. 11 (13th cent., third quarter)
V   Vatican City, Biblioteca Apostolica Vaticana Vat. Lat. 2829 (late 13th cent.)
β   *CSV*
δ   *PT*
A   *βδ*
ω   *AE*

DRAMATIS PERSONAE

MEDEA	MEDEA
NVTRIX	NURSE
CREO	CREON
IASON	JASON
NVNTIVS	MESSENGER
CHORVS	CHORUS

MEDEA

    Di coniugales tuque genialis tori,
    Lucina, custos quaeque domituram freta
    Tiphyn nouam frenare docuisti ratem,
    et tu, profundi saeue dominator maris,
    clarumque Titan diuidens orbi diem,   5
    tacitisque praebens conscium sacris iubar
    Hecate triformis, quosque iurauit mihi
    deos Iason, quosque Medeae magis
    fas est precari: noctis aeternae chaos,
    auersa superis regna manesque impios   10
    dominumque regni tristis et dominam fide
    meliore raptam, uoce non fausta precor.
    nunc, nunc adeste sceleris ultrices deae,
    crinem solutis squalidae serpentibus,
    atram cruentis manibus amplexae facem,   15
    adeste, thalamis horridae quondam meis
    quales stetistis: coniugi letum nouae
    letumque socero et regiae stirpi date.
        Est peius aliquid? quod precer sponso malum?
    uiuat! per urbes erret ignotas egens   20
    exul pauens inuisus incerti laris,
    iam notus hospes limen alienum expetat;
    me coniugem optet, quoque non aliud queam
    peius precari, liberos similes patri
    similesque matri—parta iam, parta ultio est: 25
    peperi. querelas uerbaque in cassum sero?
    non ibo in hostes? manibus excutiam faces
    caeloque lucem—spectat hoc nostri sator
    Sol generis, et spectatur, et curru insidens
    per solita puri spatia decurrit poli?   30
    non redit in ortus et remetitur diem?

---

2 domituram freta *E*: domitorem freti *A* **10** auersa *EP*: aduersa β*T* **13** nunc nunc adeste
E: adeste adeste *A* **19** est *Bentley*: mihi ω: num *Axelson* aliquid ω: aliquod *Avantius*: aliud
Gronovius **22-23** *the manuscripts have* iam notus hospes *at the start of line 23 and* me
coniugem opto *at the start of 22; Leo transposed the half-lines* **23** optet ω: opto *Axelson*
25 parta (*first*) *A*: pariat *E* ultio *A*: uitio *E* **26** sero *E*: fero *A* **28** hoc *E*: hec *A*

ACT ONE

[*Medea enters.*]

MEDEA

Gods of marriage; and you, protector of the ancestral wedding-couch,
Lucina; you who taught Tiphys to bridle
the new ship that was to tame the ocean;
you, cruel master of the deep sea;
you, Titan, who ration bright daylight for the earth;   5
you who provide conspiratorial radiance for hushed rituals,
triple-formed Hecate; gods by whom Jason
swore to me; and those to whom Medea more
rightfully prays: Chaos of endless night;
realms opposed to the gods of heaven; unholy spirits of the dead; 10
master of the grim realm, and mistress carried off
with greater faithfulness than I—to you all I pray with inauspicious words!
Now, now, come to help me, goddesses who avenge wickedness,
your hair defiled with dishevelled serpents;
grasping black torches in bloodstained hands,   15
come to help me, as grim as you were when you stood
outside my wedding chamber. Put the new wife to death,
put to death the father-in-law and the royal offspring!
   Is there something worse? What evil could be my prayer for the
                 bridegroom?
Let him live! Let him roam through unknown cities, impoverished, 20
exiled, afraid, hated, with no fixed home,
let him seek out other men's doors, already a well-known visitor;
let him long for me to be his wife and—the worst thing
that I can pray—let him long for children who resemble their father,
and resemble their mother. It's born already, vengeance is born: 25
I have given birth!
       Am I spinning out complaints and words to no effect?
Shall I not move against the enemy? Yes, I shall dash the torches from
                their hands,
and the daylight from the heavens. Does the founder of my family, the
                  Sun,
see what is happening, and yet still let himself be seen? Is he sitting in his
                 chariot
and racing along his usual course through the pure firmament? 30
Is he not returning to his rising and retracing the day's path?

48

da, da per auras curribus patriis uehi,
committe habenas, genitor, et flagrantibus
ignifera loris tribue moderari iuga:
gemino Corinthos litori opponens moras   35
cremata flammis maria committat duo.
    Hoc restat unum, pronubam thalamo feram
ut ipsa pinum postque sacrificas preces
caedam dicatis uictimas altaribus.
per uiscera ipsa quaere supplicio uiam,   40
si uiuis, anime, si quid antiqui tibi
remanet uigoris; pelle femineos metus
et inhospitalem Caucasum mente indue.
quodcumque uidit Phasis aut Pontus nefas,
uidebit Isthmos. effera ignota horrida   45
tremenda caelo pariter ac terris mala
mens intus agitat: uulnera et caedem et uagum
funus per artus—leuia memoraui nimis:
haec uirgo feci; grauior exurgat dolor:
maiora iam me scelera post partus decent.   50
accingere ira teque in exitium para
furore toto. paria narrentur tua
repudia thalamis: quo uirum linques modo?
hoc quo secuta es. rumpe iam segnes moras:
quae scelere parta est, scelere linquenda est domus.   55

CHORVS
    Ad regum thalamos numine prospero
qui caelum superi quique regunt fretum
adsint cum populis rite fauentibus.
primum sceptriferis colla Tonantibus
taurus celsa ferat tergore candido;   60
Lucinam niuei femina corporis
intemptata iugo placet, et asperi
Martis sanguineas quae cohibet manus,
quae dat belligeris foedera gentibus

---

32 patriis *E*: patris *A* **35** litori ω: litore *Gronovius* **37** pronubam *later manuscripts*: pre- ω **44** phasis aut pontus *A*: pontus aut phasis *E* **53** linques *later manuscripts*: linquis ω **55** parta ... linquenda est *E*: pacta ... linquetur *A* **59** primum *E*: primus *A*

Let me ride, let me ride through the air on my ancestral chariot,
entrust the reins to me, father, and allow me
to control your fiery horses with blazing bridle;
let Corinth, which sets up a barrier between its twin coasts, 35
be burnt up by the flames and unite the two seas.
    One thing more is needed: that I myself should carry the wedding

                                       pine-torch

to the bedroom and, after the sacrificial prayers,
should slay the victims on the consecrated altar.
Find a path to punishment through the entrails themselves, 40
if you are alive, my soul, if there is any
of your old energy left. Drive out womanly fears
and clothe your mind with the inhospitable Caucasus.
Whatever impious deeds the Phasis or the Pontus has seen,
those the Isthmus too shall see. Savage, unknown, dreadful 45
evils, which should cause heaven and earth alike to shudder,
these my mind is plotting within me: wounds and slaughter and death
that creeps limb by limb. But what I have spoken of is too feeble:
I did those things as a girl. Let anguish well up more formidably:
greater crimes suit me now, after childbirth. 50
Equip yourself with anger, and make yourself ready to wreak destruction,
with total madness. Let the story they tell of your divorce be like
the one they tell of your marriage. How will you leave your husband?
In the same way as you followed him. Cut short your slothful hesitations

                                        now:

the home that was born through wickedness, through wickedness must be

                                      abandoned. 55

[Medea exits. The Chorus enters.]
CHORUS
    May the gods who rule the sky and those who rule the sea
be present with favouring power at the marriage-chamber of the royal

                                        couple,

along with the people, who keep auspicious silence in proper fashion.
First to the sceptre-bearing Thunderers let
a white-backed bull offer his lofty neck; 60
let a female of snowy body,
one untried by the yoke, placate Lucina; and let her who
restrains the bloody hands of violent Mars,
who gives treaties to war-waging nations

et cornu retinet diuite copiam,   65
donetur tenera mitior hostia.
et tu, qui facibus legitimis ades,
noctem discutiens auspice dextera
huc incede gradu marcidus ebrio,
praecingens roseo tempora uinculo.   70
et tu, quae, gemini praeuia temporis,
tarde, stella, redis semper amantibus:
te matres auide, te cupiunt nurus
quamprimum radios spargere lucidos.
   Vincit uirgineus decor   75
   longe Cecropias nurus,
   et quas Taygeti iugis
   exercet iuuenum modo
   muris quod caret oppidum,
   et quas Aonius latex   80
   Alpheosque sacer lauat.
   si forma uelit aspici,
   cedent Aesonio duci
   proles fulminis improbi
   aptat qui iuga tigribus,   85
   nec non, qui tripodas mouet,
   frater uirginis asperae;
   cedet Castore cum suo
   Pollux caestibus aptior.
   sic, sic, caelicolae, precor,   90
   uincat femina coniuges,
   uir longe superet uiros.
   Haec cum femineo constitit in choro,
unius facies praenitet omnibus.
sic cum sole perit sidereus decor,   95
et densi latitant Pleiadum greges,
cum Phoebe solidum lumine non suo
orbem circuitis cornibus alligat.
ostro sic niueus puniceo color
perfusus rubuit, sic nitidum iubar   100

---

73 auide *A*: auidae *E* **75** uincit *E*: uicit *A* **82** *A places this line after 83* **93** femineo *E*:
uirgineo *A* **94** praenitet *E*: preminet *A* **95** sidereus *E*: sideribus *A*

and stores abundance in her rich horn,   65
let her, a more kindly goddess, be presented with a young victim.
You, too, who are present at lawful marriages,
disperse the night with augural right hand,
proceed here languidly, with drunken step,
binding your brow with a chain of roses.   70
You, star, who herald two different times of day, who
always return too slowly for lovers:
mothers keenly long for you, daughters-in-law long for you
to scatter your bright rays as soon as possible.
    The girl's beauty far surpasses   75
    the daughters-in-law of Cecrops' town,
    and those whom
    the unwalled town forces to exercise,
    like young men, on the ridges of Taygetus,
    and those who bathe in Aonian waters   80
    and in the sacred Alpheus.
    If he should wish to be judged on his appearance,
    Aeson's son, the prince, will have first place conceded to him
    by the offspring of cruel lightning,
    who puts yokes on tigers,   85
    and by the god who makes tripods move,
    the brother of the wild girl;
    along with his brother Castor,
    Pollux, who excels at boxing, will concede first place.
    Thus, thus, heaven-dwellers, I pray,   90
    may this woman surpass other wives,
    may this man far outdo other men.
When she has taken her position in the women's dance,
her face alone outshines them all.
Thus, with the sun's appearance, the beauty of the stars dies,   95
and the dense flocks of Pleiades are hidden
when Phoebe, with light not her own,
binds a solid orb with circling horns.
Thus snowy whiteness blushes when suffused with scarlet
dye; the dewy shepherd   100

pastor luce noua roscidus aspicit.
ereptus thalamis Phasidis horridi,
effrenae solitus pectora coniugis
inuita trepidus prendere dextera,
felix Aeoliam corripe uirginem   105
nunc primum soceris sponse uolentibus.
    Concesso, iuuenes, ludite iurgio,
hinc illinc, iuuenes, mittite carmina:
rara est in dominos iusta licentia.
    Candida thyrsigeri proles generosa Lyaei,   110
multifidam iam tempus erat succendere pinum:
excute sollemnem digitis marcentibus ignem.
festa dicax fundat conuicia fescenninus,
soluat turba iocos—tacitis eat illa tenebris,
si qua peregrino nubit fugitiua marito.   115

MEDEA

Occidimus: aures pepulit hymenaeus meas.
uix ipsa tantum, uix adhuc credo malum.
hoc facere Iason potuit, erepto patre
patria atque regno sedibus solam exteris
deserere durus? merita contempsit mea   120
qui scelere flammas uiderat uinci et mare?
adeone credit omne consumptum nefas?
incerta uecors mente non sana feror
partes in omnes; unde me ulcisci queam?
utinam esset illi frater! est coniunx: in hanc   125
ferrum exigatur. hoc meis satis est malis?
si quod Pelasgae, si quod urbes barbarae
nouere facinus quod tuae ignorent manus,
nunc est parandum. scelera te hortentur tua
et cuncta redeant: inclitum regni decus   130
raptum et nefandae uirginis paruus comes
diuisus ense, funus ingestum patri,
sparsumque ponto corpus et Peliae senis

---

102 horridi *E*: horridis *A* **105** aeoliam corripe *E*: aoniam prendito *A* **115** fugitiua *E*:
fugitura *A*: furtiua *Heinsius* **118** hoc *E*: hec *A* **122** credit *A*: credet *E* **123** non sana *A*:
uesana *E* **128** ignorent *E*: ignorant *A*

watches the dawn shine thus at daybreak.
Rescued from the marriage-chamber of wild Phasis,
accustomed to grasp an unbridled wife's breasts
fearfully with unwilling hand—
fortunate man, seize the Aeolian girl;   105
you are now, for the first time, betrothed with the consent of your parents-
in-law.

    Young people, enjoy the licence to be abusive;
from either side, young people, let your songs ring out:
outspokenness against your masters is rarely permitted.
    Fair, noble offspring of thyrsus-carrying Lyaeus,   110
it is now time to light the well-split pine:
wave the ceremonial flame with your languid fingers.
Let the quick-tongued fescennine pour out festive insults,
let the crowd be free with jokes—but let her depart in silent darkness,
any woman who runs away and marries a foreign husband.   115

ACT TWO

[*Enter Medea and the Nurse.*]
MEDEA
    I am ruined: the wedding song has assailed my ears.
I myself can scarcely, still scarcely credit so great an evil.
Could Jason do this, after I was robbed of my father,
my fatherland and kingdom too—could he abandon me all alone in a
foreign land, cruel man? Has he paid no heed to my good services,   120
he who saw flames and sea being overpowered by wickedness?
Does he really believe that all my evil is exhausted?
Uncertain, crazed, with demented mind, I am driven
in all directions. Where can I find vengeance?
If only he had a brother! Yet he does have a wife: let the steel   125
be plunged into her. Is this enough for my wrongs?
If the Pelasgian cities, if the barbarian ones
have discovered any misdeed that your hands do *not* know,
you must now prepare to do it. Let your crimes urge you on,
and let them all be recalled: the seizure of that famed ornament   130
of the kingdom; the impious girl's small companion
divided by the sword, the corpse that was flung at the father,
the body scattered on the sea; and old Pelias's

decocta aeno membra: funestum impie
quam saepe fudi sanguinem—et nullum scelus 135
irata feci: saeuit infelix amor.
    Quid tamen Iason potuit, alieni arbitri
iurisque factus? debuit ferro obuium
offerre pectus—melius, a melius, dolor
furiose, loquere. si potest, uiuat meus, 140
ut fuit, Iason; si minus, uiuat tamen
memorque nostri muneri parcat meo.
culpa est Creontis tota, qui sceptro impotens
coniugia soluit quique genetricem abstrahit
gnatis et arto pignore astrictam fidem 145
dirimit: petatur, solus hic poenas luat
quas debet. alto cinere cumulabo domum;
uidebit atrum uerticem flammis agi
Malea longas nauibus flectens moras.

NVTRIX

Sile, obsecro, questusque secreto abditos 150
manda dolori. grauia quisquis uulnera
patiente et aequo mutus animo pertulit,
referre potuit: ira quae tegitur nocet;
professa perdunt odia uindictae locum.

ME. Leuis est dolor qui capere consilium potest 155
    et clepere sese: magna non latitant mala.
    libet ire contra. NVT. Siste furialem impetum,
    alumna: uix te tacita defendit quies.

ME. Fortuna fortes metuit, ignauos premit.
NVT. Tunc est probanda, si locum uirtus habet. 160
ME. Numquam potest non esse uirtuti locus.
NVT. Spes nulla rebus monstrat afflictis uiam.
ME. Qui nil potest sperare, desperet nihil.
NVT. Abiere Colchi, coniugis nulla est fides
    nihilque superest opibus e tantis tibi. 165
ME. Medea superest: hic mare et terras uides
    ferrumque et ignes et deos et fulmina.

---

136 saeuit ω: suasit *Peiper.* mouit *Leo* **139** ah *(an older spelling of the exclamatory* a)
Ascensius: ha *A:* ac *E* **144** abstrahit *E:* abstrahat *A* **156** *omitted by A* **160** tunc *E:* nunc
A

limbs boiled in a cauldron. How often I have impiously
shed deadly blood—and yet I committed no crime   135
in anger: it was unhappy love that raged.
    Yet what could Jason do, finding himself under another man's sway
and authority? He ought to have exposed his breast
to face the sword. Don't say that, ah, don't say that,
mad anguish! If he can, let him live as he was, as   140
my Jason; if not, still let him live,
let him remember me and be gentle with my gift.
The fault is entirely Creon's; using his kingly power without restraint,
he unties marriages, he drags a mother away
from her children and tears apart faithfulness that was bound   145
with tight pledges: let him be the target, let him alone pay the punishment
he owes. I shall bury his house in deep ash;
a black plume driven up by flames will be seen from
Malea, whose curving coast causes long delays for ships.

NURSE

    Quiet, I beg you, hide your complaints, and   150
entrust them to a concealed anguish. When people endure severe wounds
in silence, with patience and composure,
they are able to repay them: anger that is concealed causes harm;
once made public, hatred loses the opportunity for revenge.
ME. Feeble is any anguish that can deliberate   155
and can conceal itself; great sufferings do not remain hidden.
I want to attack! NU. Restrain your Furious impulse,
my child: even silent inactivity can scarcely protect you.
ME. Fortune fears the brave, but she overwhelms the cowardly.
NU. Only if there is scope for courage should it be commended.   160
ME. There can never be no scope for courage.
NU. No hope offers any way out of your afflictions.
ME. Anyone who has nothing to hope for should despair of nothing.
NU. The Colchians have gone, your husband is not faithful,
and you have nothing left of all your great wealth.   165
ME. Medea is left: in her you see ocean and land
and steel and fire and gods and thunderbolts!

NVT. Rex est timendus. ME. Rex meus fuerat pater.

NVT. Non metuis arma? ME. Sint licet terra edita.

NVT. Moriere. ME. Cupio. NVT. Profuge. ME. Paenituit fugae.   170

NVT. Medea— ME. Fiam. NVT. Mater es. ME. Cui sim uide.

NVT. Profugere dubitas? ME. Fugiam, at ulciscar prius.

NVT. Vindex sequetur. ME. Forsan inueniam moras.

NVT. Compesce uerba, parce iam, demens, minis

    animosque minue: tempori aptari decet.   175

ME. Fortuna opes auferre, non animum potest.

    Sed cuius ictu regius cardo strepit?

    ipse est Pelasgo tumidus imperio Creo.

CREO

    Medea, Colchi noxium Aeetae genus,

    nondum meis exportat e regnis pedem?   180

    molitur aliquid: nota fraus, nota est manus.

    cui parcet illa quemue securum sinet?

    abolere propere pessimam ferro luem

    equidem parabam: precibus euicit gener.

    concessa uita est, liberet fines metu   185

    abeatque tuta.—fert gradum contra ferox

    minaxque nostros propius affatus petit.—

    arcete, famuli, tactu et accessu procul,

    iubete sileat. regium imperium pati

    aliquando discat. uade ueloci uia   190

    monstrumque saeuum horribile iamdudum auehe.

ME. Quod crimen aut quae culpa multatur fuga?

CR. Quae causa pellat, innocens mulier rogat.

ME. Si iudicas, cognosce; si regnas, iube.

CR. Aequum atque iniquum regis imperium feras.   195

ME. Iniqua numquam regna perpetuo manent.

---

171 fiam *E*: fugiam *A* uide *Heinsius*: uides ω **172** at *Ascensius*: et *A*: sed *E* **190** uade ueloci uia *A*: ualde ueloci fuga *E* **196** *R's text begins here, and continues to 274*

NU. You must fear the king. ME. My father was a king.
NU. Are you not afraid of armed men? ME. Not even if they be earth-born!
NU. You will die. ME. I long to. NU. Escape! ME. I've had enough of that.

                                                                                    170
NU. Medea ... ME. ... yes, I'll become Medea. NU. You are a mother.

                                                    ME. See for what father.
NU. Do you hesitate to escape? ME. I shall escape, but I shall have

                                                    vengeance first.
NU. An avenger will pursue you. ME. Perhaps I shall devise some obstacles.
NU. Curb your words, refrain from threats now, demented woman,
        and subdue your spirits: it is right to adjust to circumstance.   175
ME. Fortune can take away one's wealth, not one's spirit.
        [*Enter Creon and attendants.*]
        But whose banging makes the palace door-hinge grate?
        It's Creon himself, puffed up with Pelasgian power.

CREON [*To himself.*]
        Has Medea, harmful offspring of Colchian Aeetes,
        not yet begun to leave my kingdom?   180
        She is devising something: well-known is her deceit, well-known her

                                                                            power.
        Whom will she leave unharmed, whom allow to enjoy peace of mind?
        I, to be sure, was planning to destroy the evil plague
        swiftly with the sword—but my son-in-law won me over with his

                                                                        entreaties.
        She has had a reprieve; let her free the territory from fear   185
        and depart in safety.—[*He sees Medea.*] She's advancing aggressively to

                                                                    confront me,
        and menacingly seeking to speak to me face to face.
        Servants, keep her from touching or approaching me, keep her well away,
        order her to be silent. Let her learn eventually to
        submit to the king's command. [*To Medea.*] Depart speedily,   190
        and now at last set us free from a cruel, frightful monster.
ME. For what crime or what fault is exile the punishment?
CR. An innocent woman is asking what causes her expulsion!
ME. If you are judge, try me; if you are king, command.
CR. You should submit to a king's power, whether just or unjust.   195
ME. Unjust kingdoms never last for ever.

58

CR.   I, querere Colchis. ME. Redeo: qui auexit, ferat.
CR.   Vox constituto sera decreto uenit.
ME.   Qui statuit aliquid parte inaudita altera,
       aequum licet statuerit, haud aequus fuit.   200
CR.   Auditus a te Pelia supplicium tulit?
       sed fare, causae detur egregiae locus.
ME.   Difficile quam sit animum ab ira flectere
       iam concitatum quamque regale hoc putet
       sceptris superbas quisquis admouit manus,   205
       qua coepit ire, regia didici mea.
       quamuis enim sim clade miseranda obruta,
       expulsa supplex sola deserta, undique
       afflicta, quondam nobili fulsi patre
       auoque clarum Sole deduxi genus.   210
       quodcumque placidis flexibus Phasis rigat
       Pontusque quidquid Scythicus a tergo uidet,
       palustribus qua maria dulcescunt aquis,
       armata peltis quidquid exterret cohors
       inclusa ripis uidua Thermodontiis,   215
       hoc omne noster genitor imperio regit.
       generosa, felix, decore regali potens
       fulsi: petebant tunc meos thalamos proci,
       qui nunc petuntur. rapida fortuna ac leuis
       praecepsque regno eripuit, exilio dedit.   220
       confide regnis, cum leuis magnas opes
       huc ferat et illuc casus—hoc reges habent
       magnificum et ingens, nulla quod rapiat dies:
       prodesse miseris, supplices fido lare
       protegere. solum hoc Colchico regno extuli,   225
       decus illud ingens Graeciae et florem inclitum,
       praesidia Achiuae gentis et prolem deum
       seruasse memet. munus est Orpheus meum,
       qui saxa cantu mulcet et siluas trahit,
       geminumque munus Castor et Pollux meum est   230
       satique Borea quique trans Pontum quoque
       summota Lynceus lumine immisso uidet,

197 auexit *A*: aduexit *RE*   **201** Pelia *Ascensius*: pelias ω   **204** putet *E*: caput *RA*   **213** dulcescunt β: durescunt *RE*δ   **218** tunc *E*: tum *RA*   **219** nunc *RA*: tunc *E* rapida *A*: rabida *RE*   **226** Graeciae et *Studemund*: graeciae *R*: gloriae *EA*

CR. Go then, complain to the Colchians. ME. I am going back: just let him
$\qquad$ who took me away take me back.
CR. Your words come too late, the decree has been issued.
ME. If someone makes a decision without hearing the other side,
$\quad$ even if his decision is just, *he* is not just. $\qquad$ 200
CR. Did you grant Pelias a hearing before he was punished?
$\quad$ Anyway, speak, let's give you a chance to plead your outstanding case!
ME. How hard it is to deflect one's mind from anger
$\quad$ once it is aroused! and, when someone has grasped
$\quad$ a sceptre with arrogant hands, how king-like he thinks it is to stick $\quad$ 205
$\quad$ to the course on which he has embarked!—this I learned in my own
$\qquad$ palace.

$\quad$ For although I am crushed by pitiable catastrophe,
$\quad$ driven out, a suppliant, alone, abandoned, oppressed
$\quad$ from every side, once I radiated glory, thanks to my noble father,
$\quad$ and traced my resplendent family from my grandfather the Sun. $\quad$ 210
$\quad$ All the lands that the Phasis waters with its gentle meanders,
$\quad$ the lands that the Scythian Pontus sees stretching behind it,
$\quad$ the lands where the seas grow fresh with marshy waters,
$\quad$ and those that are terrorised by that regiment armed with crescent shields,
$\quad$ husbandless, fenced in by the banks of the Thermodon: $\quad$ 215
$\quad$ all these are in my father's imperial power.
$\quad$ I was noble, wealthy, endued with royal splendour,
$\quad$ I radiated glory: at that time suitors looked to marry me,
$\quad$ but now *I* am looking for suitors. Fortune—quick, fickle,
$\quad$ precipitate—wrenched me from my kingdom and sent me into exile. $\quad$ 220
$\quad$ So put your trust in kingdoms, even though fickle chance can scatter great
$\quad$ wealth in all directions! Yet kings do have this
$\quad$ great treasure that can never be taken from them:
$\quad$ helping the wretched, and protecting suppliants in a
$\quad$ faithful home. The only thing I brought from the kingdom of Colchis was
$\qquad$ this: 225

$\quad$ the great glory of Greece, its celebrated flower,
$\quad$ the bulwark of the Achaean race and the offspring of the gods—
$\quad$ I saved them. Orpheus is a gift from me,
$\quad$ he who charms rocks and transports forests with his singing;
$\quad$ Castor and Pollux are a twin gift from me, $\qquad$ 230
$\quad$ so are the sons of Boreas, and he who sees even things far distant
$\quad$ across the Pontus when he directs his gaze at them, Lynceus;

omnesque Minyae: nam ducum taceo ducem,
pro quo nihil debetur: hunc nulli imputo;
uobis reuexi ceteros, unum mihi.   235
    Incesse nunc et cuncta flagitia ingere:
fatebor; obici crimen hoc solum potest,
Argo reuersa. uirgini placeat pudor
paterque placeat: tota cum ducibus ruet
Pelasga tellus, hic tuus primum gener   240
tauri ferocis ore flagranti occidet.
Fortuna causam quam uolet nostram premat,
non paenitet seruasse tot regum decus.
quodcumque culpa praemium ex omni tuli,
hoc est penes te. si placet, damna ream;   245
sed redde crimen. sum nocens, fateor, Creo:
talem sciebas esse, cum genua attigi
fidemque supplex praesidis dextra peti;
terra hac miseriis angulum et sedem rogo
latebrasque uiles: urbe si pelli placet,   250
detur remotus aliquis in regnis locus.

CR.   Non esse me qui sceptra uiolentus geram
nec qui superbo miserias calcem pede,
testatus equidem uideor haud clare parum
generum exulem legendo et adflictum et graui   255
terrore pauidum, quippe quem poenae expetit
letoque Acastus regna Thessalica optinens.
senio trementem debili atque aeuo grauem
patrem peremptum queritur et caesi senis
discissa membra, cum dolo captae tuo   260
piae sorores impium auderent nefas.
potest Iason, si tuam causam amoues,
suam tueri: nullus innocuum cruor
contaminauit, afuit ferro manus
proculque uestro purus a coetu stetit.   265

---

240 primum *RE*: primus *A* **241** flagranti *A*: fraglanti *R*: flammanti *E* **242-3** *deleted by Zwierlein* **242** quam uolet *Watt*: quae uolet ω: quaelibet *Delz* **248** dextra *RE*: dextre *A* **249** terra hac *later manuscripts*: terram ac *RA*: terram *E*: iterum *Leo* et *RA*: ac *E* **254** haud *E*: aut *RA* **256** quippe quem *R*: quem *E*: quippe te *A* **263** nullus innocuum *E*: nullus innocuus *R*: nullum innocuum *A*

so are all the Minyans. For I do not include the chief of chiefs,
for whom no debt is owed: I charge no one for him;
I brought the rest of them back for *you*, but him alone for *myself*.   235
    Attack me now and accuse me of all my immoral deeds:
I shall admit them. Yet the charge against me is summed up in this:
that the Argo returned. Suppose the girl should opt for decency,
opt for her father: along with its leaders, the whole
Pelasgian land will fall; first of all this son-in-law of yours   240
will be killed by the blazing mouth of the vicious bull.
Let Fortune damage my case as much as she likes,
I·do not regret having saved so many glorious kings.
Any reward I gained from all my guilty deeds
is in your hands. If you so decide, condemn the accused woman;   245
but give me back my crime. I am guilty, I admit, Creon:
you knew that I was, when I grasped your knees
and, as a suppliant, with my right hand sought a guardian's protection.
I ask for some corner, for a home for my misfortunes within this land,
for a humble hiding-place: if you decide I should be driven from the city,
let me be given some remote spot within your kingdom.   251
CR. I am not one to wield the sceptre violently,
nor one to trample arrogantly over misfortunes:
I think I have proved this quite clearly enough
by choosing for son-in-law a man exiled and oppressed and cowering   255
in burdensome terror; for Acastus, who controls the kingdom of Thessaly,
demands that he face punishment and death.
He protests that his father, trembling with frail old age, and burdened with
                                                                    the years,
was murdered; the old man was struck down, and his body
was dismembered, when, taken in by your trickery,   260
the loving sisters dared commit an unloving sin.
Jason can mount his own defence, if you dissociate yours
from his: he is innocent, no blood
has stained him, his hand did not touch the sword;
he was pure, he kept well clear of your company.   265

Tu, tu malorum machinatrix facinorum,
cui feminae nequitia, ad audendum omnia
robur uirile est, nulla famae memoria,
egredere, purga regna, letales simul
tecum aufer herbas, libera ciues metu,   270
alia sedens tellure sollicita deos.

ME.   Profugere cogis? redde fugienti ratem
uel redde comitem—fugere cur solam iubes?
non sola ueni. bella si metuis pati,
utrumque regno pelle. cur sontes duos   275
distinguis? illi Pelia, non nobis iacet;
fugam, rapinas adice, desertum patrem
lacerumque fratrem, quidquid etiamnunc nouas
docet maritus coniuges, non est meum:
totiens nocens sum facta, sed numquam mihi.   280

CR.   Iam exisse decuit. quid seris fando moras?

ME.   Supplex recedens illud extremum precor,
ne culpa natos matris insontes trahat.

CR.   Vade: hos paterno ut genitor excipiam sinu.

ME.   Per ego auspicatos regii thalami toros,   285
per spes futuras perque regnorum status,
Fortuna uaria dubia quos agitat uice,
precor, breuem largire fugienti moram,
dum extrema natis mater infigo oscula,
fortasse moriens. CR. Fraudibus tempus petis.   290

ME.   Quae fraus timeri tempore exiguo potest?

CR.   Nullum ad nocendum tempus angustum est malis.

ME.   Parumne miserae temporis lacrimis negas?

CR.   Etsi repugnat precibus infixus timor,
unus parando dabitur exilio dies.   295

ME.   Nimis est, recidas aliquid ex isto licet;
et ipsa propero. CR. Capite supplicium lues,
clarum priusquam Phoebus attollat diem
nisi cedis Isthmo.—sacra me thalami uocant,
uocat precari festus Hymenaeo dies.   300

---

267 feminae *R*: feminea *EA*   audendum *A*: audende *E (before correction)*: audenda *R, E (a second hand)*   **274** *R stops after this line*   **276** pelia *A*: pelias *E*   **278** nouas *A*: nota *E*: noui *Zwierlein in his critical apparatus*   **294** infixus *E*: infelix *A*   **296** recidas aliquid ex isto *E*: et ex hoc aliquid abscidas *A*   **298** clarum *E*: clarus *A*   **300** *omitted by E*

You, you mastermind of evil crimes,
who have a woman's wickedness, and, so that you will stop at nothing,
a man's strength, and no thought of reputation—
be off, cleanse my kingdom, and also take
away with you your lethal herbs, release the citizens from fear;   270
settle in another country, and there harass the gods.
ME. You force me to flee? As I flee, give me back my ship,
or rather give me back my companion—why order me to flee alone?
I did not arrive alone. If you are afraid to suffer war,
expel us both from your kingdom. Why do you differentiate   275
between two guilty people? For *his* sake Pelias lies dead, not for mine;
add running away, robbery, my deserted father,
my mangled brother, whatever else that husband still
teaches his new wives—it is not my responsibility:
I have behaved as a criminal so often, but never for my own sake.   280
CR. You should have left already. Why keep putting it off with your talk?
ME. As a suppliant, I make this final plea as I depart:
let their mother's guilt not drag the innocent children down.
CR. Go on your way; like a parent, I shall shield them in a fatherly embrace.
ME. I pray by the royal marriage-couch, attended by good omens,   285
by your hopes for the future, and by the condition of the kingdom,
which wavering Fortune buffets with her fickle changes:
grant me, as I flee, a short delay,
while I, their mother, kiss my children for the final time—
maybe dying as I do so. CR. You just want time for your deceptions. 290
ME. What deception can be feared in a brief period of time?
CR. No time is too limited for wicked people to do harm.
ME. Do you refuse an unhappy woman even a brief time for her tears?
CR. Although deep-rooted fear rebels against your prayers,
you will be granted just one day to prepare for exile.   295
ME. That is too long, even if you subtract something from it;
I too am in a hurry. CR. You will suffer punishment of death
unless you leave the Isthmus before Phoebus raises up
the bright light of day.—The wedding rituals summon me,
Hymenaeus' festive day summons me to pray.   300
[*Exeunt Creon, Medea, the Nurse; enter the Chorus.*]

64

CHORVS

Audax nimium qui freta primus
rate tam fragili perfida rupit
terrasque suas posterga uidens
animam leuibus credidit auris,
dubioque secans aequora cursu   305
potuit tenui fidere ligno
inter uitae mortisque uias
nimium gracili limite ducto.
nondum quisquam sidera norat,
stellisque, quibus pingitur aether,   310
non erat usus, nondum pluuias
Hyadas poterat uitare ratis,
non Oleniae lumina caprae,
nec quae sequitur flectitque senex
Attica tardus plaustra Bootes,   315
nondum Boreas, nondum Zephyrus
    nomen habebant.
ausus Tiphys pandere uasto
    carbasa ponto
legesque nouas scribere uentis: 320
nunc lina sinu tendere toto,
nunc prolato pede transuersos
captare notos, nunc antemnas
medio tutas ponere malo,
nunc in summo religare loco,   325
cum iam totos auidus nimium
nauita flatus optat et alto
rubicunda tremunt sipara uelo.
    Candida nostri saecula patres
uidere procul fraude remota.   330
sua quisque piger litora tangens
patrioque senex factus in aruo,
paruo diues nisi quas tulerat
natale solum non norat opes.
bene dissaepti foedera mundi   335

CHORUS

Too audacious was the man who first broke through
the treacherous sea-waters in so fragile a boat;
he saw his own land behind his back,
and committed his soul to the fickle breezes;
cutting through the seas on an uncertain course,   305
he had the nerve to trust in thin timber,
with too slim a boundary drawn
between the paths of life and death.
Nobody yet knew the heavenly bodies,
and there was no need to use the stars   310
that are painted across the heavens; ships were not yet
able to avoid the rainy Hyades,
nor the rays of the Olenian she-goat,
nor the Attic wagon that the sluggish old man,
Bootes, follows and steers;   315
not yet did Boreas, not yet did Zephyrus
        have a name.
Tiphys was bold enough to spread the canvas sails
        on the desolate sea
and to write new laws for the winds: 320
sometimes to stretch the flax as the whole sail billows;
sometimes, with the sheet hauled forward, to catch
the slanting south-winds; sometimes to fasten
the yard safely at mid mast;
sometimes to tie it to the highest point again,   325
while the over-greedy sailor prays for
full winds, and, with the mainsail
raised, the red topsails flutter.
        Our forefathers witnessed that brilliant
age when deceit was far distant.   330
Each man lazily kept to his own shores,
and reached old age in his ancestral fields;
he owned little, yet was wealthy; he knew no riches except
what his native soil had yielded.
Laws had firmly partitioned the world,   335

66

traxit in unum Thessala pinus
iussitque pati uerbera pontum
partemque metus fieri nostri
    mare sepositum.
dedit illa graues improba poenas   340
per tam longos ducta timores,
cum duo montes, claustra profundi,
hinc atque illinc subito impulsu
uelut aetherio gemerent sonitu,
spargeret arces nubesque ipsas   345
    mare deprensum.
palluit audax Tiphys et omnes
labente manu misit habenas,
Orpheus tacuit torpente lyra
ipsaque uocem perdidit Argo.
quid cum Siculi uirgo Pelori,   350
rabidos utero succincta canes,
omnis pariter soluit hiatus?
quis non totos horruit artus
totiens uno latrante malo?
quid cum Ausonium dirae pestes   355
uoce canora mare mulcerent,
cum Pieria resonans cithara
    Thracius Orpheus
solitam cantu retinere rates
paene coegit Sirena sequi?   360
quod fuit huius pretium cursus?
    aurea pellis
maiusque mari Medea malum,
merces prima digna carina.
    Nunc iam cessit pontus et omnes
    patitur leges: 365
non Palladia compacta manu
regum referens inclita remos
    quaeritur Argo—
quaelibet altum cumba pererrat.
terminus omnis motus et urbes

---

345 arcis (*an alternative form of* arces) *Madvig*: astris *E*: astra *A* deprensum *T*: depressum
EβP **359** rates *A*: ratem *E*

but they were forced into confusion by the Thessalian pine-wood ship;
she ordered the salt-water to submit to beatings,
and ordered the sea, that had been out of bounds, to become one of
    the causes of our fear.
The shameless ship paid a heavy penalty,   340
as she was made to sail through such long-drawn-out terrors:
the two mountains, the gateway of the deep,
colliding suddenly from either side,
resounded as if with a crash from heaven;
the trapped sea spattered the crags   345
    and the very clouds.
Bold Tiphys turned pale and dropped
all the reins from his faltering hand;
Orpheus fell silent, his lyre paralysed;
even the Argo lost her voice.
What about that time when the girl of Sicilian Pelorus,   350
with her womb girded by rabid hounds,
opened all those gaping jaws in unison?
Who did not shudder in every limb
at the single monster with so many barks?
What about that time when those cursed creatures   355
soothed the Ausonian sea with melodious voice,
when, echoing on his Pierian lyre,
    Thracian Orpheus
nearly forced the Siren to follow him, though she was used
to stopping ships with her singing?   360
What was the reward for this voyage?
    the golden fleece,
and an evil worse than the sea—Medea,
fitting payment for the first ship.
    Nowadays the sea has given in, and submits to
    all our laws: 365
we do not look for something constructed by Pallas's hand,
for something famous, in which kings pull on the oars,
    for an Argo;
any little boat can wander over the deep.
Every boundary-stone has been moved, and cities

muros terra posuere noua; 370
nil qua fuerat sede reliquit
   peruius orbis:
Indus gelidum potat Araxen,
Albin Persae Rhenumque bibunt—
uenient annis saecula seris, 375
quibus Oceanus uincula rerum
laxet et ingens pateat tellus
Tethysque nouos detegat orbes
nec sit terris ultima Thule.

NVTRIX

Alumna, celerem quo rapis tectis pedem? 380
resiste et iras comprime ac retine impetum.
   Incerta qualis entheos gressus tulit
cum iam recepto maenas insanit deo
Pindi niualis uertice aut Nysae iugis,
talis recursat huc et huc motu effero, 385
furoris ore signa lymphati gerens.
flammata facies, spiritum ex alto citat,
proclamat, oculos uberi fletu rigat,
renidet, omnis specimen affectus capit;
haeret minatur aestuat queritur gemit. 390
quo pondus animi uerget? ubi ponet minas?
ubi se iste fluctus franget? exundat furor.
non facile secum uersat aut medium scelus;
se uincet: irae nouimus ueteris notas.
magnum aliquid instat, efferum immane impium: 395
uultum Furoris cerno. di fallant metum!

MEDEA

Si quaeris odio, misera, quem statuas modum,
imitare amorem. regias egone ut faces
inulta patiar? segnis hic ibit dies,
tanto petitus ambitu, tanto datus? 400
dum terra caelum media libratum feret

---

370 noua *E*: nouos *A*   **382** entheos δ: pentheos *E*: ethneosi β gressus *E*: cursus *A* **384** niualis *E*: iugalis *A*   **391** animi *E*: istud *A* uerget ... ponet *A*: uergat ... ponat *E* **394** ueteris *E*: ueteres *A*

have built walls in new territory.   370
The world is opened up to travel, and has left nothing
where it was before:
the Indian drinks the icy Araxes,
the Persians drink the Elbe and Rhine.
In later years there will be generations   375
for whom Ocean will loosen the chains
of nature, the earth will be revealed in its immensity,
Tethys will uncover new worlds,
and earth's furthest boundary will not be Thule.

ACT THREE

[*Enter Medea and the Nurse.*]
NURSE

Child, where are you rushing in haste from the house?   380
Stop, control your anger, restrain your aggression.
    Just as a Maenad moves distractedly with inspired steps
once she has let the god possess her, and she raves
on the summit of snowy Pindus or the ridges of Nysa—
so Medea keeps running to and fro with frantic movement,   385
displaying the signs of frenzied madness in her features.
Her face is ablaze, she forces her breath out from deep inside her,
she cries out, she floods her eyes with copious weeping,
she smiles, she demonstrates every kind of emotion;
she hesitates, threatens, seethes, protests, groans.   390
Which way will her heart's heaviness sink? Where will she end her
                        menaces?
Where will that wave break? Her madness is overflowing.
She is pondering no simple or moderate wickedness;
she will surpass herself: I recognise the signs of her old rage.
Something great, wild, terrible, impious is looming: 395
I see the face of Madness. May the gods prove my fears unfounded!

MEDEA

If you ask what limit you should impose on hatred, wretched woman,
take your cue from love. What, should I endure the royal wedding-torches
without revenge? Will this day pass in inactivity,
when it has been requested and won with such insistence?   400
While the earth stays at the centre and keeps the heavens balanced,

nitidusque certas mundus euoluet uices
numerusque harenis derit et solem dies,
noctem sequentur astra, dum siccas polus
uersabit Arctos, flumina in pontum cadent,   405
numquam meus cessabit in poenas furor
crescetque semper. quae ferarum immanitas,
quae Scylla, quae Charybdis Ausonium mare
Siculumque sorbens quaeue anhelantem premens
Titana tantis Aetna feruebit minis?   410
non rapidus amnis, non procellosum mare
pontusue coro saeuus aut uis ignium
adiuta flatu possit inhibere impetum
irasque nostras: sternam et euertam omnia.
     Timuit Creontem ac bella Thessalici ducis?   415
amor timere neminem uerus potest.
sed cesserit coactus et dederit manus:
adire certe et coniugem extremo alloqui
sermone potuit—hoc quoque extimuit ferox;
laxare certe tempus immitis fugae   420
genero licebat—liberis unus dies
datus est duobus. non queror tempus breue:
multum patebit. faciet hic faciet dies
quod nullus umquam taceat—inuadam deos
et cuncta quatiam. NVT. Recipe turbatum malis,   425
era, pectus, animum mitiga. ME. Sola est quies,
mecum ruina cuncta si uideo obruta:
mecum omnia abeant. trahere, cum pereas, libet.
NVT.   Quam multa sint timenda, si perstas, uide:
nemo potentes aggredi tutus potest.   430

IASON

O dura fata semper et sortem asperam,
cum saeuit et cum parcit ex aequo malam!
remedia quotiens inuenit nobis deus
periculis peiora: si uellem fidem
praestare meritis coniugis, leto fuit   435

---

408 ausonium *E*: ionium *A*   **409** quaeue *E*: quaeque *A*   **412** pontusue *E*: pontusque *A*
422 datus est *E*: datus *A*   **430** potentes *A*: potentem *E*   **432** malam *A*: mala *E*   **433**
quotiens *E*: tociens *A*

while the bright universe maintains its constant revolutions,
while the grains of sand are innumerable, while day attends the sun
and stars the night, while the pole keeps the Bears dry
as they revolve, while rivers flow down into the sea,   405
never shall my madness falter in its search for vengeance,
and it will increase constantly. What frightful breed of wild beasts,
what Scylla, what Charybdis, sucking in the Ausonian
and Sicilian sea, what Etna pressing down on a gasping
Titan will seethe with such mighty threats?   410
Not strong-flowing river, not stormy sea,
or ocean whipped by north-west wind, or mighty fire
aided by gale, could halt my aggression
and rage: I shall ruin and destroy everything.
         Was he afraid of Creon and of war with the Thessalian chief?   415
True love is strong enough to fear nobody.
But suppose he gave in and surrendered only under duress:
at least he could have gone to see his wife and spoken to her
in their final conversation—he took fright at that as well, defiant man!
At least as son-in-law he could have postponed the moment   420
of cruel exile—I have been granted just one day
for our two children. I don't protest at the shortness of the time:
it will stretch far. This day will achieve—yes, it will achieve
something that no future day will ever stop retelling—I shall assault
                                                            the gods
and throw the universe into turmoil. NU. Recover your senses,   425
which are upset by your sufferings, mistress; calm your mind. ME. My
                                        only hope of tranquillity
is if I see the universe overwhelmed by ruin along with me:
let everything be destroyed along with me. It's good to drag things with
                                        you when you are dying.
NU. Consider how many things you have to fear, if you persist:
no one can safely attack the mighty.   430
    [*Enter Jason.*]
JASON [*To himself.*]
    O, fate is ever cruel, and destiny harsh,
    equally harmful when she is violent and when she treats us gently!
    How often god devises for us remedies
    worse than the dangers: if I had wanted to keep faith with
    my wife, as she deserves, I would have had   435

caput offerendum; si mori nollem, fide
misero carendum. non timor uicit fidem,
sed trepida pietas: quippe sequeretur necem
proles parentum. sancta si caelum incolis
Iustitia, numen inuoco ac testor tuum: 440
nati patrem uicere. quin ipsam quoque,
etsi ferox est corde nec patiens iugi,
consulere natis malle quam thalamis reor.
constituit animus precibus iratam aggredi—
atque ecce, uiso memet exiluit, furit,   445
fert odia prae se: totus in uultu est dolor.

ME. Fugimus, Iason, fugimus—hoc non est nouum,
mutare sedes; causa fugiendi noua est:
pro te solebam fugere—discedo, exeo,
penatibus profugere quam cogis tuis.   450
ad quos remittis? Phasin et Colchos petam
patriumque regnum quaeque fraternus cruor
perfudit arua? quas peti terras iubes?
quae maria monstras? Pontici fauces freti
per quas reuexi nobilem regum manum   455
adulterum secuta per Symplegadas?
patruamne Iolcon, Thessala an Tempe petam?
quascumque aperui tibi uias, clausi mihi—
quo me remittis? exuli exilium imperas
nec das. eatur. regius iussit gener: 460
nihil recuso. dira supplicia ingere:
merui. cruentis paelicem poenis premat
regalis ira, uinculis oneret manus
clausamque saxo noctis aeternae obruat:
minora meritis patiar—ingratum caput,   465
reuoluat animus igneos tauri halitus
interque saeuos gentis indomitae metus
armifero in aruo flammeum Aeetae pecus,
hostisque subiti tela, cum iussu meo

---

436 nollem *E*: nolim *A*   437 carendum *E*: carendum est *A*   uicit fidem *E*: uincit uirum *A*
455 nobilem ... manum *E*: nobiles ... manus *A*   457 patruamne *Zwierlein*: paruamne ω
iolcon *later manuscripts*: folcon (*or* pholcon) *A*: colon *E*   459 exuli *A, and Ennodius (a
fifth/sixth century writer who quotes the line)*: exul *E*   465 ingratum *E*: o ingratum *A*   467-8
deleted by Leo (Richter had deleted 468)

to submit to death; if I had been unwilling to die, I would have had to
abandon my good faith, unhappy man. It was not fear that defeated my
good faith,
but anxious parental love: for after the slaughter of their parents
my children would have been next. If you dwell in heaven, holy
Justice, I invoke and call as witness your divine power: 440
the sons defeated their father. Indeed she herself too,
although she is wild at heart and intolerant of the yoke,
would put her sons before her marriage, I think.
My mind is made up to approach the angry woman with entreaties—
and look, on seeing me she has leapt forward, she is mad,   445
she parades her hatred: all her anguish shows in her expression.

ME. I have fled, Jason; I am fleeing. This is not new,
to be seeking a new home; but the reason for fleeing is new:
I used to flee for your sake—now I am departing, leaving,
because you force me to flee from your house.   450
To whom are you sending me? Should I head for the Phasis and the
Colchians,
my father's kingdom, the territory over which my brother's
blood flowed? What lands do you bid me head for?
To what seas do you direct me? The jaws of the Pontic strait
through which I brought back the noble band of kings,   455
when I followed an adulterer through the Symplegades?
Should I head for your uncle's Iolcus, or Thessalian Tempe?
Every path that I opened up to you, I closed to myself—
where are you sending me? You order an exile into exile,
but provide no destination. Let me be going—the royal son-in-law has
commanded it: 460
I have no objection! Heap terrible punishments on me:
I have deserved them! Let regal anger crush the mistress with
savage penalties, let it load her hands with chains
and bury her, imprisoned in rock and endless darkness:
I shall suffer less than I deserve!—Ungrateful creature,   465
let your mind recall the fiery panting of the bull,
and—among the unconquerable race's cruel terrors—
the flaming beasts of Aeetes in the field that sprouted armed men,
the missiles of the enemy who suddenly appeared, when at my command

terrigena miles mutua caede occidit;   470
adice expetita spolia Phrixei arietis
somnoque iussum lumina ignoto dare
insomne monstrum, traditum fratrem neci
et scelere in uno non semel factum scelus,
ausasque natas fraude deceptas mea   475
secare membra non reuicturi senis:
[aliena quaerens regna, deserui mea]
per spes tuorum liberum et certum larem,
per uicta monstra, per manus, pro te quibus
numquam peperci, perque praeteritos metus,   480
per caelum et undas, coniugi testes mei,
miserere, redde supplici felix uicem.
ex opibus illis, quas procul raptas Scythae
usque a perustis Indiae populis agunt,
quas quia referta uix domus gazas capit,   485
ornamus auro nemora, nil exul tuli
nisi fratris artus: hos quoque impendi tibi;
tibi patria cessit, tibi pater frater pudor—
hac dote nupsi. redde fugienti sua.

IA.   Perimere cum te uellet infestus Creo,   490
     lacrimis meis euictus exilium dedit.

ME. Poenam putabam: munus, ut uideo, est fuga.

IA.   Dum licet abire, profuge teque hinc eripe:
     grauis ira regum est semper. ME. Hoc suades mihi,
     praestas Creusae: paelicem inuisam amoues.   495

IA.   Medea amores obicit? ME. Et caedem et dolos.

IA.   Obicere crimen quod potes tandem mihi?

ME. Quodcumque feci. IA. Restat hoc unum insuper,
     tuis ut etiam sceleribus fiam nocens.

ME. Tua illa, tua sunt illa: cui prodest scelus,   500
     is fecit—omnes coniugem infamem arguant,

---

475 ausasque *Heinsius*: iussasque ω   477 *deleted by Zwierlein: Leo moved the line to follow 482, Delrio to follow 487*   484 agunt *E*: petunt *A*   488 tibi pater frater *Ascensius*: tibi pater. tibi frater *E*: tibi frater pater *A*   496 amores *A*: mores *E*   497-500 *E assigns the lines to Medea and Jason as in the text above: A assigns them as follows:* ME: (496) Et caedem - (497) mihi. IA: (498) Quodcumque feci. ME.: Restat - (503) nocens.   497 crimen quod potes tandem *A*: tandem quod potest crimen *E*

the earth-born soldiers fell in mutual carnage;   470
add the spoils of Phrixus' ram that you had longed for,
and the sleepless monster ordered to surrender its eyes
to unfamiliar sleep; my brother treacherously slaughtered,
and, in that single crime, a crime repeated not just once;
and the daughters, taken in by my deceit, emboldened   475
to hack the limbs of the old man—though he would not live again.
[Seeking someone else's kingdom, I deserted my own]
I beg you, by your hopes for your children, by the home you are
                                                                                              assured of,
by the monsters I defeated, by the hands that for your sake
I never refrained from using, by fears now past,   480
by sky and waves, witnesses of my marriage,
have pity! you are fortunate—give me, a suppliant, my reward.
Of those riches that the Scythians pillage from afar,
fetching them all the way from the sun-scorched tribes of India   484
(since our palace is crammed full and barely has room for these treasures,
we adorn the forests with gold)—of those riches I brought nothing
                                                                                              into exile,
except my brother's limbs: those, too, I spent on you.
To you my country yielded, to you my father, brother, honour—
with this dowry I was married. Give your wife's property back as
                                                                                              she flees.
JA. Although Creon was hostile, and wanted to have you killed,   490
     he granted you banishment, won over by my tears.
ME. I thought it a punishment: exile is a gift, I see.
JA. While you are allowed to leave, run, escape from here;
     the anger of kings is always dangerous. ME. You urge *me* to go,   494
     but you do so for *Creusa's* sake: you're getting rid of a hated mistress.
JA. So Medea accuses me of love? ME. And of slaughter and deceit.
JA. What crime can you accuse me of, I ask?
ME. Every crime that *I* committed. JA. That's all I need,
     that *I* should actually be made guilty by *your* wicked deeds.   499
ME. They are *yours*, they are *yours*: anyone who gains from wickedness
     committed it. Though everyone else accuse your wife of infamy,

solus tuere, solus insontem uoca:
tibi innocens sit quisquis est pro te nocens.
IA. Ingrata uita est cuius acceptae pudet.
ME. Retinenda non est cuius acceptae pudet. 505
IA. Quin potius ira concitum pectus doma,
placare natis. ME. Abdico eiuro abnuo—
meis Creusa liberis fratres dabit?
IA. Regina natis exulum, afflictis potens.
ME. Ne ueniat umquam tam malus miseris dies, 510
qui prole foeda misceat prolem inclitam,
Phoebi nepotes Sisyphi nepotibus.
IA. Quid, misera, meque teque in exitium trahis?
abscede, quaeso. ME. Supplicem audiuit Creo.
IA. Quid facere possim, loquere. ME. Pro me uel scelus. 515
IA. Hinc rex et illinc— ME. Est et his maior metus
Medea. nos †confligere. certemus sine,
sit pretium Iason. IA. Cedo defessus malis.
et ipsa casus saepe iam expertos time.
ME. Fortuna semper omnis infra me stetit. 520
IA. Acastus instat. ME. Propior est hostis Creo:
utrumque profuge. non ut in socerum manus
armes nec ut te caede cognata inquines
Medea cogit: innocens mecum fuge.
IA. Et quis resistet, gemina si bella ingruant, 525
Creo atque Acastus arma si iungant sua?
ME. His adice Colchos, adice et Aeeten ducem,
Scythas Pelasgis iunge: demersos dabo.
IA. Alta extimesco sceptra. ME. Ne cupias uide.
IA. Suspecta ne sint, longa colloquia amputa. 530
ME. Nunc summe toto Iuppiter caelo tona,
intende dextram, uindices flammas para
omnemque ruptis nubibus mundum quate.
nec deligenti tela librentur manu

---

506 doma *E*: domas *A* 513 exitium *Avantius*: exilium ω 514 creo *E*: creon *A* 516 his *E*: hic *A* 517 confligere ω: conflige *Avantius*: marite *Axelson*: compone*Delz* 521-2 *A* assigns all of line 521 to Jason, making Medea's speech start at the beginning of 522 522 non *E*: nolo *A* 525 quis *E*: quid *A* ingruant *A*: ingrauant *E* 534 deligenti *Ascensius*: diligenti ω

you alone should defend her, you alone should call her blameless:
you should regard as guiltless anyone who is guilty for your sake.
JA. A life one is ashamed to accept is unwelcome.
ME. One need not cling to a life one is ashamed to accept.   505
JA. Stop, tame your heart—it is tormented by anger;
be reconciled with your sons. ME. I renounce, disclaim, disown them—
will Creusa produce brothers for my children?
JA. Yes: a queen for the sons of exiles, a powerful woman for the afflicted.
ME. May there never dawn on the unhappy boys a day so foul   510
as to contaminate those renowned children with vile children,
descendants of Phoebus with descendants of Sisyphus.
JA. Why, wretched woman, are you dragging both of us to destruction?
Leave, I beg you. ME. Creon listened to my supplication.
JA. Tell me what I can do. ME. For me, even wrong!   515
JA. On this side and on that there is a king ... ME. And there is
                              something more terrifying than them—
Medea.   *   *   *   . Let us compete,
let the prize be Jason. JA. I give in, worn out by sufferings.
You, too, should fear the hazards you have often experienced in the past.
ME. Fortune, in whatever guise, has always been inferior to me.   520
JA. Acastus is closing in. ME. Creon is the nearer enemy:
run from them both. Medea isn't forcing you to arm yourself
against your father-in-law, nor to defile yourself with
family slaughter: escape with me, and be free from guilt.
JA. And who will resist, should a double war threaten us,   525
should Creon and Acastus combine their forces?
ME. Include the Colchians, include also Aeetes as commander,
combine the Scythians with the Pelasgians: I shall make them sink.
JA. I fear exalted kingly power. ME. Mind you don't desire it.
JA. Cut short these long discussions, lest they arouse suspicion.   530
ME. Now, highest Jupiter, thunder throughout the heavens,
stretch out your right arm, make ready avenging flames,
shatter clouds and shake the entire universe.
Do not keep the missiles poised while your hand selects

uel me uel istum: quisquis e nobis cadet 535
nocens peribit, non potest in nos tuum
errare fulmen. IA. Sana meditari incipe
et placida fare. si quod ex soceri domo
potest fugam leuare solamen, pete.
ME. Contemnere animus regias, ut scis, opes 540
potest soletque; liberos tantum fugae
habere comites liceat, in quorum sinu
lacrimas profundam. te noui gnati manent.
IA. Parere precibus cupere me fateor tuis;
pietas uetat: namque istud ut possim pati, 545
non ipse memet cogat et rex et socer.
haec causa uitae est, hoc perusti pectoris
curis leuamen. spiritu citius queam
carere, membris, luce. ME. Sic natos amat?
bene est, tenetur, uulneri patuit locus.— 550
suprema certe liceat abeuntem loqui
mandata, liceat ultimum amplexum dare:
gratum est. et illud uoce iam extrema peto,
ne, si qua noster dubius effudit dolor,
maneant in animo uerba: melioris tibi 555
memoria nostri sedeat; haec irae data
oblitterentur. IA. Omnia ex animo expuli
precorque et ipse, feruidam ut mentem regas
placideque tractes: miserias lenit quies.
ME. Discessit. itane est? uadis oblitus mei 560
et tot meorum facinorum? excidimus tibi?
numquam excidemus. hoc age, omnis aduoca
uires et artes. fructus est scelerum tibi
nullum scelus putare. uix fraudi est locus:
timemur. hac aggredere, qua nemo potest 565
quicquam timere. perge, nunc aude, incipe
quidquid potest Medea, quidquid non potest.
  Tu, fida nutrix, socia maeroris mei
uariique casus, misera consilia adiuua.

---

535 uel me *E*: in me *A* **538** quod *E*: quid *A* **549** sic natos *printed editions*: signatos *E*: si hic natos *A* **556** sedeat *E*: subeat *A* **567** potest ... potest *E*: potes ... potes *A*

either him or me: whichever of us falls   535
will die guilty; against us your lightning
cannot err. JA. Start thinking sensibly
and talk calmly. If my father-in-law's house can offer any source of
                                                                    comfort
to ease your exile, then ask for it.
ME. My mind is strong enough, and is accustomed, to despise   540
kingly wealth, as you know; may I simply be permitted to take my
                                                                    children
to accompany me in exile, so that I may pour out my tears
in their embrace. For you, new sons are in prospect.
JA. I admit that I want to obey your request;
but fatherly love forbids it: for not even he, both king   545
and father-in-law, could make me able to endure it.
This is my reason for living, this is my solace for a heart
burnt out with anxieties. I could sooner do without
breath, limbs, light. ME. [aside] Does he love his sons so much?
Good, he's trapped; a vulnerable spot has been exposed.   550
[aloud] As I leave, at least let me be allowed to give my final
instructions, let me be allowed to give them a last embrace.
Thank you. In my closing words I now ask this too:
if my confused anguish has said anything out of turn,
let it not linger in your mind: let the memory of the better side   555
of me stay with you; let these concessions to anger
be erased. JA. I have driven all that from my mind;
and I also have a request, that you should control your fiery mind
and treat it gently: calmness assuages miseries. [Exits.]
ME. He has gone. Is it so? Do you walk off forgetting me   560
and all my many wicked deeds? Have I vanished from your memory?
No, I shall never vanish from it! [To herself.] Come on now, summon all
your power and skill. The advantage you've gained from your crimes is
that you count nothing as a crime. There is hardly any room for deception:
they fear me. Attack at the point where no one can   565
fear anything. Go on, be bold now, begin
whatever Medea is capable of, whatever she is *not* capable of!

    [To the Nurse.] You, loyal nurse, ally in my grief
and in my varied fortunes, assist my wretched plans.

est palla nobis, munus aetheriae domus 570
decusque regni, pignus Aeetae datum
a Sole generis, est et auro textili
monile fulgens, quodque gemmarum nitor
distinguit aurum, quo solent cingi comae.
haec nostra nati dona nubenti ferant, 575
sed ante diris inlita ac tincta artibus.
uocetur Hecate. sacra letifica appara:
statuantur arae, flamma iam tectis sonet.

CHORVS

Nulla uis flammae tumidiue uenti
tanta, nec teli metuenda torti, 580
quanta cum coniunx uiduata taedis
    ardet et odit;
non ubi hibernos nebulosus imbres
Auster aduexit properatque torrens
Hister et iunctos uetat esse pontes 585
    ac uagus errat;
non ubi impellit Rhodanus profundum,
aut ubi in riuos niuibus solutis
sole iam forti medioque uere
    tabuit Haemus. 590
caecus est ignis stimulatus ira
nec regi curat patiturue frenos
aut timet mortem: cupit ire in ipsos
    obuius enses.
parcite, o diui, ueniam precamur, 595
uiuat ut tutus mare qui subegit.
sed furit uinci dominus profundi
    regna secunda.
ausus aeternos agitare currus
immemor metae iuuenis paternae 600
quos polo sparsit furiosus ignes
    ipse recepit.
constitit nulli uia nota magno:

---

570 etheree *A*: aetherium *E* **577** letifica *E*: luctifica *A* **578** statuantur *E*: struantur *A* **579** tumidiue *E*: tumidique *A* **587** impellit β*T*: pellit *EP*

I have a mantle, a gift from the heavenly palace,   570
and the glory of my kingdom, given to Aeetes by the Sun
as a guarantee of his parentage; I also have a gleaming necklace
of plaited gold, and a gold diadem, embellished with
glittering jewels, to encircle the hair.
Let my sons take these gifts of ours to the bride,   575
but gifts first smeared and impregnated by my dreadful arts.
Let Hecate be summoned. Prepare the deadly ritual:
let altars be set up, let flames now resound in the house.
[*Exit Medea and the Nurse; enter the Chorus.*]
CHORUS
No energy of flame or swelling wind,
no fearsome energy of hurled javelin, is as great   580
as when a wife, robbed of her wedding-torches,
    blazes and hates;
not when fog-soaked Auster has brought
wintry rains, and the Hister rushes
in spate, forbidding bridges to stay joined together,   585
    and roaming haphazardly;
not when the Rhone pushes against the seas,
nor when, as snows melt into streams,
while sunshine grows strong, in mid spring,
    Haemus has thawed.   590
Blind is the fire spurred on by anger:
it has no wish to be controlled, will not tolerate the bridle,
has no fear of death, but longs to go and face
    the swords head-on.
Be merciful, o gods; we pray for forgiveness,   595
that he who subjugated the sea may live in safety.
But the lord of the deep is enraged that the second
    kingdom is conquered.
When that young man dared drive the eternal chariot,
forgetful of the course his father ran,   600
he himself fell victim to the fires that he scattered
    crazily across the heavens.
The familiar road costs no one dear:

82

uade qua tutum populo priori,
rumpe nec sacro uiolente sancta   605
    foedera mundi.
quisquis audacis tetigit carinae
nobiles remos nemorisque sacri
Pelion densa spoliauit umbra,
quisquis intrauit scopulos uagantes   610
et tot emensus pelagi labores
barbara funem religauit ora
raptor externi rediturus auri,
exitu diro temerata ponti
    iura piauit.   615
exigit poenas mare prouocatum:
Tiphys in primis, domitor profundi,
liquit indocto regimen magistro;
litore externo, procul a paternis
occidens regnis tumuloque uili   620
tectus ignotas iacet inter umbras.
Aulis amissi memor inde regis
portibus lentis retinet carinas
    stare querentes.
ille uocali genitus Camena,   625
cuius ad chordas modulante plectro
restitit torrens, siluere uenti,
cui suo cantu uolucris relicto
adfuit tota comitante silua,
Thracios sparsus iacuit per agros,   630
at caput tristi fluitauit Hebro:
contigit notam Styga Tartarumque,
    non rediturus.
strauit Alcides Aquilone natos,
patre Neptuno genitum necauit   635
sumere innumeras solitum figuras:

605-6 sacro ... sancta ... mundi *E*: sancti ... mundi ... sacra *A*   **608** remos *E*: ramos *A*
nemorisque sacri *E*: nemoris sacrati *A*   **617** *Axelson moved the first comma to follow* Tiphys:
Tiphys en primus *Zwierlein (1987), supported by Kershaw (1994), 244*   **628** cui *later*
manuscripts: cum *A*: tum *E*   **631** at caput tristi fluitauit Hebro *Gronovius*: ad caput tristis
fluuitauit hebri *E*: ad caput tractus fluuialis hebri *A*

travel where it was safe for our predecessors,
and do not, violent man, break the sacred   605
    laws of the universe.
Anyone who held the noble oars
of that daring ship and stripped Pelion
of the dense shade of its sacred grove,
anyone who passed between the wandering rocks,   610
who endured so many labours on the sea
and tied the mooring-rope on the barbarian shore,
intending to plunder foreign gold and then return—
with a terrible death they all atoned for the desecration of the
    rights of the sea.   615
The sea, when challenged, exacts punishment:
Tiphys first, the tamer of the deep,
handed the steering on to an untutored master;
on a foreign shore, after dying far from his
father's kingdom, covered by a humble   620
burial-mound, he lies among unknown shades.
Since then Aulis remembers its lost king,
and confines to its sluggish harbours
    ships that complain they are standing still.
That man born of the tuneful Camena—   625
at the sound of his lyre, as his plectrum played,
torrents stopped, winds fell silent;
a bird came up to him, abandoning its
own song, and the whole forest followed behind—
that man lay in shreds all over the Thracian countryside,   630
but his head drifted down the grim Hebrus:
he reached the Styx he knew, and Tartarus,
    but with no prospect of return.
Alcides struck down the sons of Aquilo,
he slew the man, fathered by Neptune,   635
who used to assume innumerable shapes;

84

ipse post terrae pelagique pacem,
post feri Ditis patefacta regna
uiuus ardenti recubans in Oeta
praebuit saeuis sua membra flammis   640
tabe consumptus gemini cruoris,
    munere nuptae.
strauit Ancaeum uiolentus ictu
saetiger; fratrem, Meleagre, matris
impius mactas morerisque dextra   645
matris iratae. meruere cuncti—
morte quod crimen tener expiauit
Herculi magno puer inrepertus,
raptus, heu, tutas puer inter undas?
ite nunc, fortes, perarate pontum   650
    fonte timendo.
Idmonem, quamuis bene fata nosset,
condidit serpens Libycis harenis;
omnibus uerax, sibi falsus uni
concidit Mopsus caruitque Thebis.   655
ille si uere cecinit futura,
exul errabit Thetidis maritus;   657
fulmine et ponto moriens Oilei   661
<pro suo gnatus> patrioque pendet   660a
    crimine poenas.   660b
igne fallaci nociturus Argis   658
Nauplius praeceps cadet in profundum;   659
coniugis fatum redimens Pheraei   662
uxor impendes animam marito.
ipse qui praedam spoliumque iussit
aureum prima reuehi carina   665

---

643 anceum *later manuscripts*: ant(h)(a)eum ω   **644** fratrem ω: fratres *later manuscripts*
649 heu *E*: est *A*   **651** fonte timendo *Gronovius*: ponte timendo *E*: sorte timenda *A*   **653**
Lyciis *Koetschau*   **657** errabit *Gruter*: errauit ω   **658-9, 661** *Peiper moved line 661 to
follow 657, and lines 658-9 to follow 660*   **661** Oilei *Daniel Heinsius*: oyleus *E*: cyleus *A*
660a-660b *the manuscripts write* patrioque ... poenas *as a single line, but Fabricius saw that
something had been omitted, and Zwierlein suggested inserting* pro suo gnatus   **658** igne *A*:
ille *E*   **659** cadet *Gruter*: cadit ω   **663** *P.Mich. has a fragmentary text of 663-704*   **663**
impendes *Gronovius*: impendens *E*: impendit *A*

after making peace on land and sea,
after opening up the kingdom of cruel Dis,
he himself lay down, alive, on blazing Oeta,
and surrendered his limbs to the savage flames,   640
consumed by the infection of the twin gore,
    by the gift from his bride.
The violent, bristly boar struck down Ancaeus
with its impact. Impious man, Meleager, you sacrifice your mother's
brother, and you die at the hand   645
of your enraged mother. They all deserved what they got—
but what crime was expiated by the death of the young boy
whom great Hercules never found,
the boy abducted, alas, in safe waters?
Go on, then, brave people, plough across the sea,   650
    when a spring is something to be frightened of.
Idmon, even though he knew the fates well,
was sent to his grave by a serpent, in the sands of Libya.
A true prophet for everyone else, false for himself alone,
Mopsus died and was kept from Thebes.   655
If he foretold the future truly,
Thetis' husband will wander in exile;   657
killed by thunderbolt and sea, Oileus'   661
<son> will pay the penalty <for his own and>   660a
    his father's crime;   660b
as he plans to destroy Argos with a deceptive beacon,   658
Nauplius will fall headfirst into the deep;   659
to redeem the life of your spouse from Pherae,   662
you, wife, will pay for your husband with your own soul.
Even the man who commanded the booty and the golden
spoils to be brought back in the first ship,   665

86

[ustus accenso Pelias aeno]
arsit angustas uagus inter undas.
iam satis, diui, mare uindicastis:
    parcite iusso.

NVTRIX

Pauet animus, horret: magna pernicies adest.   670
immane quantum augescit et semet dolor
accendit ipse uimque praeteritam integrat.
uidi furentem saepe et aggressam deos,
caelum trahentem: maius his, maius parat
Medea monstrum. namque ut attonito gradu   675
euasit et penetrale funestum attigit,
totas opes effundit et quidquid diu
etiam ipsa timuit promit atque omnem explicat
turbam malorum, arcana secreta abdita,
et triste laeua comparans sacrum manu   680
pestes uocat quascumque feruentis creat
harena Libyae quasque perpetua niue
Taurus coercet frigore Arctoo rigens,
et omne monstrum. tracta magicis cantibus
squamifera latebris turba desertis adest.   685
hic saeua serpens corpus immensum trahit
trifidamque linguam exertat et quaerit quibus
mortifera ueniat: carmine audito stupet
tumidumque nodis corpus aggestis plicat
cogitque in orbes. 'Parua sunt' inquit 'mala   690
et uile telum est, ima quod tellus creat:
caelo petam uenena. iam iam tempus est
aliquid mouere fraude uulgari altius.
huc ille uasti more torrentis iacens
descendat anguis, cuius immensos duae,   695
maior minorque, sentiunt nodos ferae

---

666 *deleted by Peiper (but found in P.Mich. as well as* ω) **677** effundit *Heinsius, and now found in P.Mich.:* effudit ω **680** comparans *Buecheler:* complicans *A:* comprecans *P.Mich. E (see Zwierlein [1976], 205-6)* **681** feruentis *later manuscripts:* feruenti ω **683** arctoo rigens β: arcto rigens δ: arcto oriens *E* **686** saeua *E:* sera *A* **692** iam iam *Gronovius:* iam *E:* iam nunc *A* **693** mouere *E:* moueri *A* **694** *R's text resumes here, and continues to 708*

[Pelias scorched in the heated cauldron]
he burned as he tossed to and fro in the confined waves.
You have now avenged the sea sufficiently, o gods:
    spare him who acted under orders.
[*Exit Chorus.*]

ACT FOUR

[*Enter Nurse.*]
NURSE

My soul panics and shudders: great destruction looms.   670
It is dreadful how mightily her anguish grows, sets itself
aflame, and renews its bygone energy.
I have often seen her going mad and attacking the gods,
dragging down the heavens: Medea is preparing a greater horror, a greater
one than those. For once she has gone off with thunder-struck steps   675
and has reached her deathly sanctum,
she unleashes all her resources, she brings out all the things that
even she has long been afraid to, she deploys all
her host of evils—mysterious, secret, hidden things.
Preparing a sinister ritual with her left hand,   680
she summons all the noxious plagues
that the sand of burning Libya produces, and that the Taurus,
paralysed by Arctic cold, locks in perpetual snow—
and all manner of horrors. Drawn by her Magic chants,
a scaly horde comes from its abandoned lairs.   685
Here a vicious serpent drags its huge body,
keeps darting out its three-forked tongue, and looks for victims to whom
it may bring death: hearing her song it is stunned,
folds its swollen body into piled-up knots,
and forces it into coils. 'Small are the evils' she says   690
'and commonplace the weapons that the lowest earth produces:
I shall seek poisons from heaven. Now, now it is time to set in motion
something more lofty than ordinary wrongdoing.
Let that Serpent descend here that sprawls out like a vast
torrent, whose immense coils the two   695
beasts feel, the Greater and the Lesser

(maior Pelasgis apta, Sidoniis minor),
pressasque tandem soluat Ophiuchus manus
uirusque fundat; adsit ad cantus meos
lacessere ausus gemina Python numina,   700
et Hydra et omnis redeat Herculea manu
succisa serpens caede se reparans sua.
tu quoque relictis peruigil Colchis ades,
sopite primum cantibus, serpens, meis.'
    Postquam euocauit omne serpentum genus,   705
congerit in unum frugis infaustae mala:
quaecumque generat inuius saxis Eryx,
quae fert opertis hieme perpetua iugis
sparsus cruore Caucasus Promethei,
et quis sagittas diuites Arabes linunt   711
pharetraque pugnax Medus aut Parthi leues,   710
aut quos sub axe frigido sucos legunt
lucis Suebae nobiles Hyrcaniis;
quodcumque tellus uere nidifico creat
aut rigida cum iam bruma decussit decus   715
nemorum et niuali cuncta constrinxit gelu,
quodcumque gramen flore mortifero uiret,
dirusue tortis sucus in radicibus
causas nocendi gignit, attrectat manu.
Haemonius illas contulit pestes Athos,   720
has Pindus ingens, illa Pangaei iugis
teneram cruenta falce deposuit comam;
has aluit altum gurgitem Tigris premens,
Danuuius illas, has per arentis plagas
tepidis Hydaspes gemmifer currens aquis,   725
nomenque terris qui dedit Baetis suis
Hesperia pulsans maria languenti uado.
haec passa ferrum est, dum parat Phoebus diem,
illius alta nocte succisus frutex;

---

701 manu A: manus RE 711, 710 Gronovius transposed these lines 711 quis Avantius:
qui ω 710 parthi leues E: parthus leuis A 712 quos A: quo E 713 suebae E: sueui A
hyrcaniis E: (h)yrcaneis A: Hercyniis Avantius 715 decussit a manuscript reading recorded
by Ascensius: discussit ω 722 R's text resumes here, and continues to 744 724 has …
plagas EA: his … plagis R 728 est EA: omitted by R

(the Greater useful to the Pelasgians, the Lesser to the Sidonians),
and let Ophiuchus at last release his tightly gripping hands
and send the poison pouring out; in answer to my incantations, let
Python come, he who dared attack the twin deities;   700
let the Hydra return, and every serpent cut off by Hercules' hand
that grew again as it was cut off.
You too, leave Colchis and come, ever-wakeful
serpent, who were sent to sleep for the first time by my incantations.'
     When she has summoned every kind of serpent,   705
she gathers together the evil powers of ill-omened plants:
whatever inaccessibly rocky Eryx generates,
what the Caucasus, spattered with the blood of Prometheus,
grows on its ridges covered in perpetual snow;
the plants the wealthy Arabs smear their arrows with,   711
and the Mede threatening war with his quiver, or the nimble Parthians; 710
or the juices that beneath the freezing pole
noble Sueban women gather in the Hyrcanian woods;
whatever earth produces in nest-building spring,
or when stiff winter has shaken off the glory   715
of the forests and bound everything in snowy frost;
whatever herb flourishes with deadly flower,
or whatever dread sap in twisted roots
generates means of injury—all these she handles.
Haemonian Athos contributed those harmful plants,   720
mighty Pindus these; that one on the ridges of Pangaeus
shed its soft tresses before the blood-stained sickle;
these were nurtured by the Tigris, which conceals its deep current,
those by the Danube, these by the Hydaspes, which runs through parched
regions carrying gems in its warm waters,   725
and by the Baetis, which has given its name to its territory,
crashing against the Hesperian seas with its slow-moving waters.
This one fell victim to the steel as Phoebus got daylight ready,
that one's stalk was chopped down in deep night;

90

at huius ungue secta cantato seges. 730
   Mortifera carpit gramina ac serpentium
saniem exprimit miscetque et obscenas aues
maestique cor bubonis et raucae strigis
exsecta uiuae uiscera. haec scelerum artifex
discreta ponit: his rapax uis ignium, 735
his gelida pigri frigoris glacies inest.
addit uenenis uerba non illis minus
metuenda.—sonuit ecce uesano gradu
canitque. mundus uocibus primis tremit.

MEDEA

   Comprecor uulgus silentum uosque ferales deos 740
et Chaos caecum atque opacam Ditis umbrosi domum,
Tartari ripis ligatos squalidae Mortis specus.
supplicis, animae, remissis currite ad thalamos nouos:
rota resistat membra torquens, tangat Ixion humum,
Tantalus securus undas hauriat Pirenidas. 745
grauior uni poena sedeat coniugis socero mei:
lubricus per saxa retro Sisyphum uoluat lapis.
uos quoque, urnis quas foratis inritus ludit labor,
Danaides, coite: uestras hic dies quaerit manus.—
nunc meis uocata sacris, noctium sidus, ueni 750
pessimos induta uultus, fronte non una minax.
   Tibi more gentis uinculo soluens comam
secreta nudo nemora lustraui pede
et euocaui nubibus siccis aquas
egique ad imum maria, et Oceanus graues 755
interius undas aestibus uictis dedit,
pariterque mundus lege confusa aetheris
et solem et astra uidit et uetitum mare
tetigistis, ursae. temporum flexi uices:
aestiua tellus horruit cantu meo, 760

---

735 his *EA*: hic *R* **740** *EA indicate that Medea is speaker, R has no indication* comprecor *E*: uos precor *A* uosque *EA*: uos quoque *R, apparently* **742** ripis ω: tenebris *Billerbeck (1987)* **743** supplicis *editors*: suppliciis ω **746** *deleted by Axelson* grauior uni *E*: grauiorum *A* sedeat ω: cedat *Grotius* **747** uoluat ω: soluat *Gronovius* **754** nubibus ω: rupibus *Heinsius* **760** horruit *Markland*: floruit ω

but this one's stem was cut by her enchanted finger-nail.   730
   She plucks the deadly herbs, squeezes
venom from the snakes, and adds birds of ill-omen too,
the heart of an inauspicious owl, and the innards cut out
from a screech-owl that was still alive. The expert in wickedness
lays these out separately: these have the devouring energy of fire,   735
these the frosty iciness of immobile cold.
To her poisons she adds words no less
terrible than them.—Listen, there's the noise of her crazed footsteps,
and her singing! The universe shudders as she begins to speak.
[*Enter Medea.*]

MEDEA
I pray to the host of silent ones, and to you funereal gods,   740
to dark Chaos and the impenetrable house of shadowy Dis,
to the caverns of ugly Death, confined by the river-banks of Tartarus.
Souls, with your torments suspended, hurry to the new wedding:
let the wheel that racks Ixion's limbs stand still, let him touch the ground;
let Tantalus gulp down the waters of Pirene without fear;   745
let punishment continue—and more severely—only for my husband's
                                                                                    father-in-law,
let the stone slip backwards and roll Sisyphus down over the rocks.
You too, whose fruitless efforts mock you with hole-riddled urns,
daughters of Danaus, gather here: this day needs your hands.
Now, summoned by my rituals, come, star of the night,   750
assuming your most terrible aspect, menacing with each of your faces.
   For you, I have unfastened my hair, as is my people's custom,
I have paced the hidden forests with bare foot,
I have summoned water from dry clouds
and driven the sea to its depths: Ocean,   755
his tides defeated, has drawn his sluggish waters deep within.
The laws governing the heavens have been overturned, the world
has seen both sun and stars at once; and you, Bears, have dipped into the
forbidden sea. I have changed the courses of the seasons:
the summer earth has shivered at my chant,   760

92

coacta messem uidit hibernam Ceres;
uiolenta Phasis uertit in fontem uada
et Hister, in tot ora diuisus, truces
compressit undas omnibus ripis piger;
sonuere fluctus, tumuit insanum mare   765
tacente uento; nemoris antiqui domus
amisit umbras uocis imperio meae.
die relicto Phoebus in medio stetit,
Hyadesque nostris cantibus motae labant.—
adesse sacris tempus est, Phoebe, tuis.   770
    Tibi haec cruenta serta texuntur manu,
      nouena quae serpens ligat,
tibi haec Typhoeus membra quae discors tulit,
      qui regna concussit Iouis.
uectoris istic perfidi sanguis inest,   775
      quem Nessus expirans dedit.
Oetaeus isto cinere defecit rogus,
      qui uirus Herculeum bibit.
piae sororis, impiae matris, facem
      ultricis Althaeae uides.   780
reliquit istas inuio plumas specu
      Harpyia, dum Zeten fugit.
his adice pinnas sauciae Stymphalidos
      Lernaea passae spicula.—
sonuistis, arae, tripodas agnosco meos   785
      fauente commotos dea.
Video Triuiae currus agiles,
non quos pleno lucida uultu
      pernox agitat,
sed quos facie lurida maesta,   790
cum Thessalicis uexata minis
caelum freno propiore legit.
sic face tristem pallida lucem
      funde per auras,
horrore nouo terre populos

---

761 coacta messem *E*: messem coacta *A* **766** domus *A*: decus domus *E* **767** umbras *E*: umbram *A* **775** uectoris *E, after correction*: uictoris *A* **785** tripodas *E*: tripodes *A* **793** face *E*: fac *A*

Ceres has been compelled to watch a winter harvest.
The Phasis has turned its violent waters back to its source,
and the Hister, that branches out into so many mouths,
has held back its sullen waters, reluctant to move in any of its channels.
Waves have roared and the frenzied sea has churned   765
though the wind stayed silent; the ancient forest's home
has lost its shade at a command from my voice.
Phoebus has abandoned the day and stopped in mid course,
and the Hyades waver, shaken by my chant.
It is time, Phoebe, to attend your rites.   770
 For you these garlands are woven with bloody hand
   (nine serpents intertwine them),
 for you these limbs that belonged to rebellious Typhoeus,
   who made Jupiter's kingdom tremble.
 Here is the blood of the treacherous ferryman,   775
   which Nessus gave as he breathed his last.
 The pyre on Oeta, which drank the poison given to Hercules,
   died down into these ashes.
 You see the torch of the loving sister, the unloving mother,
   avenging Althaea.   780
 The Harpy left behind these feathers in an inaccessible cave
   while fleeing from Zetes.
 Add to these the feathers of a wounded Stymphalian bird
   that was victim of the Lernaean arrows.
 Altars, you made a noise; I recognise that my tripods 785
   shook as the goddess showed her favour.
I see the swift chariot of Trivia,
not the one that she drives all through the night,
   when bright with full face,
but the one that she drives when she is lurid with mournful 790
expression, as, troubled by Thessalian threats,
she crosses heaven with a tighter rein.
 With just such a pallor, diffuse a grim light from your torch
   through the atmosphere,
 terrify the nations with new dread,

inque auxilium, Dictynna, tuum   795
pretiosa sonent aera Corinthi.
tibi sanguineo caespite sacrum
    sollemne damus,
tibi de medio rapta sepulcro
fax nocturnos sustulit ignes,   800
tibi mota caput flexa uoces   801a
    ceruice dedi,   801b
tibi funereo de more iacens
passos cingit uitta capillos,
tibi iactatur tristis Stygia
    ramus ab unda,   805
tibi nudato pectore maenas
sacro feriam bracchia cultro.
manet noster sanguis ad aras:
assuesce, manus, stringere ferrum
carosque pati posse cruores—   810
sacrum laticem percussa dedi.
quodsi nimium saepe uocari
quereris uotis, ignosce, precor:
causa uocandi, Persei, tuos
    saepius arcus   815
una atque eadem est semper, Iason.
    Tu nunc uestes tinge Creusae,
quas cum primum sumpserit, imas
urat serpens flamma medullas.
ignis fuluo clusus in auro   820
latet obscurus, quem mihi caeli
qui furta luit uiscere feto
dedit et docuit condere uires
arte, Prometheus; dedit et tenui
sulphure tectos Mulciber ignes,   825
et uiuacis fulgura flammae
de cognato Phaethonte tuli.
habeo mediae dona Chimaerae,
habeo flammas usto tauri

---

803 cingit *E*: uincit *A*   **814-5** tuos ... arcus *ω*: tuas ... artes *Axelson*   **819** serpens *E*: repens *A*

and, Dictynna, let the   795
precious bronzes of Corinth ring out to aid you.
For you, on the bloodstained turf,
     we make the customary offering,
for you a torch snatched from the middle of a funeral-pyre
sends out nocturnal fires,   800
for you, I toss my head, I arch my neck,
     and utter my cries,
for you a headband, worn in funereal fashion,
circles my flowing hair;
for you I brandish a sinister branch from beside
     the waters of the Styx;   805
for you, with bared breast, like a Maenad,
I shall slash my arms with a sacred knife.
Let my blood flow on the altar:
grow used, my hands, to unsheathing the steel
and managing to endure the shedding of your own dear blood— 810
the blow is struck, I have offered up the sacred liquid.
But if you complain that you are invoked too often
by my prayers, forgive me, I pray:
the reason, daughter of Perses, for my invoking your
     bow so often   815
is always one and the same: Jason.
     Now impregnate the garments for Creusa,
and as soon as she puts them on,
let creeping flame burn right to the marrow of her bones.
Enclosed in the yellow gold there   820
lurks hidden the fire that was given to me
by the one who pays for his theft from heaven with entrails
that reproduce themselves, by the one who taught me to conceal fire's
power artfully, Prometheus; Mulciber, also, gave me
fire concealed in fine-ground sulphur,   825
and I received lightning-flashes of living flame
from my kinsman Phaethon.
I have gifts from the middle of the Chimaera,
I have flames snatched from the scorched

gutture raptas, 830
quas permixto felle Medusae
tacitum iussi seruare malum.
  Adde uenenis stimulos, Hecate,
donisque meis semina flammae
  condita serua:
fallant uisus tactusque ferant, 835
meet in pectus uenasque calor,
stillent artus ossaque fument
uincatque suas flagrante coma
  noua nupta faces.
uota tenentur: ter latratus 840
audax Hecate dedit et sacros
edidit ignes face luctifera.
  Peracta uis est omnis: huc gnatos uoca,
pretiosa per quos dona nubenti feram.
  Ite, ite, nati, matris infaustae genus, 845
placate uobis munere et multa prece
dominam ac nouercam. uadite et celeres domum
referte gressus, ultimo amplexu ut fruar.

CHORVS

Quonam cruenta maenas
praeceps amore saeuo 850
rapitur? quod impotenti
facinus parat furore?
uultus citatus ira
riget et caput feroci
quatiens superba motu 855
regi minatur ultro.
  quis credat exulem?
flagrant genae rubentes,
pallor fugat ruborem.
nullum uagante forma 860
seruat diu colorem.
huc fert pedes et illuc,

---

841 audax ω: uindex *Watt (1996), 250* **842** luctifera *later manuscripts (see Zwierlein [1976], 208-9)*: lucifera ω **844** feram *Bentley*: feras ω **847** ac *E*: et *A*

throat of the bull,
which I mixed with the bile of Medusa,
and commanded to keep their evil hidden.
    Spur on the poisons, Hecate,
and guard the seeds of flame
    concealed within my gifts:
let them elude the eye and permit touch,   835
let the heat go into breast and veins,
let limbs melt and bones smoke,
and with blazing hair let the new bride
    eclipse her wedding-torches.
    My prayers are being granted: three times bold Hecate   840
has barked and has shot out sacred
fires from her torch that brings grief.
    The potent mixture is all completed: summon my sons here,
so that through them I may convey the precious gifts to the bride.
[*Enter the sons.*]
    Go, go, my sons, offspring of an ill-fated mother;   845
with this gift and with many prayers appease
your mistress and stepmother. Set off, and quickly make your way
back home, so that I may enjoy a last embrace.
[*Exit Medea, Nurse and children. Enter the Chorus*]

CHORUS

Where is the blood-stained Maenad
rushing, swept headlong by cruel   850
love? What deed is she
planning in her uncontrollable madness?
Her face, driven by anger,
is set firm; haughtily
tossing her head in wild movements,   855
she deliberately threatens the king.
    Who would believe she is an exile?
Her reddened cheeks are ablaze,
then pallor banishes the redness.
Her appearance shifts, she   860
maintains no colouring for long.
She paces to and fro,

ut tigris orba natis
cursu furente lustrat
   Gangeticum nemus. 865
frenare nescit iras
Medea, non amores;
nunc ira amorque causam
iunxere: quid sequetur?
quando efferet Pelasgis 870
nefanda Colchis aruis
gressum metuque soluet
regnum simulque reges?
nunc, Phoebe, mitte currus
nullo morante loro, 875
nox condat alma lucem,
mergat diem timendum
   dux noctis Hesperus.

NVNTIVS

     Periere cuncta, concidit regni status;
     nata atque genitor cinere permixto iacent. 880
CH.   Qua fraude capti? NVN. Qua solent reges capi:
     donis. CH. In illis esse quis potuit dolus?
NVN. Et ipse miror uixque iam facto malo
     potuisse fieri credo. CH. Quis cladis modus?
NVN. Auidus per omnem regiae partem furit 885
     ut iussus ignis: iam domus tota occidit,
     urbi timetur. CH. Vnda flammas opprimat.
NVN. Et hoc in ista clade mirandum accidit:
     alit unda flammas, quoque prohibetur magis,
     magis ardet ignis; ipsa praesidia occupat. 890

NVTRIX

     Effer citatum sede Pelopea gradum,
     Medea, praeceps quaslibet terras pete.

---

866 nescit ω: non scit *Bentley (but see Zwierlein [1986], 165)* **871** nefanda ω: infanda *L. Müller* **882** *A begins the Chorus's response at* in illis, *E begins it at* donis. **886** ut iussus ω: inmissus *Gronovius* **889-890** *A omits* quoque … ignis **891** *A indicates that the Nurse speaks here, E does not (making this a continuation of the Messenger's speech)*

as a tigress bereft of her children
with insane speed roams
    the forests of the Ganges.   865
Medea does not know how to rein in
anger, nor love.
Now anger and love have made
common cause: what will result?
When will the unspeakable   870
Colchian woman depart from Pelasgian
lands and release from fear
the kingdom, and the king's family too?
Now, Phoebus, drive your chariot onwards;
don't let your reins delay it,   875
let life-giving night bury the light,
let Hesperus, usher of night,
    drown this frightful day.

ACT FIVE

[*Enter Messenger.*]
MESSENGER
    All is lost! The kingdom is in ruins.
    Daughter and father lie in mingled ashes.   880
CH. Trapped by what deceit? MESS. The kind by which kings are usually
                                           trapped—
    by gifts. CH. What trickery could there be in them?
MESS. I too am amazed, and even after the horror *has* occurred
    I can scarcely believe it could have. CH. What limit is there to the
                                           disaster?
MESS. Greedily fire rages through every part of the royal palace,   885
    as if under orders; the building has already collapsed completely,
    people fear for the city. CH. Let water smother the flames.
MESS. In this catastrophe this further paradox occurs:
    water feeds the flames, and the more they try to check the fire,
    the more it blazes: it seizes even our means of defence.   890
    [*Exit Messenger and Chorus, enter Nurse and Medea.*]
NURSE
    Depart with all speed from Pelops' home,
    Medea, and make haste for whatever lands you choose.

MEDEA

Egone ut recedam? si profugissem prius,
ad hoc redirem. nuptias specto nouas.
quid, anime, cessas? sequere felicem impetum.   895
pars ultionis ista, qua gaudes, quota est!
amas adhuc, furiose, si satis est tibi
caelebs Iason. quaere poenarum genus
haut usitatum iamque sic temet para:
fas omne cedat, abeat expulsus pudor;   900
uindicta leuis est quam ferunt purae manus.
incumbe in iras teque languentem excita
penitusque ueteres pectore ex imo impetus
uiolentus hauri. quidquid admissum est adhuc,
pietas uocetur. hoc age, et faxo sciant   905
quam leuia fuerint quamque uulgaris notae
quae commodaui scelera. prolusit dolor
per ista noster: quid manus poterant rudes
audere magnum, quid puellaris furor?
Medea nunc sum; creuit ingenium malis: 910
iuuat, iuuat rapuisse fraternum caput,
artus iuuat secuisse et arcano patrem
spoliasse sacro, iuuat in exitium senis
armasse natas. quaere materiam, dolor:
ad omne facinus non rudem dextram afferes.   915
    Quo te igitur, ira, mittis, aut quae perfido
intendis hosti tela? nescioquid ferox
decreuit animus intus et nondum sibi
audet fateri. stulta properaui nimis:
ex paelice utinam liberos hostis meus   920
aliquos haberet—quidquid ex illo tuum est,
Creusa peperit. placuit hoc poenae genus,
meritoque placuit: ultimum magno scelus
animo parandum est: liberi quondam mei,
uos pro paternis sceleribus poenas date.   925

---

897 furiose *Bentley*: furiosa ω   901 purae *E*: parue *A*   905 agam et *Richter*: age! en
Axelson (but see Kershaw [1994], 245-6)   912 artus *A*: ortus *E*   913 spoliasse *E*: spoliare
A   923 ultimum magno *later manuscripts*: ultimum agnosco *E*: ultimo magno *A*

MEDEA
Should I leave? If I had fled earlier,
I would return for this. I am watching a new kind of wedding.
Why, my soul, do you hold back? Follow up your successful attack. 895
How small a part of your revenge is this you are enjoying now!
You are still in love, mad soul, if you are satisfied now that
Jason is unmarried. Look for a form of punishment
out of the ordinary, get yourself ready now, like this:
let all morality depart, let honour be expelled; 900
it's a trifling retribution that *pure* hands achieve.
Work at your anger, rouse your feeble being,
and savagely draw up old impulses from deep in the well
of your breast. Whatever you have perpetrated up till now
should be called love. Come on, I shall make them recognise 905
how trifling and how commonplace are
the crimes I have committed to oblige others. My anguish has been
practising on those crimes: what mighty deed could unskilled hands,
could the madness of a *girl* dare to achieve?
Now I *am* Medea; evils have increased my talent: 910
I'm glad, I'm glad I tore off my brother's head,
I'm glad I cut up his limbs, and robbed my father of
his secret relic, I'm glad I armed the daughters
to destroy the old man. Look for your opportunity, anguish:
for every crime you will have hands that are well trained. 915
     What target will you launch yourself at, rage, what missiles
will you aim at your treacherous enemy? My mind has secretly made
some hideous decision, and does not yet dare
confess it openly to itself. Fool, I have been in too much haste:
if only my enemy had some children 920
from his mistress! Yet whatever offspring *you* have by him,
Creusa is their mother. I have decided on this form of punishment,
and decided rightly; I must plan the ultimate crime
with courageous heart: children, once mine,
you must pay the penalty for your father's crimes. 925

Cor pepulit horror, membra torpescunt gelu
pectusque tremuit. ira discessit loco
materque tota coniuge expulsa redit.
egone ut meorum liberum ac prolis meae
fundam cruorem? melius, a, demens furor!   930
incognitum istud facinus ac dirum nefas
a me quoque absit; quod scelus miseri luent?
scelus est Iason genitor et maius scelus
Medea mater—occidant, non sunt mei;
pereant, mei sunt. crimine et culpa carent,   935
sunt innocentes, fateor: et frater fuit.
quid, anime, titubas? ora quid lacrimae rigant
uariamque nunc huc ira, nunc illuc amor
diducit? anceps aestus incertam rapit;
ut saeua rapidi bella cum uenti gerunt,   940
utrimque fluctus maria discordes agunt
dubiumque feruet pelagus, haut aliter meum
cor fluctuatur: ira pietatem fugat
iramque pietas—cede pietati, dolor.
     Huc, cara proles, unicum afflictae domus   945
solamen, huc uos ferte et infusos mihi
coniungite artus. habeat incolumes pater,
dum et mater habeat—urguet exilium ac fuga:
iam iam meo rapientur auulsi e sinu,
flentes, gementes—osculis pereant patris: 950
periere matris. rursus increscit dolor
et feruet odium, repetit inuitam manum
antiqua Erinys—ira, qua ducis, sequor.
utinam superbae turba Tantalidos meo
exisset utero bisque septenos parens   955
natos tulissem! sterilis in poenas fui—
fratri patrique quod sat est, peperi duos.
     Quonam ista tendit turba Furiarum impotens?
quem quaerit aut quo flammeos ictus parat,

---

930 ah *Ascensius*: ha *A*: *omitted by E* (*compare on line 139*) **939** diducit *A*: deducit *E*
940 rapidi *E*: rabidi *A* **942** feruet pelagus *E*: pelagus feruet *A* meum *E*: metu *A* **950**
patris *A*: patri *E* **951** periere *A*: pariere *E* matris *later manuscripts*: matri ω **952** inuitam
Gronovius: inuisam ω **958** furiarum *E*: funerum *A*

    Shudders have rocked my heart, my limbs are going numb with cold,
my breast has been trembling. Anger has deserted her post,
the wife in me is driven out, the mother is completely reinstated.
Should I spill the blood of my children,
of my offspring? Ah, insane madness, better to   930
let that unheard-of crime and terrible wickedness
remain remote even from me. For what crime will the poor boys atone?
Their crime is having Jason for father, and a greater crime is
having Medea for mother—if they are *not* mine, let them die;
if they *are* mine, let them perish. They are without sin and guilt,   935
they are innocent, I admit: so was my brother.
Why, soul, do you vacillate? Why do tears water my cheeks
and, as I waver, why does anger now drag me off in one direction, love
                                           now

in another? An undecided tide sweeps me along in my uncertainty;
just as, when violent winds wage cruel war,   940
the quarrelling billows drive the sea-water in two directions at once,
and the swell seethes indecisively, just so my
heart is surging: anger banishes love,
love anger—anguish, surrender to love.
    Here, my dear offspring, sole comfort amid the   945
ruin of my home, come over here and throw your arms
around me in an embrace. Let your father keep you, unharmed—
provided your mother does too. But exile and flight threaten me:
soon, soon they will be torn and snatched away from my embrace,
weeping, groaning—let them be lost to their father's kisses,   950
for they are lost to their mother's. Anguish increases again
and hatred boils up, the ancient Erinys again demands
my reluctant hand: anger, where you lead, I follow.
If only the brood of Tantalus's arrogant daughter
had issued from my womb, and I had been mother to   955
twice seven children! I've been infertile when it comes to punishments—
yet I have given birth to two, which is enough for my brother and my
                                       father.

    Where is that violent brood of Furies heading?
Whom is it seeking? where is it poised to direct its fiery blows?

aut cui cruentas agmen infernum faces 960
intentat? ingens anguis excusso sonat
tortus flagello. quem trabe infesta petit
Megaera? cuius umbra dispersis uenit
incerta membris? frater est, poenas petit:
dabimus, sed omnes. fige luminibus faces, 965
lania, perure, pectus en Furiis patet.
    Discedere a me, frater, ultrices deas
manesque ad imos ire securas iube:
mihi me relinque et utere hac, frater, manu
quae strinxit ensem—uictima manes tuos 970
placamus ista. quid repens affert sonus?
parantur arma meque in exitium petunt.
excelsa nostrae tecta conscendam domus
caede incohata. perge tu mecum comes.
tuum quoque ipsa corpus hinc mecum aueham. 975
nunc hoc age, anime: non in occulto tibi est
perdenda uirtus; approba populo manum.

IASON

Quicumque regum cladibus fidus doles,
concurre, ut ipsam sceleris auctorem horridi
capiamus. huc, huc, fortis armiferi cohors, 980
conferte tela, uertite ex imo domum.
ME.   Iam iam recepi sceptra germanum patrem,
spoliumque Colchi pecudis auratae tenent;
rediere regna, rapta uirginitas redit.
o placida tandem numina, o festum diem, 985
o nuptialem! uade, perfectum est scelus—
uindicta nondum: perage, dum faciunt manus.
quid nunc moraris, anime? quid dubitas? potens
iam cecidit ira? paenitet facti, pudet.
quid, misera, feci? misera? paeniteat licet, 990
feci. uoluptas magna me inuitam subit,

---

961 intentat *A*: intendat *E* ingens anguis *A*: igne sanguis *E* 977 approba *E*: approbo *A*
982 recepi β: recipi *E*: recepti δ 985 numina *A*: nomina *E* 987 *omitted by A* 989
Axelson first punctuated the first half of the line as a question 991 inuitam δ: inuisam β: et
inuitam *E*

at whom is the hellish band pointing its bloody
torches? A huge serpent writhes and hisses
as the whip is cracked. Whom is Megaera hunting with menacing
brand? Whose shade is approaching, indistinct,
dismembered? It is my brother, he seeks revenge:
we shall provide it—all of us shall. Plunge your torches into my eyes, 965
hack, burn; see, my breast is exposed to the Furies.

    Brother, command the avenging goddesses to let me alone,
and to go to the shades below, their minds at rest:
leave me to myself, brother, and use this hand of mine
which has drawn its sword—[*She kills one of the sons.*] with this victim
I placate your shade. [*Jason and armed attendants approach.*]
                                What does that sudden noise mean? 971
Armed men are being marshalled, and are seeking to destroy me.
I shall climb the lofty roof of our house—
the slaughter is unfinished. [*To the remaining son.*] You go on, keep next
                                          to me.
[*To the dead son.*] Your body, too, I shall carry off with me. 975
Come on, now, my soul: you must not waste your
courage in secret; have your handiwork applauded by the people.
[*Medea climbs on to the roof, carrying the dead son and making the other
son go with her. Enter Jason and attendants.*]

JASON
    All you who loyally grieve at the disastrous sufferings of the king's
                                         family,
    gather swiftly, so that we may seize the perpetrator of this
    grisly crime herself. Here, here, men bearing arms, brave band, 980
    bring weapons, destroy the house from its foundations up.

ME. Now, now I have regained sceptre, brother, father;
    the Colchians keep the golden creature's spoils;
    my kingdom has been restored, my raped virginity is restored.
    O divine powers, favourable at last, o festive day, 985
    o wedding day! Go, your wickedness is complete—
    but not yet your vengeance: finish it, while your hands are on good form.
    Why do you now hold back, my soul? Why hesitate? Has potent
    anger now abated? I feel regret and shame for my deed.
    What, wretched woman, have I done? Wretched? Even if I feel regret,
    I have done it. Great pleasure is stealing over me against my will, 991

et ecce crescit. derat hoc unum mihi,
spectator iste. nil adhuc facti reor:
quidquid sine isto fecimus sceleris perit.

IA. En ipsa tecti parte praecipiti imminet.   995
huc rapiat ignes aliquis, ut flammis cadat
suis perusta. ME. Congere extremum tuis
natis, Iason, funus ac tumulum strue:
coniunx socerque iusta iam functis habent
a me sepulti; gnatus hic fatum tulit,   1000
hic te uidente dabitur exitio pari.

IA. Per numen omne perque communes fugas
torosque, quos non nostra uiolauit fides,
iam parce nato. si quod est crimen, meum est:
me dedo morti; noxium macta caput.   1005

ME. Hac qua recusas, qua doles, ferrum exigam.
i nunc, superbe, uirginum thalamos pete,
relinque matres. IA. Vnus est poenae satis.

ME. Si posset una caede satiari manus,
nullam petisset. ut duos perimam, tamen   1010
nimium est dolori numerus angustus meo.
in matre si quod pignus etiamnunc latet,
scrutabor ense uiscera et ferro extraham.

IA. Iam perage coeptum facinus, haut ultra precor,
moramque saltem supplicis dona meis.   1015

ME. Perfruere lento scelere, ne propera, dolor:
meus dies est; tempore accepto utimur.

IA. Infesta, memet perime. ME. Misereri iubes.—
bene est, peractum est. plura non habui, dolor,
quae tibi litarem. lumina huc tumida alleua,   1020
ingrate Iason. coniugem agnoscis tuam?
sic fugere soleo. patuit in caelum uia:
squamosa gemini colla serpentes iugo
summissa praebent. recipe iam gnatos, parens;
ego inter auras aliti curru uehar.   1025

---

993 iste *E*: ipse *A* **1005** dedo *E*: dede *A* **1006** doles *E*: dolet *A* **1009-27** *omitted by A*
1009 satiari manus *later manuscripts*: satiariamanus *E* **1014** perage *later manuscripts*:
perge *E* haut *later manuscripts*: aut *E* **1016** scelere *later manuscripts*: sceleri *E*

and, see, it is increasing. This is the one thing that I lacked,
to have him watching me. I think nothing has yet been achieved:
every crime I have committed without him was wasted.

JA. See, she looks down menacingly from the steep-sloping roof.   995
Someone bring fire here quickly, so that she may fall, burnt up
by her own flames. ME. Heap up for your sons a final
funeral, Jason, and build a burial-mound:
your wife and father-in-law already have what is owed to the dead,
they have been buried by me; this son has met his fate,   1000
this one will be despatched to a like death as you watch.

JA. By every divine power, by the banishments we shared,
and by the bed that was not violated by my faithfulness,
spare our son now. If there is any crime, it's mine:
I surrender to death; sacrifice my guilty life.   1005

ME. Where you protest, where you feel anguish, there I shall plunge the steel.
Go on now, arrogant man, chase after marriage to girls,
abandon mothers. JA. One son is sufficient to punish me.

ME. If my hand could have been satisfied with just one slaughter,
it would not have sought any. Even if I destroy two sons, still   1010
the number is too limited for my anguish.
If any pledge even now lurks unseen within its mother,
I shall probe my womb with the sword and tear it out with the steel.

JA. Complete the deed you have begun. I entreat you no further;
at least don't let my tortures be drawn out.   1015

ME. Relish a leisurely crime, anguish, do not hurry:
the day is mine; I am enjoying the time I have been granted.

JA. Savage woman, destroy *me*. ME. You're telling me to have pity.
[*She kills the second son.*]
Good, it is finished. I had nothing else, anguish,
to sacrifice to you. Raise your swollen eyes towards me,   1020
ungrateful Jason. Do you recognise your wife?
I'm used to escaping in such a fashion. A path to the heavens has opened
up:

twin serpents offer their scaly necks
in submission to the yoke. Now take your sons back, parent;
I shall ride on my winged chariot among the winds.   1025

108

IA.Per alta uade spatia sublime aetheris,
testare nullos esse, qua ueheris, deos.

1026 sublime aetheris *Bothe*: sublimi aetheri *E*: sublimi aetheris *later manuscripts*

JA. Travel up above through the high expanses of the heavens;
     bear witness that wherever you go there are no gods.

Commentary

ACT ONE: 1-55

1-55   Seneca's (S.'s) play opens with a soliloquy from Medea (M.) that expresses her anger against Jason and the royal family of Corinth. She does not give any narrative of what has happened, and her allusive references to the new wife and the father-in-law presuppose that the audience knows the story of Jason abandoning M. in order to marry Creon's daughter (see Introduction §3.2(c)). M. does not state clearly that the wedding has not yet taken place: that emerges at 37-9 as she speaks of participating in the ceremony herself (in Euripides the wedding has taken place before the play starts, cf. Eur. *Med.* 18-9). The sequence of thought in her speech may be analysed as follows (but such analysis runs the risk of disguising the unpredictable swings in her emotions and thoughts):

1-12	Prayer to the gods.
13-18	Prayer to the Furies for the death of Creusa, Creon and the royal family.
19-26a	Prayer for a living punishment for Jason.
26b-36	Appeal to the Sun to help, and to lend her his chariot to destroy Corinth.
37-43	She will play a part in the wedding ceremony and seek vengeance there.
44-55	She must equal or surpass her past crimes, now that she is a mother.

Euripides' play starts with the Nurse wishing that the Argo had never been built and had never set sail, and Ennius' Latin version of the play followed him closely (208-16 Jocelyn, 205-13 Ribbeck, 253-61 Warmington). The Nurse's opening speech obliquely provides some of the background to the play; but her argument was treated by Roman authors as an example of a rather distant causal relationship—the connection between the felling of the trees on Mount Pelion, with which the Nurse starts, and the suffering of M., is a remote one (cf. Cic. *Fat.* 34-5). S., by contrast, plunges straight into the suffering and anger of M. herself.

1-12   The first twelve lines are a single sentence, consisting of a series of addresses to deities in the vocative case, with the main clause in the second half of line 12. Several of the deities are referred to by descriptive phrases rather than proper names, so the reader is required to draw on knowledge of myth and religion to identify them (see Introduction §5.1). In Greek tragedy, the opening speaker's identity is usually established clearly in the first couple of lines, but that does not always happen in S. Here, the concern for marriage and for the Argo (1-5) could come from M. or her Nurse; but the prayer to Hecate in 6-7 points to M., immediately establishing her as a witch figure, and her identity is clinched by the phrase 'gods by whom Jason swore to me' in 7-8. In a written text, of course, the speaker is named at the start of the speech, and in stage performance her identity could be established by costume and mask.

1   **Gods of marriage**: the phrase suggests various deities associated with marriage—Juno and Hymenaeus in particular, perhaps also Jupiter and Venus (cf. Eur. fr. 781.17N 'Aphrodite goddess of marriage'). But it is noteworthy that neither Venus nor Cupid is mentioned individually by name in this speech, or elsewhere in the play (see, however, on 62-5 and 219-20). The phrase 'gods of marriage' is used by S. also at *Thy.* 1102-3; and Tac. *Germ.* 18 uses it in the context of a German tribe. It is a phrase that was apparently used in Roman cult, and Varro (ap. Non. 528 M.; Wissowa [1912], 281) called the agricultural deities Pilumnus and Picumnus gods of marriage, though they are most unlikely to be relevant here. **and you**: repetition of the second person pronoun is characteristic of classical—and Christian—prayers and hymns (see on 71-4). **the ancestral wedding-couch**: literally 'the bed of the *genius*.' The *genius* by S.'s time was regarded as the individual divine spirit who protected each man; women had a corresponding protecting spirit called the *iuno*. In household religion the *genius* of the paterfamilias was worshipped, and was associated with the special bed that was used at weddings. (See *OCD³* on 'genius'.)

2   **Lucina**: whereas several other deities in the list are referred to by description, Lucina is named; yet her identity is uncertain. (1) Originally in Roman religion Lucina was a title of Juno, in her role as protectress of childbirth. However, in the choral ode at line 61 it is likely that Lucina is not to be identified with Juno, who has already been referred to two lines earlier (see on 59 'sceptre-bearing Thunderers'). (2) In Latin poetry Lucina had been identified with Diana from Catullus onwards (Catul. 34.13, cf. Pease on Cic. *N.D.* 2.68). The identification perhaps arose because of the associations with childbirth of Diana's Greek counterpart, Artemis; and because of Diana's association with the moon, for the name Lucina was connected etymologically by the Romans with Moon—*Luna*—, and with light—*lux, lucis*—(cf. Var. *L.* 5.69; Maltby [1991] on *Lucina, luna*). (3) S. may treat Lucina as an independent goddess who is not necessarily to be identified with either Juno or Diana. (4) He may deliberately leave the identity of Lucina obscure (a learned paradox, since her name was connected with light).

The first one and a half lines show M.'s preoccupation with marriage and childbirth. These preoccupations pervade the whole speech, and are reflected in the imagery of birth used at 25 and 55.

2-3   M. next invokes gods associated with the voyage of the Argo, and hence with her own past. **you who taught Tiphys**: Tiphys, the steersman of the Argo, was taught by Pallas Athena, Roman Minerva, the goddess here addressed, who was one of the chief divine supporters of the Argonauts. Tiphys first appears on the Argo in Pherecydes (*FGH*3F107; in Aeschylus fr. 21 Radt he is called Iphys). In S.'s play he appears again at 318-28, 616-24. Pallas also helped Argus construct the Argo (see on 366). **to bridle … tame the ocean**: the ship is like a young animal that Tiphys must bridle; and the sea is regarded as a wild creature that must be tamed, or an enemy that must be conquered or mastered (for the verb *domituram* can have either meaning). Jason had been called the charioteer (*auriga*) of the Argo by Varro of Atax (fr. 4 Courtney; cf. Ovid *Tr.* 1.4.16), and the metaphor of bridling (*frenare*) a ship had been used by the poet Manilius (4.283; the metaphor of the reins of a ship was fairly common, see on 346-7). Here 'new' ship probably means 'the first-ever', see introductory note to 301-79.

4   **you, cruel master of the deep sea**: Poseidon, the Roman Neptune. The word 'master' (*dominator*) is similar to the word 'that was to tame' (*domituram*), and ancient scholars thought both words were related to *domus*, 'home' (on the ancient etymologies see Maltby [1991] on *dominus* and *domo*; on the modern, see *OLD*). Thus there is a suggestion that the role of Neptune as master of the sea has been usurped by the Argo; and the word 'cruel', although a conventional description of the sea, and of Neptune,

may also hint at the punishment of the Argonauts for their invasion of Neptune's preserve (described by the Chorus in the second and third odes).

5-12 M. now prays to a series of deities with whom she has more personal links.

5   **Titan:** the Sun-god, Helios in Greek, Sol in Latin, who is M.'s grandfather; he is called Titan because his father was Hyperion, one of the Titans, the earlier generation of gods who were overthrown by Zeus and succeeded by the Olympian gods (see *OCD*[3] on 'Titan'; 409-10 below). **ration:** literally 'divide'; the sun 'rations' daylight because at any moment half of the earth faces the sun's light and half is in darkness, and as the sun revolves round the earth (on the geocentric model of the universe) the areas in light and darkness keep changing. Cf. Germanicus *Aratea* 498 *diuidit aequali spatio noctemque diemque*, '(the sun) divides up night and day with equal area'; Lucr. 1.1067.

6-7   **triple-formed Hecate:** Hecate was often represented in art with three heads or three bodies; she was the goddess of cross-roads (called 'three roads' in Greek, τρίοδος, and Latin, *triuium*), at which such representations were set up; and she appeared in all three regions of the mythological world, in the heavens as the Moon, on earth as Diana, and in the underworld as Hecate. By S.'s day Hecate was also associated with magic and witchcraft, hence she provides 'conspiratorial radiance for hushed rituals', that is for magical and chthonic rituals, which were conducted in silence (cf. Gow on Theocritus 2.38), unlike normal rituals; for even private prayers were normally said out loud. Hecate is invoked later at 577, 787-842. M. has a close relationship with her at Eur. *Med.* 395-7, and invokes her at Ovid *Met.* 7.194-5. She is a priestess of Hecate in Ap. Rh. 3.251-2, but S. does not describe her as such. Other witches in literature invoke her (e.g. Theocr. 2.14), and she often appears in *defixiones* (curse tablets or binding spells, usually together with Hermes, cf. *IG* III.3, 104-7), and in the magical papyri. For the historical development of the cult see *OCD*[3] on 'Hecate'.

7-8   **gods by whom Jason swore to me:** the oaths sworn by Jason are a regular feature of the story from Euripides onwards (*Med.* 21-2, 161-3, 168-70, etc.; see also Sophocles *Colchides* fr. 339 Radt). Perhaps S. is not thinking of any specific gods, but in Ovid *Epist.* 12.78-9 and *Met.* 7.94-7 Jason swears by Hecate and the Sun. In Apollonius' version, when M. offered to help Jason, he promised to take her with him and marry her when he returned home (Ap. Rh. 4.95-8, cf. 355-90, 1042, 1084-5; in Diodorus 4.46.4 it is an oath of lifelong marriage). To break an oath sworn by the gods was bound, in ancient religious thought, to lead to retribution, so Jason's sufferings are here foreshadowed.

8-9   **and those to whom Medea more rightfully prays:** because of her association with the underworld and magic, she particularly prays to the deities listed in lines 9-17.

9   **Chaos of endless night:** the modern editor or translator has to decide whether Chaos should have a capital letter or not (see on 44 for the lack of initial capitals in S.'s day). The same phrase is found at *Her. F.* 610 (see Fitch's comm.); that passage, and the next phrase here, 'realms opposed to the gods of heaven', would suggest that 'chaos of endless night' is here a general description of the underworld. On the other hand, it is more appropriate in a prayer that Chaos is a deity, for which there are precedents starting with Hesiod *Th.* 116 (see West's comm.); Chaos is invoked, along with Erebus and Hecate, by Dido in Vergil *A.* 4.510, and by the poet in *A.* 6.265; Chaos the deity is also found in the magical papyri (e.g. *PGM* IV.443, 1459). Cf. 741 below.

10   **unholy spirits of the dead**: probably equivalent to 'spirits of people who were impious
during their life on earth' (who will make suitable helpers for M.), rather than implying
that all spirits of the dead are unholy. One ancient etymology of *manes* ('spirits of the
dead') was that it meant 'good' (see Maltby [1991] on *manes* (a); *OLD* s.v. *manus*²,), in
which case the adjective 'unholy' is almost an oxymoron (i.e. a short, paradoxical, even
self-contradictory phrase; cf. on 419).

11-12 **master of the grim realm**: Hades (see *OCD*³ s.v.) or Pluto, god of the underworld, in
Latin Dis. **and mistress carried off with greater faithfulness than I**: Persephone, in
Latin Proserpina, the daughter of Zeus and Demeter who was abducted from Sicily by
Hades and taken to the underworld, where she became Hades' wife and queen (*OCD*³ on
'Persephone/Kore'; *LIMC* 8.1, 956-78, 8.2, 640-53—the rape is a common theme in
Roman art). 'with greater faithfulness than I' because Hades remained faithful to
Persephone, unlike Jason, who is now abandoning M. Her words suggest that she was
'carried off' or 'raped', and did not accompany Jason entirely willingly, which is
perhaps how she views it in her present embittered state of mind; but some earlier
versions stress that M. was overwhelmed by the power of Aphrodite (see on 219-20),
and M. acknowledges her love for Jason below at 135-6, cf. 140-2, 235. ('than I' is not
in S.'s elliptical Latin, see Introduction §5.2; Billerbeck [1988], 128-9.)

12   **I pray with inauspicious words**: literally 'I pray with voice not well-omened (*fausta*).'
M. overturns the normal conventions of Roman religion. At religious rituals those
attending were ordered to keep quiet and avoid words of ill-omen with the command
fauete linguis, literally 'be well-omened with your tongues' (see *OLD* s.v. *faueo* 5;
below on 58). M.'s word 'well-omened' (*fausta*) is etymologically related to *fauete*: her
words would disrupt any normal religious ritual, and effectively do disrupt the prayer of
the Chorus at 56-74, but they are also appropriate in her own prayer to underworld
deities.

          We have now reached the end of the first sentence of M.'s prayer. A prayer is a
standard opening for ancient dramas (cf. Aeschylus *Supp.*, *Ag.*, *Cho.*, *Eum.*, Euripides
Cycl., *Suppl.*, *Phoen.*), but M.'s prayer so far is unusual in that it makes no request of
the deities invoked—it just leads up to 'I pray with inauspicious words.' However, the
invocation of a series of deities well evokes M.'s mood—her preoccupation with her
marriage and Jason's unfaithfulness, and her readiness to appeal to the forces of the
underworld and of magic. But her prayer continues with specific requests. (Her barrage
of vocatives might be compared with the lists of deities and magical words that
regularly begin magical spells: e.g. see *PGM* XIXa, and a phylactery—a magical
charm—published by F. Heintz in *ZPE* 112 [1996], 295-300.)

13   **Now, now**: such immediate repetition (iteration or gemination), especially of
monosyllables (here *nunc*), is typical of the tragedies (cf. below 32, 90, 266, 911, 949);
here it reinforces M.'s impatience. Emphatic monosyllables tend to stand out more in
an inflected language like Latin than they do in English. (Compare the formula 'now,
now, quickly, quickly' frequently found in magical tablets and papyri; e.g. Gager
[1992], 115, or the papyrus quoted below on 673.) **come to help me**: literally 'be
present' (*adeste*), repeated in line 16. The repetition is characteristic of prayers and
hymns, and the expression is a standard one in ancient prayers, which treat the gods as
localised, so that they must be where the worshipper is, and not somewhere else (see
Tarrant on *Ag.* 348). **goddesses who avenge wickedness**: a summons to the Erinyes,

identified with the Latin Furies (*OCD³* on 'Erinyes'). The Erinyes primarily avenge wrong done to members of one's family—so it is implied that Jason's behaviour is a wicked crime deserving to be punished by them (cf. Ap. Rh. 4.385-7, where M., believing Jason is going to abandon her on the journey home, says 'May my Furies drive you straight from your homeland, because of what I have suffered through your heartlessness' (trans. Hunter)). The whole of this sentence recalls Horace *Epode* 5.49-54, where the witch Canidia summons Night and Diana to her magic rites; thus S.'s M. is placed in the tradition of Latin poetic witchcraft from very early in the play.

14 **your hair defiled with dishevelled serpents**: the Erinyes are regularly portrayed with snakes writhing in their hair, and carrying torches (cf. 958-66). Note the alliteration of *s*, suggesting the snakes' hissing, *solutis squalidae serpentibus*; cf. on 118-20, 190, 238-9, 362-3, 933-4. S. uses alliteration sparingly (in contrast to Republican tragedians), so it is the more striking when it occurs. (*crinem* is accusative indicating in what respect they are *squalidae*; the construction is mainly poetic in Latin, and imitates Greek syntax; see Woodcock [1959], 13.)

15 **black torches**: i.e. very smoky torches; the striking, almost paradoxical phrase is found earlier in Verg. *A.* 9.74, 10.77. (Compare phrases like 'black fire', *atri ignes*, which are not uncommon; see Pease on Verg. *A.* 4.384; *TLL* 2.1020.39-50.) The torches of the Erinyes are a sinister substitute for the torches usually carried at weddings (see on 37-9).

16-17 **come to help me**: see on 13. **as grim as ... my wedding chamber**: the idea that the Furies preside at a marriage that turns out unhappily is found at *Oed.* 644 (of Oedipus' marriage), and earlier in Ovid (e.g. *Epist.* 2.117-20, 6.45-6, 7.96, *Met.* 6.428-32, where see Bömer, cf. 10.313-4; also Lucan 8.90 and [Sen.] *Oct.* 23-4); compare also Aesch. *Ag.* 744-9. The Furies effectively usurped the role of the *pronuba* or matron-of-honour (see on 37-9; and compare the idea of Bellona, goddess of war, being *pronuba* at the marriage of Turnus and Lavinia, Verg. *A.* 7.319).

17 **the new wife**: Creusa, whom Jason is about to marry. In Euripides she is not named; in some versions she is called Glauke (e.g. Hyg. *Fab.* 25.2; Apollod. 1.9.28). S., like Ovid (*Epist.* 12.53), calls her Creusa, a name which stresses her relationship to Creon.

18 **the father-in-law and the royal offspring**: Creon and his whole family (implying that Creon had other children besides Creusa; Hyg. *Fab.* 25.2 calls her the younger daughter; Schol Eur. *Med.* 19 talks of a son). M. already, at the start of the play, firmly wishes to see Creon and Creusa dead. But her intentions regarding Jason are less clearly formed, as the following lines show.

19-55 Up to now M.'s train of thought is clear, and her speech has some of the formality of religious language. From now on her thought twists and turns unexpectedly as she debates with herself what punishment is appropriate for Jason, and what she herself should do.

19 **Is there something ... for the bridegroom?**: M. wants to punish Jason with something worse than death. Near the start of Euripides' *Medea*, the Nurse expresses fears that M. could kill Jason and his new wife (39-42), though in the event Jason is not killed. But S.'s M. begins by searching for something even worse than death for Jason. (The lines of Euripides are believed by some editors to be interpolated, but they were probably present in copies of the Roman period; see on 893-977.) [*est* is a conjecture of Richard Bentley: with the manuscript reading, *mihi*, the sense is something like 'do *I* have something worse ...?' But the emphasis on *mihi*, in first position, seems misplaced. For other conjectures see Zwierlein (1986), 131-2.]

20-1 Let him live: *uiuat*, jussive subjunctive. This is a paradoxical answer to the question in the previous line, and we wait to hear how life will be worse than death for Jason. The paradox is emphasised by the sense pause after the first word of the line. S. is fond of the idea that continuing to live may sometimes be a fate worse than death. Tyrants in his tragedies regularly think that a swift death is too lenient a punishment. For example, Aegisthus at *Ag.* 995 says *rudis est tyrannus morte qui poenam exigit*, 'he is an inexperienced tyrant who punishes with death' (see Tarrant's comm.); cf. Lycus in *Her. F.* 511-2 (see Fitch's comm.). Similar attitudes are found in Eur. *Hipp.* 1047 and other writers, and are attributed to the emperors Tiberius (Suet. *Tib.* 61.5) and Gaius (S. *Nat.* 4a.praef.17). (S. is also fond of a positive version of the same basic idea, that sometime it takes courage and virtue to carry on living in the face of sufferings: cf. *Epist.* 78.2; *Her. F.* 1316-7 and Fitch's comm.; *Phoen.* 319 and Frank's comm.) **impoverished ... no fixed home:** the string of adjectives in asyndeton (i.e. without 'and' or other connecting words) is a favourite technique of S.'s; cf. 45, 123, 207-8, etc.; Canter (1925), 169-70. It is also found in Republican drama; cf. Accius *trag.* 415 Ribbeck, 407 Warmington (maybe M., or someone else, speaking about Jason?) *exul inter hostes expes expers desertus uagus*, 'an exile among the enemy, hopeless, helpless, abandoned, wandering'; and in Greek tragedy, cf. *Trag. Adesp.* 284 Nauck 'cityless, homeless, deprived of fatherland, begging, wandering, living from day to day.' The lines also echo Aeneas' description of himself as *ignotus, egens*, 'unknown, impoverished' in Verg. *A.* 1.384. Exile was a real fear in the Greco-Roman world; Ovid and S. himself both experienced long periods of exile, and one species of consolation literature dealt with exile (see *OCD³* on 'exile'; cf. comm. on 459-60).

22   a well-known visitor: because he has visited before, having been a wandering exile for so long; or it could mean 'a notorious visitor', i.e. his reputation (for deserting M.) has gone before him.

23-5 let him long for ... resemble their mother: a difficult sentence. With the text as translated here (with the beginnings of lines 22 and 23 interchanged), M. wants Jason to become so lonely that he will even wish to be married to her again, and will long for children even if they resemble both M. and Jason—i.e. even if they are just as unfaithful as he and just as wicked as she. This interpretation assumes that the 'mother' in 25 is M. Some take the mother to be Creusa, in which case the point is that Jason should long for children by her, but not have them; but this is weaker, for 'who resemble their father, and resemble their mother' has less point. It was conventionally regarded as good fortune for parents to have children who resembled them; see e.g. Hes. *Op.* 235; Catul. 61.214-8; Hor. *Carm.* 4.5.23; Mart. 6.27.3. [Zwierlein prints Axelson's conjecture *opto*, meaning 'I long for ...', because he thinks that Jason could never pray for something so terrible as he does in the transmitted text. But this misses the characteristically paradoxical point, that M. wants Jason to become so desolated that he will pray even for this. For another view of the passage see Krafft (1994).]

25-6 It's born already ... given birth: the enigmatic language probably operates at three levels: (1) The birth is metaphorical: she has hatched a plan of vengeance (i.e. she has conceived a suitable form of punishment for Jason). In Latin the verb *pario*, 'give birth', is applied to all sorts of achievements and products (see *OLD* s.v. 5-6). First she expresses her idea in the passive, as though the idea has occurred to her in response to her question in 19; but then she turns it into the active ('I have given birth'), appropriating the credit to herself. (2) She is also literally a mother, and already has children who are likely to grow up to be as bad as both Jason and herself; so Jason need not long for such terrible children, because he already has them. (3) The audience, who expect that M. is going to murder her children, will probably see an allusion to their fate when M. says she has given birth. But we should not imagine that this is in M.'s mind at the moment. There is no hint of the idea of murder in her words; possibly the idea of taking the children away from Jason is implicit, but it is not clearly expressed. So the words mean more to the audience than to her. There is also an echo of Ovid's M., *Epist.* 12.208 *ingentes parturit ira minas*, 'my anger gives birth to great threats', which also alludes to the killing of the children (see Heinze's comm.). (In Euripides' play the idea of killing her own children does not occur to her until line 792.) **It's born ... is born**: for iteration (see on 13) with an intervening word *(parta iam, parta)* compare 423; Wills (1997), 103.

27   **Shall I not move ... from their hands**: her thoughts turn from the future prospect of Jason suffering to the present moment, and to an attack on the wedding party, who will be carrying torches. This is the first indication in the play that the wedding ceremonies have not yet taken place (whereas in Euripides they are over before the play starts, see on 1-55). The passage recalls Ovid's M. in *Epist.* 12.155-6: after receiving word that the wedding procession is passing, M. describes how *ire animus mediae suadebat in agmina turbae, / sertaque compositis demere rapta comis*, 'my mind urged me to attack the procession, passing through the crowd, and to snatch and tear the garlands from their well-groomed hair.' In Ovid, M.'s impulse is a natural reaction to the procession as it is passing by: in S. it is an unexpected impulse that recalls the passage of Ovid (but we must constantly remember that we do not know what happened in Ovid's play *Medea*). On Roman weddings see *OCD*[3] under 'marriage ceremonies'; Treggiari (1991), 161-70; for torches carried in the wedding procession see on 37-9.

28   **and the daylight from the heavens**: her meaning is explained in the lines that follow, but the jump from dashing 'torches from their hands' to dashing 'daylight from the heavens' is typical of S.—where human actions are regularly linked to cosmic effects and events—and characteristic of M., whose magical powers may affect even the heavens (see on 46, 121, 166-7, 407-14, 674, 889; Introduction §4.8).

28-9 **Does the founder ... what is happening**: the Sun and Perse were parents of Aeetes, who was father of M.; cf. 209-10. The Sun traditionally saw everything that happened on earth (cf. Aesch. (?) *Prom.* 91 'the all-seeing circle of the sun'). **and yet still let himself be seen**: the implications of this phrase are explained in the next two lines: the Sun ought not to stay in view, but should retreat out of sight in horror at the way in which M. is being treated. (Contrast M.'s attitude to Titan, another name for the Sun, in 5.) The Sun retreated at the sight of the cannibalistic banquet served up by Atreus to Thyestes (S. *Thy.* 789-804), and Hippolytus prays that the Sun would hide from Phaedra's wickedness at *Phaed.* 677-9. For the play on active and passive forms of the same verb (*spectat ... spectatur*), one form of paronomasia, cf. 218-9 *petebant ... petuntur*; Canter (1925), 162; Wills (1993), 296; it is a feature of S.'s prose too, and of contemporary oratory, see Bonner (1949), 70, 167.

29-30 Is he sitting ... the pure firmament: the image is of a race course. The firmament is pure, i.e. bright and free from clouds that would impede his view, and free from other impurities and disturbances found in the sublunary atmosphere; but there is also a suggestion of moral purity that ought not to be sullied by earthly wickedness. People normally stand in chariots, in literature and life (including *Tro.* 188, *Dial.* 7.25.4), but for sitting in a chariot cf. *Oed.* 424; Naevius *com.* 107 Ribbeck, *inc.* 28-9 Warmington.

32-6 Let me ..., let me: iteration (*da, da*), see above on 13. **Let me ... unite the two seas**: M.'s request to drive her ancestor's chariot is reminiscent of Phaethon's request to his father, the Sun, to drive his chariot. Phaethon came to grief, causing conflagration on the earth—until Jupiter struck him with a thunderbolt. M. echoes the destruction caused by Phaethon in her wish (35-6) to burn up the Corinthian isthmus. She, too, is descended from the Sun, and therefore related to Phaethon. However, Phaethon caused his own destruction when he drove the Sun's chariot (cf. 599-602), whereas at the end of the play M. will ride away in her chariot without being destroyed. (The story of Phaethon was familiar in Rome from Lucr. 5.396-405 and Ovid *Met.* 2.1-328, and was popular in art; for other ancient sources see Eur. *Phaethon* [ed. Diggle]; Gantz [1993], 31-4; in art, *LIMC* 7.1.350-4, 7.2.311-3.)

33   father: as 'founder of my family' (28) she can call him 'father'. He is in fact her grandfather, and *genitor* is not usually applied to a grandfather (there may be a parallel at Accius *trag.* 277 Ribbeck, 260 Warmington, but the context is far from certain).

35   Corinth, which sets ... its twin coasts: Corinth is on the isthmus that joins the Peloponnese to northern Greece, and separates the Corinthian gulf from the Saronic gulf, and hence the Aegean from the Ionian sea. There were several unsuccessful ancient attempts to cut a canal through the isthmus (see Pliny *Nat.* 4.10; the modern canal was completed in 1893). Nero was one of those who attempted to build a canal, but even if we knew that this play post-dated his attempt—and we do not know that (see Introduction §1.3)—it would be hazardous to see an allusion to it in M.'s wish to unite the two seas. *Corinthos*: -*os* is a Greek nominative singular feminine ending, cf. on 45, 81, 457. **coasts**: in Latin *litus* can refer to the sea along the coast-line as well as, or instead of, the dry land (see e.g. Clausen on Verg. *Ecl.* 2.25-6; Zwierlein [1986], 134). Here Corinth is imagined keeping apart the two seas on either side of the isthmus.

37-9 One thing more ... should carry ... should slay: *restat* is followed by a pair of consecutive clauses, with the conjunction *ut* postponed until after the first verb *feram*; *caedam* is the second verb. Cf. 498-9, and for consecutive clauses after *restare* cf. *OLD* s.v. *resto* 4b, 5d. **the wedding pine-torch**: a torch made of pine wood was an integral part of the Roman wedding ceremony (cf. 111, 27, 67; *OLD* s.v. *fax* 2a; Treggiari [1991], 163, 166, 168-9). Here it will be carried by M., acting as a *pronuba*, the 'matron-of-honour' who accompanied the bride at Roman weddings (Treggiari [1991], 164, 168, 229, 233). **should slay the victims on the consecrated altar**: she is probably thinking of animal sacrifices performed during the wedding ceremony (cf. 59-66; Serv. *A.* 3.136, 4.374; Tac.*Ann.* 11.27; Treggiari [1991], 164). By performing them herself she will ensure that they are ill-omened. But to the audience the words can suggest the human victims who will die, Creon, Creusa and M.'s children.

40   Find a path ... the entrails themselves: This is an enigmatic sentence whose interpretation is disputed—and it very likely bears more than one meaning. (1) The primary meaning probably picks up the literal sense of the previous sentence, the entrails being those of the sacrificial animals: i.e. she urges herself to devise some vengeance that can be achieved while she is sacrificing. (2) It is not specified what this vengeance might be: perhaps she is thinking of killing Jason and Creusa, and the entrails are also theirs. (In the event, Jason is not killed, but for fears that M. may kill him see Eur. *Med.* 39-42.) (3) Alternatively, she may mean her own entrails, i.e. her own life, and her meaning is 'seek punishment, even if it costs you your own life' (so Zwierlein [1986], 135). (4) The audience, however, may think of the entrails of the human victims they expect her to kill—Creon, Creusa, and her own children. (Murder was regularly described as sacrifice, especially in Senecan tragedy; see on 970-1.)

41 **my soul**: address to her soul is a recurrent feature of M.'s soliloquies (cf. 895, 937, etc.). Such self-address goes back to Homer (*Od.* 20.17-8 'Be patient, heart'), and is widespread in later poetry, including Euripides' *Medea* (see Page on 1056; Tarrant on *Ag.* 108f.).

42 **Drive out womanly fears**: i.e. she must behave like a man (cf. on 160). In S.'s play there is not much stress on the female gender of M. (which is in contrast to Euripides' play, where M. identifies with the unequal treatment and oppression that all women suffer [230-51], and the female Chorus, together with the Nurse, shares a strong bond of female sympathy with her). On the whole, S.'s M. sees herself as a wife and mother, rather than as a woman. Other speakers in the play contrast her with women: in the first choral ode the bride is a 'woman' (*femina*, 91), there is a 'women's dance' (93), and one of the sacrificial animals is a 'woman' (see note on 61-2), whereas towards the end of the ode the Chorus is openly hostile towards M.; later Creon characterises M. as far from an 'innocent woman' (193, using another word, *mulier*, see comm.), and as combining 'a woman's wickedness' and 'a man's strength' (267-8).

43 **and clothe ... inhospitable Caucasus**: literally 'put on the inhospitable Caucasus in/with your mind' (cf. 708-9). It was commonplace in classical literature to say that someone's heart was like stone (e.g. such similes are used at Eur. *Med.* 28-9, 1280), but S. uses a much bolder metaphor: M. will put on the mountain-range, and hence the character, of her home region. The Caucasus was traditionally associated with wildness and inhospitability (cf. *Thy.* 1048-9; Nisbet and Hubbard on Hor. *Carm.* 1.22.6-7, where the same adjective 'inhospitable' is used, an adjective that was also applied to the Black Sea, cf. Plin. *Nat.* 6.1). The Caucasus mountain range stretches between the Black Sea and the Caspian Sea, along the northern border of modern Georgia. Colchis, M.'s home, was the region to the south of the Black Sea end of the range; the river Phasis (modern Rioni) rises in the Caucasus and flows into the Black Sea (see 44, and on 762). The mountains, rising to 5642 metres, form a formidable barrier between Europe and Asia, hence they are 'inhospitable'.

44 **impious deeds**: principally her desertion of her father and the murder of her brother Apsyrtus, also spelt Absyrtus (see on 452-3). **Phasis**: see on 43. **Pontus**: the Greek noun *pontos* just means 'sea', but it was also used of 'the Sea', meaning the Black Sea. Latin prose adopted the word both for the Black Sea and for the land region between Bithynia and Armenia, which was incorporated into the province of Pontus in 63 B.C. In Latin poetry *pontus* was also used for the sea in general; hence in our play, and elsewhere, it is sometimes hard to know whether the reference is to the sea in general or the Black Sea in particular, and whether the word should be printed with a capital letter or not. (Ancient Greek and Latin poetic manuscripts made no distinction between small and capital letters at the start of words, so the last issue did not arise; cf. on 9.)

45   **the Isthmus**: i.e. the Corinthian isthmus, see on 32-6 (*Isthmos* is a Greek nominative singular ending, cf. on 35). **Savage, unknown, dreadful**: see on 20-1.

46   **heaven and earth**: perhaps meaning 'gods and men'; but not necessarily, or not solely, since M. can literally make the heavens and earth tremble (see on 28).

49   **as a girl**: 'girl' translates Latin *uirgo*, which can mean 'virgin' or 'girl' or 'young woman'; cf. 87, 105, 131, 238, 350, 984, 1007 (and the adjective *uirgineus* at 75). **anguish**: Latin *dolor*, one of the key terms of the play (recurring at 139, 151, 155, 446, 554, 671, 907, 914, 944, 951, 1011, 1016, 1019; and the related verb *doleo* at 978, 1006); the translation 'anguish' has been used throughout the play where the noun occurs. The Romans (like the modern Italians) were typically more demonstrative about their feelings than the northern Europeans, and *dolor* is not just the inner feeling of grief or pain, but usually signifies the accompanying outward behaviour as well; so 'indignation' or 'anger' are sometimes appropriate translations. (*exurgat* is present subjunctive of *ex-(s)urgo*.)

51   **Equip yourself**: *accingere*, 2nd person sing. passive imperative, in a reflexive sense; literally 'gird yourself'.

52-55 **Let the story ... must be abandoned**: the series of three comparisons between past and present displays M.'s obsession with making sure her behaviour in the current situation will match her behaviour in the past.

52-3   **your divorce**: the word *repudium* in S.'s day applied only to the husband divorcing his wife, not vice versa (Treggiari [1991], 435-41). M. inhabits the mythological world, not the Roman world, but Roman attitudes to marriage and divorce may have coloured Roman responses to Jason's treatment of M. Marriage in the ancient world was not a religious bond (although religious rituals could form part of a wedding); it was more a legal contract, and a contract that could be terminated. Divorce was relatively easy and common in S.'s world, and not in itself a focus of moral debate; but in some circumstances divorces could be regarded as particularly harsh or callous; see Treggiari (1991), 464-5, 471-2, 480-1. What particularly distinguishes M.'s situation from that of the Roman wife, however, is that the divorced Roman women could always return to her father, or her nearest male relative—or she might even have the relative freedom of living independently—but M. has nowhere to go.

54   **Cut short your slothful hesitations now**: a Vergilian phrase, from *G*. 3.42-3 (*segnes / rumpe moras*). The Vergilian context is an exhortation by the poet to himself to get down to his subject; this may remind the reader that, parallel to M.'s ambition to equal her previous actions, there runs the poet's ambition to equal his predecessors' poetry. Similarly 'the story they tell' in 52 refers primarily to her reputation, but for the audience it can also suggest poetic accounts of her story. See Introduction §5.5.

55   **that was born through wickedness**: M.'s preoccupation with her motherhood emerges not just in the explicit reference to childbirth in 50, but also in the metaphor here. After the final line of her speech it is best to imagine that M. leaves the stage before the Chorus comes on; otherwise it could scarcely ignore her presence throughout most of the ode. We should perhaps imagine that she reappears at line 114 (see on 114-5), or else after the end of the ode. Alternatively we may imagine that she remains on stage, overhearing the Chorus, but unseen by it until 114.

FIRST CHORAL ODE: 56-115

The Chorus prays for the forthcoming marriage, sings the praises of the bride and groom, and addresses the crowd. The structure of the ode, which is partly articulated by changes of metre (see Introduction §5.7), is as follows:

56-74	Prayers to the gods to attend the marriage.	(lesser asclepiad)
75-81	Praise of the bride.	(glyconic)
82-92	Praise of the groom.	
93-101	Further praise of the bride.	(lesser asclepiad)
102-6	The groom is instructed to take his new bride.	
107-9	Instructions to the young people to joke and sing.	
110-2	Prayer to Hymenaeus.	(dactylic hexameter)
113-5	Instructions to the crowd.	

At the start of the next act, M. says (116) that she has heard the wedding song (*hymenaeus*), referring presumably to this choral ode. The ode contains elements of the wedding song, or epithalamium, a part of Greek wedding ritual that is already mentioned in the *Iliad* (18.493), and is represented by surviving Greek examples from Alcman onwards. The wedding song is not known to have been a part of the traditional Roman wedding, but it was developed as a literary genre, particularly by Catullus (poems 61 and 62, cf. 64), and was perhaps sometimes performed at weddings. The epithalamium continued as a literary genre throughout Greek and Latin antiquity (see Costa on 56-115; OCD^3 on 'epithalamium').

In the Greek world songs could be sung at various stages of the wedding proceedings: at the wedding-banquet, during the procession to the groom's house, outside the wedding chamber on the wedding night, and on the following morning. But these distinctions were not always observed in literature, and it is not possible to assign a precise occasion to S.'s ode, nor does he indicate any precise sequence of ritual events in the way that Catullus does in poems 61 and 62. In line 56 the word *thalamos*, 'marriage-chamber', need not imply that the ode is sung outside the bridal chamber, for it can be a metonymy for 'wedding'. In the play as a whole there is no clear sense of the timing of the wedding ceremony. The Chorus at 59-66 talks of the sacrifices as though they are imminent: these normally took place at the first stage of a wedding, before the procession. The jocular obscenities sung by the crowd (107-9, 113-5) best fit during the procession. M. at 116 has heard the wedding song. But later, at 299-300, after Creon's long dialogue with M., he goes off to the wedding rites; and in the next act, at 431-559 Jason appears for a long dialogue with M. that can scarcely be fitted in to the wedding rituals. In S.'s predecessors the internal chronology is more straightforward: in Euripides the wedding has already taken place before the play begins (18-9); in Ovid M. describes her feelings on hearing the wedding procession (*Epist.* 12.137-58). S. is more concerned with the effect the wedding song has on M., and with the dynamics of her relationships with Creon and Jason, than with exact dramatic time.

The ode contains elements of the traditional wedding-song: prayers to the gods, praise of the bride and groom, address to the onlookers, are all traditional elements, and S. gives the ode a distinctively Roman flavour with the reference to chanting of rude Fescennine verses (see on 107-9 and 113)—though it is debatable whether a Roman audience would have felt that this element was distinctively Roman and out of place in a Greek heroic context. But the references to M., the first and now discarded bride (102-6, 114-5), do not belong, obviously enough, in the epithalamium tradition.

The members of the Chorus are plainly citizens of Corinth, well-disposed to the royal family and hostile to M., but their age and sex are not made clear. Richard Bentley suggested that the Chorus in this ode is divided into two separate groups of young women and young men, as in Catullus 62; he assigned 75-81 to the women, 82-92 to the men, and 93-106 to the women. The address to young men, *iuuenes*, in 107-8, fits into this scheme. But it makes the division between men and women unbalanced, with a much smaller contribution from the men (who in Catullus make an equal contribution), which seems unsatisfactory. It seems that S. does not give a clear lead on the identity of the Chorus or on the mechanics of a stage performance of this ode. There is a further question who constitutes the crowd mentioned in 114, which is apparently distinct from the Chorus, and is perhaps the whole citizen body.

Whereas Euripides' Chorus is friendly to M., S.'s is hostile to her, and here speaks with the civic voice of Corinth. Weddings bring people together; they are one of the central rituals that mould a society, keep it united, and reinforce its values. M.'s opening speech has sought the opposite: it did not just express her bitterness at her own personal plight, but it was also full of threats and images of the disruption of Corinthian society and of the whole cosmic order—of relationships between humans and gods, and indeed between gods and gods (since the powers of the underworld are summoned to invade the world above). The first choral ode is in sharp contrast, expressing longing for the integration of society, for proper, stable relationships between humans and gods. In the first three lines gods, rulers and people are united in their proper places and functions. Individual gods are duly invoked, the bride and groom receive praises. Structurally the ode is clearly and conventionally articulated, in contrast to the passionate, clever, unpredictable veering of M.'s speech. Only briefly, towards the end (102-6), does the Chorus allude to M., to celebrate Jason's rescue from such a repugnant marriage.

But even before the Chorus remembers about M., the audience may realise that its longing for order is implicitly undermined from at least four directions:
1. M.'s impious words have already, in Roman terms, invalidated the religious ceremonies that are taking place (see on 12, 58). That she is in competition with the Chorus is subtly emphasised by the correspondences between her prayer and the Chorus's (see below on 56-74).
2. M. has recalled the oaths that Jason once swore to her by the gods (7-8), but has now broken. However unreasoning and excessive her thirst for vengeance may be, she has a just grievance against him. But the Chorus fails to acknowledge this, seeing M. as a foreigner, wild, repugnant to Jason, married against her parents' will (102-6; cf. also on 64).
3. The choral ode, for the audience, contains ironic pointers to the murders that they know M. will perform (see on 66).
4. It may be suggested more tentatively that there are points where the Chorus unconsciously offends the deities whose favour it seeks: some of its comparisons of Jason and Creusa to the gods verge on the dangerous and blasphemous, blurring or threatening the proper distinction between human and divine (see on 82-9).

Cumulatively these elements in the ode show that the Chorus's hopes are doomed.

[On this ode see further Davis (1993), 189-95; Fife (1983), 78-9; Hine (1989); Biondi (1984), 25-34.]

56-7 the royal couple: *regum*, plural of *rex*, 'king', could mean either 'the royal family' or 'the royal couple' (*OLD* s.v. 6b for the former). The word *regum* is etymologically linked to *regunt*, 'rule', in the same sentence: kings rule in human society as gods rule in the universe, in the harmonious world desired by the Chorus. **with favouring power**: the Latin *numen*, connected with the verb *nuo*, 'I nod' (which is only found in compound forms such as *abnuo, adnuo*), from meaning 'a nod of the head', came to mean 'divine power', 'divinity', and sometimes 'deity'. **the gods who ... the sea**: M., too, has prayed to the god of the sea, and the language she used suggested his hostility to the infringement of his domain by the Argo (see on 4). A later choral ode will speak of the Argo's voyage as a crime (605-6, 616, 668, cf. 361-3), so the support of the gods of the sea—which is vital to Corinth, a sea power—cannot be taken for granted. The shape of the line suggests harmony and co-operation between gods of sea and land: there are two clauses of three words introduced by *qui*, 'who'; *superi*, 'the gods', the antecedent of the relative 'who', is placed inside the first clause; the verb *regunt*, 'rule', placed in the second clause, is understood with the first clause too.

58   **along with ... in proper fashion**: the word *fauentibus*, 'who keep auspicious silence', echoes M.'s prayer 'with inauspicious (*non fausta*) words' (12). As the comm. there said, her words invalidate in advance the Chorus's prayer. In ancient religion it was essential not to disrupt rituals with words of ill omen, so *fauere*, meaning basically 'be favourable', came to mean 'keep silent', as S. himself explains at *Dial.* 7.26.7: 'this phrase is not derived from "favour", as most people think, but it commands silence, so that a sacred ritual can be performed without any ill-omened utterance disrupting it.' A well-known example is the phrase *fauete linguis* in the second line of Horace's third book of *Odes*. See *OLD* s.v. *faueo* 5; Pease on Cic. *Diu.* 1.102.

59-74: The Chorus invokes a series of deities. Only Lucina (61) is addressed by name (as by M. at 2), the rest are invoked allusively by epithet or description (cf. Introduction §5.1).

59   **the sceptre-bearing Thunderers**: the Thunderers are Jupiter and Juno (elsewhere the epithet is commonly found in the singular, referring to Jupiter alone). For their invocation at a wedding cf. Plut. *Quaest. Rom.* 2; Zeus is invoked in a wedding hymn at Theocr. 18.52-3. 'sceptre-bearing' is a poetic compound adjective (see Introduction §5.6), already used by Ovid (*Fast.* 6.480, of a king's hands).

60   **a white-backed bull**: a sheep (Serv. *A.* 4.374; Treggiari [1991], 21-4) or pig (Var. *R.* 2.4.9) could be sacrificed at real-life weddings; sacrifice of a bull suits a grand mythological wedding, and a sacrificial bull appears on reliefs of wedding scenes on sarcophagi of the second century A.D. (*LIMC* 5.2, 336 no. 77, and perhaps no. 74c, though there the bull may belong to a different scene; cf. 5.2, 541 no. 189). All sacrificial animals had to be unblemished, which is implied by 'white-backed'. Animals sacrificed to Jupiter had to be white (Paul. Fest. 10 M., cf. Verg. *A.* 3.20-1), and normally, in Greece and Rome, white animals were sacrificed to the gods of the upper world, black animals to the gods of the underworld and the dead (Tarrant on *Ag.* 364 [353]; Frazer on Ovid *Fast.* 1.720; though Latte [1967], 210 warns that this is an oversimplification for the Roman world, as does *RE* 18.1.594 for the Greek).

61-2   **Lucina**: see on 2; here identification with Juno, already referred to in 59, is unlikely, and identification with Diana is unnecessary. **a female of snowy body**: the heifer (a female animal is sacrificed to a female goddess) is called *femina*, 'woman'. The use of this word adjectivally to denote a female animal was part of farming language, and used in religious contexts (*TLL* 2.2141.54-8, 6.1.462.39-44); it was taken up by the poets (see

OLD s.v. 3a), but this use as a noun is unusual (cf. Ovid, *Met.* 2.701), and, taken with the description 'untried by the yoke', creates strong personification of the animal (see further below on 66). **untried by the yoke**: the requirement that the sacrificial animal should not have done ordinary work was a standard one; cf. *Ag.* 354 (366) and Tarrant, *Oed.* 299-300. The 'yoke' can be a metaphor for marriage (*OLD* s.v. *iugum* 2b).

62-5   **her who restrains ... her rich horn**: it is debated whether this description refers to Venus, or to the goddess Peace (Pax), or to an amalgamation of the two. Venus was a well-established goddess, Peace a very minor one, but she was given prominence in the Augustan period, and so would be familiar to S. and his audience (see *OCD*³ o n 'Eirene', 'Pax'). Near the start of Lucretius' poem (1.31-40) there is a famous description of how Venus cradles Mars in her arms and brings peace, which may be recalled here. On the other hand 'who gives treaties to war-waging nations and stores abundance in her rich horn' suggests Peace, who is regularly portrayed with a cornucopia, a horn of plenty (cf. e.g. Horace, *Carm. Saec.* 57-60, and, in art, *LIMC* 7.1, 204-12, 7.2, 134-8; and on Greek Eirene, *LIMC* 3.1, 700-5, 3.2, 540-2); Aphrodite, the Roman Venus, on the other hand, is not represented with a cornucopia. Nevertheless it would be quite in S.'s allusive manner, and in accord with the synthesising tendencies of Roman religion, to see elements of both goddesses in the description. The link between Venus and marriage is clear enough (cf. Theocr. 18.51-2 for invocation of Aphrodite in a wedding hymn); Peace is linked with marriage or child-bearing in Aristoph. *Peace* 975-6, Eur. *Suppl.* 490, Tib. 1.10.53-4. In this play the reference to peace may have political overtones, for there is a military threat from Acastus, which the banishment of M. is meant to remove (see on 256-7). If Venus is referred to, it is the only reference to her in the play, and it has nothing to do with M.'s love for Jason (see on 1, 219-20; Introduction §3.3).

64   **who gives treaties**: the Chorus here addresses the goddess who gives treaties, but at 335-6 it describes the Argo breaking the treaties or laws of the universe, cf. 606. In the present ode the Chorus does not acknowledge Jason's faults. **war-waging**: a poetic compound (first found in Ovid, *Ars* 2.672, *Tr.* 3.11.13); see Introduction §5.6.

66   **with a young victim**: Peace/Venus is given an appropriately tender victim. Three victims are mentioned in all, the bull for Jupiter and Juno, the heifer for Lucina, and the young victim (a calf?) for Peace/Venus. It is noteworthy that there are just three victims, though more than three deities are mentioned, and normally each would receive a sacrifice. The strong personification of the second victim (see on 61-2) suggests that, for the audience, the sacrificial victims anticipate M.'s victims: the bull is Creon, the unmarried heifer is Creusa, the young victim represents the sons. So the Chorus's prayers foreshadow their own futility. When M. kills the first of her sons she describes it as a sacrifice to placate her brother's ghost (see on 970-1). **more kindly**: this translation takes *mitior* to be attributive (i. e. to describe a fixed attribute of the goddess); alternatively it could be proleptic, indicating the effect of the sacrifice on the goddess ('let her be presented with a young victim, becoming more kindly'). It is more tactful for the Chorus to assume that the goddess is kindly to begin with. On the other hand the passage recalls a line of Horace where the adjective is definitely proleptic, *Carm.* 1.19.16 *mactata ueniet lenior hostia*, 'she (Venus) will come more gently when a victim has been sacrificed'; but the context there is different, for the poet has been under attack by Venus, whereas here, if Venus is present at all, she is assimilated to Peace.

67-70 Hymen is addressed, identified by his association with marriage, and by his torch and garland (cf. 111, and e.g. Bion 1.87-8; Catul. 61.6-7, 14-5; Ovid *Epist.* 6.44; in art cf. *LIMC* 5.1, 583-5, 5.2, 401). By S.'s date Hymen or Hymenaeus was regarded as a marriage god. From Homer onwards the Greek *hymenaios* can denote a wedding song (*Il.* 18.493), and *hymen hymenaie* was a Greek ritual cry used at weddings. Already in the fifth century Hymenaeus was regarded as a god (cf. Eur. *Tro.* 310, 314, and perhaps already Pi. *fr.* 128c7-9), but *hymen* continued to be regarded as a ritual cry, and the earliest certain use of Hymen as the name of the god is in Ovid (*Epist.* 6.44).

67   **who are present at lawful marriages**: literally '... at lawful marriage-torches'; the torches are a metonymy for the marriage itself (cf. 398, 581). The phrase 'lawful torches' is echoed by Lucan 2.356; cf. Quint. *Decl.* 291.5 and Winterbottom. On torches at weddings see on 37-9; on the torch carried by Hymen see 111-2.

68   **with augural right hand**: at a Roman wedding, at least at a proper, formal one, there was an *auspex*, originally someone who took the auspices to ensure the favour of the gods before the ceremony went ahead (Cic. *Diu.* 1.28; V. Max. 2.1.1); but this seems to have become a formality before the end of the Republic (see *OLD* s.v. *auspex* 2; Treggiari [1991], 164-5). This translation assumes that Hymen is acting as *auspex*, the term being applied to his right hand.

69   **languidly**: for *marcidus* and the verb *marceo* associated with drunkenness, cf. Sen. *Suas.* 6.7 *ipse uino et somno marcidus*, 'he, languid with wine and sleep'; and applied to Bacchus, Stat. *Theb.* 4.652, 667. **drunken step**: drunkenness is not a regular feature of Hymen, but it is appropriate to a son of Bacchus (see on 110; Myth. Vat. 3.11.2 says his parentage represents the connection between drunkenness and sexual desire).

71-4 **You, star, who ... as soon as possible**: ancient weddings took place in the evening, and so Hesperus, the evening star (see on 727), Vesper in Latin, is a regular feature of wedding songs: cf. Sappho fr. 104a 'Hesperus, bringing everything that the shining dawn scattered'; Catul. 62.1-35, including vocative addresses to Hesperus at 20, 26, 35. From an early date the Greeks knew that the evening star and the morning star are the same, the planet Venus, which is visible only just after sunset or just before sunrise. The phrase 'who herald two different times of day' alludes learnedly to this. (See Pease on Cic. *N.D.* 2.53; Nisbet and Hubbard on Hor. *Carm.* 2.9.10.) **You ... for you ... for you**: this repetition of the second personal singular pronoun (starting with 'You, too' in 67) is a feature of hymnic language both classical and Christian; cf. 1-4, 797-807, and in Latin poetry e.g. Lucr. 1.6-40; Catul. 34.13-20; Nisbet and Hubbard on Hor. *Carm.* 1.10.9. In the Latin, 'times' (71 *temporis*) echoes 'temples' (70 *tempora*), though the senses are different, and the echo looks coincidental.

75-81 Praise of the bride's beauty is a standard feature of wedding songs; cf. e.g. Theocr. 18.19-38; Catul. 61.86-95. Creusa is compared to the women of other Greek towns. Note the allusiveness: none of the towns is referred to by name, nor is Creusa or Jason (see Introduction §5.1).

76   **Cecrops' town**: i.e. Athens. In mythology Cecrops was an early king of Attica, sometimes said to be the first king (see *OCD³* on 'Cecrops').

77-9 **whom the unwalled town ... of Taygetus**: i.e. the women of Sparta. Taygetus is the mountain range to the west of the town of Sparta, separating it from Messenia. In classical times the town had no walls; some were built in the Hellenistic period, and in other respects Spartan life had become more conventional by the Roman period, but

mythological poetry looks back to the traditional image of Sparta (see *OCD*³ on Sparta').
forces to exercise the severe regime imposed on Spartan boys and girls alike was part
of the traditional Spartan image, and Spartan women in the classical period had greater
economic rights and social freedom than most Greek women (cf. Plut. *Lyc.* 14-16; P.
Cartledge, *CQ* 31 [1981], 84-105). The lack of segregation between the sexes was
shocking to conventional Greek and Roman opinion (cf. Eur. *Andr.* 595-601), though
attractive to a love-poet like Propertius (3.14); the Chorus here makes no evaluative
comment.

80-1 and those who bathe ... sacred Alpheus: i.e. the women of Thebes (Aonian is another
word for Boeotian) and Olympia (though the reference may be to a larger area, since the
Alpheus rises in Arcadia and flows through Elis). The cult of river-gods was frequent in
Greece and Rome, hence Alpheus is 'sacred' (see *OCD*³ on 'river-gods', 'Alpheus').
Alpheos is a Greek nominative singular form (cf. on 35).

82-9 The Chorus praises the bridegroom's handsome appearance. Praise of the groom is also
a conventional part of wedding songs; cf. Sappho fr. 105(b) (the groom is compared to
Achilles), 111 (he is compared to Ares), 112, 115; Catul. 61.196-200. The Chorus says
that Jason surpasses gods in appearance: four gods who will yield the first place to him
are referred to, the first two allusively, Castor and Pollux by name. In poetry and
rhetoric there was a tradition of saying that people equal or surpass the gods, but there
was also a religious sense—found in some poetry—that such high praise was impious
and could bring down punishment on the person praised (see for example Catul. 51.1-2
ille mi par esse deo uidetur, / ille si fas est, superare diuos, 'He seems to be to be equal
to a god, he, if it is right to say so, seems to surpass the gods', where the conditional
clause guards against causing offence by an impious comparison). So the Chorus's
words may in their own eyes be justified praise, but equally the audience may think they
are excessive and dangerous, foreshadowing Jason's sufferings. See Hine (1989), 416-
9, for further parallels.

83 **Aeson's son:** Aeson was father of Jason, and half-brother of Pelias, who, in some
versions, deprived him of the kingship of Iolcus (see on 133-4).

84-5 by the offspring ... yokes on tigers: Dionysus, also called Bacchus, the child of
Jupiter and Semele, a mortal woman. When Semele, still pregnant, asked to see Jupiter
in all his glory, he appeared as lightning, which killed her, but made her son immortal;
Jupiter sewed the unborn child in his thigh for the rest of the gestation period. After the
eastern campaigns of Alexander the Great, the myth of Dionysus included a journey to
India, where he yoked panthers or tigers or other exotic animals to his chariot. (See
*OCD*³ on 'Dionysus'; on Roman portrayals of Dionysus/Bacchus see *LIMC* 3.1, 540-66,
3.2, 428-56.) Hippolytus is said to be more handsome than Bacchus at *Phaed.* 753-60,
and in *Oed.* 403-508 there is a long choral ode in praise of the god, describing his
appearance (403-23), and his driving a chariot—this time pulled by lions—in the east
(424-8).

86 **the god who makes tripods move:** Apollo, god of prophecy, at whose oracular
sanctuary at Delphi a priestess sat on a tripod and was inspired by the god to prophesy
(see *OCD*³ on 'Apollo', 'Delphic oracle'). Pindar (*Pyth.* 4.87) and Apollonius (3.1283)
compare Jason to Apollo, and Verg. *A.* 4.143-50 compares Aeneas to the god (see Pease
on 4.143 for other such comparisons). The form *tripodas* (with a short *a*) is a Greek
accusative plural.

87   **the wild girl**: Artemis, the Roman Diana, the virgin huntress.

88-9 **with his brother Castor, Pollux**: literally 'with his Castor', 'brother' being understood (cf. the use of *sui* to denote relatives, *OLD* s.v. *suus* B6b). Castor and Pollux (Greek Polydeuces), known as the Dioscuri, were twin gods worshipped throughout Greece, and introduced to Rome early in the fifth century B.C. In myth they were brothers of Helen and Clytemestra, and were renowned, respectively, as a horse-rider and a boxer (cf. Hom. *Il.* 3.237; Nisbet and Hubbard on Hor. *Carm.* 1.12.25-7). Their paternity was disputed, their father being variously said to be Zeus or the mortal Tyndareus. This ambiguous status is reflected in the play: here the Chorus prays to them, but they were also Argonauts for whose safety M. can claim credit at 230. (See *OCD*³ on 'Castor and Pollux', 'Dioscuri'.)

90   **Thus, thus**: see on 13. This repetition (*sic, sic*) is found earlier at Verg. *A.* 4.660 (see Wills [1997], 118-9). **heaven-dwellers**: *caelicolae* is a poetic compound word, found in Ennius (*Ann.* 445 Skutsch, 292 Warmington), and frequent in epic (see Introduction §5.6).

91   **surpass other wives**: 'wives' implicitly includes M.

92   **man ... men**: *uir ... uiros* can also mean 'husband ... husbands' (as at 53, the only other occurrence in the play; *maritus*, which only means 'husband', is used at 115, 279, 657, 663).

93-8 The bride's beauty is compared to the brightness of the sun and moon, which outshine the other stars. In Theocr. 18.26-8, a wedding-song, Helen is compared to Dawn. Here the audience may remember that the sun is M.'s ancestor (cf. 28-34), that she claims to control the heavenly bodies (27-8; cf. 757-8), and that her magic closely involves the moon (cf. 770); so the comparisons can be read as implying M.'s superiority to Creusa, in contradiction of the Chorus's meaning.

95   **with the sun's appearance**: i.e. the stars are no longer visible when the sun appears. The literal meaning is just 'with the sun', a phrase also found at Verg. *A.* 3.568 (cf. *OLD* s.v. *cum*¹ 6a).

96   **the dense flocks of Pleiades**: Sappho fr. 34 described the moon out-shining other stars; cf. Nisbet and Hubbard on Hor. *Carm.* 1.12.48 for other examples, and S. *Phaed.* 743-8. The prominent star-cluster of the Pleiades lies in the constellation Taurus; seven of the stars were supposed to be visible to the naked eye. Thus the 'dense flocks' are only seven in number, but the phrase could refer to them being close together; or S. perhaps alludes to the ancient etymology of Pleiades from the Greek *pleiones*, 'more' (see Maltby [1991] on *Pleiades*). In mythology they were normally identified as the seven daughters of Atlas and Pleione (see Bömer on Ovid *Fast.* 5.81-4; Gantz [1993], 212-8). However, a rare variant tradition said that they were daughters of the queen of the Amazons, and introduced choral dancing and nocturnal festivals (Callim. fr. 693 Pfeiffer); this would have a particular relevance to Creusa 'in the women's dance' (93).

97-8 **Phoebe**: a Greek nominative singular ending (with long final *-e*). In early Greek poetry she was a Titan (see above on 5, and West on Hes. *Th.* 136), mother of Leto and grandmother of Artemis (Gantz [1993], 37-40; *LIMC* 8.1., 984, 8.2, 655), but by Roman times she was identified with Artemis, the Roman Diana (see *OLD* s.v. *Phoebe*; Bömer on Ovid *Fast.* 2.163). M., with her magical powers, is a devotee of Phoebe (770), who was also identified with Hecate, so again the Chorus's words suggest the sinister, superior power of M. **with light not her own**: from an early date the Greeks knew that the moon does not generate light of its own but reflects the sun's light, and the poets liked to describe the moon's borrowed light in novel ways (e.g. Catul. 34.15-6; Lucr. 5.575). **binds a solid orb with circling horns**: an elaborate description of the full moon, with the horns of the crescent moon imagined as joining in a full circle. (The past participle *circuitis* is used intransitively; see Hillen [1989], 246, n. 668; K-S 1.97-9; H-Sz 290-1.)

99-101 Creusa's red and white complexion is compared to red dye on white material, and to early morning light. The juxtaposition of red and white was regarded as a mark of beauty: cf. Catullus's wedding song 61.186-8; Verg. A. 12.64-9; Davis [1993], 193. For the audience the red may here suggest blood, foreshadowing Creusa's death. **the dewy shepherd**: the description of a person as dewy is striking, and apparently original; it suggests the shepherd has been outside all night.

102-6 Jason is well rid of his previous wife, M. This is the first explicit reference to M. by the Chorus (though she may be implicitly included in the wives of 91). The Chorus describes her as Jason's wife (103), not denying the legitimacy of the relationship, but its hostility is unmistakable. In its eyes, Jason has been saved from a grim marriage in which he was an unwilling partner; and the Chorus's words suggest he loves Creusa in a way he has never loved M. This gives a quite different motive for the new marriage from the political ones that Creon and Jason later give: but of course they are speaking to M., and are less likely to talk of personal repugnance to her face (see Introduction §4.1).

102 **the marriage-chamber of wild Phasis**: i.e. marriage to a Colchian; the river Phasis (see on 43) here denotes the Colchis region, 'wild' because cold and barbaric.

103 **an unbridled wife**: the Argo could be bridled (2-3), and the moon can keep a tight rein on her chariot (792), but M. is unbridled here and at 866 (cf. also 592). M. has control over the world around her, but she herself is uncontrolled. (The image of the bridle is also found in S.'s philosophy: e.g. *Dial.* 3.7.3 *deinde ratio ipsa, cui freni traduntur, tam diu potens est quam diu diducta est ab adfectibus*, 'then reason itself, which is given the reins, is effective for just so long as it is separated from the emotions'.)

105 **seize**: the word evokes Jason's eagerness, but it also suggests a violent act (it is the only example of the word in an amatory context in *TLL* 4.1040.51). **Aeolian**: i.e. Corinthian; Aeolus, son of Hellen, was father of Sisyphus, founder of Corinth (see on 512; *Neue Pauly* on 'Aiolos' 1).

106 **now, for the ... parents-in-law**: by helping Jason and escaping with him, M. betrayed her father Aeetes (see Introduction §3.2(a)). In Greece and Rome a daughter had to marry with the consent of her parents, if they were still alive (*OCD*[3] on 'marriage law'; Treggiari [1991], 164); indeed a daughter would not normally leave the family home except to get married with that consent. See on 115.

107-9 **Young people**: for the question whether the young people are members of the Chorus, or a half-chorus, or are distinct from the Chorus, see introductory note on 56-115. **enjoy the licence ... is rarely permitted**: at Greek and Roman marriages the onlookers traditionally chanted obscene abuse at the bridal couple, cf. Aristoph. *Pax* 1336-57; Theocr. 18.9-15; in Rome the abuse was called 'Fescennine verses', see 113 below, Catul. 61.119-20. An ancient etymology (Paul. Fest. 85 M.) linked the word to *fascinum*, 'evil spell', because the abuse was supposed to avert the harmful power of jealousy and the evil eye. The etymology is wrong, but this may have been the function of the chanting (*OCD*[3] on 'Fescennini'). **from either side**: this may suggest two half-choruses (see on 56-115), or it could refer to crowds that line the street on either side of the procession.

110-5 The ode ends with six lines of dactylic hexameters, the metre primarily associated with epic, and very rare in S.'s tragedies (otherwise it is only used in *Oed.*: 233-8, an oracle; 403-4, 429-31, 445-8, 467-71, 503-8, in a long ode). The metre was also used in hymns, including Catullus 62, a wedding-hymn, which makes it appropriate here.

110 **offspring of thyrsus-carrying Lyaeus**: Lyaeus is a title of Dionysus or Bacchus, whose worshippers, like the god himself, carried a thyrsus; this was a special staff which had a pine-cone at the end, or ivy or vine-leaves twined round it. The word Lyaeus means 'loosener', describing the effect of wine, and also appropriate in the context of the wedding and especially of the unrestrained chanting of Fescennines that has just been described. Dionysus' offspring is Hymen; see on 67-70, where he has already been invoked. There were various accounts of his parentage: most commonly he was said to be son of Apollo and a Muse (see *LIMC* 5.1, 583-5), but S. follows the version that his father was Dionysus: see Eur. *Phaethon* 233-4 and Diggle's comm.; Donatus on Ter. *Ad.* 905; Serv. *A.* 4.127; Myth. Vat. 3.11.2 (most of these make Aphrodite/Venus his mother, but Mart. Cap. 1.1 makes him son of Bacchus and a Muse). **thyrsus-carrying**: a poetic compound (see Introduction §5.6), used at *Phaed.* 753, and earlier in Naevius (*trag.* 32 Ribbeck, 34 Warmington), based on the Greek *thyrsophoros* (Eur. *Cycl.* 64; Ion of Chius fr. 26.1 West).

111 **it is now time**: the Latin uses the imperfect tense, *tempus erat*, to refer to the present, probably expressing impatience; this is chiefly poetic, but also found in Livy 8.5.3; cf. Nisbet and Hubbard on Hor. *Carm.* 1.37.4. **the well-split pine**: see on 37-9. 'well-split', meaning frayed at the end to make it burn better, is a poetic compound adjective (see Introduction §5.6), first found in Ovid, who applies it to the torches used by M. while performing the rejuvenation of Aeson, Jason's father (*Met.* 7.259; also 8.644). The Ovidian echo, and M.'s hope that she would carry the torch herself (37-8), suggest that even Hymen's torch is tainted by association with M.

112 **languid**: see on 69. The contrast with the vigorous verb 'shake' shows the impatience of the Chorus, an impatience characteristic of wedding songs: cf. Catul. 61.90 (to the bride) 'but you delay; the day is passing', cf. 192-3, 62.2-3.

113 **fescennine**: see on 107-9; S. probably did not feel any anachronism in applying a Latin term to the Greek mythological age, and in any case the practice of such chanting at weddings was also Greek. This is a golden line, with the verb in the middle, two adjectives at the beginning, and their two nouns at end of the line (well-established in Catullus and Vergil, and very popular in Ovid and later epic poets; see Williams on Verg. *A.* 5.46; Wilkinson [1963], 215-7).

114-5 **let her depart ... a foreign husband**: this parting shot is directed against M.; possibly we are to imagine the Chorus catching sight of her as she comes on stage. **in silent darkness**: the Chorus speaks as if M. will be safely out of the way if banished to darkness, forgetting her magical powers that flourish in darkness. **any woman who runs away and marries**: brides were usually married from their parents' home, as is Creusa (see on 106), but M. broke convention by running away from home with Jason. Men, by contrast, were free to leave home to find a bride. The word *fugitiuus* is rare in poetry, but is found at Ovid *Epist.* 5.91.

ACT TWO: 116-300

This Act consists of a soliloquy by M. (116-49), followed by two dialogues, first between M. and the Nurse (150-76), then between M. and Creon (177-300). The arrival of Creon on stage is firmly signalled by M.'s words at 177 (see comm.). Her own entry on stage *may* be indicated by the Chorus's words at 114-5 (see comm.). In her soliloquy at 116-49 she does not acknowledge the Nurse's presence, but since the Nurse has heard what M. has been saying (150-1), or at least some of it, it is natural to assume that she has come on stage with M.; it is less likely that she appears part-way through M.'s soliloquy.

116-49   M.'s second soliloquy reveals the complexity of her feelings for Jason. In the first half (116-36) she repeats her accusations against him, and again considers how she can adequately punish him. But in the final word of 136, *amor*, 'love', she acknowledges that she has loved Jason: she probably refers to the past (see on 135-6), but her words leave it open to the audience to suppose that she still feels that love in some measure. This supposition is confirmed by an unexpected change of direction at 137: the wedding is not really Jason's fault, she says, for he is under Creon's power; she must not speak of Jason dying, but must let him live; for Creon alone deserves punishment (137-49). Here we see M.'s former love for Jason resurfacing.

116   **I am ruined ... assailed my ears**: M. now realises that the wedding really is taking place. (In the Latin, *occidimus* is first person plural, referring to herself alone, but *meas* in the same line is the first person singular possessive adjective; this shows how interchangeable first person singular and plural were in such contexts in S.; cf. 142.)

117   **scarcely ... scarcely**: anaphora of *uix*, 'scarcely', i.e. repetition of the same word at the start of two parallel phrases or clauses; see 127, 272-3, 309-17, 321-8, 502, 634, 643, 674-5, 911-3; cf. 228, 230. The repetition need not be at the start of the phrase, see 238-9. (Compare on 13 for another form of repetition, iteration.) **scarcely credit so great an evil**: Ovid's M., in *Heroides* 12, describes her initial reaction to hearing the wedding-song and procession as partial incredulity: *ut subito nostras Hymen cantatus ad aures / uenit, ... / tibiaque effundit socialia carmina ... / pertimui; nec adhuc tantum scelus esse putabam: / sed tamen in toto pectore frigus erat*, 'As the cries of "Hymen" suddenly reached my ears ... and the pipes rang out the wedding-song ... I was afraid; I didn't yet think the wickedness had grown so great, but still a chill gripped my whole heart' (137-42).

118   **robbed of my father**: Aeetes. She speaks of being robbed of her father, as though it was not her fault that she betrayed him in order to help Jason.

118-20   There is marked alliteration in these angry lines: *... potuit, erepto patre / patria atque regno sedibus solam exteris / deserere durus?* Cf. on 14.

120   **my good services**: *merita*, meritorious actions which deserve gratitude or a reward; cf. 435, 465. *Merita* can have political associations, when applied to the services that create obligations between men in public life, and M. may imply that she is a political equal of Jason.

121   **flames and sea ... by wickedness**: flames and sea represent two of the four elements, fire and water: M. can control the natural world (see on 28, 755). She overcame flames when she protected Jason against the fire-breathing bulls, and overcame the sea when she helped the Argonauts to sail back to Greece safely, scattering the pieces of her dismembered brother on the sea (see on 452-3, 528).

123-4 I am driven in all directions: this resembles one of the two surviving lines of Ovid's *Medea: feror huc illuc, uae, plena deo*, 'I am driven this way and that, ah!, filled with the god' (fr. 2 Ribbeck; see Heinze [1997], 247-51).

125 If only he had a brother: i.e. then I could murder *his* brother, just as I murdered my own (see on 121). **he does have a wife:** Creusa.

126 my wrongs: *meis malis*; this could mean either 'the wrongs I have suffered' (in 117 'evil' translates the same word *malum*) or 'the wrongs I have committed.' Probably both senses are present, for she has been speaking both of her sufferings and of her crimes: she means both 'will that be sufficient vengeance for what I have suffered?' and 'will that equal my previous crimes?'. Cf. on 910.

127 If the Pelasgian ... barbarian ones: in the *Iliad* the Pelasgi are a tribe associated with northern Greece; later 'Pelasgi' is a poetic equivalent for 'Greeks' in general (see *OCD³* on 'Pelasgians'); thus here 'Pelasgian cities' are contrasted with 'barbarian ones', with anaphora of *si quod* ('if ... any'; cf. on 117). Notice how this contrast of Greek and barbarian is put in the mouth of M., herself a 'barbarian' from Colchis; in her eyes either side may provide an inspiration for her crimes. Euripides' M. had also referred to Colchis as a barbarian land (*Med.* 256). The Greek/barbarian distinction is less important in a Roman writer than in a Greek—the Romans, after all, were originally counted as barbarians themselves—but it would probably be going too far so suggest that 'barbarian' may mean little more than 'eastern' (as Fitch claims of *Her. F.* 475 in his comm.). However, the barbarian origin of M. is not prominent in S.'s play: Colchis is called barbarian by the Chorus at 612 (see comm.), and its disparaging description of M. at 102-3 suggests barbarian stereotyping. M. herself describes her origins in civilised terms, see on 209-19, and there may be a contemptuous note in her use of 'Pelasgian' in 178 (see comm.). The comment of Kerrigan (1996), 101, on Euripides' M. could also apply to S.'s: she has 'scarcely ... internalized Greek values.'

129-130 Let your crimes ... all be recalled: 'let them be recalled', *redeant*, is sometimes taken to mean 'let them be repeated'; but it can also mean 'let them be remembered' (as an inspiration for new crimes, see Zwierlein [1986], 139), and this seems more appropriate after 'Let your crimes urge you on.'

130-4 There follow allusive references to her major crimes.

130 that famed ornament of the kingdom: the golden fleece.

131 the impious girl's: i.e. her own, M.'s. By using the third person she sets herself up as an example, and by describing herself as 'impious' she spurs herself on to more wickedness. **small companion:** Apsyrtus, see next note.

132 the corpse that was flung at the father: this is explained in the next phrase—it refers to the dismembering of her brother Apsyrtus and the scattering of the pieces to delay Aeetes' pursuit of the Argo (see on 452-3).

133-4 old Pelias: Pelias was the half-brother of Jason's father, Aeson, and M. was responsible for his death. That much is common to all versions of the story of Pelias, but there are major variations, of which the main ones are as follows.

(a) Pelias' status in Iolcus: according to the version first found in Pindar (*Pyth.* 4.138-67), Aeson was rightful ruler of Iolcus, but Pelias usurped the throne and ruled himself; another version said Pelias held the throne lawfully as regent after Aeson's early death (Schol. Hom. *Od.* 12.69). In both versions Pelias had received a prophecy warning him to beware of a man wearing one sandal, and Jason arrived in Iolcus minus one sandal.

(b) Pelias, Jason and the golden fleece: according to the Pindaric version, when Jason returned to reclaim the throne, Pelias devised the mission to fetch the golden fleece as a way of getting rid of him. In other versions, Pelias was the rightful ruler, and devised the mission because Jason fulfilled the prophecy (Pherecydes *FGH*3F105; Apollod. 1.9.16; Ap. Rh. 1.5-17); or, in Diodorus, Jason was an adventurer out for glory (D. S. 4.40.1-3).

(c) The motive for the murder of Pelias: Jason wanted to avenge either Pelias' usurping of the throne (Pindar), or the death of his father Aeson, who in some versions was killed, or driven to suicide, by Pelias after the Argo set sail (D. S. 4.50.1-3; Apollod. 1.9.27); or Hera sought revenge because Pelias did not honour her (Pherecydes *FGH*3F105; Ap. Rh. 1.12-4, cf. 3.64-5, 4.241-3; Hera/Juno has no such role in S., see Introduction §3.3).

(d) M. and the death of Pelias: on the return of the Argo, M. deceived the daughters of Pelias: pretending that she would help them to rejuvenate their father, she got them to kill and dismember him and boil the pieces in a cauldron. It was variously said that M. had first demonstrated her power by successfully rejuvenating Jason, or Aeson, or a ram (*LIMC* 5.1, 634-5, 5.2, 432; 7.1, 274-6, 7.2, 215).

In S. Pelias was punished (201), for Jason's benefit (276), and M. deceived his daughters into killing him (256-61, 475-6), but otherwise the brief allusions leave it unclear which version(s) S. was familiar with. (See further Gantz [1993], 189-94, 341-3, 365-7.)

135-6 and yet I ... love that raged: 'unhappy (*infelix*) love' denotes irrational, crazed love, cf. Verg. *Ecl.* 6.47, on Pasiphae's passion for the bull, *a uirgo infelix, quae te dementia cepit*, 'ah, unhappy girl, what madness possessed you?', *A.* 4.68-9 *uritur infelix Dido totaque uagatur / urbe furens*, 'unhappy Dido burns [with love], and wanders all over the city raging.' (These and other parallels show that we cannot take *saeuit* to be present, meaning: 'my unhappy love (unhappy because Jason has abandoned me) is filling me with rage.' See Zweirlein [1986], 139-41.)

137-49 M. changes direction (signalled by 137 *tamen*, 'Yet'): after the mention of her love for Jason in 136, she says that Creon is really to blame, and he deserves all the punishment, not Jason (see on 116-49). This sympathy for Jason is not found in Euripides; but in Ovid *Epist.* 12.135-6 M. still expresses love for Jason: *iussa domo cessi, natis comitata duobus / et, qui me sequitur semper, amore tui*, 'When I was ordered to, I left your house, accompanied by my two sons and by the love for you that always follows me.'

137-8 finding himself ... sway and authority: Roman legal language, though not applied in a strict legal context; as the following lines show, Creon has a *de facto* hold over Jason. (*arbitri* is genitive of *arbitrium*, not of *arbiter*; for the *-i* genitive form of nouns in *-ium* or *-ius*, cf. on 481. For the genitive as a predicate after *factus* cf. *Epist.* 77.15 *fac tui iuris quod alieni est*, 'bring under your own power what is under somebody else's'; Woodman on Vell. 2.108.2; *TLL* 6.1.112.64-113.15.)

139-40 mad anguish: M. feels the tension within herself: her pain was going too far in wishing that Jason had killed himself rather than submit to Creon. 'mad', *furiose*, is the adjective from *furor*, 'madness', one of the recurrent themes of the play; I have consistently translated these terms 'mad' and 'madness' (cf. 52, 386, 392, etc.). Words closely related in sense are: *demens* (174, 930), *insanio* (383), *insanus* (765), *lymphatus* (386), *non sanus* (123), *uesanus* (738). In the play 'mad(ness)' is used with various nuances. It is not meant in the strict medical or legal sense, of permanent incapacity to act rationally and responsibly, which would have implied that M. was not really responsible for her actions. It is used more in the layman's ill-defined sense, describing behaviour or a state of mind that is impelled by extremes of emotion and unable to see reason, or that holds beliefs which normal people would never hold, or that spectacularly transgresses the normal rules of moral or social behaviour. Not only do others recognise madness in M. (e.g. the Nurse at 380-96), but she recognises it in herself (e.g. 123 and here): sometimes, as here, she is aghast at her madness, sometimes she embraces or desires it (e.g. 52). Other characters sometimes treat her madness as something quite uncontrollable (e.g. 849-73), sometimes as amenable to persuasion and reason (e.g. 157-8, 537-8). The audience is left to decide to what extent, and in what precise sense, M. is mad. Madness was also a prominent theme in S.'s philosophy and in Stoicism generally, and the behaviour of M. in the play in important ways resembles the behaviour associated with madness in S.'s philosophical works (see on 380-96). But the Stoics offered a persuasive redefinition of madness: they wanted it to be recognised that everyday faults such as anger or greed, which in mild forms are regularly condoned or tolerated by society, are really forms of madness, because they are not governed by reason. This was the basis of the Stoic paradox that we are all mad, and all equally mad, until we become Stoic sages. S. acknowledges the gap between Stoic and everyday perceptions of madness e.g. at *Ben.* 2.35.2: 'We [the Stoics] say that everybody is insane, and yet we do not treat everybody with hellebore [a medicine]; we give both the vote and judicial powers to those very people whom we call insane.' In the play there is no hint of this wider Stoic sense of madness: other characters than M. may act wrongly or unwisely, but madness is ascribed only to her. (On her behaviour and the Furies, see on 157. On 'anguish', see on 49. On various ancient views on madness, see Herschkowitz [1998], 1-16.)

140-2 If he can ... with my gift: the traces of M.'s love for Jason are clear in these lines. **let him remember me**: implying 'remember with affection'; cf. how Aeneas, in his last speech to Dido, says (Verg. *A.* 4.335-6) *nec me meminisse pigebit Elissae / dum memor ipse mei*, 'I shall not be sorry to remember Dido while I remember myself'; also Hom. *Od.* 8.461-2; Sappho fr. 94.7-8; Hor. *Carm.* 3.27.14. **be gentle with my gift**: i.e. the gift of life that M. gave him when she saved him from Aeetes and from Pelias; cf. Ovid *Epist.* 12.203, 205-6.

143 The fault is entirely Creon's: in Euripides M. says Creon is not to blame (306-11); but she says it to Creon himself, so it does not necessarily represent her truest feelings.

144-5 he drags ... her children: in S.'s play it is not clear at exactly what point M. hears that she must leave Corinth and be parted from her children. The natural implication of 144-5 is that she already knows that she must lose her children, and perhaps also that she is banished (but the loss of the children is compatible with her remaining in the kingdom while they remain in Jason's household). Costa thinks she first learns of her banishment in 190. However, at 179-80 Creon is indignant that she has not already left, which suggests that the order has already been given. At 170 the Nurse urges her to escape to avoid death, which may or may not imply a sentence of banishment. In Euripides, M. is banished along with her children; the sentence is first reported to the Nurse by the Tutor as a rumour (67-73), and Creon himself pronounces the sentence on M. at 271-6. It is as though S. need not include an explicit statement of her banishment because the audience, who know the traditional story, will take it for granted. See further on 192, 283.

145   **faithfulness ... tight pledges**: an elusively abstract phrase: the faithfulness is probably that between Jason and M., and the pledges are their children (see 1012 and *OLD* s.v. *pignus* 4 for children as pledges or guarantees of a marriage); alternatively the pledges are the promises that Jason and M. exchanged (see on 7-8).

147   **I shall bury ... deep ash**: in Euripides, too, M. thinks of burning the palace, but rejects the idea as too risky for herself (378-83). In S. the palace is set on fire by the gifts sent to Creusa (885-90).

149   **Malea**: the most easterly of the three southern promontories of the Peloponnese. In literature it is always described as dangerous, because of the sudden veering of the winds. The idea that the fire will be seen from as far away as Malea shows the magnitude of the revenge that M. desires.

150-76   The Nurse must have been listening to M. (see on 116-300). In her opening speech she urges M. to keep her complaints hidden, in order that her revenge may be more effective. This is surprising, since servants in tragedy often seek to dissuade their masters or mistresses from any wrongdoing (in S. cf. *Ag.* 108-225, and the male servant at *Thy.* 176-335; cf. *Oct.* 1-272); though compare the Nurse in *Phaedra*, who first argues that Phaedra must resist her passion for Hippolytus, but then changes her mind at the end of the second act, and promises to try to win Hippolytus over (*Phaed.* 255-73); and in *Her. O.* 233-582 the Nurse is persuaded to assist Deianira's plans to use magic against Hercules. However, as this scene of *Medea* continues, the Nurse tries more and more to dissuade M. from acting at all, so that her opening words, while appearing to go along with M.'s desire for revenge, could be read as a ploy to gain M.'s attention at the start. Her arguments throughout are practical and prudential rather than moral, and to that extent she is consistent. Nurses were a familiar figure in literature from Eurycleia in the *Odyssey* onwards (see Pease on Verg. *A.* 4.632).

150   **hide your complaints**: the participle *abditos* is translated as an imperative ('hide') because it is predicative, a description of something the Nurse wants M. to do, not of something she is already doing.

151-4   **When people endure ... opportunity for revenge**: there are similar ideas in Euripides' *Medea*, where Creon at 319-20 says that outspokenness is easier to guard against than silent cunning; and Jason at 448-50 says that M. could have stayed in Corinth if she had not been so outspoken. For the general idea compare Sen. *Contr.* 1.pr.21 *magis nocent insidiae quae latent: utilissima est dissimulata subtilitas, quae effectu apparet, habitu latet*, 'Concealed plots are more harmful: the most useful acuteness is hidden; its effect is seen, its nature is concealed'; Tac. *Hist.* 4.24. **endure ... are able**: *pertulit ... potuit*: the Latin verbs are gnomic perfects, see on 199-200.

155-76   There follows a rapid dialogue between M. and the Nurse; it is similar to Greek stichomythia, where the speeches are each one line long. Sometimes, as at 157, there is speaker-division in mid-line, called antilabe; it is found in Sophocles and Euripides, Old and

New comedy, and is frequent in Senecan tragedy. Down to 167, M. and the Nurse exchange whole lines or longer speeches; from 168 they speak alternate half-lines, and in 170-1 quarter-lines (also found at *Thy.* 257 and *Her. O.* 438; earlier in Soph. *Phil.* 753, and Menander, e.g. *Dysc.* 85). In this sort of rapid dialogue one speaker regularly echoes the words of the other and twists or contradicts them. In the present passage M. insistently answers all the Nurse's points, sometimes echoing the Nurse's words to reinforce her reply (cf. 160-1 'scope for courage'; 162-3 'no hope', 'nothing to hope for'; 165-6 'nothing left', 'Medea is left'; 168 'king'). The fact that M. picks up and answers the Nurse's points, while the latter moves on to new points, shows that M. has the better of the argument (cf. Tarrant on *Ag.* 131, 284ff.). For other dialogue features see on 159, 168, 176, and for similar dialogue later in the play see 192-202, 490-530.

156 **conceal**: *clepere* is rare in S.'s period (it is also used at *Her. F.* 799, where manuscript *E* has the more familiar *tegit*, and at Manil. 1.27). It is found in early Latin drama, and may have been used in legal (cf. Cic. *Leg.* 2.22, *Rep.* 4.3) and religious (cf. Livy 22.10.5) language. It may have an archaic flavour here, something not very common in Senecan tragedy (see Carlsson [1926], 43-4, 57-62; Billerbeck [1988], 28-9).

157 **Restrain your Furious impulse**: the adjective is not *furiosus*, the normal word for 'furious, mad', but *furialis*, literally 'Fury-like', linked to the Furies, *Furiae*; hence the capital letter in the translation. So the Nurse sees that M. is behaving like a Fury (and the audience realises that M.'s invocation of the Furies at 13-8 has borne fruit in her behaviour). *furialis* has the same connotations at *Thy.* 94, its only other occurrence in S.

159 **Fortune fears the brave**: it was a proverbial commonplace that fortune helps the brave (Ter. *Ph.* 203 *fortes fortuna adiuuat*; Verg. *A.* 10.284 *audentis fortuna iuuat*; Plin. *Ep.* 6.16.11; Otto [1890], s.v. *fortuna* 9). M. gives a new twist, Fortune *fears* the brave; i.e. M. can arouse fear even in Fortune. On Fortune in the play, see on 520. The pithily expressed moral generalisation in this line is an example of a *sententia* or epigram, Greek *gnome*; there are other examples in 161 and 163, and they are a regular feature of rapid dialogue (see on 163, 559; Tarrant on *Ag.* 145ff.; Fitch on *Her. F.* 433-7).

160 **courage**: *uirtus* is not easy to translate effectively; here 'courage' is the basic meaning, but (a) *uirtus* is etymologically linked to *uir*, 'man' (as opposed to 'woman'); 'manliness' would sound too strange to English ears in this context, but M. is advocating what is originally a male quality (see on 42); (b) *uirtus* can also mean 'virtue', both in ordinary moral discourse and in Stoic ethics (see Introduction §1.2). Here and in the next line the moral sense is hardly present, but some would detect it at 977 (see comm.).

163 **Anyone who ... despair of nothing**: close to ideas expressed in S.'s philosophical works: *Epist.* 5.7 (quoting the Stoic Hecato) *desines timere si sperare desieris*, 'you will stop being afraid if you stop hoping.' The line is a typical Senecan *sententia* (see on 159): note the parallelism and antithesis, *nil ... sperare, desperet nihil*. (For the two forms *nil* and *nihil* in parallel, see Verg. *Ecl.* 2.6-7 *nihil mea carmina curas? / nil nostri miserere?*, 'Do you not care at all for my songs? Do you have no pity at all for me?'; Wills [1996], 464.)

166-7 **Medea is left ... and thunderbolts**: M. appeals to her own past achievements, and to her power over the elements (already hinted at in 28 and 121, see comm.) and over the gods (cf. 271, 424).

168   NU: You must fear the king: Creon. **ME: My father was a king**: i.e. 'I dealt with
Aeetes, so I can deal with Creon.' Here and in 169 M. meets the Nurse's warnings
about the present with references to what she has done in the past, a regular feature of
such dialogue (see 527-8; Tarrant on *Ag.* 791ff.). (Literally M. says 'My father had
been a king', for *fuerat* is a pluperfect, but here it is used indistinguishably from the
imperfect; this usage, and the more frequent use of pluperfect for perfect, was originally
colloquial, and is found in S.'s prose as well as his plays; see on 371; H-Sz 320-1;
Axelson [1933], 44-5.)

169   Not even if they be earth-born: literally 'Let them be produced from the earth (sc. I
shall still not fear them).' When Jason sowed the dragon's teeth, they grew up into
armed men (cf. 470). M. told him to throw a stone into the middle of the armed men,
and they would start killing each other. So M. means 'I coped with weapons produced
from the earth, and I can cope with any others.'

170   I long to: S.'s M. does not elsewhere express a wish to die, but she has these starkly
vacillating swings of mood; Euripides' M. expresses such wishes more frequently (*Med.*
97, 144-7, 226-7, cf. 153-4).

171   NU: Medea ... ME: ... yes, I'll become Medea: just two words in Latin, (*Medea ...
fiam*, 'Medea ... I'll-become'); the Nurse is presumably addressing M. in the vocative,
but M. interrupts and completes the sentence differently, asserting that she will renew
all her powers. The audience will hear the further meaning 'I shall become the
proverbially infamous Medea.' The words are picked up at 910 (see Introduction §5.5).
See for what father: i.e. 'Jason is the only one who will benefit from the children,
since I am going to lose them.' (*cui* is dative of advantage, and *cui sim* is an indirect
question dependent on *uide*.)

173   some obstacles: alluding, again, to the killing of Apsyrtus, which delayed Aeetes'
pursuit of the Argo (see on 452-3); for the audience this foreshadows the murders they
expect M. to commit in the play, but her own ideas are probably not so clear-cut.

175   your spirits: the plural of *animus*, 'spirit', can mean, among other things, 'passion',
'pride', or 'anger' (see *OLD* s.v. 9, 11, 12); here, after mention of her threats, the last
seems most appropriate.

176   Fortune can ... one's spirit: another *sententia* (see on 159, 163) rounds off the
dialogue between M. and the Nurse (for *sententiae* rounding off a section of a speech or
dialogue cf. Tarrant on *Ag.* p. 160). Similar sentiments are found in earlier tragedy: Eur.
fr. 1066 Nauck 'Indeed we are lacking in possessions, but nobility and excellence
remain'; Accius *trag.* 619-20 Ribbeck, 625-6 Warmington *nam si a me regnum Fortuna
atque opes / eripere quiuit, at uirtutem non quiit*, 'for if Fortune has been able to take
from me my kingdom and possessions, still she has not been able to take my courage.'
S. expresses similar ideas in his philosophical works: e.g. *Ben.* 4.10.5 *cum omnia illi
(uiro bono) deerunt, supererit animus*, 'when he (the good man) has nothing, his spirit
will survive'; *Dial.* 7.26.3; *Epist.* 36.6. But despite the superficial similarity of the
sentiments, there is a world of difference between M.'s aims and those of the Stoic sage.
(See on 520.)

177-8   But whose banging ... with Pelasgian power: the sound of the palace door opening
interrupts M.'s conversation with the Nurse, and M. announces the arrival of Creon.
References to doors creaking appear in late plays of Euripides and twice in
Aristophanes, and become a standard part of such entry-announcements in Hellenistic

drama; see Tarrant [1978], 246-7, for references and discussion, showing that S. is in some respects closer to the post-classical writers than to Euripides; Sutton (1986), 16. **banging**: *ictus* is literally a 'blow', and it is not clear exactly what it refers to here. Since Creon is coming out of the palace, it may refer to him pushing the door open noisily; on the assumption that the door opens inwards, we should perhaps imagine that the door has first to be pulled open slightly, then it can be pushed fully open. Compare the passages in new comedy where somebody coming out of the house is said to strike the door: see Gomme-Sandbach on Menander *Samia* 300-1, with addenda; Gratwick on Ter. *Ad.* 788; Beare (1964), 285-94. There is no parallel for *ictus* of pushing a door open at *TLL* 7.1.165.5-6, but *impulsus* is used similarly at Apul. *Met.* 1.11; [Quint.] *Decl.* 2.19. **door-hinge grate**: Tarrant loc. cit. shows that the phrase *cardo strepit* can be paralleled most closely in Ovid *Met.* 14.782, and references to the door-hinge occur in two of the four fragments of the Augustan tragedian Gracchus (frr. 1-2 Ribbeck). **Pelasgian**: see on 127. On the lips of M. the non-Greek, the word may be scornful.

179-300 M. and Creon: Creon's first eleven and a half lines are a monologue, not addressed to M. (see on 179-90). The first words he addresses to her (190-1) order her to leave, just as in Euripides Creon's first words are a sentence of banishment (271-6). But in S. it is not clear that Creon's words at 190-1 are the first M. has heard of her banishment (see on 144-5). In any case Creon provokes a heated debate, in three phases: first there is rapid dialogue, with speeches of no more than two lines (192-202); then M. is allowed a long speech in her defence (203-51), provoking a shorter response from Creon (252-71), which ends with a renewed command that she must leave; thirdly, in the final stretch of dialogue M. manages to persuade Creon to give her one day's reprieve (272-300). The corresponding scene in Euripides is shorter (271-356), and comparison with S.'s scene will illustrate well the distinctive features of the two writers.

179-90 From the content, especially the third person references to M., it is clear that lines 179-86a are not addressed to M., but are a monologue. Creon probably notices her on stage at 179-80 (though he could still ask this question even if he has not yet noticed her); then he describes her approaching him and gives orders to his servants, at 186b-190a, and finally addresses her at 190b. For such monologues in which a newly arrived character ignores those already on stage, compare Jason at 431-44, *Her. F.* 332-53, *Tro.* 861-71a, *Thy.* 491-507; see the discussion in Tarrant (1978), 231-41, who examines the antecedents of S.'s practice in late Euripides and comedy, particularly new comedy.

183-4 **I, to be sure ... with his entreaties**: later, at 490-1, Jason too says that he requested that the sentence of death be commuted to exile. Here, coming from Creon himself, the admission could be a sign of weakness. In Euripides Jason says that he did not want M. to be exiled (*Med.* 455-8).

186 **and depart in safety**: literally 'and depart safe', where 'safe' means both 'suffering no harm' and 'posing no threat' (see *OLD* s.v. *tutus* 1 and 6).

188 **Servants**: Creon is to be imagined coming on with attendants; on these ever-present servants in Senecan tragedy see Tarrant on *Ag.* 787, and on their antecedents in Greek tragedy, Bain (1981). Here they are told to stop M. approaching. If the play is being staged, M. will probably have to move towards Creon swiftly before the servants can react. The order thus turns out to have been futile, but this crude attempt to silence M.

shows both Creon's weakness and her power. **keep her from touching**: as she would do if she seized him by the knees in formal entreaty, as M. does in Euripides *Med.* 324; Creon perhaps fears that she will be violent, or that he will be ritually tainted by contact with her.

189 **order her to be silent**: by telling his slaves to give the order, instead of giving it himself, Creon may appear feeble. (In real life it may have been appropriate for rulers to delegate such tasks, but it is not the same in tragedy.) *iubete sileat*: here *iubeo* is not followed by the accusative and infinitive construction, but by the jussive subjunctive in parataxis (i.e. two clauses are juxtaposed without a subordinating conjunction, which in this case would have been *ut*; see on 905, 934-5); this is common in poetry and imperial prose, cf. *OLD* s.v. *iubeo* 3b; K-S 1.718; H-Sz 530.

190 **Depart speedily**: striking alliteration, *uade ueloci uia*. Cf. on 14.

191 **now at last**: *iamdudum* with imperative means 'now after all this time, now at last', see *OLD* s.v. *dudum* 3.

192-202 M. and Creon accuse each other of having acted unjustly, but Creon is persuaded to allow M. to state her case. Disputes about the nature of kingship are frequent in Senecan tragedy, and here some of the most common themes are briefly touched upon. Sometimes readers want to detect contemporary Roman resonances in such disputes, but it is hard to detect them here (though cf. on 196). The rapid dialogue characteristically contains *sententiae* at 195-6, and the speakers echo each other's words as they counter each other's arguments (194-6 'king', 'kingdoms'; 195-6 'unjust'); see on 155-76, 159, 163.

192 **For what crime ... the punishment?**: in Euripides, when M. hears the sentence of exile, she breaks into lament (277-9) before asking for an explanation (280-1), but here she asks for an explanation immediately. This may be another indication that, whereas in Euripides she is hearing the sentence for the first time, in S. she already knows it (see on 144-5); but in any case this must be her first opportunity to question Creon about it.

193 **An innocent woman ... her expulsion**: ironic, for he means that the reasons for her expulsion are staring her in the face.

195 **You should ... or unjust**: a traditional sentiment, cf. *Trag. Adesp.* 436 Nauck 'slaves, obey your masters' orders, just and unjust'; Soph. *El.* 340; Prop. 2.3.50.

196 **Unjust kingdoms never last for ever**: a similar point is made by the servant to Atreus in *Thy.* 215-7, cf. *Tro.* 258-9 (and Boyle), *Phoen.* 660, *Her. F.* 341-5, 737-45. It is also a theme of the *De Clementia* (*On Mercy*), addressed to the young emperor Nero (*Clem.* 1.11.4, 1.25.3-26.1), perhaps written later than *Med.* (see Introduction §1.3).

197 **Go then**: ironic, cf. on 650-1, 1007-8.

199-200 **makes a decision ... is not just**: the Latin verbs (*statuit, fuit*) are perfect, but are translated with present tenses, because Latin regularly uses the perfect in such generalising statements that always have been and always will be true (it is sometimes called the gnomic perfect, because it is used in *gnomai* or proverbial sayings; it corresponds to the gnomic aorist in Greek). See 151-4, 603-4.

201 **Pelias**: see on 133-4. (*Pelia* is a Latin nominative form, as in 276.)

202 **outstanding case**: 'outstanding' is ironic. S.'s tragedies regularly speak of characters having a quasi-legal case to defend: cf. 262-3, *Her. F.* 401, *Tro.* 905-6, 922-3, *Oed.* 695, 697, *Thy.* 514, 1087.

203-51 M.'s speech. At the risk of over-simplification, the argument may be analysed as
follows:

> 203-6   Introduction: I learnt about the power of anger, and about how difficult it is
>   for a king to change his mind, in the palace where I grew up.
>
> 207-19a In my early years I was a noble princess.
>
> 219b-20 Then fortune forced me into exile.
>
> 221-5a   Kings are subject to fortune: the only thing that fortune cannot take from them
>   is their ability to help and protect the weak.
>
> 225b-35 I protected the Argonauts, I alone, although you, Creon, reap the benefit;
>   except that I rescued Jason for my own sake.
>
> 236-51   Therefore condemn me, if you like, even though you have known all along
>   about my crimes; but give me back Jason, or at least allow me to live in some
>   remote part of your kingdom.

Creon's language in 201-2 invites M. to give a speech in her defence (cf. 194), as though she
is on trial, and we can see elements of the traditional forensic speech:

> (i)   203-19a can be seen as a *captatio beneuolentiae*, a bid to secure the audience's
>   sympathy, by giving a sympathetic picture of her early life, in a royal court similar
>   to Creon's.
>
> (ii)   219b-35 describes how her fortunes were reversed, but she still managed to save the
>   lives of the Argonauts—this is like a *narratio* giving her slant on the events crucial
>   to the charges against her (see *OCD*³ on '*narratio*').
>
> (iii) In 236-48 she admits the crimes she is charged with, but also says that the real
>   crime, if any, was saving the Argonauts, for her criminal deeds were simply means
>   to that end—this can be seen as the *argumentatio*, and it uses the *status generalis*, or
>   the strategy of re-labelling the actions of which she is accused (i.e. she claims her
>   actions were not a series of murders, but a glorious rescue of the cream of Greek
>   manhood); or, in the terminology of declamation, this is her *color* or 'spin' (see
>   *OCD*³ on '*color*', 'declamation').
>
> (iv)   Finally in 249-51 there is a brief peroration, in which she asks that her punishment
>   should be reduced so that she can be allowed to remain in a remote part of Creon's
>   kingdom.

The content, however, is as important as the structure. There is a striking contrast between
M.'s description of her early years (recalling the M. we meet in Apollonius of Rhodes) and
her behaviour and reputation in the rest of the play. But she hastens over the details of the
crimes she committed in order to rescue the Argonauts, and, most important, says nothing to
answer Creon's fears about what she might do next. But her emphasis on a king's duty to
protect the weak, and on her protection of the Argonauts, puts moral pressure on Creon to
grant her protection now.

203-6 How hard ... my own palace: her speech opens with a sentence that is four lines
long, and has a close-knit grammatical structure that is not complete until the last few
words (though the translation masks this—see below): such sentence structure is not
frequent in Senecan tragedy, and it clearly marks this as the beginning of a long
oratorical speech. By keeping us waiting for the main verb *didici*, 'I learned', which is
almost at the end, the sentence also throws emphasis on 'in my own palace', which
leads into the next section of the speech, about M.'s early years.

208-9 driven out ... from every side: asyndeton, see on 20-1.

209-19 M. describes her early life, stressing her noble birth and her father's power and wealth. In Ovid *Heroides* 12 M. describes her position when Jason arrived in Colchis as just like Creusa's now: *iussus inexpertam Colchos aduertere puppim, / intrasti patriae regna beata meae. / hoc illic Medea fui, noua nupta quod hic est: / quam pater est illi, tam mihi diues erat. / hic Ephyren bimarem, Scythia tenus ille niuosa / omne tenet, Ponti qua plaga laeua iacet*, 'Commanded to steer the untried ship to the Colchians, you [i.e. Jason] entered the prosperous kingdom of my fatherland. There I, Medea, was what your new bride is here: I had a father as wealthy as hers is. He has Ephyra [= Corinth] with two seas, mine had everything, where the left-hand coast of the Pontus lies, as far as snowy Scythia' (12.23-8). S.'s M. refers to the Pontus and Scythia in 212.

209 **I radiated glory**: one word in Latin, *fulsi*, literally 'I shone' (repeated at 218); the application of this verb to a person is uncommon and striking, and particularly apt for M., a descendant of the Sun (see on 28-9).

211 **Phasis**: see on 43 and 762, and compare the language of 44.

212 **Scythian Pontus**: on Pontus see on 44. Scythia was a vague term used by the Greek and Romans for their neighbours east of the Danube, and north and east of the Black Sea; Scythia and the Scythians were associated with cold climate and barbaric way of life. (See *OCD*³ on 'Scythia'.) At 483 and 528 M. regards the Colchians as Scythian.

213 **the seas grow fresh**: ancient authors commented on the freshness of the water of the Black Sea, particularly near the mouth of the Danube; cf. *RE* Suppl. 9.930-2.

214-5 **by that regiment ... the Thermodon**: the Amazons, the mythical race of female warriors with no husbands, were archetypal barbarians; here Colchis seems civilised, by contrast with them. Their kingdom was said to have been at various points on the edge of the known world. S. here follows the commonest version, that they lived on the river Thermodon, a river in the Roman province of Pontus, part of modern Turkey, that flows into the south shore of the Black Sea; thus they were the western neighbours of the Colchians. The association with the Thermodon goes back to the fifth cent. B.C. (Aesch. (?) *Prom.* 723-5; Pherecydes *FGH*3F15), and was familiar to the Romans (Verg. *A.* 11.659; Prop. 3.14.13-4; Ovid *Pont.* 4.10.51; S. *Her. F.* 246), and in poets 'Thermodontic' was a synonym for 'Amazonian' (Ovid *Met.* 12.611). See *OCD*³ on 'Amazons'. **with crescent shields**: for the distinctive crescent shields of the Amazons cf. e.g. Verg. *A.* 1.490; Tarrant on *Ag.* 217-8; there are illustrations at *LIMC* 1.2, 471 no. 242, 503 nos. 551-2.

218 **I radiated glory**: the repetition of the striking word used in 209 frames this section.

218-9 **at that time ... looking for suitors**: for the contrast between active and passive forms of the same verb (*petebant, petuntur*), see on 28-9. Here the point is elliptically expressed: then men came seeking marriage with M., but now that she has been abandoned by Jason, she must go seeking men if she is to find someone to protect and marry her. In this play M. nowhere else speaks of remarriage, so some think that, despite the plural, she is really speaking of Jason: he wanted her to marry him then, now it is *she* who wants *him*, but she cannot bring herself to speak his name to Creon (cf. 233, 240, 273, 276, 279, 415). However, there were versions of the myth where she subsequently married Aegeus in Athens (Gantz [1993], 255-6), or eventually married Achilles in Elysium (Ap. Rh. 4.814-5 and Scholia, quoting Ibycus 291 and Simonides 558), so there is no need to restrict the reference to Jason. In the past, also, she could have had other suitors besides Jason: a fragmentary papyrus may refer to an earlier version in which the Argonauts came as, or posed as, suitors for M.'s hand, and the yoking of the fire-breathing bulls was a suitors' trial (see Rusten [1982], 62-3; *Suppl. Hell.* 339A.23-5).

219-20 Fortune—quick, ... sent me into exile: she treats the arrival of the Argonauts and all its consequences as the work of Fortune; for Fortune elsewhere in the play see on 520. By attributing her own downfall to Fortune, M. here makes her precarious life an example of the precariousness of all royal power, including Creon's (221-2, cf. 286-7). Fortune, Greek Tyche, was widely worshipped as a goddess (see *OCD³* on 'Fortuna/Fors', 'Tyche'). As Costa suggests, M.'s mention of her speed may suggest the common portrayal of her as winged; cf. e.g. Hor. *Carm.* 3.29.53-4; *LIMC* 8.1, 115-41, 8.2, 85-109. Earlier accounts regularly stressed the intervention of Aphrodite (Venus) or Eros (Cupid) to make M. and Jason fall in love (Pi. *Pyth.* 4.213-9; Eur. *Med.* 526-31, 627-62; Ap. Rh. 3 passim, especially 275-98), but in S.'s play neither deity is ever mentioned by name (see on 1, 62-5), and any mention of their power over her would have detracted from her superiority to the gods (see on 166-7). Admittedly other characters, or the poet, are more likely to talk of the action of Venus or Cupid than M. herself is; thus Ovid's M. does not talk of the action of the deities in *Epist.* 12; in *Met.* 7.55, however, she says *maximus intra me deus est*, 'there is a very powerful god [sc. Cupid] within me.'

221 So put your trust in kingdoms: ironic, implying 'So it's foolish to trust ...'.

224-5 helping the wretched ... faithful home: cf. Ovid *Pont.* 2.9.11 *regia, crede mihi, res est succurrere lapsis*, 'believe me, it is a king-like thing to help the fallen.'

226 the great glory ... celebrated flower: 'flower' is a standard metaphor in Latin, meaning the best or the pick of a group of people. The metaphor is more common in prose than poetry; cf. e.g. Cic. *Phil.* 11.39 *tirones milites, flos Italiae*, 'new recruits, the flower of Italy'; *OLD* s.v. *flos* 10.

227 the bulwark of the Achaean race: not because the Argonauts were defending Greece against any threat (at least not until the Colchians pursued them to recover M.), but because all the leading fighting men of Greece were on the Argo. In Apollonius (4.202-5), after Jason has got the golden fleece, and as the Argonauts prepare to escape from the Colchians, taking M. with them, Jason says to them: 'Now we have in our hands the fate of our children, our dear country, and our aged parents; upon our success rests whether Hellas will reap despair or great glory' (trans. Hunter); so here in S., M. claims that the safety of all Greece ultimately depended on herself. **and the offspring of the gods**: a number of the Argonauts were descended from the gods, though by no means all: Hercules, Castor and Pollux were sons of Zeus (see on 88-9), Orpheus was usually said to be son of the Muse Calliope, Echion and Eurytus were sons of Hermes, Calais and Zetes were sons of Boreas; for others sometimes given divine parentage see Gantz (1993), 343-4. (*deum* is genitive plural.)

228-9 I saved them: in earlier versions too M. recalls how she saved the lives of Jason or the Argonauts; see Eur. *Med.* 476-85, 515; Ovid *Epist.* 12.173, 203, *Met.* 7.55-61; cf. Ovid *Medea* fr. 1 Ribbeck *seruare potui: perdere an possim, rogas?*, 'I was able to save: do you ask whether I am able to destroy?' (see Heinze [1997], 245-7). **Orpheus ... his singing**: on Orpheus see 355-60, 625-33. He is found among the Argonauts from Pindar onwards (*Pyth.* 4.176-7). His singing's power over nature was traditional since at least the time of Simonides (fr. 567); see *OCD*³ on 'Orpheus'; S. *Her. F.* 572-4 and Fitch.

228, 230 gift ... gift: repetition (cf. on 117). Compare the anaphora in Ovid *Epist.* 12.203, when M. writes to Jason *dos mea tu sospes, dos est mea Graia iuuentus*, 'Your safe return is my dowry, the young men of Greece are my dowry' (see on 489).

230 Castor and Pollux: see on 88-9. They are regularly Argonauts from Pindar onwards (*Pyth.* 4.172).

231 the sons of Boreas: Zetes and Calais, sons of the north wind, Boreas, and included among the Argonauts from Pindar onwards (*Pyth.* 4.181-3). Like their father they had wings, and their most prominent part in the Argonaut story was when they pursued the winged Harpies (Ap. Rh. 2.240-300). See 634; *OCD*³ on 'Calais'.

231-2 and he who sees ... Lynceus: an identifying description is followed by the name of Lynceus. He was son of Aphareus, and renowned for his keen sight, which could even penetrate underground; cf. Pi. *N.* 10.62-3; Ap. Rh. 1.151-5, 4.1466-84; *LIMC* 6.1, 319-22, 6.2, 165-6.

233 the Minyans: a Greek people of the heroic age, descendants of Minyas; here, as often, applied to the Argonauts generally; cf. Pi. *Pyth.* 4.69; Ap. Rh. 1.229-33 (who makes Minyas great-grandfather of Jason); *OCD*³ on 'Minyans', 'Minyas'. **chief of chiefs** cf. Tarrant on *Ag.* 39 *rex ille regum, ductor Agamemnon ducum*, 'that king of kings, chief of chiefs, Agamemnon'; H-Sz 55; Wills (1996), 193. This is an example of polyptoton, repetition of the same word in different cases; cf. 474, 511, 563-4, Canter (1925), 161; cf. on 28-9 for repetition of different verb forms.

235 for *you*: plural, i.e. for Creon and the Greeks. **for *myself*:** another reminder of her love for Jason.

236-48 M. anticipates charges that can be brought against her and answers them; this is the rhetorical figure of thought called *prolepsis* by the Greeks and by Quint. *Inst.* 4.1.49-50, and *anteoccupatio* by Cic. *de Orat.* 3.205; later there were various other labels for it, including *anticipatio* and *occupatio*. Cf. *Her. F.* 401-8.

237 Yet the charge ... in this: the implied thought is that all her immoral deeds were done solely as a means to the end of rescuing the Argonauts, so this is what she should really be accused of.

238-9 Note the alliteration (see on 14) and anaphora (see on 117): *uirgini placeat pudor / paterque placeat.*

240 Pelasgian: see on 127.

241 of the vicious bull: S. uses the singular 'bull' here, and at 466, 829. It could be poetic singular for plural, since traditionally Jason had to plough with two bulls (e.g. Ap. Rh. 3.409-10; Apollod. 1.9.23).

242-3 Fortune: see on 219-20, 520. **as much as she likes:** *quam uolet*. Zwierlein (1976), 192-4, and in the Oxford text, deletes these two lines. Delz (1989), 507, defends the lines, proposing *quaelibet* instead of the manuscripts' *quae uolet*. Watt (1996), 249-50, proposes instead *quam uolet*, equivalent to *quamuis*, with *uis* altered to suit the subject. This is palaeographically easier, and is accepted here, though such variations on *quamuis* are not common outside Cicero, and not found elsewhere in S. See K-S 2.443; H-Sz 603; Pease on Cic. *N.D.* 2.46; for such expressions after Cicero, see Col. 2.10.28 *quam uoles teneram (sc. Medicam) ... deseces licet*; Plin. *Epist.* 1.20.25 *quam uoles* *breui epistula*; for the expression with a verb rather than adjective, cf. Ter. *Hec.* 634 *turbent porro quam uelint*.

246 **but give me back my crime**: i.e. 'give me back what I am accused of, i.e. Jason (whom I rescued thanks to my alleged crimes)', a case of abstract for concrete (see Introduction §5.6).

247 **I grasped your knees**: in Greece suppliants (see the next line) traditionally knelt or prostrated themselves and touched the knees, or the chin or beard, of the person they were supplicating; cf. Eur. *Med.* 324 (M. to Creon) 'Do not, I beg you by your knees and by your newly-married daughter', 709-10 (M. to Aegeus) 'But I beg you by this beard and by your knees and I make myself a suppliant'; see 282, 482; Fantham, and Boyle, on S. *Tro.* 691f.; J. Gould, *JHS* 93 (1973), 74-103.

248 **sought**: *peti*, contracted form of the perfect *petii*. Cf. on 984, 994.

249-51 Similarly in Eur. *Med.* 313-4 M. asks Creon to let her stay somewhere in the kingdom: 'But let me live in this land.' The words of S.'s M. are more emotive at this point, but Euripides' M. goes on immediately to kneel and supplicate Creon (324-6), which in S. she does not do until 282.

252-71 Creon's speech rejects M.'s accusations of arrogance (252-3). She has stressed that a king should protect the exile and the needy (222-5): Creon responds that he is doing just that in protecting Jason—who is an exile, and is being pursued by Acastus (252-61). However, it will be much easier to protect Jason if M. is out of the way, for she alone is to blame for the death of Acastus' father, Pelias (262-5). Creon is also afraid of what M. may do with her magical powers, and so orders her to leave (266-71). He ignores most of M.'s speech, not surprisingly, for she dwelt on the past, ignoring the present situation and the threat she is perceived to pose.

252-3 **sceptre ... arrogantly**: Creon echoes M.'s opening sentence (205). Creon defends his behaviour in similar terms in Euripides (348-9).

256-7 **for Acastus ... punishment and death**: this is the first reference to Acastus in the play; the motif of fear of Acastus recurs at 415, 521, 526. There is no mention of Acastus in Euripides' *Medea*, and no suggestion of Jason being influenced by fear of him. He was son of Pelias (the father of line 258). When, through M.'s deceit, Acastus' sisters caused the death of their father, Acastus sought revenge on her and Jason, in the version followed by S. (see on 133-4; Apollod. 1.9.27). But there were other versions: sometimes Jason seemingly remained on good terms with Acastus after the death of Pelias (Hes. *Th.* 992-1002; Paus. 5.17.10), or handed the kingdom over to him voluntarily before leaving for Corinth (D. S. 4.53.1-2; Hyg. *Fab.* 24). Sometimes Acastus had sailed with the Argonauts, against his father's wishes (first in Ap. Rh. 1.224-7, 321-8, etc.; Hyg. *Fab.* 24). See Gantz [1993], 194, 344, 365-8.

261 **the loving sisters ... an unloving sin**: 'loving' and 'unloving' here translate *pius* and *impius*. No single English word adequately translates every use of *pius* and its noun *pietas*, which is the central other-regarding virtue of the Romans: towards the gods *pietas* can be translated 'piety', but towards members of one's family *pietas* is nearer to 'devotion, loyal affection'. In the present translation, different English equivalents are used as appropriate in each context, but it is important to be able to trace the theme through the play: cf. 10, 134, 395, 438 (*pietas* translated 'parental love'), 545, 645, 779, 905, 943-4. For the words in the context of Pelias' daughters cf. Ovid *Epist.* 12.129

quid referam Peliae natas pietate nocentes, 'Why should I mention the daughters of Pelias doing harm through *pietas*'; in *Metamorphoses* 7 M. urges the daughters to kill Pelias 'if you have any *pietas*' (*si pietas ulla est*), and when she finishes speaking, *his, ut quaeque pia est, hortatibus inpia prima est / et, ne sit scelerata, facit scelus*, 'At these urgings, as each (daughter) is *pia*, she is first to be *impia*, and, so that she may not be wicked, she commits wickedness' (7.336, 339-40); S. uses the paradoxical antithesis more sparingly than Ovid on this occasion. For such antitheses in general cf. 163 'hope ... despair', 472-3 'sleepless ... sleep', 503 'guiltless ... guilty'; Canter (1925), 162.

262-3 Jason can mount ... from his: i.e. if you go elsewhere, then Jason, left to defend his own case on his own, can establish his innocence; but if you stay here and his case is heard along with yours, he is likely to be found guilty with you (see on 202). In S.'s play M. never argues that Pelias deserved to die because he had wronged Jason, although Creon calls his death a punishment at 201 (see on 133-4).

265 your company: the Latin, like the English, can mean either 'association with you' or 'your circle of associates'. In either case, 'your' is plural, which is puzzling. The simplest explanation is that Creon is thinking of M. and the daughters of Pelias; or perhaps he means M. and her Nurse, who is presumably still on stage (there is nothing to suggest she leaves after 178); or, more vaguely, he means M. and everybody she consorts with. Alternatively, this could be another of the rare cases where one might argue that *uester* is used like *tuus*, to mean 'your (singular)'; see Housman [1972], 790-4, who defends the usage; Fordyce on Catul. 39.20 is more cautious; there may be another case at *Her. O.* 1513, but see Watt (1989), 344. (*noster* and *nos*, by contrast with *uester* and *uos*, are frequently used with singular meaning, cf. on 116.)

266 You, you: see on 13. **mastermind of evil crimes**: the feminine form *machinatrix*, 'deviser, mastermind', is found only here; the masculine *machinator* is regularly used of devising evil, from Cicero onwards, including S. *Tro.* 750 (see Fantham). S. likes such coinages, in prose as well as verse, but they are characteristic of the age as much as of S.; for his neologisms in prose see Bourgery (1922), 249-91; Summers (1910), xlvi-xlix.

267-8 a woman's wickedness ... a man's strength: see on 42.

269-70 be off ... from fear: there is an echo of Cicero's appeal to Catiline to leave Rome (in 63 B.C.): *Catil.* 1.10 *Quae cum ita sint, Catilina, perge quo coepisti: egredere aliquando ex urbe; patent portae; proficiscere... Educ tecum etiam omnis tuos, si minus, quam plurimos; purga urbem. Magno me metu liberaueris, modo inter me atque te murus intersit*, 'Since this is so, Catiline, carry on the way you have begun: be off at last from the city; the gates are open; get started. Take all your men away with you, too, or at least as many as possible; cleanse the city. You will release me from great fear, so long as there is a wall between me and you.' The echo suggests that M. is a threat to the whole city, just like Catiline; both threats must be driven out from the city. **your lethal herbs**: the first explicit reference by another character to M.'s magical powers. **release the citizens from fear**: in contrast to Euripides' Creon, who openly admits to M. his fear of her (282-3, 316-7), S.'s Creon never expresses his own fear to her face. Before directly addressing her, he described his apprehensions about what she might do (181-6), but there (185 'let her free the territory from fear') and here he admits only to a general fear in the population.

271 settle in ... harass the gods: but the audience know that she has already harassed the gods in Corinth, in the opening scene (see on 12). For M.'s power over the gods see on 166-7.

272-80 M.'s response challenges Creon's claim that Jason is completely free of guilt for the crimes that she has committed for his sake.

272-3 give me back ... give me back: anaphora, see on 117. **my companion**: Jason; she denies Creon's claim that Jason was not closely involved with her (a denial reinforced by her word *comes*, 'companion', which echoes, and is etymologically related to, the word *coetus*, 'company', that Creon used in 265; see *OLD* on the two words).

276-8 A dense series of allusions to the murder of Pelias, her flight from Colchis, the stealing of the golden fleece, the desertion of Aeetes, and the killing of Apsyrtus. *Pelia*: see on 201.

278-9 whatever else ... his new wives: M. refers primarily to the other crimes Jason got her to commit, but the plural 'wives', and 'still', sarcastically insinuate that he is likely to get Creusa to commit crimes too, and will do the same with any future wives (cf. the plurals 'girls' and 'mothers' at 1007-8).

280 I have behaved ... own sake: cf. Ovid *Epist.* 12.132 *pro quo sum totiens esse coacta nocens*, '(you) on whose behalf I have so often been forced to be guilty'; 503 below.

282 As a suppliant: this indicates that she entreats him formally (see on 247 and 249-51), a very solemn form of request.

283 the innocent children: the children were first mentioned explicitly at 144-5 (see also on 23-6, 37-40 and 66 for allusions to them). In Euripides they are more prominent early on in the play: they appear on stage, as mute characters, with their tutor (*paedagogus*) at 49-105; in contrast to S.'s play, the children in Euripides have been banished along with M. (70-1, 273), but she from the start has rejected them (36, 92-3, 112-3); the Nurse is afraid that M. may do them harm (117-8), while M. herself later expresses fears that her enemies will harm them if she does not kill them herself (1059-61). At this point in S.'s play it is unclear exactly what M. fears for the children, and what she is asking of Creon. Is she asking that they should not be taken away from her? or that they should not suffer death or some other punishment at Creon's hand? Probably the latter, for that is the more natural meaning of her request that they should not be dragged down, and when Creon assures her that he will look after them and they will come to no harm (284), she ostensibly accepts this assurance (285-90). This acquiescence may be part of her strategy to win a short delay, ostensibly in order that she can say goodbye to the children properly. Later on, however, at 541-3, she asks Jason to let her take the children with her into exile.

285-99 In Euripides (*Med.* 340-56) M. asks for a day's delay before she goes into exile, and Creon grants it, against his better judgement. M. soon sets out her plans to kill Creon, his daughter, and Jason (364-85); in the end she does not kill Jason, and at this point she says nothing about killing her children (see the Introduction §3.2(c) on the question whether her murder of the children was an innovation by Euripides, or was first found in Neophron). In S. Creon initially rejects her request, but finally gives in. S.'s audience will certainly be expecting M. to kill the bride and Creon and murder her children, which makes Creon's resistance seem the more natural, and his eventual weakness the more apparent. (See on 189 for earlier signs of his weakness.)

285-8 I pray by ... grant me: *per ego auspicatos ... precor*: in such entreaties in poetry it is common for the unemphatic pronoun *ego* to come second word, even though it separates *per* from its noun; cf. Gratwick on Plaut. *Men.* 990 and 34; Austin on Verg. *A.* 4.314. Such expression probably had an archaic feel (Jocelyn on Ennius *trag.* 3). There are similar entreaties with 'by', *per*, though without *ego*, below at 478-82, 1002-4. **attended by good omens**: literally 'preceded by favourable auspices', referring to the traditional wedding auspices (see on 68). **Fortune**: see on 520.

293 even a brief time: *temporis* is partitive genitive with *parum*, literally 'a very little amount of time.' *parum* can mean 'very little' as well as 'too little', and the latter seems less natural here, especially when M. in 296-7 says that a day is longer than she needs (on *parum* see *TLL* 10.1.571.53-61, 575.68-83).

296-7 That is too long ... in a hurry: Euripides' M. says nothing like this, and it seems out of keeping with any genuine concern to bid her children a proper farewell. On the other hand, whereas Euripides' M. asks for one day (340), S.'s has asked less specifically for a short delay (288), and it is Creon who grants her a day (295). In any case, for the audience, the surprising perversity of the sentiment gives the sort of clever twist to the dialogue that S. loves, and the words contain an implicit threat that M. is in a hurry to get revenge.

297 You will suffer punishment: Creon's threat of punishment is found also in Euripides, *Med.* 352-4 (see Jocelyn on Enn. *trag.* p. 349 for caution about attributing to Ennius' *Medea* the lines generally so attributed, e.g. in 224-5 Ribbeck and 272-3 Warmington). The expression is similar to that used when Opis addresses the dying female warrior Camilla in Verg. *A.* 11.841-2: *heu nimium, uirgo, nimium crudele luisti / supplicium*, 'Alas, virgin, you have suffered too cruel, too cruel a punishment ...' (cf. also *Her. F.* 511).

299-300 The wedding rituals ... to pray: Creon's thoughts return to the wedding, and he implies that the ceremony is not over (for S.'s vagueness about the exact course of events see introductory comm. to 56-115). **Hymenaeus**: see on 67-70.

Creon clearly exits at this point, and presumably M. and the Nurse do too, for at the start of the next Act (380) they emerge from the house.

SECOND CHORAL ODE: 301-379

While Creon returns to the wedding ceremonies, which were the concern of the first Choral Ode, the second Ode takes a quite different direction, reflecting on the voyage of the Argo: before people sailed on the seas there was an age of innocence; the voyage of the Argonauts was a bold enterprise that incurred punishment, in the form of a series of dangers, the worst of which was M. The structure may be analysed as follows:

301-8	The first sailor was too audacious.
309-17	Before him, nobody recognised the stars or the winds.
318-28	Tiphys learnt the techniques of sailing.
329-34	Before that men lived innocent lives.
335-9	The Argo violated solemn boundaries.
340-60	The Argo suffered terrible dangers.
361-3	For what reward? For the golden fleece, and M.
364-79	Since then, all the world's boundaries have been broken down.

The ode begins by talking generally about the person who first sailed over the seas in a ship. The audience may assume that this refers to Jason or Tiphys, but at this point in the ode it could be an anonymous first sailor (see on 301-2; cf. on 2-3). For such an unknown first sailor, compare e.g. Hor. *Carm.* 1.3 (and Nisbet and Hubbard on line 12); Prop. 1.17.13-18; Ovid *Am.* 2.11.1-6; Pease on Cic. *N.D.* 2.89. Only later in the ode, at 318, is Tiphys introduced as the person who wrote 'new laws' for the sea; the Argo is mentioned in 335-6, and later called the first ship at 363. So it becomes clear, by that stage of the ode, that S. follows a tradition that the Argo was the first ship to sail the seas. This tradition was not unanimous: Minos, Danaus and others were rivals for the distinction of having invented sailing (see Phaedr. 4.7.17-20; Plin. *Nat.* 7.206-7; *RE* 2.722-3; Pease loc. cit.). But the Argo is often, without qualification, the first ship (e.g. Catul. 64.11; Ovid *Am.* 1.15.21; Pease loc. cit.). In Apollonius there are already sea-going ships, but the Argo is far superior to them because of the part that Athena played in its construction (cf. Ap. Rh. 1.111-4, 2.1187-91, 3.340-6; however, the people living at the mouth of the Ister had never seen a ship before, 4.316-22).

In antiquity the voyage of the Argo was evaluated in different ways, both positively and negatively. It was seen as an example and a symbol of the growth of civilisation, because the Argonauts overcame a series of barbarian opponents on their voyage (so Ap. Rh., see Hunter [1993], 162-9). But sea-faring was often viewed in a negative light, a view found in S.'s prose works (*Nat.* 5.18; cf. Hesiod *Op.* 236-7; Nisbet and Hubbard on Hor. *Carm.* 1.3, pp. 43-4), and was associated with the end of the Golden Age (e.g. Arat. *Phaen.* 110-1; see Smith on Tib. 1.3.37-40). Adopting the second perspective, S.'s Chorus sees in the Argo a symbol of the decline of civilisation and the disruption of the cosmic order, a view found earlier, and more briefly, in Vergil and Horace: Verg. *Ecl.* 4.34-5 *alter erit tum Tiphys et altera quae uehat Argo / delectos heroas*, 'then (at the end of the new golden age) there will be a second Tiphys, and a second Argo to carry select heroes'; Hor. *Epod* 16.57-8 (talking of the Isles of the Blessed) *non huc Argoo contendit remige pinus, / neque impudica Colchis intulit pedem*, 'the pinewood with the Argo's oarsmen did not voyage here, nor did the immoral Colchian woman set foot here.' However, the end of S.'s ode is more ambivalent, talking of the opening of the earth to navigation in what can be interpreted as a more positive tone, and in terms that apply to the Roman empire better than to the world of mythology (see on 364-79).

Furthermore, the Chorus, by suggesting that M. is a consequence of, or punishment for, the sailing of the Argo, puts her in a broader context, as not just an individual bent on vengeance and evil-doing, but also the instrument of a wider purpose. This perspective is developed in the next chorus.

[On this ode see further Lawall (1979), 421-3; Davis (1993), 78-84; Romm (1992), 165-71; Biondi (1984), 87-141, gives a full commentary.]

301-2 Too audacious ... fragile a boat: the opening of the ode has various echoes of Hor. *Carm.* 1.3, which is addressed to a ship on which Vergil is sailing, and prays that he may have a safe voyage. At lines 9-16 Horace describes the boldness of the first sailor (phrases echoed by S. are highlighted): *illi robur et aes triplex / circa pectus erat, qui fragilem truci / commisit pelago ratem / primus*, 'he had oak and three-layered bronze round his breast, the man who entrusted a *fragile boat* to the fierce sea *first*'; and at 25-40 Horace protests more generally about the audaciousness of humankind. The first word of S.'s ode, 'audacious', *audax*, introduces the last section of Horace's ode (25, repeated at 27). Ovid's M. describes the Argonauts as audacious (*Epist.* 12.14).

303 behind his back: *posterga* is an abbreviated form of *post terga* that is found occasionally in the manuscripts of Senecan tragedy (see Zwierlein's Oxford text p. 462 for details).

306 to trust in thin timber: the thinness of boats' hulls was a traditional theme; cf. Arat. *Phaen.* 299 'a small plank keeps death away' and Kidd's comm.; Diog. Laert. 1.103; S. *Epist.* 49.11 *erras si in nauigatione tantum existimas minimum esse quo <a> morte uita diducitur: in omni loco aeque tenue interuallum est*, 'You're wrong if you think it's only in sea-faring that a minimal distance separates life from death: the gap is just as narrow everywhere'; Mayor, and Courtney, on Iuu. 12.57-9.

309-17 Nobody yet knew ... have a name: S. seizes the opportunity for a learned, allusive lists of stars and constellations, all associated with bad weather. For knowledge of the stars going back to the first sailor see Verg. *G.* 1.137-8 *nauita tum stellis numeros et nomina fecit / Pleiadas, Hyadas, claramque Lycaonis Arcton*, 'a sailor then counted and named the stars, Pleiades, Hyades, and Lycaon's bright bear'; there were various accounts of how human beings, who at first were ignorant of the stars, began to distinguish and name them, see Mynors ad loc. S. adds that the winds, too, did not yet have names. **Nobody yet ... not yet ...:** fourfold anaphora of *nondum* (see on 117).

310 stars ... painted: for the metaphor cf. Manil. 1.445; Tarrant on S. *Thy.* 834.

312 the rainy Hyades: a cluster of five stars in the constellation Taurus (cf. 769); their morning risings and settings were associated with rain. In Greek the name *Huades* is connecting with *huein*, 'to rain', so 'rainy Hyades' is a bilingual pun, already found in Verg. *A.* 1.744. On myths about the Hyades see Gantz (1993), 218; *LIMC* 5.1, 543-6, 5.2, 375-6.

313 rays of the Olenian she-goat: Capella, the brightest star in the constellation Auriga; *capra*, the word S. uses here, and *capella*, both mean 'she-goat'. The star was linked to stormy weather, see Hor. *Carm.* 3.7.6; Ovid *Met.* 3.594; Bömer on Ovid *Fast.* 5.113; Kidd on Arat. *Phaen.* 157. S. describes Capella by a piece of mythological learning. The infant Zeus was fed on goat's milk: according to some versions the goat was called Amalthea, according to others Amalthea was a nymph to whom the goat belonged; in both versions Amalthea became the star Capella (see Gantz [1993], 41-2; *LIMC* 1.1, 582-4, 1.2, 437-8). The adjective 'Olenian' was explained in various ways: either Amalthea was daughter of Olenus, son of Hephaestus; or she came from the town of Olenus or Olene; or the star was on the arm (Greek *ôlenê*) of the constellation Auriga (see Kidd on Arat. *Phaen.* 164, who first applies the adjective to Capella; Bömer on Ovid *Fast.* 5.113). For *lumina* (plural) of the rays of a single heavenly body see *OLD* s.v. *lumen* 1.

314-5 nor the Attic ... follows and steers: the constellation Bootes, meaning 'Ploughman' (often also called Arctophylax, meaning 'bear-guard'), was supposed to steer the Wagon (also called the Plough, Big Dipper, or Great Bear; see Pease on Cic. *N.D.* 2.109). He was traditionally described as slow-moving because of the time the constellation takes to set below the horizon (Hom. *Od.* 5.272 ὀψὲ δύοντα Βοώτην, 'slow setting Bootes'; Catul. 66.67-8; Ovid *Met.* 2.176-7). The wagon is Attic because Bootes was sometimes identified with the Athenian Icarius, father of Erigone, a genealogy that appeared in Eratosthenes' *Erigone* (see Mayer [1990], 401-2). The rising and setting of Arcturus, the brightest star in the constellation, was associated with bad weather in poetry from Aratus onwards (see Kidd on Arat. *Phaen.* 745, and e.g. Plaut. *Rud.* 70-1; Ovid *Epist.* 18.187-8).

316   Boreas ... Zephyrus: the north and west winds.

318   Tiphys: see on 2-3.

320   write new laws for the winds: there is something sacrilegious about men writing laws for the forces of nature (cf. 365). It resembles the Giants at *Aetna* 45 who try to attack the gods and *uicto leges imponere caelo*, 'to impose laws on a defeated heaven', or the old woman at Prop. 4.5.13 who is bold enough to *cantatae leges imponere lunae*, 'to impose laws on the bewitched moon.' M. too breaks the existing laws of the cosmos, see on 757. The attitude of S.'s Chorus to sailing here may be compared with other Choruses that use the metaphor of sailing to recommend a cautious and quiet life (see *Oed.* 882-91, *Ag.* 90-107 and Tarrant, *Her. O.* 694-9).

321-8   sometimes to stretch ... topsails flutter: a brief description of how the sails were adjusted to cope with different winds. Ancient sailing ships had a single mast and a rectangular sail, attached along its top edge to the yard (*antemna*), a horizontal pole that was attached at its centre to the mast (*malus*). To each of the two bottom corners of the sail was attached a rope called the sheet (*pes*), whose other end was attached to the side of the ship's hull. By attaching the sheets at different points along the side of the hull, the sail could be swivelled round to catch the wind; and the yard could be raised or lowered to unfurl more or less of the sail. S. describes several different configurations of the rigging: the full sail billowing (321, presumably with the sheets square?); one sheet moved forward to catch a side-wind (322-3); the yard lowered to mid-mast for safety in strong winds (323-4); and, for maximum speed, the full sail assisted by an additional top-sail (*siparum*), a triangular sail fastened to the top of the mast and to the two ends of the yard (325-8). (See Casson [1971], 229-45, and figs. 143-4, 149, 171; S. shows his knowledge of the technicalities of sailing ships at *Epist.* 77.1-2.) **sometimes ... sometimes ...**: fourfold anaphora of *nunc* (see on 117).

321   to stretch the flax: it is disputed whether *linum* here means flaxen ropes, or linen sails (linen is made from flax). *OLD* s.v. *linum* 3 and *TLL* 7.2.1471.22-3 say 'sails', but Bömer on Ovid *Met.* 14.554 is probably right to argue for 'ropes'; this is certainly the sense at Ovid *Fast.* 3.587 *parant torto subducere carbasa lino*, 'they prepare to lower the sails with twisted flax (sc. ropes)', and *Met.* 14.554, where, as ships are metamorphosed into nymphs, the 'linen' becomes their hair. See Casson (1971), 231 and n. 27.

322-3   the slanting south-winds: ancient poets often choose a specific wind, pretty much at random, instead of using a generic word for 'wind'.

326   over-greedy: this phrase (*auidus nimium*) echoes 'too audacious' (*audax nimium*) at the start of the ode (301), continuing the theme of excess; and, although the sailor's greed here is for full winds, it anticipates the theme of financial greed hinted at in 333-4 and 361-3. *auidus* and *audax* are etymologically related, as the ancients knew (Paul. Fest. p. 20 M).

329-30   that brilliant age ... far distant: the Golden Age, the imagined early stage of human history that was free from the need to work and from wrongdoing; it was first described in Hesiod.*Op.* 109-26 (see West's comm.; Greek authors talk of a golden *race*, the term golden *age* being introduced by the Romans); other famous descriptions include Plato *Polit.* 271d-272b; Arat. *Phaen.* 100-14; Verg. *Ecl.* 4, *G.* 1.125-8, 2.532-40; Ovid *Met.* 1.89-112. (See *OCD*[3] on 'golden age'; Blundell [1986], 135-64.) For S. the golden age had been a historical reality, even if not in exactly the form described in myth, cf. *Epist.* 90.36-46. In the tragedies cf. *Phaed.* 525-39. **brilliant age**: S. avoids the hackneyed term 'golden' (see *Aetna* 9-16 on how hackneyed the topic had become). *candidus*, here translated 'brilliant', can also mean 'prosperous, happy'.

331 **lazily kept to his own shores**: i.e. people were content, but did not make undue effort, to travel by land down to their own shores, but they never crossed the seas to other shores. Cf. *Phaed.* 530-1 *nondum secabant credulae pontum rates: / sua quisque norat maria*, 'trusting ships did not yet cut through the sea; each man knew just his own seas'; Ovid *Met.* 1.96 *nullaque mortales praeter sua litora norant*, 'and mortals knew no shores except their own', *Am.* 3.8.43-4.

333 **he owned little, yet was wealthy**: literally 'wealthy on little', just two words in Latin: the happiness of the unambitious who stay at home was a traditional idea (Eur. fr. 793.1 Nauck 'blessed is the man who stays at home, enjoying good fortune'; Hor. *Epod.* 2.1-3 *beatus ille qui procul negotiis, / ut prisca gens mortalium, / paterna rura bubus exercet suis*, 'happy is he who, far from troubles, like the ancient race of mortals, farms his ancestral land with his own oxen'). It was a philosophical commonplace that true wealth lay in being content with whatever one had, that one needed very little to achieve contentment, and that immense riches would not satisfy if one still wanted more. For the phrase 'wealthy on little', cf. the phrase 'content with little', e.g. S. *Epist.* 110.18 *ad ueras potius te conuerte diuitias; disce paruo esse contentus et illam uocem magnus atque animosus exclama: habemus aquam, habemus polentam; Ioui ipsi controuersiam de felicitate faciamus*, 'Turn rather to true wealth; learn to be content with little, and nobly, bravely cry out "We have water, we have flour; let us dispute with Jupiter himself who is the happier".' See below on 603-4.

335 **Laws had firmly partitioned the world**: the expression implies that the laws of nature originally prescribed that there should be a fixed frontier between sea and land; but the Argo's voyage violated those laws. For the world being organised according to laws (*foedera*, which most commonly means 'treaties'), cf. 606. The unusual verb 'partitioned' (*dissaepti*) was also applied by Ovid, in his creation narrative, to the division of the world between the four elements (*Met.* 1.69). The idea that the first ship linked up places that had been separated by god is found in Hor. *Carm.* 1.3.21-4 (see Nisbet and Hubbard).

336 **Thessalian pine-wood**: because the Argo was made of pine-wood from mount Pelion in Thessaly. Cf. 608-9; Eur. *Med.* 3-4 'would that pine trees had never been cut down and fallen in the glens of Pelion'; Ennius *Med.* 208-9 Jocelyn (205-6 Ribbeck, 253-4 Warmington); Catul. 64.1.

336-7 **... forced ... ordered ... to submit to beatings**: 'beatings' are oar-strokes, but the language suggests that the Argo was doing violence to the natural order.

338-9 **ordered the sea ... of our fear**: for the idea that the sea was a new source of fear cf. Prop. 3.7.31-2 *terra parum fuerat, fatis adiecimus undas: / fortunae miseras auximus arte uias*, 'the earth was too small, we have added the waves to fate: by our skill we have added to the dreadful paths to doom'; Lucan 3.193-7.

342-6 the two mountains ... the very clouds: in myth the Clashing Rocks (Symplegades) were two moving rocks on either side of a narrow sea-channel that regularly crashed together. The Argo had to pass between them, which it did, sustaining slight damage to the stern, and thereafter the rocks became fixed, forming the Bosporus. There was uncertainty and confusion in antiquity on whether the Clashing Rocks (Symplegades, a name first found in Eur. *Med.* 2, who also calls them 'blue', *kyaneai*) were the same as the Wandering Rocks (Planctae, a name first found in Hom. *Od.* 12.59-72), and there were various conjectures about the location of the latter. Different accounts of the Argo's route involved encounter with one or both sets of rocks on either the outward voyage or the homeward voyage. S. mentions the wandering rocks at 610, where it is not clear whether they are the same as the Symplegades or not. (See *OCD*[3] on 'Symplegades'; Gantz [1993], 356-7; Moreau [1994], 28, 36-7, 40.)

345 the trapped sea ... the very clouds: *E*'s text *spargeret astris nubesque ipsas* is ungrammatical; with *A*'s *astra* the meaning is that the sea 'spattered the stars [*astra*], and the clouds themselves'; it is a commonplace of stylised poetic descriptions of storms that the waves are said to reach the stars (see Hardie [1986], 261-3; Tarrant on S. *Ag.* 471), but here, after the sea-water has struck the stars, striking 'the very clouds' seems an anti-climax; and *A*'s *astra* could well be an attempt to get meaning from *E*'s *astris*. The text prints Madvig's conjecture *arces* (he actually proposed the form *arcis*), meaning 'peak, crag' (*OLD* s.v. *arx* 5). [But for a defence of *astra* see Fitch (1987), 36-7.]

346 Bold ... turned pale: the two words are juxtaposed in Latin (*palluit audax*), reinforcing the paradoxical contrast. The same two words were used by Horace to describe the fear of the young girl Europa when she was carried off across the sea by Jupiter in the guise of a bull (*Carm.* 3.27.28); Tiphys is as fearful as she. **Tiphys**: see on 2-3.

346-7 dropped all the reins: the phrase is metaphorical for 'lost control', probably specifically referring to losing control of the ship's ropes; for 'reins' in that sense see *TLL* 6.3.2392.79-2393.3, e.g. Verg. *A.* 6.1 *classique immittit habenas*, 'and he gave the fleet its reins.' Pindar, in his account of Jason and the Argonauts, calls the Argo's anchor its bridle (*chalinos*; *Pyth.* 4.25; cf. Eur. *IT* 1043). For *mittere habenas* in the sense of dropping the reins see Furius Bibaculus fr. 8 Courtney *ille graui subito deuictus uolnere habenas / misit equi*, 'overcome by a serious wound he suddenly dropped the horse's reins.'

348 Orpheus: see on 228-9.

349 even the Argo lost her voice: the prow of the Argo was made of a piece of the oak of Dodona supplied by Athena, and it had the power of speech and prophecy (e.g. Aesch. *Argo* fr. 36 Mette = fr. 20, 20a Radt; Ap. Rh. 4.580-92, cf. 1.526-7; Moreau [1994], 63 n. 17, 269 n. 23). The idea that the Argo lost its voice in fright is not found before S. (Mayer [1990], 404).

350-4 the girl of ... so many barks: Scylla, the mythological sea-monster who lived in the straits of Messina, between Sicily and Italy; Pelorus is the north-eastern promontory of Sicily. In Homer (*Od.* 12.85-100) she is a monster with six heads that devour fish and sailors, and she has a voice like a young dog (for which *skulax* is the Greek word, cf. 'Scylla'). Later, from the fifth century onwards, she regularly has the lower body of a fish with dogs' heads round it, and the upper body of a beautiful woman (*OCD*[3] on

'Scylla (1)'; in Roman poetry see e.g. Lucr. 5.892; Catul. 60.2; Verg. *Ecl.* 6.75). *uirgo*: the final *o* is scanned short.

350   **What about that time when ...**: for this elliptical use of *quid cum*, see *OLD* s.v. *quis*[1] 13b.

351   **with her womb girded by rabid hounds**: literally 'having girded on rabid hounds around her womb'; the participle *succincta* is used with a direct object, *canes*, a survival of the Latin middle voice, which had a quasi-reflexive sense (like the Greek middle voice). Cf. 751 *pessimos induta uultus*, 'assuming your most terrible aspect'; Woodcock (1959), 13-4; H-Sz 36-7. With our passage compare the description of Scylla at Verg. *Ecl.* 6.75 *(Scyllam) candida succinctam latrantibus inguina monstris*, 'having surrounded her white groin with barking monsters' (similar sense, but a different construction, see Coleman ad loc.).

355-60   **those cursed creatures ... with her singing**: the Sirens, half-woman, half-bird, who by their singing lured sailors to their deaths on the rocky coast of the island where they lived (see *OCD*[3] on 'Sirens'). When the Argo passed, Orpheus sang so sweetly that none of the Argonauts was attracted by the Sirens' song, except Butes (Ap. Rh. 4.891-921; Apollod. 1.9.25); S. adds the conceit that Orpheus nearly lured the Siren (or Sirens, see on 360) away with his singing. **Ausonian sea**: 'Ausonian' is a poetic equivalent for Italian or Roman (the Ausones were the earliest inhabitants of Campania), and here refers to the Tyrrhenian Sea, the sea between the west coast of Italy, Sardinia and Sicily.

357   **Pierian**: Pieria was an area of north-east Greece between Mount Olympus and the river Haliacmon; from early times it was associated with the Muses, who were called Pierides (Hes. *Op.* 1, *Th.* 53; Solon 13.2), and Orpheus, as a singer, was associated with the Muses. He had a grave and cult at Pieria, though he came from Thrace (see *OCD*[3] on 'Orpheus').

360   **the Siren**: perhaps singular for plural, meaning all the Sirens, or else meaning that one of the Sirens almost broke ranks and followed the Argo (compare how in Ap. Rh. 4.912-9 Butes alone of the Argonauts swims off towards the Sirens).

361-3   **What was the reward ... for the first ship**: the voyage is treated as a mercenary enterprise for profit. By suggesting that M. was the sort of reward that the voyage deserved, the Chorus puts her in a wider context, as an instrument of cosmic justice.

362-3   note the alliteration, *maiusque mari Medea malum, merces* ... Cf. on 14.

364-79   **Nowadays ... Thule**: 'Nowadays' is ostensibly from the Chorus's point of view; though not all that many years can have elapsed since the Argo returned to Greece. But colonisation (369-70), and the Araxes, the Elbe, the Rhine, and Thule belong to the geo-political world of Rome rather than of mythology; so the Chorus's reflections have a bearing on S.'s Rome. During his lifetime there were wars in Germany and Armenia, and 'Thule' may allude to Claudius' invasion of Britain (see on 379; Romm [1992], 167-71). The Roman ethos of the lines marks them out from the rest of the ode, but so does the tone, for the Chorus up to now has spoken of sailing as transgressive, but here speaks more positively of the prospect of the whole earth being opened up to human knowledge. But even here at the end of the ode there are hints of the earlier adverse opinions on sailing: the sea 'submits to all our laws' (364-5), and 'Every boundary-stone has been moved' (369). Although up to this point the Chorus may have expressed nothing but deep unease about the voyage of the Argo, the audience may see it differently: for the Argonauts heroically overcame all the dangers, and they returned successfully.

364-5 submits to all our laws: cf. 320.

366 something constructed by Pallas's hand: there were different traditions about the builder of the Argo. S. mentions only Pallas Athena's role in building the ship, as do Antimachus fr. 57 and Catul. 64.8-10. In S.'s context, where the Argo is contrasted with ordinary ships of a later period, only the assistance of the goddess is relevant, but other accounts mention various human builders too, usually Argus, but sometimes Glaucus, or Jason himself. (See Gantz [1993], 343; Moreau [1994], 63 n. 17; *LIMC* 2.1, 600-2, 2.2, 433-4.)

367 in which kings pull on the oars: literally 'pulling back the oars of kings'; the ship itself, not the crew, is said to pull the oars back (see Zwierlein [1986], 145; Hillen [1989], 227).

369-70 boundary-stone: a *terminus* was originally a stone set up to mark a boundary; such stones were sacred to the god Terminus (*OCD*³ on 'Terminus'), and there were laws against fraudulent removal of boundary-stones (see Nisbet and Hubbard on Hor. *Carm.* 2.18.24), so there is a suggestion here that moving all boundary-stones is wrong.

371 where it was before: literally 'where it had been'; *fuerat* is pluperfect where perfect would be more usual (see on 168).

373-4 the Indian ... and Rhine: peoples were regularly identified by the local rivers from which they drank, as was natural enough in a world where rivers were more important than they are today in the west for transport, drinking water and other daily needs. The usage goes back to Homer (*Il.* 2.825-6 'the Trojans who drink the dark water of the Aesepus'), cf. e.g. Nisbet and Hubbard on Hor. *Carm.* 2.20.20; Tarrant on S. *Ag.* 318ff.; *TLL* 2.1964.39-66. Here, however, the Chorus describes peoples drinking from rivers in lands far distant from their own. This is something that was traditionally regarded as impossible: cf. Verg. *Ecl.* 1.59-63 *ante leues ergo pascentur in aethere cerui, / et freta destituent nudos in litore piscis, / ante pererratis amborum finibus exsul / aut Ararim Parthus bibet aut Germania Tigrim, / quam nostro illius labatur pectore uultus,* 'Sooner, then, will nimble stags feed on the air, and the seas leave fish stranded and exposed on the shore, sooner will the Parthian drink the Saône or Germany the Tigris, wandering in exile across each other's boundaries, than memory of his face will fade from my heart.' That passage contains a series of *adynata*, or proverbial natural impossibilities (see on 401-5; for *adynata* in general cf. Nisbet and Hubbard on Hor. *Carm.* 1.29.10; Henry and Henry [1985], 14-20, 197-200; Rosenmeyer [1989], 194-203). The voyage of the Argo in effect, according to the Chorus, achieved a miracle. Later on M. will achieve comparable miracles, making *adynata* happen (see on 762, 889), and thus her actions are foreshadowed by the Argo. **the Indian drinks**: when he travels to the Araxes, which marked the ancient trade-route, used by Indian merchants, between the Caspian and Asia Minor. S. was familiar with the geography of India, for he himself wrote a work, now lost, on the topic (frr. 9-11 Haase, T20-1 Vottero; fr. 11=T21a, from Serv. *A.* 9.31, is about the river Ganges). **the icy Araxes**: the chief river of Armenia, modern Aras, which flows into the Caspian Sea; 'icy' because it rises in the high Ararat mountains, and is fed by melting snows. S. uses exactly the same phrase 'drinks the icy Araxes' at *Phaed.* 58 (of wild animals). (See *OCD*³ on 'Araxes'.) **the Elbe and Rhine**: the Rhine marked the eastern boundary of Roman Gaul; there were various attempts, all ultimately unsuccessful, to extend Roman control eastward across Germany as far as the Elbe. Again both rivers were major trade-routes. (See *OCD*³ on 'Germania', 'Rhenus'.)

376 **Ocean**: in ancient geography Ocean was the sea surrounding all the known land-masses of Europe, Africa and Asia; there was speculation whether there were other unknown land-masses across the Ocean. In mythology Oceanus was son of Uranus (Sky) and Ge or Gaia (Earth), and husband of Tethys. (See West on Hes. *Th.* 133; *OCD*³ on 'Oceanus (geographical)' and 'Oceanus (mythological)'.)

378 **Tethys**: a sea-goddess, sister and wife of Ocean(us), and mother of rivers and Oceanids. (See West on Hes. *Th.* 136; *OCD*³ on 'Tethys'.)

379 **Thule**: the most remote northern land known to the Greeks and Romans, first described by Pytheas in the late 4th cent. B.C.; perhaps he referred to Iceland or Norway, though later writers identify it with the Shetlands. See *OCD*³ on 'Thule'. Nisbet (1990), 96-7, argues that the reference to Thule here is a compliment to Claudius' invasion of Britain in 43 A.D. In the Renaissance these lines were regarded as a prophecy of the discovery of America (see P. H. Damsté, *Mnemosyne* 2.46 [1918], 13; Costa ad loc.; cf. E. G. Bourne, 'Seneca and the discovery of America', *The Academy* 43 [1893], 130).

ACT THREE: 380-578

The structure of this act resembles that of the second: first there is a dialogue between M. and the Nurse, this time with the Nurse speaking first (380-430), then a dialogue between M. and Jason (431-559), corresponding to the dialogue with Creon in the previous act. But most of the encounter between M. and the Nurse consists of two long speeches; they do not properly converse until 425-30.

380-96 The Nurse and M. emerge from the house, and the Nurse addresses her first two lines to M., but in 382-396 she describes M.'s behaviour in the third person. The portrayal of M. pacing to and fro, distracted, changeable and indecisive, is a traditional feature of her portrayal, cf. Ap. Rh. 3.645-55 (as she wonders whether to go to her sister Chalciope). In his philosophical discussions of anger S. is interested in its physical symptoms, cf. *On Anger* 1 (= *Dialogues* 3).1.3-4: 'You can see that men possessed by anger are insane, if you look at their expression. The sure signs of raving madness are a bold and threatening look, a gloomy countenance, a grim visage, a rapid pace, restless hands, change of colour, heavy and frequent sighing. The marks of anger are the same: eyes ablaze and glittering, a deep flush over all the face as blood boils up from the vitals, quivering lips, teeth pressed together, bristling hair standing on end, breath drawn in and hissing, the crackle of writhing limbs, groans and bellowing, speech broken off with the words barely uttered, hands struck together too often, feet stamping the ground, the whole body in violent motion, "menacing mighty wrath in mien" [an otherwise unknown verse quotation], the hideous horrifying face of swollen self-degradation—you would hardly know whether to call the vice hateful or ugly' (trans. Cooper and Procopé); cf. 2.35.3-36.2. But the portrait of M. here has an additional element, her indecisiveness. Robin (1993), 107-8, more speculatively links the present passage with medical descriptions of hysterical female disorder, comparing *Ag.* 234-8, *Phaed.* 360-83; but the behaviour described in the medical writers there quoted only partially matches the behaviour described in these passages of tragedy. (On madness in the play see further on 139-40.)

The long description of the behaviour of M. while she herself is on stage is regularly taken as a sign that the plays were not really meant for stage performance (e.g. Costa on 382ff.; Zwierlein [1966], 61-2). Certainly if M. is supposed to be acting out all the behaviour as the Nurse describes it, then the whole passage, and line 390 in particular, represents a histrionic obstacle course that in performance could well become comic; and if the actors wore masks, there could be no question of changes of facial expression. But it is possible to regard the Nurse's description at 382-96 as a long aside (on Senecan asides, see Tarrant [1978], 242-6). The Nurse could be giving a general description of how M. has been behaving recently, rather than a specific description of her present behaviour on stage; compare the Nurse's description of Phaedra's recent behaviour at *Phaed.* 360-83, though that is before Phaedra comes on stage. For the paradoxical changes of behaviour see Pomponius *com.* 124 Ribbeck <*Flet*>, *fit desubito hilarus; tristis saltat; ridens ringitur*, 'he weeps, suddenly becomes happy; is sad, dances; laughing, bares his teeth.' On the general question of descriptions of characters' behaviour while they are on stage see Fitch on *Her. F.* 1044-8; and compare Plaut. *Mil.* 200-14.

382-4 Just as a Maenad ... of Nysa: Maenads or Bacchants were worshippers of Bacchus or Dionysus (the god of 383). The Greek word 'Maenad' means 'mad woman', being etymologically related to the verb *mainomai*, 'I am mad', so it is an appropriate comparison for M. S. is fond of such similes in his tragedy, see Primmer (1976); Fitch on *Her. F.* 1046-8, 1088-93; Boyle on *Tro.* 537. For comparisons to Maenads, cf. 806, 849; Fantham, and Boyle, on *Tro.* 672ff.; Verg. *A.* 4.300-3, describing Dido (see Pease on line 301); Ovid *Met.* 7.258 (comparing M. to a Bacchant), 9.640-1. Maenads were also a popular subject in art (cf. Catul. 64.61; Cic. *Fam.* 7.23.2; *LIMC* 8.1, 780-803, 8.2, 524-50).

382 inspired: the adjective (*entheos*) is a Greek loan-word that is first found in Senecan tragedy, and in later poetry (see *OLD* or *TLL* s.v. *entheus*).

384 Pindus: a mountain between Thessaly and Macedonia; cf. 721. For Bacchants there see *Oed.* 435; elsewhere the mountain is not particularly linked to Bacchic worship, but at *Oed.* 435 and *Her. F.* 1285 (see Fitch) S., with characteristic geographical vagueness, calls Pindus Thracian, and Thrace was linked with Bacchus. **Nysa:** the mythical mountain on which Dionysus was born, often thought to be in India, though other sites, from Egypt eastwards, were suggested (see Austin on Verg. *A.* 6.805).

389 she smiles: her smile may anticipate the joy she feels later (see on 896).

391 Which way ... heaviness sink?: the image is of a balance which is evenly poised at the moment, but one side or other must soon be weighed down.

392 Where will that wave ... is overflowing: the metaphor of the 'wave' of emotion is first found in Latin in Lucr. 3.298, 6.74 (see *TLL* 6.1.948.26-48; in Greek cf. Aesch. *Cho.* 183-4, *Eum.* 832); the metaphor 'overflowing' (*exundare*) is first found in S., in tragedy and prose (*Oed.* 924, *Dial.* 3.7.1, *TLL* 5.2.2110.81-2111.9). It recalls M.'s claim to control the waves (121, 166), and picks up the Chorus's words that M. is a worse evil than the sea (362).

394 she will surpass herself: cf. 49-50, 904-10.

396 I see the face of Madness: von Winterfeld suggested printing *Furoris* with a capital; for madness (*furor*) personified, cf. *Her. F.* 98, *Oed.* 590; Verg. *A.* 1.294-6; Serv. *A.* 1.294 refers to Furor in chains in a painting in the Forum of Augustus.

397-425 M.'s speech: M. ignores the Nurse and soliloquises (at 397 'wretched woman' is herself, not the Nurse). In her speech she vehemently insists that she will achieve a terrible revenge, and at 415-22 attacks Jason.

397-8 If you ask ... from love: M. may be appealing to the general principle that love knows no limits, but more likely she is thinking of her own experience: in the past her love for Jason was unrestrained, and led her to evil actions; accordingly, her present hatred should know no restraint.

398-9 What, should I endure: an indignant rejection of the very idea that she should endure it. The construction (*egone ut* and subjunctive *patiar*) is originally a colloquial one, found in two more speeches of M.'s (893, 929-30), and in *Her. F.* 372-3, *Oed.* 671. In each passage of *Med.*, M. indignantly rejects a suggestion coming from the Nurse or (in the last case) herself. The construction is otherwise found frequently in comedy (e.g. Plaut. *Aul.* 690, *Mil.* 962), in Accius *trag.* 427 Ribbeck (415 Warmington), in dialogue at Cic. *Tusc.* 2.42, and in letter writing (Cic. *Att.* 15.4.3; Fronto *ad M. Caes.* 5.74.1).

401-5 While the earth ... into the sea: i.e. as long as nature runs its unchanging course, she will continue to seek vengeance. She uses standard examples of things in the natural world that cannot be otherwise—things that feature in lists of *adynata*, proverbial impossibilities (see on 373-4; on counting grains of sand see Nisbet and Hubbard on Hor. *Carm.* 1.28.1)—but the last two have an added piquancy coming from M., for her magical powers can deflect the stars from their course and make rivers run upstream (see 757-9, 762-4). The earth is 'at the centre' of the (geocentric) universe, and the heavens are 'balanced', because in ancient cosmology the fixed stars are equidistant from the earth, carried on a sphere whose centre is the earth.

404-5 while the pole ... as they revolve: in the Mediterranean region and further north, the circumpolar constellations of the Great and Little Bear never sank below the horizon, and never touched the sea (a regular idea, going back to Hom. *Il.* 18.489, *Od.* 5.275): cf. Ovid *Met.* 2.171-2, where Phaethon risks making them touch the sea; and for the use of the motif in an adynaton cf. *Thy.* 476-7. Later we learn that M. has made the Bears touch the sea (758-9), something that the Chorus fears may happen in *Thy.* 867-8. (Today, because of the precession of the equinoxes, the Great Bear is seen dipping into the sea in parts of the Mediterranean region.)

407-14 Her anger is more powerful than wild beasts, than Scylla and Charybdis, than Etna and other powerful natural forces—a continuation of the theme that her powers rival those of the physical world (see on 28).

408-9 Scylla: see on 350-4. **Charybdis, sucking ... Sicilian sea**: Charybdis is the whirlpool, opposite Scylla, encountered by Odysseus (Hom. *Od.* 12.101-7). It was later located near the straits of Messina, between Italy and Sicily; there is no dangerous whirlpool there, but there are strong currents (see *OCD*[3] on 'Charybdis'). For 'Ausonian', see on 355; the 'Sicilian sea' is between the toe of Italy and Sicily. S., in a letter to Lucilius, procurator of Sicily, published in the early 60s A.D., asked him to investigate whether Charybdis lived up to its name, and if so, what caused the whirlpool (*Epist.* 79.1).

409-10 what Etna ... a gasping Titan: there were rival mythological accounts of the monster imprisoned below Etna. Pindar said it was Typhoeus (Pi. *Pyth.* 1.16-28; see further below on 773-4), but a later tradition had the giant Enceladus buried there (Callim. fr. 1.36 Pfeiffer; Williams on Verg. *A.* 3.578). Neither was originally a Titan (an earlier race of gods, see on 5), but later the distinction between Titans, Giants, and similar monsters was often forgotten (see Fitch on *Her. F.* 79; *LIMC* 4.1, 192-6). S. may have Enceladus in mind, following Virgil. (*Her. O.* 1157-9 also puts Enceladus under Etna.)

415 **Was he afraid**: referring to Jason; the omission of his hated name is a sign of contempt (cf. on 218-9). **the Thessalian chief**: Acastus, see on 256-7.

418-9 **at least ... final conversation**: cf. Eur. *Med.* 586-7 (M. addressing Jason) 'If you were a man of honour, you should have won my consent to this new marriage instead of keeping it a secret from your own family.' Compare also Dido's reproach to Aeneas for trying to leave without speaking to her (Verg. *A.* 4.305-6).

419 **he took fright ... defiant man!**: 'defiant man' is ironic, and the juxtaposition with 'he took fright' is an oxymoron (see on 10).

421-2 **for our two children**: for the audience this foreshadows their death.

423 **will achieve ... will achieve**: see on 25-6.

424 **I shall assault the gods**: by magic; see on 166-7.

426-8 **My only hope ... when you are dying**: M. owes something to the idea that when you suffer death yourself, it is some consolation if you know that other people are dying at the same time as you. This regular theme of consolatory literature is extended to the mortality of the natural world at *Nat.* 6.2.9: 'So we can say, "If I must die, may I die as the world is shaken [by earthquake], not because it is right to hope for public disaster, but because it is a powerful consolation for death when one sees that even the earth is mortal"'; Sen. *Contr.* 9.6.2. However, M. goes further than that, anticipating actively causing destruction herself. Compare how S. believed that thwarted anger picks its targets indiscriminately: cf. *Dial.* 4 (*On Anger* 2).35.5 (in a long comparison of anger to a Fury) *... et omnium odio laborantem, sui maxime, si aliter nocere non possit, terras maria caelum ruere cupientem*, '... consumed with hatred of all, especially of itself, if it can find no other way to do harm, ready to confound earth, sea and sky' (trans. Cooper and Procopé); in other Senecan plays cf. Hercules in *Her. F.* 1167, 1284-93. (On the distinct but related thought 'I don't mind dying myself as long as I kill X too', see Tarrant on *Ag.* 201 and on *Thy.* 190-1; *Dial.* 3.1.1.) **when you are dying**: *cum pereas*; the present subjunctive is descriptive or characterising, i.e. 'at *a* time when you are dying', 'at a time *such that* you ...'; see Woodcock (1959), 191; *OLD* s.v. *cum²* 3. Here the second person singular is indefinite (see Fordyce on Catul. 22.9): that is, M. is not talking about the Nurse, but means 'when one is dying.'

431-46 Enter Jason, unannounced (unlike Creon at 177-8). He first speaks to himself (see on 179-90), then at 445-6 he describes M. approaching him. So far we have had conflicting impressions of Jason from the Chorus, Creon and M. In his opening speech he acknowledges his debt to M., but loyalty to her would mean death not just for himself, which is less important, but also for his sons: it is for their sake that he has rejected M. He does not say where the danger comes from, but the audience knows, from the dialogue between Creon and M. in the previous act, that it comes from Acastus. His affection for his sons is to prove the inspiration for M.'s revenge, and his confidence that M. too would put the sons before her marriage (441-3) is ironically misplaced.

431 **O, fate ... destiny harsh**: Jason at once reveals himself as someone who feels at the mercy of fate or fortune, and of god (433); yet he also expresses doubt whether Justice is a god (439-40). By contrast M. is someone who believes she is superior to fortune (see on 520). The difference is reflected in their vocabulary: Jason talks of fate, *fata*, which is usually something fixed and preordained (at 652 Idmon the prophet 'knew the fates well'; otherwise the word *fatum* is used only at 662 and 1000, with the meaning 'death'); the word 'destiny' (*sors*) has similar associations (it is not used elsewhere in the play). By contrast M. just talks of fortune and chance, terms which usually imply that events are not foreordained. Jason also sees god controlling men (433-4); on the other hand M., though she may pray to the gods, also attacks them, and is as powerful as they are (see on 166-7).

433-4 remedies worse than the dangers: cf. Sen. *Contr.* 6.7 *quaedam remedia grauiora ipsis periculis sunt,* 'some remedies are worse than the dangers themselves'; S. *Oed.* 517 *ubi turpis est medicina sanari piget,* 'when the medicine is shameful, being healed is odious.'

434-9 if I had wanted ... would have been next: the imperfect subjunctives (*uellem, nollem, sequeretur*) are here used in past unreal conditions, as in early Latin. The pluperfect subjunctive had become more usual by S.'s day, so here the expression has an archaic flavour; see Woodcock (1959), 154-6. *fuit* with the gerundives *offerendum* and *carendum* is equivalent to the potential subjunctive in such sentences; see Woodcock (1959), 156. It may seem disingenuous of Jason to say, in an unreal condition, 'I would have had to abandon my good faith', when he has in fact broken faith with M. But his point is that he was not unwilling or afraid to die, so the protasis (the 'if'-clause) does make an untrue supposition. Nevertheless the strained expression suggests a man struggling to justify his actions.

435 with my wife, as she deserves: literally 'with the deserts (*merita*) of my wife', see on 120.

438 parental love: *pietas*; see on 261, and on 545. Jason stresses the children's interests in Euripides at *Med.* 559-67, but there he speaks with more detachment about wanting to improve their lot, and does not show the strong emotions of S.'s Jason.

439-40 If you dwell in heaven, holy Justice: Jason calls on Justice, who appears personified, as a goddess, only here in S.'s plays, and once in *Oct.* (398). In Euripides' *Med.* M. appeals to Themis (Justice) at 160, cf. 208-9. The Romans identified personified Justice with the Greek Astraea (daughter of Themis) or Dike, who was the last deity to leave earth at the end of the silver age, when she became the constellation Virgo (cf. Arat. *Phaen.* 96-136; Verg. *G.* 2.473-4 and Thomas; Ovid *Met.* 1.150, *Fast.* 1.249-50; *LIMC* 3.1, 388-91, 3.2, 280-1, 8.1, 661-3, 8.2, 412). Jason says 'If you dwell in heaven', as though there is some doubt whether she really is a goddess. For such doubts in Senecan tragedy compare Thyestes' more general scepticism at *Thy.* 406-7 *patrios deos / (si sunt tamen di) cerno,* 'I see ... the gods of my fatherland (if gods do exist)'.

441 she herself: *ipsam*. Just as M. cannot utter Jason's name to Creon (see on 218-9), so he can scarcely bring himself to utter hers; he does so only at 496, and then in a third person sentence. She, however, uses his name in this scene at 447 and 518, for she wants to work on his former love for her.

444-6 As Jason is about to speak to M., she approaches him; cf. the Nurse's description of M.'s behaviour at 382-96.

447-89 M. delivers a long tirade against Jason, full of bitter irony and reproach. First (447-60) she accuses him of sending her into exile when there is nowhere for her to go; secondly (460-76) she reminds him of all she has done for him in the past, services for which he now shows no gratitude; finally (478-89) she appeals to him to have pity on her—but her concluding demand, that he return her country, father, brother, and honour to her (488-9), is not one that Jason can fulfil, so the plea is a vehicle for further reproach.

447 I have fled ... I am fleeing ...: metre requires us to take the first *fugimus* as perfect tense, with a long first *u*, and the second as present tense, with a short first *u*; and the sense is better with different tenses. (If the first were also present tense, the first foot would be a self-contained tribrachic word, which is not found elsewhere in S. or earlier Roman drama, though it is found in Greek; see Axelson [1967], 42 n. 26.) On such repetition of forms with different vowel lengths, see Wills (1996), 465.

449-50 for your sake ... from your house: there is a pointed contrast between these two phrases (in Latin *pro te* and *tuis* are at opposite ends of the two lines).

451-9 To whom are you ... sending me?: the series of angry questions that M. fires at Jason is traditional. Compare Eur. *Med.* 502-4 'Where am I to turn now? To my father's house that I betrayed together with my homeland when I came here? Or to Pelias' wretched daughters?'; part of Ennius' version survives, *Med.* 217-8 Jocelyn (231-2 Ribbeck, 284-5 Warmington) *quo nunc me uertam? quod iter incipiam ingredi? / domum paternamne? anne ad Peliae filias?*, 'where can I now turn? what journey shall I embark on? to my father's house? to Pelias' daughters?' In Apollonius M. says to Jason, while escaping with him, 'How shall I face my father? Will it be with a good name? What revenge, what heavy calamity shall I not endure in agony for the terrible deeds I have done? And will you win the return that your heart desires?' (4.378-81). Other deserted lovers complain in similar ways, cf. Ariadne at Catul. 64.177-83, Dido at Verg. *A.* 4.534-52, Scylla at Ovid *Met.* 8.113-8, and their speeches will all repay detailed comparison with M.'s here: Ariadne and Scylla, like M., have deserted their fathers; Catullus, Vergil, Ovid and S. all know their predecessors' works, so a complex web of intertextuality links S. to the others.

452-3 the territory ... blood flowed: S. several times alludes briefly to the killing of Apsyrtus, without ever naming him (see 121, 131-3 and comm., 173, 278, 486-7, 911-2, 936, 957, 964-71). The numerous references by M. herself suggest a sense of guilt. There were different accounts of the place and the circumstances of his death:

(i) he was killed in Colchis, in the palace, before the Argo set sail (Soph. *Colchian Women*, fr. 343 Radt; Eur. *Med.* 1334);

(ii) Jason and M. took him with them, and he was killed on the journey; he was dismembered and his limbs were scattered on the river Phasis or on the sea, so that the Colchians had to slow down their pursuit to collect the pieces;

(iii) Apsyrtus joined in the Colchian pursuit, and was lured by M. into an ambush where Jason killed him (Ap. Rh. 4.452-81).

In the present passage of S. it sounds as though Apsyrtus was killed on land ('territory over which ...'), but at 133 the body is scattered on the sea; line 487 possibly, but not necessarily, indicates that Apsyrtus was already dead when Jason and M. set sail, and that they took the corpse with them. Perhaps S. follows a combination of (i) and (ii): Apsyrtus was killed before they left Colchis, and his body was scattered first on the land, then on the sea. (On the myth see Gantz [1993], 363-4; Bremmer [1997].)

453 What lands ... head for?: Quintilian (*Inst.* 9.2.8) quotes this half line to show how a rhetorical question can express indignation; this is the earliest surviving quotation of any of the Senecan tragedies by a later author.

454 The jaws of the Pontic strait: the Bosporus, or the Hellespont (Dardanelles), or both; cf. V. Max. 2.8.pr. *fauces Pontici sinus. fauces*, literally 'throat' or 'jaws', is a common term for straits and other narrow entrances, in prose and verse (see *OLD* s.v. *fauces* 3a).

456 I followed an adulterer: elsewhere M. has stressed that she was married to Jason (see on 1), but here she talks as though he seduced her in an immoral fashion (cf. on 11-12); or she may be thinking that he is now literally an adulterer (as she views it), having taken a second wife. **Symplegades**: see on 342-6. The ending *-adas* is a Greek accusative plural form.

457 your uncle's: Pelias's. (*patruam* is a very fine conjecture by Zwierlein [1977], 160, for the manuscript reading *paruam*, 'small', which has little point.) **Iolcus**: see on 133-4 and 256-7. Iolcus was an important Mycenaean site, but insignificant in the historical period (see *OCD³* on 'Iolcus'). *Iolcon* is a Greek accusative ending (nominative *Iolcos*, cf. on 35). **Thessalian Tempe**: Tempe was the valley of the Peneus, between mounts Ossa and Olympus; it is here regarded as part of Pelias's, now Acastus's, kingdom. (*Tempe*, with long final *-e*, is a Greek neuter plural form, either nominative or, as here, accusative.)

459-60 You order ... no destination: imperial Rome was familiar with emperors ordering people into exile—but they always specified the destination, unlike Creon and Jason.

460-5 Let me ... than I deserve: with bitter irony, M. for the moment pretends that she deserves the punishment of exile, or worse.

462 the mistress: here, and at 495, M. ironically applies to herself the word 'mistress' (*paelex*), adopting Creusa's viewpoint. At 920, talking to herself, she applies the same word to Creusa.

464 and bury her ... endless darkness: burial alive is reminiscent of Antigone's punishment (Soph. *Ant.* 773-80), and of the punishment for unchaste Vestal Virgins at Rome (see *OCD³* on 'Vesta, Vestals'). Antigone suffered at the hands of another king called Creon (the name just means 'ruler').

465 than I deserve: literally 'than my *merita*', see on 120. **Ungrateful creature**: literally 'ungrateful head'; *caput*, like Greek κάρα and κεφαλή, is used in emotive expressions like this, to express hatred or affection (see Tarrant on *Ag.* 953; Fitch on *Her. F.* 920, 1334; in Greek, Barrett on Eur. *Hipp.* 651).

466-76 M. reviews all that she has done for Jason, just as at Eur. *Med.* 476-87, Ovid *Epist.* 12.107-18. Cf. trag. inc. 172-3 Ribbeck (Ennius 282-3 Warmington, but see Jocelyn on Enn. *trag.* p. 350 for the uncertainty of the text and the attribution to Ennius) *non commemoro quod draconis saeui sopiui impetum, / non quod domui uim taurorum et segetis armatae manus*, 'I don't remind you that I put to sleep the attacks of the cruel dragon, or that I conquered the power of the bulls and the strength of the armoured harvest.'

467-8 and—among the ... sprouted armed men: here S.'s allusiveness has caused doubts about the meaning and the genuineness of the lines. Leo thought 'the unconquerable race' referred to the warriors who sprang from the dragon's teeth, which is an awkward anticipation of the description of them in 468-70, and he thought the double mention of the fire-breathing bulls in 466 and 468 was awkward too; so he deleted 467-8. But

Costa and Zwierlein (1986), 146-7, rightly take 'the unconquerable race' to be the
Colchians themselves; and the two references to the bulls are no more awkward than the
two references in 469 and 470 to the warriors who sprang from the dragon's teeth. **that
sprouted armed men**: see on 169. Literally 'weapon-bearing', *armifer*, a poetic
compound adjective, used also at 980 and *Phaed.* 909, and first found in Ovid (*Am.*
2.6.35, *Ars* 2.5, etc.).

470 **earth-born**: *terrigena*, a poetic compound, corresponding to Greek γηγενής, first
found in a verse quotation in Cic. *Diu.* 2.133, and in Lucr. 5.1411, 1427. The whole
line recalls Ovid *Met.* 7.141: *terrigenae pereunt per mutua uulnera fratres*, 'the earth-
born brothers perish by mutual wounds.'

471 **the spoils of Phrixus' ram**: the golden fleece. Phrixus and his sister Helle were about
to be sacrificed by their father Athamas when they were rescued by a golden ram, sent
by Jupiter (or in other versions by Nephele their mother), which flew off with them.
Helle fell into the sea and drowned, giving her name to the Hellespont, but Phrixus
reached Colchis, where he sacrificed the ram to Zeus, and he, or Aeetes, hung up its
golden fleece on a tree (cf. 485-6). (See *OCD*[3] on 'Athamas', 'Helle'.)

472-3 **the sleepless monster**: the dragon that guarded the golden fleece (different from the
dragon whose teeth Jason had to sow). In the earliest versions Jason seems to have
dealt with this serpent without M.'s help: a vase by the painter Douris, ca. 470 B.C.,
shows Jason half swallowed by a serpent, with Athena standing next to him, and similar
scenes are found on two earlier paintings (see *LIMC* 5.1, 632 nos. 30-32, 5.2, 427-8,
nos. 30, 32); Pindar (*Pyth.* 4.249) and Pherecydes (*FGH*3F31) describe Jason killing the
snake. In Euripides, however, M. claims that she killed the snake (480-2), which is
perhaps Euripides' invention (Gantz [1993], 359-60). Later Ap. Rh. 4.123-82 and V. Fl.
8.64-108 describe M. putting the serpent to sleep, as she does here and at 703-4.
ordered to surrender its eyes ...: i.e. M. put the dragon to sleep with her magic.
sleepless ... sleep: for the word-play cf. on 261.

474 **in that single crime, ... not just once**: maybe this means that the killing, the
dismembering and the scattering of Apsyrtus were three separate crimes. But the phrase
is more ingenious, more macabre, and therefore more Senecan, if it means that each
sword-blow, each piece tossed overboard, was a separate crime. S. is fond of
polyptoton (see on 233) with *scelus*, see 563-4, Wills (1996), 220.

476 **old man—though he would not live again**: Pelias, whom his daughters believed they
were rejuvenating (see on 133-4; 261).

477 **[Seeking someone ... my own]**: the square brackets indicate that this verse, which is
found in the manuscripts, is spurious and ought to be omitted. Zwierlein (1976), 194-5,
argues that the sentence interrupts the sequence of thought, and M. cannot be described
as 'seeking someone else's kingdom' when she left Colchis.

481 **by sky and ... of my marriage**: since she had fled her home, M. did not have a proper
wedding in a domestic setting, and the elements had to stand in for witnesses; compare
the union of Dido and Aeneas in the cave, attended by Earth, Juno, aether, lighting, and
nymphs (Verg. *A.* 4.166-8). **marriage**: *coniugi* is the genitive of *coniugium*, equivalent
to *coniugii*. (Cf. on 137-8 and 743.)

482 **a suppliant**: implying that she formally supplicates Jason, see on 247. **reward**: *uicem*,
see Fitch on *Her. F.* 1338; *OLD* s.v. *uicis* 5.

483   the Scythians pillage from afar: M. regards the Colchians as Scythians (see on 212; Serv. *G*. 2.140 calls Colchis a Scythian city), and she here describes their wealth as plundered in foreign raids.

484   the sun-scorched tribes of India: in Roman times a trade-route from India passed through Colchis (Plin. *Nat*. 6.52; S. wrote a lost work on India, see on 373-4). 'sun-scorched' is one of the varied expressions used to refer to the dark skins of the inhabitants at *Thy*. 602, *Oed*. 122-3, *Phaed*. 345; for all dark-skinned peoples were thought to be burnt by the sun; cf. e.g. Lucr. 6.722; Plin. *Nat*. 6.70. In the fifth century B.C. the Colchians themselves were sometimes described as black-skinned (Pi. *Pyth*. 4.212; Hdt. 2.103-4).

485-6   (since our palace ... with gold): literally 'which treasures since the crammed-full palace barely holds, we adorn ...', 'which treasures' being object of 'holds'. M. ingeniously speaks as though the golden fleece was hung on a tree because there was not enough room for so much gold in the palace. In fact, according to the standard story, it was hung up as a religious dedication, see on 471.

486-7   I brought nothing ... my brother's limbs: see on 452-3 for the circumstances of the murder of Apsyrtus. This claim to have brought nothing is strictly incompatible with her having ancestral gifts to send to Creusa later in the play, for at least some of these were brought from Colchis (570-4). The Roman reader is unlikely to have been bothered by this any more than by the gifts that, in the *Aeneid*, Aeneas turns out to have brought with him as he escaped from Troy (*A*. 1.647-55, 7.243-8).

489   with this dowry: the dowry was the gift given by the bride's family to the groom (see *OCD³* on 'marriage law'). In Homer the man has to pay a price for his bride, but in later poetry the contemporary practice of the wife's family paying a dowry is regularly introduced into the mythological age, e.g. Eur. *Hipp*. 627-9. In stories of the 'Tarpeia type', where a young woman tries to betray her country for love (see Graf [1997a], 23-5; *OCD³* on 'Tarpeia'), the woman traditionally refers to her country as a dowry: cf. Prop. 3.19.23 (Scylla), 4.4.56 (Tarpeia); Ovid *Met*. 8.67-8 (Scylla), and *Epist*. 12.199-203, where M. writes to Jason *dos ubi sit, quaeris? campo numerauimus illo / qui tibi laturo uellus arandus erat. / aureus ille aries uillo spectabilis alto / dos mea; quam dicam si tibi 'redde,' neges. / dos mea tu sospes; dos est mea Graia iuuentus*, 'You ask where the dowry is? I counted it out on the field that you had to plough to win the fleece. The golden ram, resplendent in his thick coat, was my dowry; if I said "Give it back", you would refuse. Your safe return is my dowry, the young men of Greece are my dowry'; but, whereas in Ovid M. lists benefits she brought to Jason, here in S. she lists sacrifices she made, things that Jason can never give back. **Give your wife's property back**: literally 'Return her own things.' This is an echo of a traditional Roman divorce formula: the husband said to the wife *tuas res tibi habe*, 'take your things for yourself', or something similar. Occasionally in literature the wife speaks as M. does here; so in Plaut. *Amph*. 928 Alcmena says to Jupiter, who is disguised as her husband, *ualeas, tibi habeas res tuas, reddas meas*, 'farewell, keep your things to yourself, give back mine', and compare Ovid *Epist*. 12.202 quoted above. See Treggiari (1991), 446-8, for other examples.

490-530   The rapid dialogue between Jason and M. has some of the regular features of such passages (see on 155-76): M. picks up Jason's words (499-500 'your wicked deeds', 'yours

... wickedness'; 504-5 'one is ashamed to accept'), she appeals to her past deeds to answer his present fears (527-8, see on 168), delivers *sententiae* (503, 505), and there are conspicuous examples of repetition, antithesis and balance (500, 502, 503, 509, 512, 527).

490-1 In Euripides Jason defends his behaviour at length, but not in S. Here he says he has saved M.'s life, but she has already heard that from Creon at 183-4, which reduces the impact of Jason's argument on her. In Euripides Jason says he pleaded with Creon to let M. stay (455-8).

495 **mistress**: see on 462.

496 **So Medea accuses me of love?** this is the only time that Jason uses M.'s name, and then only in the third person (cf. on 441). It comes at a crucial point where she has, in effect, accused him of being in love with Creusa, and not just bowing to overwhelming political pressures. His reply effectively admits the charge.

496-503 **And of slaughter ... for your sake**: the issue of Jason's share of guilt for M.'s past crimes was debated by Creon and M. at 262-80, where Creon initiated the argument by claiming that Jason could defend himself with M. out of the way; here M. initiates the exchange.

497 **I ask**: *tandem*, see *OLD* s.v. 1b.

501 **your wife**: M. switches from bitterly calling herself a mistress (495) to calling herself Jason's wife, as she appeals to his former feelings for her.

503 **you should regard ... your sake**: cf. on 280.

504 **A life one ... is unwelcome**: Jason speaks in detached, general terms, as though reluctant to admit that he is ashamed that his own life has been saved through M.'s crimes.

505 **One need not ... to accept**: i.e. if his life is unwelcome, Jason can kill himself. M.'s words bear some resemblance to Stoic ideas about suicide: one of the reasons for which Stoics thought suicide justified was to avoid being coerced into doing or saying something disgraceful (Griffin [1976], 379-80). S. expresses such ideas fairly loosely in his philosophical works: *Epist.* 70.6 *bene autem mori est effugere male uiuendi periculum*, 'to die well is to escape the danger of living badly', cf. 14.2, *Ben.* 1.11.4. But while there is some resemblance to Stoic thinking, M.'s motives for speaking as she does could not be more remote from those of the Stoic. Jason understandably ignores her.

506 **Stop, tame**: *quin ... doma*: *quin* with the imperative expresses an impatient request; the construction is first found in comedy and Cicero's letters, then in Vergil and later poets (see Austin on Verg. *A.* 4.99).

507 **I renounce, disclaim, disown them**: M. has not previously disowned her sons so vehemently in this play. In Euripides she had cursed them early on (116-8).

512 **descendants of ... of Sisyphus**: for M.'s descent from Phoebus, identified with the Sun, see on 28-9. In some versions Sisyphus was founder of Ephyre, the original name of Corinth (see on 105; *OCD*³ on 'Sisyphus'), hence Creon's descendants can be called descendants of Sisyphus (no blood descent is necessarily implied in the tradition, though Schol. Eur. *Med.* 19 may imply that Creon was descended from Bellerophon, grandson of Sisyphus). Sisyphus was one of the arch-sinners of Tartarus, condemned to roll a stone perpetually uphill (see on 746-7): M. therefore uses the contrast between Phoebus, god of light and prophecy, and Sisyphus, to symbolise the contrast between her own children and Creusa's. Disparaging allusion to Sisyphus was a traditional feature of M.'s argument, found in Euripides 404-6 (M. speaking) 'You must not suffer mockery from this Sisyphean marriage of Jason, you who are sprung from a noble father and have Helios for your grandsire' (trans. Kovacs), and Ovid *Epist.* 12.204, *i nunc, Sisyphias, improbe, confer opes*, 'go on, wretched man [M. is addressing Jason], compare your Sisyphian wealth [sc. with what I have done for you].'

516 On this side and on that there is a king ...: referring to Creon and Acastus. The terseness of the Latin is difficult to convey in English, for M. interrupts Jason before he finishes his sentence, which in the Latin has no verb: literally he says 'A king on this side and on that side...', and in his mind the verb might be something like 'threatens', but M. interrupts him in mid-sentence, assumes the verb was going to be 'there is', and caps Jason's point with her own: 'There is something more terrifying ...'

517 Medea. * * * Let us compete: after 'Medea' the text of the manuscripts is corrupt, for *confligere* makes no sense in the context, and does not scan. No correction is certain, but the run of the sense is not affected (see Zwierlein [1986], 148-9).

518 I give in, worn out by sufferings: i.e. because of his past sufferings, Jason has already given up the fight against Creon and Acastus.

519 hazards: *casus*, see on 520.

520 Fortune ... inferior to me: in Stoic philosophy the wise man is superior to fortune, and this can be expressed in the image of him looking down from a high vantage point at fortune, cf. S. *Epist.* 84.13 *Quaecumque uidentur eminere in rebus humanis, quamuis pusilla sint et comparatione humillimorum exstent, per difficiles tamen et arduos tramites adeuntur. Confragosa in fastigium dignitatis uia est; at si conscendere hunc uerticem libet, cui se fortuna summisit, omnia quidem sub te quae pro excelsissimis habentur aspicies, sed tamen uenies ad summa per planum*, 'Whatever seems to stand out in human affairs, even if it is tiny and stands out only in comparison to the most insignificant things, still it is approached by difficult and laborious paths. The road to the pinnacle of honour is a rocky one; but if you want to climb this peak, before which fortune bows low, you will see at your feet all the things that are regarded as most elevated; all the same you will reach the summit by a level route'; *Dial.* 10.5.3. The image of the philosopher looking down on the world is a traditional one, cf. Tarrant on *Thy.* 366; Lucr. 2.7-13; Cic. *Rep.* 1.28, *Tusc.* 3.15. So M.'s claims for her magical powers ape the claims of philosophy. Fortune (*fortuna*) and chance (*casus*) are recurrent themes in the play, and usually on M.'s lips: she acknowledges the power of fortune over worldly power and wealth (221-2, 287), and when it suits her she acknowledges the power of fortune over her own life (219-20, in her appeal to Creon for sympathy, cf. 242; and 568-9, when appealing to the loyal Nurse; cf. Jason in 519); but at 159 she says she will challenge fortune, at 176 she is undeterred by fortune, and here she boldly asserts her superiority. Jason, by contrast, feels at the mercy of fate (see on 431).

521 the nearer enemy: Jason does not regard Creon as an enemy, but M. wants Jason to regard him as the enemy of them both.

522-4 Medea isn't forcing ... free from guilt: i.e. though *she* had to commit crimes when she fled with Jason from Colchis, *he* will not need to commit crimes for her sake. **family slaughter:** Acastus is Jason's cousin (see on 83, 133-4).

526 should Creon ... their forces: at present Acastus is threatening Creon, because he is harbouring M.

528 **Scythians**: see on 212. **Pelasgians**: see on 127. **I shall make them sink**: not a reference to any particular past deed of hers, but a claim based on her supernatural powers in general (cf. on 121). (For the construction, *dare* = 'make, cause to be' with a perfect participle, see *OLD* s.v. *do¹* 24b.)

529 **Mind you don't desire it**: M. insinuates that Jason, having lost the throne of Iolcus, may be marrying Creusa to gain royal power for himself once Creon dies.

531 **Now, highest Jupiter, thunder ...**: several characters in Senecan tragedy pray to Jupiter to strike them down with lightning (Hercules at *Her. F.* 1202-5, Hippolytus at *Phaed.* 671-83, Thyestes at *Thy.* 1077-92). Those prayers are all in immediate response to intense suffering or moral outrage, or both; in our play Jason does not pray in such a fashion at the end, but M. prays at this stage that Jupiter would strike down one or the other of them. It is noteworthy that elsewhere in the play M. does not pray to Jupiter, but to other deities, and especially to underworld powers. This prayer powerfully expresses her feeling that her case is just, and that Jason is equally as guilty as she is, both because he shares the guilt of her crimes against the Colchians and Pelias (e.g. 497-503), and because he has betrayed her (e.g. 7-8, 11-2, 496). Jupiter does not respond to her prayers any more than the Sun satisfied her expectations at 28-36, but her eventual vengeance on Jason could be seen as an indirect response. In Euripides' play M. repeatedly appeals to Zeus (332, 516, 764, 1352).

532 **avenging flames**: i.e. lightning; Ovid puts the same phrase (in the singular) into the mouth of Jupiter at *Met.* 1.230, as he describes how he punished the wicked Lycaon.

535-7 **whichever of us ... cannot err**: compare Thyestes' prayer at *Thy.* 1087-90 and Tarrant's comm.

538-9 **If my father-in-law's ... ask for it** Jason means 'if money or other material assistance can help'; in Euripides Jason had made a similar offer of money, but there, significantly, it was his own money (610-3, cf. 459-64). S.'s Jason is more dependent on Creon.

541-3 **may I simply ... in their embrace**: at 282-3 M. asked Creon to protect the children in Corinth; here, in response to Jason's invitation to ask for some comfort to take with her, she asks him to let her take them into exile. We may well imagine that she does not really expect him to accede to this request, but there is no reason to doubt at this stage the sincerity of her wish to keep her children; cf. 945-6 'sole comfort.'

545 **but fatherly love forbids**: cf. 438 (and for the vocabulary see on 261). In Euripides, M. was allowed to take the children into exile, but decided to ask that they might stay, so that they might be instrumental in killing Creon's daughter (780-6, 939-40). In S., Jason's love for his children helps M. reach her decision to murder them. In the Roman world it was normally expected that the father would keep the children after a divorce (Treggiari [1991], 467), so a Roman audience would not be surprised that Jason wanted to keep his; but his claim that they will benefit from association with children of Creusa's (509) seems naïve, and offends M. (he makes a similar claim in Eur. *Med.* 562-5, 593-7). His declaration of his dependence on them for solace says little for his affection for Creusa, and perhaps supports the impression that he is forced into the marriage; on the other hand, he may be reluctant to acknowledge before M. that he loves Creusa (see on 496).

549-50 **Does he love ... has been exposed**: for the audience this must suggest that she plans to kill her children, but that plan does not take further shape until 921-5 (though see on

808-9 and 848). In fact her words here need mean no more than that she could abscond with them. 550 combines an image from hunting (the phrase 'Good, he's trapped' also occurs at *Tro.* 630) with one from warfare or gladiatorial fights (a gap has appeared where he is not protected by his armour).

551-2 my final instructions: the phrase suggests the final instructions of someone on his or her deathbed, as though M. is about to die (in Senecan tragedy *supremus*, as opposed to *summus*, usually refers to death or funerals, cf. *Oed.* 60, *Phoen.* 487, *Phaed.* 1113, 1273, *Tro.* 374, 761; but *Phaed.* 949 is different). The phrases 'a last embrace' (cf. 848) and 'my closing words' (553) could be taken similarly (as opposed to the latter just meaning 'the last words I say to you now'). Jason may take M.'s words, after her prayer at 531-7, as a sign that she is in a mood to commit suicide. But her next lines (553-7) serve to reassure him.

553 Thank you: literally 'it is pleasing' (*gratum est*), which can mean 'thank you', 'I'm much obliged' (*OLD* s.v. *gratus* 2d). The implication is that Jason has silently indicated his assent.

554-7 if my confused ... be erased: likewise in Euripides (869-70) M. says 'Jason, I ask forgiveness for what I said earlier.'

559 calmness assuages miseries: as elsewhere, an epigram rounds off a scene (see on 159, and Tarrant on *Ag.* p. 160 for the *sententia* or epigram as a marker of the end of a section). The shallow sententiousness of 558-9 shows Jason's lack of understanding of the depth of M.'s feelings—or his unwillingness to face it.

560 He has gone: M. indicates Jason's departure from the stage.

560-2 Do you walk ... vanish from it: i.e., though you may for the moment have forgotten what I have done up till now, you shall never forget what I am going to do.

562 Come on now: *hoc age*, literally 'do this', a colloquial phrase urging someone to concentrate and get on with something that needs doing; cf. 905, 976, *Ben.* 3.36.2; for examples where another imperative follows, as here, cf. Plaut. *Cist.* 693 *Halisca, hoc age, ad terram aspice et despice*, 'Halisca, come on, look at the ground, look down'; S. *Her. O.* 1717; Quint. *Decl.* 349.13. The phrase was also said to magistrates and priests conducting religious rituals, including sacrifices (Plut. *Coriol.* 25.2, *Numa* 14.5; cf. Suet. *Calig.* 58.2, *Galb.* 20.1); there is no good reason to think the religious use was the original or primary one (Professor Gratwick suggests that the religious phrase may originally have been *hoc* (= *huc*) *age*, 'lead (the victim over) here'), but there may be a hint here that M. is embarking on a sacrifice (cf. Fitch on *Her. F.* 104).

565-6 Attack at the point ... fear anything: i.e. do something so terrible that no one will be expecting it.

567 is capable ... is *not* capable: a polar expression, cf. Catul. 76.16 *siue id non pote, siue pote*, 'whether that is not possible, or it is possible' (and Fordyce ad loc.).

568-78 M. now addresses the Nurse, who, we should probably imagine, has remained on stage throughout the dialogue between M. and Jason.

569 varied fortunes: see on 520.

570-4 I have a mantle ... encircle the hair: in S., M. sends three gifts, a mantle, a necklace, and a diadem or tiara (see below on 573). In Euripides there were two gifts, a robe and a crown; in Hyginus (*Fab.* 25) there is just a crown. Apollodorus (1.9.28), though paraphrasing Euripides, omits the crown. S.'s M. outdoes her literary predecessors in generosity, a characteristic piece of Roman literary inflation, and one that may draw on the list of gifts that Aeneas gives Dido in Verg. *A.* 1.647-55, which include a mantle (*palla*), a necklace (*monile*) and a crown (*corona*). Later, however, in S.'s messenger speech, no distinction is made between the individual gifts. The costliness of the gifts is here stressed; for the theme of luxury in the play see on 795-6. On the Colchian origin of the gifts see on 486-7; in Euripides the gifts had a similar origin (954-5 '... the finery that Helios, my father's father, once gave to his offspring').

570 **from the heavenly palace**: this could mean either the palace of the Sun, who gave the mantle (571), or the heavens themselves.

571-2 **as a guarantee of his parentage**: the Sun was father of Aeetes. The origin of the mantle adds to its value, but also reminds of M.'s dangerous and divine origins. Similarly the gifts in Verg. *A.* 1 (see above on 570-4) include clothes that have an uncomfortable history, for they had belonged to Helen.

573-4 **and a gold diadem, embellished ...**: the Latin says just 'and gold, embellished ...'; S. again substitutes general for specific. (Costa rightly argues against thinking that this clause is a further description of the necklace, instead of a third item; for the necklace cannot encircle the hair.)

575 **Let my sons ... to the bride**: in S. the role of the children in taking the gifts is explained in a single line; it can be assumed that the audience will know about their role. In Euripides M. explains at greater length her plan to use the children (780-9).

576 **impregnated by my dreadful arts**: i.e. by magic, or with poisons; another general term instead of a specific one.

577 **Hecate**: see on 6-7. **deadly**: *letifica*, literally 'death-producing', a poetic compound adjective, first found here, and then in Lucan (9.901). The word was perhaps coined by S. himself as a variant on *letifer*, 'death-bearing', which is found in earlier poets from Catullus onwards (see *OLD*).

578 **let altars be ... in the house**: this is her own house (see Introduction §6). On the question of the altar's location, see on 797; on theatrical altars see on 785. S.'s acts regularly end in a line charged with more than one meaning: here M. is talking about an altar for the performance of her magic ritual, but her words also suggest that the death of the bride—she has not here mentioned Creon—will be a human sacrifice; and for the audience the flame also suggests the fire that will burn down Creon's palace.

We may assume that at this point M. and the Nurse leave the stage and go inside (see on 675-6).

THIRD CHORAL ODE: 579-669

This long choral ode may be analysed as follows:

579-94	The anger of an abandoned wife is more powerful than the forces of nature.
595-8	May the conqueror of the sea be spared;
599-602	though Phaethon is not an encouraging precedent.
603-6	It is safer to stick to familiar paths and not transgress the laws of nature.
607-15	The Argonauts have met terrible deaths:
616-24	Tiphys
625-33	Orpheus
634-42	Calais and Zetes, Periclymenus, Hercules

643-51   Ancaeus, Meleager, Hylas
652-67   Idmon, Mopsus, Nauplius, Oileus, Pelias
668-9   Gods, spare the one who was under Pelias's orders.

The Chorus is obviously speaking about M. and Jason at the beginning and end of the ode, yet does not use their names: it speaks of an unnamed wife (581), of the man who subjugated the sea (596) or was under Pelias's orders (669).

This ode picks up many themes from earlier in the play. The second choral ode had spoken of the voyage of the Argo as a transgression, one that had as its reward the golden fleece and M. herself; the third ode follows up with more sombre reflections on the fate that awaited the individual Argonauts—a fate that they pray Jason may avoid. Before the second ode M. had reminded Creon that it was only thanks to her that the Argonauts returned from Colchis alive (225-35); here the frame is larger, and we see that, in the Chorus's view, despite what M. did, the Argonauts were exposed to punishments less readily avoided than the wrath of Aeetes. The comparison of M. to fire, wind, sea and river picks up the themes of M.'s powers over nature and her rivalry of nature.

[On this ode see further Davis (1993), 84-93; Henderson (1983); Biondi (1984), 142-99, gives a full commentary.]

579 **flame**: this picks up the flame of M.'s last sentence in 578, and recalls M.'s own powers over flame (see 36, 121, 148, 167, 387, 466, 468, and later in the play). **wind**: M. is also superior to winds (412, and later at 766), and though Tiphys may have known how to handle the winds (318-28), she is something more powerful.

580 **javelin**: M. can deal with javelins too (469).

581 **a wife, robbed ...**: in Euripides, M. herself describes the anger of a wronged woman: 'Women are timid creatures for the most part, cowards when it comes to fighting and at the sight of steel; but wrong a woman in love and nothing on earth has a heart more murderous' (263-6, trans. Davie). Ovid, *Ars* 2.373-86, describing the anger of a woman who discovers a rival, says it is wilder than a boar or lioness or viper; the woman charges against sword and flame (*in ferrum flammasque ruit*, 379). S. elevates the comparisons in Euripides and Ovid: he does not talk of cowardice or courage in the face of weapons, but the woman's anger is itself compared to weapons; it is not compared to wild animals, but to the most powerful forces of nature. **wedding-torches**: *taedae*, another word for torch (cf. on 37-9 on *pinus*), metonymy for marriage.

583-4 **fog-soaked Auster**: Auster was the south wind, closely associated with rain and fog (cf. Sil. 12.2, winter has a 'foggy brow and Auster-bringing head', *austrifero nebulosam uertice frontem*; Prop. 2.16.56; Ovid *Pont.* 2.1.26).

585 **Hister**: originally the lower Danube, later applied to the whole river. The name in Greek can be etymologised as 'stopper' (in the sense of 'that which brings something to a stop'); S. exploits the paradox of the swift river being so called. Of course M., as a witch, can stop rivers (762-4).

590 **Haemus**: a mountain-range in northern Thrace. There is perhaps a play on the Greek *haima*, 'blood' (see on 720), and *tabuit*, 'melted'; the corresponding noun *tabes* often refers to blood and other fluids oozing from wounds (cf. 641). The imagery has connotations of death.

591 **fire**: i.e. the fire of love; cf. 135-6, 866-9 for the combination of love and anger.

592-3 **it has no ... of death**: the negative in *nec* carries over into the next two clauses, which are linked by *-ue* and *aut*. Cf. *OLD* s.v. *neque* 7f. **tolerate the bridle**: see on 103.

593-4 to go and face the swords: as M. does, cf. 27, 157.

596 he who subjugated the sea: expressed in general terms, but Jason is meant; the Chorus seems reluctant to acknowledge his guilt openly.

597 the lord of the deep: the phrase is similar to that used in line 4, in M.'s prayer, which has effectively pre-empted this prayer. There, too, Neptune's displeasure was suggested, by the verbal echo of line 2 (see on 4). The idea that Neptune was offended by the Argonauts is not found before S.

598 the second kingdom: when Cronus was overthrown, the gods drew lots, and Zeus/Jupiter won first prize, control of the heavens, Poseidon/Neptune second prize, control of the sea, and Hades/Dis, control of the underworld (so Hom. *Il.* 15.187-92); S. has several references to one or more of the three kingdoms, see *Her. F.* 599, 833, *Phaed.* 904, 1212, *Tro.* 344-6, 879-80.

599-600 that young man: Phaethon, see on 32-6. He also undertook a journey that he should not have, he was punished for it, and a similar fate threatens the Argonauts. By contrast M. traditionally drives a chariot of the Sun, but without the disaster that Phaethon caused—another example of her supernatural powers. **forgetful of the course his father ran:** literally 'forgetful of his father's turning-post', treating the course of the Sun's chariot as a race-course (just as in 30), where the chariots turn at a turning-post.

601-2 he himself fell victim to the fires: the audience may anticipate that M. will cause the palace to go up in flames, though without suffering harm herself (see on 885-7 for earlier versions in which the palace went up in flames).

603-4 The familiar road ... our predecessors: the Chorus, with its advice to stick to the familiar and the safe, sounds like the ordinary man or woman, advocating an unambitious life; see 331-4. We have here a variant on the common contrast between the tranquil life of the humble and unambitious and the more precarious existence of the powerful and ambitious, a contrast regularly found in Senecan tragedy, particularly in the choral odes, and sometimes in his prose works; see Tarrant on *Thy.* 391-403, 446-70; Fitch on *Her. F.* 196-201; Tarrant on *Ag.* 57-107 (especially p. 183); S. *Epist.* 90.41. Such thoughts go back to Greek tragedy, for instance the Nurse at Eur. *Med.* 122-30: 'It is better to be accustomed to live on terms of equality. At any rate, may I be able to grow old in modest state and with security. For modest fortune has a name that is fairest on the tongue, etc.' (trans. Kovacs). **costs ... dear:** *constitit* is a gnomic perfect; see on 199-200. *magno* is ablative of price.

605-6 and do not ... break: *rumpe nec: nec* is postponed to second word, and the prohibition, following the positive command in the previous line, is expressed by *nec* with the present imperative. S. in the tragedies never uses the normal prosaic *noli(te)* plus infinitive for prohibitions, but *ne* (or *nec*) plus present imperative (as at 1016 *ne propera*). Cf. Tarrant on *Ag.* 796; H-Sz 340. **violent man:** this could be addressed, together with the preceding line, to Phaethon, or it could be a generic singular for humankind in general. **the sacred laws of the universe:** see on 335. *sacro* and *sanctus* go together; normally *sacrosanctus* is printed as a single word, so this is an example of tmesis, when a compound word is divided with another word or words intervening; cf. Plin. *Nat.* 7.143 *sacroque sanctum*, and for other examples of tmesis in poetry e.g. Verg. *G.* 3.381 *septem subiecta trioni*, *A.* 10.794 *inque ligatus*, and Housman on Manil. 1.355.

607-67   The Chorus catalogues the fates of various Argonauts who died either during the voyage or after they returned home to Greece. Apollonius had narrated the fates of some of these (Tiphys, see below on 617; Calais and Zetes, see on 634; Hylas, see on 647-9; Idmon, see on 652-3; Mopsus, see on 654-5); Hyginus (*Fab.* 14.25-9) catalogues those who died on the outward journey (Hylas, Polyphemus, Tiphys, Idmon, Butes) and the return journey (Eurybates, Canthus, Mopsus). S.'s catalogue does not correspond exactly to either of these. There were various catalogues of the Argonauts, sometimes given at the start of accounts of the voyage (Pi. *Pyth.* 4.169-83; Ap. Rh. 1.23-227, listing 53 men; V. Fl. 1.353-486; Orph. *Arg.* 129-231), or in handbooks (Apollod. 1.9.16; Hyg. *Fab.* 14; POxy 53.3702 fr. 2; Gantz [1993], 343-5; *LIMC* 2.1, 597-8). On poetic catalogues in general see introductory comm. on 670-848.

608-9 Pelion: see on 336. **its sacred grove:** woods are sacred in Roman religion as well as in mythology, and inscriptions survive prescribing punishments for anyone who desecrated sacred woods (see Wissowa [1912], 469-70). At the start of Euripides' *Medea* the Nurse regrets the felling of the trees on Pelion (see on 336).

610   the wandering rocks: see on 342-6.

612   the barbarian shore: for Colchis as barbarian see on 127. Here the emphasis may be on geographical remoteness as much as moral connotations, but it is incongruous that such a long and arduous journey should be directed towards a barbarian land.

617 Tiphys: see on 2-3. **first:** with the manuscript text and this punctuation (adopted by Zwierlein in the corrected edition of the OCT) there is an ellipse in the thought: 'Tiphys first <suffered punishment when he died and> handed the steering over ...' This seems acceptable. **the tamer of the deep:** echoing 597 'lord of the deep', and implying Tiphys' impious rivalry and infringement of Neptune's role (the echo is closer in Latin: 'tamer' is *dominator*, 'lord' is *dominus*, the words being etymologically related; compare the similar word play in lines 2 and 4). Tiphys' death and burial is narrated in Ap. Rh. 2.851-7; cf. Hyg. *Fab.* 14.26.

618   handed the steering on to an untutored master: S. stresses that there was nobody else to match Tiphys as steersman. Apollonius' account is less bleak: at first the Argonauts despair of getting home with Tiphys dead (2.859-63), but several Argonauts volunteer to steer the ship, and Ancaeus, who is said to be very skilled at steering (867-8), is selected (864-98; cf. Hyg. *Fab.* 14.26, and below on 643-4). Later, in Valerius Flaccus (5.63-6), Erginus is the successful contender (as in Herodorus, *FGH*31F55). **the steering:** i.e. the rudder, abstract for concrete.

619-20 his father's kingdom: see on 622.

621   among unknown shades: i.e. he is buried among strangers (whose shades or spirits are assumed to inhabit the vicinity of their graves).

622   Aulis remembers its lost king: Tiphys came from Boeotia, but there were different accounts of his exact home region (see Schol. Ap. Rh. 1.105): Potniae according to Pherecydes (*FGH*3F107), Siphae according to Apollonius (1.105; Orph. *Arg.* 122-4), or Thespiae, of which Siphae was a deme (V. Fl. 1.124, 2.368, 5.44; Orph. *Arg.* ibid.). He is not elsewhere said to have been king of Aulis, which is the natural interpretation of S.'s words, and may reflect an otherwise unattested tradition; but it is not necessarily implied by S.'s words, for all the Argonauts were of kingly family (they are collectively called kings at 243, 367, 455), and Aulis, as the famous port of Boeotia in mythology, would mourn any Boeotian who was a prominent sailor.

623-4 and confines ... standing still: the Chorus here speaks in general terms of Aulis delaying ships, but clearly S. is forging a causal link between the voyage of the Argo and the Trojan war. The Greek fleet prepared against Troy was delayed at Aulis by lack of winds, until Agamemnon sacrificed his daughter Iphigenia. For Roman authors the standard story was that Artemis delayed the fleet and demanded the sacrifice because of her anger at Agamemnon—for which various explanations were given; see OCD^3 on 'Iphigenia'. The suggestion that Aulis' behaviour was affected by grief for Tiphys is likely to be an invention, and a very Senecan one, linking one famous mythological story to another.

625 The man born of the tuneful Camena: Orpheus (see on 227-9), son of the Muse Calliope. The Camenae (see OCD^3) were Roman goddesses who were identified with the Greek Muses from Livius Andronicus onwards. The equivalence was so well-established by S.'s time that it is unlikely to have a distinctively Roman resonance here.

627 torrents stopped, winds fell silent: Orpheus can control nature by his singing, somewhat as M. can by her magic (cf. 405, 762-70); but his benign control of nature was ultimately inadequate, and he died. (By S.'s time Orpheus himself was associated with magic: there were magical works that circulated under his name, for example, the one quoted at *PGM* XIII.933-46.)

630-1 that man lay ... the grim Hebrus: Orpheus was (in most versions) torn apart by the women of Thrace. Many different motives were ascribed to them, none related to the voyage of the Argo. Usually they are said to have thrown all the pieces into the river Hebrus, but S. follows a version that only the head was thrown in, and the rest was left scattered over the countryside (so Verg. *G.* 4.522; Ovid *Met.* 11.50; compare the deaths of Pentheus or Hippolytus or Phaethon). The head was generally said to have floated separately, reaching Lesbos in some versions. (See Verg. *G.* 4.520-7; Ovid *Met.* 11.1-66; OCD^3 on 'Orpheus'.)

632-3 he reached the Styx ... prospect of return: alluding to Orpheus' previous journey to the underworld to recover the dead Eurydice: he had been allowed to take her back to the upper world, but when he broke the condition that he must not turn round and look at her, he lost her for ever (Verg. *G.* 4.464-506; Ovid *Met.* 10.11-77; S. *Her. F.* 569-89, *Her. O.* 1061-89). 'Tartarus' is a poetic name for the underworld (cf. 742), and the Styx is one of the rivers of the underworld (cf. on 742, 804-5).

634 Alcides: Hercules is regularly one of the Argonauts from Pindar onwards (*Pyth.* 4.171-2), though some said that he never boarded the ship because he was too heavy for it (Pherecydes *FGH*3F111; Antimachus fr. 58; Apollod. 1.9.19). 'Alcides' was taken to mean 'descendant of Alcaeus', the father of Amphitryon, Hercules' mortal father; it was applied to Amphitryon in Hesiod (*Scut.* 112), and to Hercules himself in Callimachus (*Hy.* 3.145) and later writers. There were rival explanations of the name: some said that Hercules himself was originally called Alcaeus (S. E. *M.* 9.36; Schol. Hom.*Il.* 14.324; D. S. 4.10.1) or Alcides (Apollod. 2.4.12), and only later acquired the name Hercules (Schol. Pi. *Ol.* 6.115b). **struck down the sons of Aquilo:** Aquilo is the Latin equivalent of Boreas, the north wind, whose sons were Calais and Zetes (see on 231). S. follows the version that Hercules killed them after the funeral games of Pelias because they had persuaded the Argonauts to leave him behind when he went off on a prolonged search for Hylas (cf. 647-9; Ap. Rh. 1.1298-1308).

635-6 he slew the man ... innumerable shapes: Periclymenus from Pylos; he was son of Neleus, son of Neptune, and was able to change himself into any shape. When Hercules attacked Pylos, he changed into a bee (or in other versions an eagle), but Hercules saw through the disguise and killed him (cf. Bömer on Ovid *Met.* 12.556-76; Apollod. 1.9.9). Here S. calls Neptune his father, whereas elsewhere he is his grandfather, and the apparent discrepancy has provoked discussion. One view is that S. has simply made a mistake, confusing the Argonaut Periclymenus with another Periclymenus, son of Neptune, and one of the seven defenders of Thebes (Eur. *Phoen.* 1156-7); but the mythological tradition was not uniform in distinguishing the two of them (see Gantz [1993], 184-5 with n. 23; *LIMC* 7.1, 322-3), and S. may follow a tradition that identified them.

637 after making peace on land and sea: literally just 'after peace on...'; for such expressions see Nisbet and Hubbard on Hor. *Carm.* 1.18.5 *post uina*, 'after the drinking of wine', and cf. above on 95. For Hercules as peace-maker in S., cf. *Her. F.* 250, 882-90.

638 after opening ... cruel Dis: on Dis, see on 11, 740-1. Hercules went down to the underworld to capture Cerberus, the three-headed guard-dog of Hades.

639-42 he himself lay ... from his bride: the death of Hercules took place on mount Oeta in southern Thessaly. His wife Deianira had given him a tunic dipped in what she believed was a love potion, but was in fact a poison (see on 641). Hercules could not remove the tunic, and the agony was so great that he built a funeral pyre on top of Oeta and threw himself onto it to end the pain. (Cf. Soph. *Trach.*; Ovid *Met.* 9.103-272; *Her. O.*; Gantz [1993], 457-63.) **on blazing Oeta**: S. writes as though the whole mountain were blazing; cf. Stat. *Theb.* 12.67 *laetus in accensa iacuit Tirynthius Oeta*, 'the Tirynthian hero (Hercules) gladly lay on lighted Oeta.'

641 by the infection of the twin gore: the poison was given to Deianira by Nessus, a centaur—half-horse, half-man—and ferryman on the river Evenus. When he tried to rape Deianira, Hercules shot him, but as he died Nessus told Deianira to take some of his blood (see 775-6), saying it would be a love-potion. The gore was 'twin' because Nessus' blood was contaminated with the blood of the Lernaean Hydra, another of Hercules' victims (see on 701-2), which Hercules used to poison his arrows (see e.g. Soph. *Trach.* 569-77; Ovid *Met.* 9.129-33; Apollod. 2.5.2). The death of Hercules anticipates the death of Creusa, who will also put on a robe that is impregnated with poison.

643-4 The violent, bristly ... with its impact: Ancaeus, an Arcadian, was killed in the hunt of the Calydonian boar (Bacchyl. *Ode* 5.115-20; Ovid *Met.* 8.315, 391-402; Gantz [1993], 332-3). In Apollonius there are two Argonauts called Ancaeus, this one from Arcadia, son of Lycurgus (1.163-5), the other one son of Poseidon (1.185-9), and Tiphys' successor as steersman (see on 618). **bristly**: *saetiger*, a poetic compound, earlier found only in Ovid's narrative of the hunting of the Calydonian boar, *Met.* 8.376. **struck down**: picking up 634 in anaphora (see on 117); in Latin *strauit* is the first word of each sentence.

644-6 Impious man ... your mother's brother ... your enraged mother: the impious man is Meleager. After killing the Calydonian boar, Meleager gave the spoils to Atalanta, who had inflicted the first wound. This enraged his mother's brothers, who said they should have had the spoils if Meleager did not want them; a dispute arose, leading to a fight in which Meleager killed them. His mother, Althaea, then caused his death by burning a magic log on whose preservation his life depended. The principal manuscripts here make Meleager kill just one brother, and they should be followed, for Homer *Il.* 9.567 refers to 'the death of a brother' (κασιγνήτοιο φόνοιο; though a scholiast ad loc. took this to mean 'brotherly death', leaving the number of brothers open); later versions (Bacchyl. 5.127-9; Ovid *Met.* 8.432-44; Paus. 8.45.6; Apollod. 1.8.2-3) mention two brothers, and later manuscripts here read 'brothers' (*fratres*), probably a deliberate attempt to bring S. into line with the usual version. Meleager and Althaea here both anticipate M.'s murders of her relatives, as the wording emphasises: the imagery of sacrifice is picked up later (1005 uses the same verb *mactare*, 'sacrifice'), and M. is another 'enraged mother' who kills her own offspring. (See *OCD*³ on 'Meleager'.)

647-9 but what crime ... safe waters: Hylas, a handsome young man with whom Hercules was in love, accompanied him on the Argo. When Hylas was sent to fetch water from a spring, the Nymphs seized him. Hercules, distraught, went off in search of him, and took so long that, on the suggestion of the sons of Boreas, the Argonauts sailed on and left him behind. (See on 634; *OCD*³ on 'Hylas'; Ap. Rh. 1.1207-1357; Theocr. 13.) **boy ... boy:** *puer* is repeated at the same position in successive lines. The repetition of the name *Hylas* in successive lines occurs in Verg. *Ecl.* 6.43-4, Prop. 1.20.48-52 (and later, see V. Fl. 3.183-4, 596); S., without using the proper name, achieves a similar pathos by the repetition of 'boy'.

650-1 Go on, then, ... to be frightened of: i.e. there is no need to sail the high seas in order to place yourself in danger—a spring (such as the one where Hylas died) can be quite dangerous enough. For this use of the imperative *i* or *ite* (often *i(te) nunc*) ironically to make an inappropriate suggestion, cf. 197, 1007, *OLD* s.v. *eo*¹ 10b. (*fonte timendo* is an ablative absolute, with the participle of 'to be' understood, and the gerundive *timendo* as complement.)

652-3 Idmon ... sands of Libya: Idmon was the seer on the Argo (already in Pherecydes *FGH*3F108 and Carcinus (?) *Naupactia* fr. 6 Kinkel = fr. 5 Davies); he joined the ship despite knowing that he would die (Ap. Rh. 1.139-145)—in fact in Greek his name means 'knowing' (cf. Schol. Ap. Rh. 1.139). There were various accounts of his death. In Apollonius he is killed by a boar in the land of the Mariandyni on the way to Colchis (2.815-34, cf. Apollod. 1.9.23, Hyg. *Fab.* 18), whereas in S. he is killed by a snake on the sands of Libya; in V. Fl. 5.2-3 he dies of illness on the way to Colchis. It has been suggested either that S. has confused him with Mopsus who *was* killed by a snake in Libya (see on 654-5; Leo I.24-5), or that S. deliberately changes the nature of his death to avoid confusion with the Calydonian boar (Biondi [1984], 187-8; Henderson [1983], 107). P. Koetschau, *Philologus* 61 (1902), 137-8, proposed emending 'Libyan' to 'Lycian' (*Lyciis*), for Idmon's death is near the river Lycus in Apollonius; other emendations are reviewed by Leo loc. cit. However, one should be cautious about talking of confusion or alteration, when the ancient tradition was so fluid (cf. on 654-5): as regards the timing of his death, there were accounts in which Idmon was still alive when the expedition reached Colchis (cf. Eumelus fr. 4 Davies; Carcinus loc. cit.), so S. may follow such a tradition which placed his death on the return journey.

654-5 A true prophet ... from Thebes: Mopsus was another Argonaut with prophetic powers, able to interpret bird omens (Ap. Rh. 1.65-6; cf. Pi. *Pyth.* 4.191), who was killed by a snake in Libya, where the Argo had been driven off-course by a storm (Ap. Rh. 4.1502-36, cf. 1.79-85). Apollonius (4.1503-4) said that his prophecies could not save him, and S. makes him actually prophesy falsely about himself. In Apollonius, Mopsus is not from Thebes, and it is commonly suggested that S. has confused a second Mopsus, son of Manto, from Thebes; but the ancient tradition is initially hazy about whether there is one Mopsus or more than one, and S. may be following some unifying version (see *OCD*[3] on 'Mopsus'; *LIMC* 6.1, 650-4, 6.2, 381-2).

656 If he foretold the future truly: this reference to prophecies by Mopsus makes an elegant transition from misfortunes that are already in the past as the Chorus speaks, to those that still lie in the future (Zwierlein [1978b], 149).

657 Thetis' husband will wander in exile: Peleus, who suffered exile several times: he and his brother Telamon were exiled from Aegina after the death of Phocus, his half-brother; he was exiled from Phthia after accidentally killing Eurytion, his father-in-law, in the Calydonian boar-hunt (both these occurred before the events of this play); and later he was exiled by Acastus or his sons. For Peleus as an archetypal exile, see Hor. *Ars* 96 *Telephus et Peleus ... pauper et exsul*, 'Telephus and Peleus ... poor and exiled' (where probably Telephus is poor and Peleus exiled); *OCD*[3] on 'Peleus'.

657-62 The text, following Zwierlein, adopts Peiper's transposition of lines, and assumes a half line is omitted by the manuscripts at 660a, in order to continue the stanzaic structure of lines 607-651. The effect of the transposition is to put the lines about Ajax before the lines about Nauplius. In 660a Zwierlein's supplement is adopted, to show the kind of sense required. For full discussion of the text see Zwierlein (1978b), 148-51.

661, 660a, 660b killed by thunderbolt ... father's crime: Oileus from Locri was an Argonaut, and his son was Ajax, know as 'lesser' Ajax, to distinguish him from 'great' Ajax the son of Telamon, from Salamis (see *OCD*[3] on 'Aias' (1) and (2)). Both Ajaxes fought in the Trojan war, where the lesser offended Athena, who ensured that as the Greek fleet sailed home from Troy it was struck by a storm in which Ajax died—hit by a thunderbolt sent by Athena, in a version to which S. here alludes (see the detailed narrative in *Ag.* 528-56; cf. Verg. *A.* 1.39-45; contrast Hom. *Od.* 4.499-511). S. characteristically makes the death of Ajax a punishment not only for his own sacrilege but also for his father's involvement with the Argonauts. If S. knows the idea found later in Valerius Flaccus (1.372-3) that Oileus survived and grieved over his son's death, then the death is effectively a punishment for the father. (This text and interpretation adopts Heinsius' conjecture *Oilei* for *Oileus*. See Zwierlein [1978b], 151.)

658-9 as he plans ... into the deep: Nauplius (see *OCD*[3] s.v.), another Argonaut (Ap. Rh. 1.133-8), was father of Palamedes. The son went with the Greek expedition to Troy, and was killed by the Greeks on a charge of treachery. To avenge his son's death, when the Greek fleet returned, Nauplius lured it onto rocks at the southern end of Euboea by lighting a huge fire, which the Greeks took as a sign that it was a harbour (see Apollod. *Epit.* 6.7-11 and Frazer's notes). S. here seems to say that Nauplius died before or while the fleet was wrecked; no other account links Nauplius' own death to that of the Greeks, although Apollod. 2.1.5 says that he died by the same sort of death he inflicted on others, whom he used to lure to their deaths with false beacons (implying that he did this more than once). In S. the 'deceptive beacon', literally 'deceptive fire', foreshadows M.'s burning of the palace. **Argos**: the town of Argos stands for the whole of Greece, just as the Argives are often the Greeks (see *OLD* on *Argiuus* 2).

662-3 to redeem ... your own soul: Alcestis, one of the daughters of Pelias (the only one who did not participate in his killing), married Admetus, king of Pherae in Thessaly, who was an Argonaut. Alcestis was the only person willing to die in her husband's place (see *OCD*³ on 'Alcestis'). Similarly Creusa will die—though unwittingly— because of her husband; just as in the ode Alcestis' death is treated as a punishment for Admetus, so Creusa's death will be a punishment for Jason.

664-7 Even the man ... confined waves: after the long list of Argonauts, the Chorus concludes with Pelias, who sent Jason to get the golden fleece (see on 133-4).

666-7 [Pelias scorched ... cauldron] ... confined waves: in order to restore the stanzaic structure of lines 652-69, it is necessary not only to transpose some lines (see on 657-62 above), but also to delete one line. There have been various suggestions about which line to delete (including 656 and 657), but here Peiper's deletion of 666, accepted by Zwierlein, is adopted. Lines 666 and 667 both describe the death of Pelias, chopped into pieces and boiled in a pot, but 666 does so in clear, simple terms, using Pelias' name (which is not needed after his identification by the description in lines 664-5), whereas 667 refers to his death in oblique terms. So 666 looks like an explanatory insertion, and is a prime candidate for deletion. 667, with the grotesque 'tossing to and fro' of the pieces in 'the confined waves' of the pot, draws a parallel between Pelias' fate and the sailing of the Argo.

668-9 You have now ... under orders: the Chorus's final prayer for Jason seeks to deflect blame and punishment from him. It suits the Chorus's argument to present Jason as acting under orders, but at the same time it conveys a picture of a passive, weak figure. For the plea that Jason acted under compulsion see Ap. Rh. 3.388-90; V. Fl. 5.480-90; in this play M. at one stage regards him as acting under duress (137-49), and he argues that he is compelled by circumstances to abandon her (431-43). For the general idea compare S. *Tro.* 870-1 (Helen speaking): *quid iussa cessas agere? ad auctorem redit / sceleris coacti culpa*, 'Why delay carrying out your orders? The guilt of an enforced crime rebounds on its initiator.'

ACT FOUR: 670-848

This act describes the magical rituals by means of which M. prepares the poisoned gifts for Creusa. First there is a speech from the Nurse (670-739), then a long polymetric lyric song by M. (740-842), at the end of which M., changing to dialogue metre (843-8), summons her sons and gives them the gifts to take to the bride.

The Nurse first appears on her own, and launches into a long description of M.'s preparations, including a report of some of M.'s words in direct speech (see on 670-739 for an analysis). At 738-9 she hears M. approaching, then at 740 M. herself comes on stage and delivers her long magical song (740-848). If we imagine the play being staged, M.'s entry at this point is a vivid dramatic surprise. The audience would be used to long messenger speeches reporting what has happened indoors: a good parallel is the long scene in S.'s *Thyestes* where the messenger describes how Atreus has murdered and cooked Thyestes' sons (623-788). In this act the Nurse appears to be reporting in a similar way on the actions M. has performed indoors, when suddenly M. is heard and then seen coming on stage herself.

Rosenmeyer (1993), 239-40, argues that the things described by the Nurse could not be acted on stage, and are described as the Nurse, on stage, watches them happening off stage out of the audience's sight. Certainly some of the actions described in the Nurse's speech could not have been performed on stage in anything like a realistic fashion: snakes are summoned from remote regions of the earth, and from the heavens (680-704). The actions performed after M. appears are more manageable on stage: at 771-2 she has a garland wreathed in snakes for Hecate, at 773-84 she lists poisonous ingredients of her mixture, and at 785-6 acknowledges the favourable crackling of the fire on the altar; she then describes the lurid appearance of the moon, then waves a torch, a Stygian branch, and, finally and most dramatically, cuts her arm and sheds her own blood (787-811). At 817-42 a prayer accomplishes the poisoning of the robe and gifts. At 843-8 the sons are summoned to take them.

The speeches of the Nurse and M. allow S. to offer long lists or catalogues—of snakes, herbs, and so on. Such catalogues were a popular feature of poetry from Homer onwards, and were much favoured by S. (see Canter [1925], 74-6; Rosenmeyer [1989], 160-77; above on 607-67). Despite the need for haste, if she is to complete her business by the end of her day's grace (cf. 296-7), M. takes her time and performs her rituals thoroughly.

Magical practices were a popular literary theme from Homer onwards; in the *Odyssey*, for example, Circe changes Odysseus' companions into pigs. In Euripides the human aspect of M. is emphasised, and her magical powers are relatively inconspicuous, but in Apollonius her magical activities are prominent (3.844-68, 1026-51, etc.). In Augustan poetry magic is found, for instance, in Vergil's *Eclogues* and Horace's *Epodes*, and M. has a long magic scene in Ovid (*Met.* 7.179-293). In the later years of S.'s life his nephew Lucan included a lengthy magic scene in his epic (6.413-830).

Magic was not just a feature of literary tradition associated with M. and others, but had a place in real life in the Greek and Roman worlds (see Graf [1997b]). At Rome the 5th century B.C. law-code of the Twelve Tables prohibited using songs (or chants) to harm a neighbour's crops. In the early empire, accusations of magic several times featured in the charges brought against prominent public figures. For instance, magical substances were supposed to have been found in the house where Germanicus died (Tac. *Ann.* 2.69); and in the 2nd century A.D. Apuleius was accused of magic (Apul. *Apol.*). Magic was especially associated with Persia and with Egypt (cf. the account in Plin. *Nat.* 30.1-13, written in the 70s A.D.), and is known to us especially from the magical papyri from Egypt. Most of these are later than the first century A.D., and do not necessarily represent closely what was happening in other parts of the empire; but there are *defixiones* (curse tablets) from various parts of the Greek and Roman world, dating from the 5th century B.C. to late antiquity. In the commentary some parallels to the magical papyri and *defixiones* are noted. For there is a genuine question whether S.'s portrayal of magic in the play is based entirely on the literary tradition, or also draws on knowledge of contemporary practice. Since he spent some years in Egypt as a young man convalescing, and since he wrote a work, now lost, on the geography and religion of the Egyptians (*de situ et sacris Aegyptiorum*, fr. 12 Haase, T19 Vottero, ap. Serv. *A.* 6.154), it is likely he knew something about magic in Egypt, for it had a role in traditional Egyptian religion. But Egypt does not feature in the geographical catalogues in this act.

670-739 The Nurse describes M.'s magical preparations in the following stages: M. gets out her magical paraphernalia and makes general preparations for the ritual (677-80); she summons various snakes (681-90), and the Nurse reports in direct speech a long, prayer-like invocation of famous mythological snakes (690-704); then M. gathers all kinds of plant and herb (705-30); having gathered the herbs, squeezed the venom from the snakes, and included other magical birds (731-6), she speaks her magical formulae (737-8). At 738-9 the Nurse hears M. approaching.

670 The first foot is a rare proceleusmatic, four short syllables (*pauet ani-*), which may reflect the Nurse's panic.

673 **and attacking the gods:** for M.'s attacks on the gods see 167, 271, 424. Magic is an attack on the gods of the upper world because it invokes the underworld powers, and because the magician tries to control the gods directly. The last idea, although it has been prominent in some modern approaches to magic, is not frequent in antiquity, but one may compare what Pliny says of Nero, that in his fascination with magic he 'yearned to command the gods' (*Nat.* 30.14 *imperare dis concupiuit*); Lucan writes that in Thessaly *plurima surgunt / uim factura deis*, 'many plants grow that will do violence to the gods', and the witches' voices *uerba ... ad inuitum perfert cogentia numen*, 'cause coercing words to reach the unwilling deity' (6.440-1, 446). Such a view of magic as compelling or doing violence to the gods is not common in magical documents, but for an example of a demon being threatened with punishment from a more powerful god, see *PGM* XII.140-3 'If you (the demon) disobey me and don't go to him, <the name of the human target is inserted here>, I will tell the great god, and after he has speared you through, he will chop you up into pieces and feed your members to the mangy dog who lies among the dungheaps. For this reason, listen to me immediately, immediately; quickly, quickly, so I won't have to tell you again' (Betz [1992], 158). But M. herself attacks the gods directly, not through the agency of other gods.

674 **dragging down the heavens:** one of the powers traditionally attributed to witches was the ability to pull down the moon (since Aristoph. *Clouds* 749-52; Plato *Gorg.* 513a; cf. D. E. Hill, *RhM* 116 [1973], 221-38); they could also make the sun disappear (Hippocr. *On the sacred disease* 4; Ovid *Epist.* 6.86, *Rem.* 256, *Met.* 7.208-9), and the stars too (Ap. Rh. 3.528-33; Hor. *Epod.* 5.45-6; cf. Verg. *A.* 4.489); S. extends this to pulling down the heavens. For M.'s power over the heavens cf. 28.

674-5 The alliteration of *m* is striking, reinforcing the repetition of *maius*, 'greater', and the link between M.'s name and *monstrum*, 'horror' or 'portent' (originally a religious term for an unnatural event or object that indicates the hostility of the gods). See Segal (1982).

675-6 **she has gone ... deathly sanctum:** it is not clear whether her departure to her 'sanctum' refers just to her going off stage into her house at 578, or to a specific place where she went subsequently to perform her rituals (presumably in any case it was somewhere within her house).

677 **unleashes ... brings:** here, and in the rest of her speech, the Nurse uses the present tense to describe all M.'s actions. This may be the vivid present describing past events, for which a past tense sounds more natural in English; but it might be a genuine present tense, as the Nurse describes what she sees happening while she speaks; see introductory note to 670-848.

678-9 deploy all her host: perhaps a military image. **mysterious, secret, hidden things**: for the string of adjectives (here used as nouns) in asyndeton, see on 20-1.

680   with her left hand: the ill-omened hand, and appropriate for magic, because social and religious convention normally prescribed use of the right hand, which was more honourable than the left (cf. Plin. *Nat.* 33.13); similarly Tiresias uses his left hand in the necromancy scene of S.'s *Oed.*, 566-7; cf. Lucan 6.563; Stat. *Theb.* 4.502. The left hand was not used in Roman religion (Latte [1967], 376), and it was associated with thieving (Plaut. *Pers.* 226; Ovid *Met.* 13.111; Catul. 12.1). It was used for sinister actions such as removing a snake's heart (Plin. *Nat.* 30.100, cf. 28.33), and in the magical papyri see *PGM* XXXVI.256-7 'Taking a three-cornered sherd from the fork of a road—pick it up with your left hand—...' (Betz [1992], 275).

681   plagues: the word can mean any source of death and destruction—illness, natural disaster, animal or human being. Here it is as yet non-specific, like 'horrors' in 684; at 720 it refers to harmful herbs.

682-3 Libya ... Taurus: extremes of hot and cold climate, symbolising M.'s universal power. The Taurus mountain range stretches for nearly 500 km in south-east Asia Minor, south-central modern Turkey, and rises to a height of 3910 metres. Taurus in Latin means 'bull', and that sense may be felt. Libya abounded in snakes that reputedly grew from the drops of blood that fell there from the Gorgon's head (Ap. Rh. 4.1513-7; Ovid *Met.* 4.614-20 and Bömer's comm.; Lucan 9.619-99). **Arctic**: Greek *arktikos* is the adjective from *arktos*, 'bear', referring to the northern polar constellations (see on 404-5). Latin *arctous* is a rare, poetic form, first found in Senecan tragedy; Latin *arcticus* is more prosaic, but rare, the usual adjective being *septentrionalis*.

684   Drawn by her Magic chants: this is the only occurrence in the play of the Latin word *magicus* or related words; the adjective is found elsewhere in the Senecan corpus at *Oed.* 561 and *Her. O.* 452. In Latin the adjective always denotes magical ritual, usually sinister, and the derivation of the word from Magi, Persian priests, was well known; so the adjective has been given a capital letter in the translation. S.'s M. draws all the snakes to her by means of her magic chants, and gives a further demonstration of her magical prowess. The power to charm, control, or destroy snakes was a feature of magic (Verg. *Ecl.* 8.71; *PGM* XIII.261-5), and was particularly associated with the Marsi tribe in Italy, the Psylli of north Africa, and the family of Ophiogeneis in the Bosporus (see Dench [1995], 154-74; O. Phillips in Meyer and Mirecki [1995], 391-400; A.-M. Tupet, *Aufstieg und Niedergang der römischen Welt* II.16.3, 2591-2675, at 2617-26). Snakes or snake-venom are ingredients in magic in Roman poetry (Hor. *Epod.* 3.6, 5.15; Prop. 3.6.28; Lucan 6.679), but not in papyri or curse tablets, though for pictures of snakes on curse-tablets cf. Gager (1992), 53-4, 68-9.

685   a scaly horde: in poetry, and sometimes prose, snakes are regularly, though incorrectly, said to have scales (like fish); cf. 1023, and e.g. Acc. *trag.* 517-8 Ribbeck, 513 Warmington; Verg. *G.* 2.154, 3.426. The adjective *squamifer*, 'scaly', is a poetic compound, first found here, and then in Lucan 9.709 (whereas *squamiger* is found from Cicero's poetry and Lucretius onwards, see *OLD*—S. has a preference for adjectives in *-fer* over adjectives in *-ger*, but at 1023 below *squamosus* is used, a word first found in Plautus, see *OLD* s.v.).

687   three-forked tongue: snakes in Latin poetry from Vergil onwards (*G.* 3.439, *A.* 2.475) regularly have three-forked tongues; see Bömer on Ovid *Met.* 3.34. In Plautus (*As.* 695) and occasionally elsewhere they have an anatomically correct two-forked tongue. 'three-forked' is another poetic compound adjective, first found in Ovid (*Met.* 2.325, of the flame from a thunderbolt).

688   it may bring death: literally 'it may come death-bringing', another compound adjective (*mortifera*), but this one is equally at home in S.'s prose and verse (and in Cicero's prose, e.g. *Sull.* 73, *Sest.* 44).

690-704   Reported direct speech is a regular feature of S.'s dramas, in messenger speeches and elsewhere, but the Nurse's repetition of M.'s words here is strikingly unusual, in that M. herself appears on stage shortly afterwards (see on 670-848). Some of the longer examples of reported direct speech in S. include e.g. *Tro.* 452-6 (there at 452 is the only other occurrence of *inquit* in Senecan tragedy, outside *Her. O.*); *Ag.* 517-26, 545-52, *Her. F.* 582-7, *Oed.* 626-58, 926-34, 936-57, 975-7. On Greek tragedy see Bers (1997).

691   the lowest earth: in the ancient geocentric cosmos the earth was called the lowest part of the universe (because heavy things fall down to earth), and the heavens were the highest (see *TLL* 7.1.1397.15-22; Pease on Cic. *N.D.* 1.103).

692   Now, now: the same iteration at 949, 982 (cf. on 13; there the Latin is *nunc, nunc*, here it is *iam iam*—actually a conjecture by Gronovius, see the apparatus).

694-704   In the rest of the speech M. summons various supernatural snakes. Servius on Verg. *G.* 1.205 says that there are three serpent-constellations in the sky: Draco; Serpens, the snake held by Ophiuchus; and Hydra. All three are summoned by M., and so are other mythological serpents: Python, killed by Apollo and cremated or buried, and the snake that guarded the golden fleece. The form of the speech resembles that of a cletic hymn, i.e. a hymn summoning a deity to be present, with the snakes as the deities; the size and power of the snakes enhance M.'s power. On cletic hymns see Nisbet and Hubbard on Hor. *Carm.* 1.30.

694-5   Let that Serpent ... vast torrent: the northern constellation Draco, compared to a river also at *Thy.* 869-70, Arat. *Phaen.* 45-6 (see Kidd's comm.); earlier Hesiod (fr. 70.23) had compared a winding river to a snake.

695-6   whose immense coils ... and the Lesser: the Greater and Lesser Bear, Ursa Major and Ursa Minor; Draco circles round the Lesser Bear and stretches towards the Greater (cf. *Thy.* and Arat. mentioned on 694-5; Ovid *Met.* 3.45; Manil. 1.305-6).

697   the Greater useful ... to the Sidonians: on Pelasgians, see on 127; the Sidonians were the inhabitants of Sidon, on the coast of Phoenicia, hence sometimes Sidonian meant 'Phoenician' in general. It was said that Greek sailors used the Great Bear to navigate, and the Phoenician sailors used the Lesser; cf. e.g. Arat. *Phaen.* 36-9 and Kidd's comm. on 39; Cic. *N.D.* 2.105-6 and Pease's comm. (Because of the precession of the equinoxes, what we call the pole star was not near the celestial pole in antiquity, so these constellations were the best indicators of north.) It may seem that the learned comment is out of character for the Nurse, but she is reporting M.'s words, which are a kind of prayer, in which the stylistic formality is not inappropriate, for the extended description of the Serpent is analogous to a description of a deity's attributes and past actions. The phrase also suggests the universal scope of M.'s magic powers.

698-9   and let Ophiuchus ... poison pouring out: Ophiuchus is a constellation pictured as a man wrestling with a snake that is coiled round his middle, but he holds its head and tail in his hands (cf. Arat. *Phaen.* 74-87; Cic. *Arat.* fr. 15; Germ. *Arat.* 73-89; the snake is Serpens, distinct from Draco; on the ancient terminology see Kidd on Arat. *Phaen.* 45-62, 74-87). M. asks him to release it so that she can make use of its poison; possibly S. envisages the snake's poison being in its throat, rather than in its fangs (see Gow on Theocr. 24.28).

700　Python ... the twin deities: Python was a huge serpent killed by Apollo; the 'twin deities' are Apollo and Diana. Python, or a chest containing his ashes, was said to be buried at Delphi (Var. *L.* 7.17; Hyg. *fab.* 140), so M. summons him from the dead; compare how witches were reputed to be able to raise human beings from the dead, usually to obtain a prophecy by necromancy (see e.g. Pease on Cic. *Diu.* 1.132 and on Verg. *A.* 4.490; Cic. *Vatin.* 14; Verg. *Ecl.* 8.98; Hor. *Epod.* 17.79). There were various accounts of how Apollo killed Python. The earliest versions said that Python had prophetic powers and lived near Delphi, so Apollo had to eliminate him before founding his own prophetic sanctuary there. S. probably follows a later development of the story, which said that Python tried to kill Leto when he heard she was pregnant with the 'twin deities', but he failed and she gave birth safely to Apollo and Diana; subsequently Apollo killed Python in revenge (see e.g. Lucan 5.79-81; Hyg. *Fab.* 140).

701-2　let the Hydra ... as it was cut off: the killing of the Hydra of Lerna was one of Hercules' twelve labours. The Hydra became a constellation of that name, see Arat. *Phaen.* 443-50 and Kidd's comm.; Cic. *Arat.* 214-22; Manil. 1.612. The Hydra had many heads, each of which immediately grew again when it was cut off (or in some versions two or three grew in its place), and Hercules only defeated the monster by burning the stump as soon as each head was severed. (See on 641; Gantz [1993], 384-6; *LIMC* 5.1, 34-43, 5.2, 52-60). Here 'every serpent ... as it was cut off' refers to the individual heads of the Hydra.

703-4　You too ... by my incantations: the serpent that guarded the golden fleece, see on 472-3. At the climax of her reported speech, M. addresses the last serpent, the one she has already overcome, in the vocative. **ever-wakeful**: another poetic adjective (*peruigil*) already applied to a sleepless snake by Ovid *Met.* 7.149. (The noun *peruigilium* and verb *peruigilo* are used in prose.)

705-30 After summoning snakes, M. mixes together plants from all over the world. Knowledge of magic herbs was traditionally the most prominent feature of M.'s magic. Here none of the plants is given a species name, but they are categorised by the place of origin or manner of collection: the catalogue includes different mountains (707-9), peoples (711-3), seasons (714-6), parts of the plant (717-9), mountains again (720-2), rivers (723-7), and times and methods of gathering (728-30). Ovid gives a catalogue of mountains and rivers from which M. collected herbs to rejuvenate Aeson (*Met.* 7.220-33), but M.'s journey is there confined to Greece, and the only place shared with S.'s list is Pindus.

707　inaccessibly rocky Eryx: Eryx is the second highest mountain of Sicily (751m), in the west, above Drepana. (See *OCD³* on 'Eryx'.) It was chiefly famous for its sanctuary of Venus. Since the temple was on the summit, the mountain was not inaccessible in historical times; S. has given a conventional description that reinforces M.'s prowess (for inaccessibility as a feature of mountains, see *TLL* 7.2.237.26-31). The translation takes *saxis* with *inuius*, as the word-order suggests; but the meaning might be 'whatever inaccessible Eryx generates from its rocks.'

709 Caucasus ... Prometheus: on Caucasus, see on 43. S. here alludes to the punishment of Prometheus: because he had given fire to humankind (see 821-2), Jupiter had him chained to a rock on the Caucasus, and sent an eagle to feed daily on his liver, which constantly grew again. Prometheus was eventually rescued by Hercules. (See *OCD*³ on 'Prometheus'.) In Ap. Rh. M. uses a potion made from the flower which grew up where Prometheus' blood dripped on the ground, a potion that gives protection against weapons and fire (3.844-57). What previously was used for Jason's protection is here used for Creusa's destruction. See also 821-4.

711 the plants ... their arrows with: the Arabs were proverbially wealthy (Otto [1890], s.v. 'Arabs'), and are here assumed, along with the Medes and Persians, to use poisoned arrows, a practice that the ancients regularly associated with barbarians (see Pease on Cic. *N.D.* 2.126; Nisbet and Hubbard on Hor. *Carm.* 1.22.3). [Gronovius' transposition of lines 711 and 710 is here accepted, for otherwise line 710 has no construction; see Zwierlein (1969), 768.]

710 the Mede ... the nimble Parthians: Media was a region south-west of the Caspian sea, and the centre of the Median empire in the 6th-5th centuries B.C., until the Medes were overthrown by the Persians. In Roman times they were a small tribe. The Parthians were Rome's powerful neighbours to the east, with an empire stretching from the Indus to the Euphrates. They specialised in horse-riding and archery, and one of their favourite tactics was to feign retreat and then shoot at their pursuers. The Medes were sometimes said to be descended from Medus, who was either a son or a later husband of M. (see Introduction §3.2(e)), but we are presumably not meant to think of that story, which would make the reference here anachronistic. The Parthians belong to later history rather than to Greek mythology, but they appear regularly in the mythological world of Senecan tragedy (*Oed.* 119, *Phaed.* 816, etc.).

712-3 or the juices ... the Hyrcanian woods: the Suebi were a group of German tribes who originally lived east of the river Elbe, but many of them gradually migrated west. Elsewhere in S. (cf. *Epist.* 113.29) and other writers the Hyrcanians are an eastern people living on the south-east of the Black Sea, nowhere near the Suebi. Either S. is very confused, or the text is corrupt. Avantius changed 'Hyrcanian' to 'Hercynian' (*Hercyniis*), after the Hercynian forest and mountains in Germany (see *OCD*³ on 'Hercynian Forest'). However, in Greek and later Latin poetry *Hercynius* is scanned with a short *y*, whereas here a long *y* would be required by the metre. That is not inconceivable, but it is safer to stick with the transmitted text and its geographical confusion. For other geographical confusions in S. see Leo I.202-3. (In the other passages of Senecan tragedy where 'Hyrcanian' occurs, the context does not make it entirely clear what region is referred to: on *Thy.* 630-1 see Tarrant; *Phaed.* 70 gives no clue to the location.)

714 nest-building: a poetic compound adjective, found only here. The verb *nidificare* is found in the prose of Columella and the elder Pliny (see *OLD* s.v.).

715-6 when stiff winter ... of the forests: i.e. when the trees have lost their leaves; for the description of leaves falling cf. Verg. *G.* 2.404 *frigidus et siluis aquilo decussit honorem*, 'and cold Aquilo has shaken off the pride of the woods', a line that, according to Servius, was borrowed from Varro of Atax's *Argonautica* (fr. 8 Courtney); Hor. *Epod.* 11.6 (*December*) *siluis honorem decutit*, '(December) shakes off the pride of the woods.' S. varies the phrase, using *decus* and *nemorum*, echoing Ovid *Met.* 8.317 *nemorisque decus*, though that phrase describes a person.

718 or whatever dread sap: 'whatever' is not in the Latin, and *quicumque* must be understood from the *quodcumque* of the previous clauses. (Compare how sometimes, in a series of relative clauses describing the same noun, the relative pronoun is omitted even when a different case has to be understood, e.g. Plaut. *Amph.* 425 ... *quod egomet solus feci nec* [sc. *cui*] *quisquam alius adfuit*; K-S 2.323-4; H-Sz 565.)

720 Haemonian Athos: Haemonian is a poetic equivalent of 'Thessalian'. Originally Haemonia was one region of Thessaly, but it was used by poets to denote the whole of Thessaly, and acquired a legendary founder called Haemon (see *RE* 7.2217, 2219-20). Athos is the mountain at the southern tip of the peninsula of Acte in the Chalcidice (historically not part of Thessaly, so S. has made a mistake, or conceivably he uses 'Haemonian' more loosely for any part of northern Greece; for in Roman times Thessaly had been absorbed into the province of Macedonia). Thessaly was widely associated with magic and witchcraft (see 790; *OLD* s.v. *Thessalia* and related words; Nisbet and Hubbard on Hor. *Carm.* 1.27.21); also 'Haemonian' may suggest the Greek *haima*, 'blood' (see on 590).

721 mighty Pindus: see on 384. **the ridges of Pangaeus**: a mountain in southern Thrace, near Amphipolis.

722 the blood-stained sickle: *cruenta*, 'blood-stained', implies either that some of the plants ooze blood, or that the sickle has been used on animals or humans; it could also mean 'cruel' (because used by M.; cf. *OLD* s.v. *cruentus* 3), or it could be proleptic, i.e. anticipatory, thinking of the deaths that will be caused in future by the herbs M. is gathering (cf. on 849). The *falx*, sickle, was a traditional tool for gathering magic herbs, cf. Soph. *Rhizotomoi* fr. 534 Radt 'And she [M.], looking back as she did so, caught the white, foamy juice from the cut in bronze vessels ... And the hidden boxes conceal the cuttings of the roots, which she, uttering loud ritual cries, naked, was severing with bronze sickles' (trans. Lloyd-Jones); Ovid *Met.* 7.227; Delatte (1961), 166-7, 171.

723-7 The Nurse describes four rivers by whose banks M. collects her herbs. They range from the far east to the far west of the known world, and three of the four have unusual features: the Tigris plunges underground and hides its course; the Hydaspes is warm (rivers are usually cool) and gems are found in its bed; the Baetis is described with oxymoron, as *crashing against* the Atlantic with its *slow* waters.

723 Tigris, which conceals its deep current the Tigris, one of the two great Mesopotamian rivers (the other being the Euphrates), was believed to flow underground for part of its course (like various other rivers); S. refers to the belief in *Nat.* 3.26.4, 6.8.2. (See *RE* 6A.1009-10; R. Mayer, *CQ* 28 [1978], 241-2.)

724 Danube: in the tragedies the older, Greek name Hister is more frequently used, as at 585 and 763, but *Danuuius* is used here and at *Thy.* 376. (See Syme [1987], 50.)

724-5 the Hydaspes ... its warm waters: the Hydaspes, modern Jhelum, is a tributary of the Indus. The river was prominent in Alexander's campaigns, and in Roman poetry its name is evocative of the east. (See *OCD*[3] on 'Hydaspes'; Nisbet and Hubbard on Hor. *Carm.* 1.22.8.) **carrying gems**: a poetic compound, first found in Propertius 3.4.2, of the Indian ocean. India was conventionally regarded as wealthy, the source of gems, as well as spices, ivory, pearls and other luxury goods. (For precious stones from the Hydaspes see [Plut.] *De fluuiis* 1.2; from India generally, Plin. *Nat.* 37.200; *OCD*[3] on 'India'.)

726 **the Baetis, which has given its name to its territory**: the Spanish province of Baetica in southern Spain got its name from the river Baetis, modern Guadalquivir.

727 **crashing against ... slow-moving waters**: the Baetis flows west into the Atlantic. Once it reaches the plains, it is broad and slow-moving, flowing through Cordoba (ancient Corduba, S.'s birth place) and Seville (ancient Hispalis); it is tidal below Seville, hence 'slow-moving waters'. Martial, another native of Spain, calls it *placidus*, 'peaceful' (9.61.2). There is a paradox in 'slow-moving' waters 'crashing against' the sea. ('Hesperian' means 'western'; the evening star, Venus, is called Hesperus because it is only seen in the west, just after sunset; cf. on 71-4.)

728-30 The herbs have been gathered in different ways, all appropriate to magical practices.

728 **This one fell ... got daylight ready**: i.e. the plant was gathered just before dawn. There was a wealth of tradition about the appropriate time of day or night to collect different plants (see Delatte [1961], 39-72). For collecting just before dawn see e.g. Columella 10.294, telling the nymphs to gather plants either *iubare exorto iam nocte suprema*, 'as day rises at the end of the night', or as the sun sets; *PGM* IV.286 'Spell for picking a plant: Use it [i.e. the spell] before sunrise' (Betz [1992], 43; the words of the spell follow); Delatte (1961), 50-4. On 'Phoebus' see on 512. **the steel**: in magic the use of iron was often avoided: according to Plin. *Nat.* 24.12, some thought mistletoe more effective if collected at a new moon without iron (cf. also 19.177, 23.163, 24.103; Delatte [1961], 166-8). Bronze implements were widely used, and iron ones avoided, in all kinds of religious ritual, since the use of bronze was of greater antiquity than the use of iron (e.g. Macr. *Sat.* 5.19.6-14; Soph. fr. 534 Radt; Verg. *A.* 4.513; Frazer's comm. on Ovid *Fasti*, vol. 4, pp. 48-50, 95). However, M.'s use of iron, though unusual, is not unparalleled, for iron was occasionally used in magical and religious ritual (see e.g. Marcellus, *De medicamentis* 27.87; Plin. *Nat.* 26.24; *OLD* s.v. *secespita*; Fest. p. 158 M.; Faraone & Obbink [1991], index s.v. 'iron').

729 **that one's stalk ... in deep night**: for collecting magical herbs at night see e.g. Ap. Rh. 3.863; Verg. *A.* 4.513-4; it was often said that they should be gathered by moonlight (Delatte [1961], 42-50). The phrase 'deep night' (*alta nox*) is first found in S., both in plays (*Tro.* 197, *Phoen.* 144, *Ag.* 727, *Thy.* 51) and in prose (*Dial.* 6.26.3, *Nat.* 1.16.6), unless the pseudo-Ovidian *Am.* 3.5.46 is earlier. The normal prose expression is *multa nox*.

730 **this one's stem ... finger-nail**: in Ovid *Epist.* 6.84 M. uses an 'enchanted sickle', *cantata falce*; here *ungue* is most naturally taken to be M.'s own finger-nail, although there seem to be no parallels for incantations applied to one's own finger-nail in ancient literature, and Delatte (1961), 167 n. 1, suggests it may be an implement (see *OLD* s.v. *unguis* 3 for the meaning 'metal hook or claw').

732 **of ill-omen**: the basic sense of *obscenus*, 'ill-omened', is appropriate here, applied to birds, but the sense 'foul, loathsome', is present too.

733-4 **owl ... screech-owl**: the *bubo* is the eagle-owl, the *strix* probably a generic term for various species of owl (the elder Pliny was unable to identify it with certainty, *Nat.* 11.232); see Capponi (1979), s.v. *bubo* and *strix*. The *bubo* was associated with death (Verg. *A.* 4.462 and Pease; Plin. *Nat.* 10.34). Ovid's M. adds the wings and flesh of a *strix* to her brew (*Met.* 7.269; cf. Hor. *Epod.* 5.20; Prop. 3.6.29). Also witches were believed to turn into owls (Ovid *Fast.* 6.139f.; Apul. *Met.* 3.21), and a *strix* or *striga*

was sometimes a kind of vampire or child-killing demon, appropriate for the infanticide
M. (see Mankin on Hor. *Epod.* 5.20; Dench [1995], 166-73).

734-6 these ... these ... these ...: the reference is unclear, but probably the first 'these'
refers back to all the things mentioned in 731-4, and the next two clauses distinguish
two different categories within these things.

738   Listen, there's the noise of her crazed footsteps: an announcement of M.'s arrival on
stage.

739   and her singing: the vocabulary of singing is applied to magical chants and
incantations throughout Greek and Latin: for instance, the Greek ἐπαοιδή or ἐπῳδή,
'spell', means literally 'a song sung to, over'; in the Twelve Tables (the early Roman
law code, see *OCD*[3] s.v.) the word for enchanting crops is *occentare*, a compound of
cantare, to sing (Table VIII.1, in M. Crawford, ed., *Roman Statutes,* II [London, 1996],
677-9); in this play the verb *cantare* is used of enchantment at 730, and the noun *cantus*
means magical incantation at 684, 699, 704, 760, 769. But the verb *cano* is unusual in
this sense (see *OLD* s.v. 1b.) **The universe shudders:** cf. 46.

740-848 M.'s magical song. Her sudden appearance on stage is a surprise, see the
introductory comm. on 670-848. Her song is a long one, of over 100 lines, which can be
compared for length with *Her. F.* 1-124, *Phoen.* 80-181, 480-585, *Phaed.* 1000-1114, *Oed.*
530-658, *Ag.* 421-578; but the polymetric form is unique in S. It is divided into four sections
by its different lyric metres:

> 740-51   trochaic tetrameter
> 752-70   iambic trimeter (normal dialogue metre)
> 771-86   iambic trimeter + iambic dimeter in couplets
> 787-842   anapaests

A final section of iambic trimeters, the normal dialogue metre, rounds off the act (843-8).
The conventional term 'magical *song*' has been used, but we do not know whether any of it
would have been sung or chanted if performed on stage in S.'s lifetime. In Republican drama
passages of trochaic tetrameters, iambic dimeters and anapaests would have been chanted, and
iambic trimeters were spoken, but such distinctions may have disappeared before S.'s time.
The changes of metre correspond to changes of content, which can be analysed as follows:

> 740-51   Invocation of the shades and gods of the underworld.
> 752-70   Invocation of the moon/Hecate, with a description of M.'s power over
>   nature.
> 771-86   M. makes her offerings to Hecate, and receives favourable signs.
> 787-842   Continued invocation of Hecate, and preparation of the poisoned gifts.
> 843-8   M. sends her sons off bearing the gifts to Creusa.

There is no magical song in Euripides' play, and we do not know whether any other tragedian
included one before S. In Ovid *Met.* 7.192-219 M. has a shorter song, in a different context,
and later one can compare the long magic scene with the witch Erictho in Lucan 6.413-830.
The Greek magical papyri contain a number of verse hymns, prayers and incantations, which
are set out as verse in the translations in Betz (1992).

740-51   Invocation of the shades and gods of the underworld.

740-1 I pray ... Chaos ... Dis: the wording recalls M.'s briefer prayer at 8-12; the present
prayer is longer, more detailed, and more sharply focused. **host of silent ones:** for the

dead characterised as silent, cf. e.g. Verg. *A.* 6.264-5, 432. **funereal gods:** *ferales deos*, a collocation found only in S., here and at *Thy.* 668 (see Tarrant); it is a poetic variant on the usual Roman term for the collective spirits of the dead, *di Manes*. **dark Chaos:** see on 9; in this invocation it is clear that Chaos is a deity. *caecum* might therefore be translated 'blind', its basic sense, rather than 'dark'. (S. has the same phrase at *Oed.* 572, and it is found at *Her. O.* 1134, *Oct.* 391.) **Dis:** see on 11.

742   **the caverns of ugly Death:** the underworld was entered through a cave (cf. *Phaed.* 120-1), and there is also a cave within the underworld at *Her. F.* 718. Here, however, the whole underworld is probably envisaged as a huge cave or cave-system, bounded by the underworld rivers (see next note). **the river-banks of Tartarus:** Tartarus is the underworld (see on 632-3), so 'banks' must be metonymy for the rivers of the underworld; their banks are referred to e.g. at Verg. *A.* 9.104-6 *dixerat idque ratum Stygii per flumina fratris, / per pice torrentis atraque uoragine ripas / adnuit,* 'Jupiter had spoken, ratifying his words by the waters of the Styx, his brother's river, by the banks and dark whirlpools of that pitch-black torrent' (trans. D. West); Zwierlein (1976), 207-8, gives more parallels. The underworld had no fixed topography, and the river(s) here cannot be identified with certainty: traditionally the river Phlegethon (or Pyriphlegethon) enclosed Tartarus (see Verg. *A.* 6.550-1), but at *Her. F.* 716-7 Styx and Acheron surround the palace of Dis.

743-9   Ixion, Tantalus and the Danaids, the canonical wicked prisoners of the underworld, are invited to the wedding. They all murdered close relatives (see notes below), so they are appropriate guests for M. to summon. They usually appear in the lists of the sinners punished in Tartarus that were popular from Homer onwards in literature (*Od.* 11.576-600; Verg. *A.* 6.548-627) and art (*LIMC* 7.1, 786-7), and were popular with S., see Tarrant on *Ag.* 15ff., Fitch on *Her. F.* 750-9. Orpheus was able to give the sinners a rest from their punishments when he was in the underworld (Ovid *Met.* 10.41-4, cf. *Her. O.* 1068-74); here M. assumes that their torments will be suspended in response to her prayer.

743   **torments:** *supplicis* is a contracted form of the ablative *suppliciis*; cf. 1015, and on 481. **new wedding:** 'new' may imply 'novel, strange'.

744   **Ixion:** Ixion was punished by being attached to a revolving, burning wheel. His crimes were, first, murdering his father-in-law, and then attempting to rape Hera; but Zeus made a phantom Hera from cloud, and from it was born the first centaur. (See *OCD*³ on 'Ixion'; *LIMC* 5.1, 857-62, 5.2, 554-7—where no. 5 is a wall-painting from Pompeii showing Ixion on the wheel.)

745   **Tantalus:** Tantalus was punished by eternal hunger and thirst: water and fruit that were close to him receded out of reach whenever he tried to eat or drink. There were several accounts of the crime for which he was punished: revealing the secrets of the gods, or stealing their nectar and ambrosia, or killing his son Pelops and feeding him to the gods at a banquet. It is the last that S. refers to at *Thy.* 62-3 and elsewhere. (See *OCD*³ on 'Tantalus'.) **the waters of Pirene:** Pirene is a fountain in Corinth, so this is an invocation to Tantalus to come to Corinth. He was normally associated with Lydia or Argos, but in late antiquity there was a tradition that he was king of Corinth, so there could be an allusion to that too—but the tradition may be post-Senecan (Serv. *A.* 6.603; *Myth. Vat.* 2.102, 3.6.21; see below on 891).

746-7 let punishment continue … over the rocks: Sisyphus, who is regarded as Creon's ancestor (see on 512; 'father-in-law' is used for 'grandfather-in-law'), is not to be let off his punishment, but rather is to be punished more severely: instead of him perpetually pushing a rock uphill, it will roll downhill taking him with it. Sisyphus was the arch-trickster, and his punishment was associated with various deceits he practised against the gods and men (see *OCD³* on 'Sisyphus'; *LIMC* 7.1, 781-7, 7.2, 564-7). [The text has often been doubted and emended (Zwierlein accepts Axelson's deletion of 746), because (i) the idea that Sisyphus should be subjected to worse punishment interrupts the series of sinners who are to be let off; (ii) elsewhere in Senecan tragedy Sisyphus carries his rock, and does not push it; (iii) 'You *too* … gather here' in 748-9 shows that the person mentioned just before was also summoned to attend. But in response it can be argued that (i) an outburst from M. against Creon's ancestor is understandable; (ii) it is true that elsewhere in S.'s tragedies Sisyphus carries the rock, but he frequently pushes it in other ancient accounts, including S. *Epist.* 24.18, and carrying and pushing are both found in art (see *LIMC* loc. cit.); in any case, the rock presumably rolls back down the hill even in the versions where Sisyphus carries it; (iii) 'You *too*' in 748 can mean 'you, just like Ixion and Tantalus'; and there is a pattern in the manuscript order: Ixion, Tantalus and Sisyphus are males who endure physical ordeals, the Danaids are females who suffer endless frustration.]

748-9 You too … needs your hands: the fifty daughters of Danaus, or Danaids, all (with the sole exception of Hypermestra) murdered their husbands and were punished in Tartarus. Their hands killed their husbands, so they can help M. punish Jason. The punishment of the Danaids is perhaps not found before the Roman period ([Plato] *Axiochus* 371e is not necessarily pre-Roman), and it can take two forms: (a) the standard version involves them trying to fill up a large water jar that is leaking (e.g. Lucr. 3.1008-10, Hor. *Carm.* 3.11.26-7); (b) a later version has them trying to carry the water in leaking pitchers (Zenobius 2.6; cf. Porphyry *De Abstinentia* 3.27; Juvenal 6.614A-B—probably interpolated, see Courtney's comm. and C. D. N. Costa, *Mnemosyne* 26 [1973], 289-91). Here the plural 'hole-riddled urns' (these are usually small portable vessels) indicates the second version; but *Her. F.* 757 refers to the first, as argued by Fitch ad loc. (See *OCD³* on 'Danaus and the Danaids'.)

750 star of the night: the moon. The phrase is unusual: plural 'stars of the night' is found for the stars shining at night (cf. Lucr. 1.1065; Ovid *Am.* 1.6.44; V. Fl. 1.416, 4.82), but with the present passage compare *Phae.* 410 *clarumque caeli sidus et noctis decus* ('(moon) bright star of heaven and glory of the night'). The Greeks and Romans regarded the moon, sun and planets as stars, all orbiting round the earth (cf. on 401-5).

751 assuming your most … of your faces: the moon is here identified with Hecate, who was often portrayed with three faces, see on 6-7. For the construction, see on 351.

752-70 The metre changes to iambic trimeter, and the invocation to the moon continues with the emphatic 'For you' at the start of 752. The next eighteen lines describe what M. has done for the Moon in the past, and 770 repeats the request of 750-1 for Phoebe to come to M.'s assistance. The passage echoes 401-5: the regularities of nature to which M. there appealed are here overturned by her magic. It was common in ancient prayers to recall honours paid to the deity by the speaker in the past, for these provided evidence that it would be worth the deity's while to grant the current request (this has been called the 'da quia dedi' prayer—'give because I have given'—in contrast to the 'do ut des' prayer—'I give in order that you may give'). Most of the evidence for this kind of prayer is literary, but there is reason to think such prayers were used in real life too, at least in Greece (see Pulleyn [1997], 16-38; Appel [1909], 149-51; Hickson [1993], 11). Normally previous sacrifices and gifts to the god were recalled (e.g. Hom. *Il.* 1.39-41; Verg. *A.* 9.406-8), but M. describes her past magical actions, before at 771-83 describing the offerings she is making to the goddess now. There are similar accounts of M.'s achievements in Ovid *Met.* 7.199-214; compare, in a different context, Hypsipyle's list of M.'s activities in Ovid *Epist.* 6.83-92; also Ap. Rh. 3.528-32. For such lists of magical powers see Bömer on Ovid *Met.* 7.199-200; for power over nature in the magical papyri cf. *PGM* I.120-5 'he will quickly freeze rivers and seas and in such a way that you can run over them firmly, as you want. And [especially] will he stop, if ever you wish it, the sea-running foam, and whenever you wish to bring down stars and whenever you wish to make [warm things] cold and cold things warm, he will light lamps and extinguish them again' (Betz [1992], 6); XIII.871-6 (Betz [1992], 192).

752-3 unfastened my hair ... with bare foot: because knots have magical power, the practitioner of magic (and of conventional religious ritual) often has hair untied, and bare feet, because sandals need to be tied (and in addition there were sometimes religious prohibitions on the wearing of leather). Cf. the witch Canidia in Hor. *Serm.* 1.8.24 *pedibus nudis passoque capillo*, 'with bare feet and loose-flowing hair'; Pease on Verg. *A.* 4.509, 518; Bömer on Ovid *Fast.* 3.257. (The singular *nudo ... pede* is probably singular for plural, as e.g. at Hor. *Serm.* 1.2.132, *Epist.* 1.19.12, but it might mean she has just one foot bare, as does Dido at Verg. *A.* 4.518.) **as is my people's custom:** by her people she probably means the Colchians; it is sometimes thought she means witches, but witches did not usually think of themselves as a group (except for the small covens of hag-like witches one finds e.g. in Hor. *Serm.* 1.8; *Epod.* 5; Apul. *Met.* 2.21-30; but M. is in a different class).

754 I have summoned water from dry clouds: 'dry cloud' is cloud that does not produce rain: cf. Verg. *G.* 3.196-8 *Aquilo ... arida differt / nubila*, 'the north wind ... scatters the dry clouds'; Plin. *Nat.* 2.131; S. *Nat.* 2.30.4 *nubem ... tam arida quam umida conserunt* 'clouds are formed from dry matter no less than moist' (see Zwierlein [1986], 155-7). For magical power over the clouds cf. Ovid *Met.* 7.201-2, *Am.* 1.8.9-10; Tib. 1.2.49.

755 sea ... Ocean: the Ocean (see on 376) is tidal, by contrast with the seas (principally, for the Romans, the Mediterranean, Black Sea, and Caspian), which are not noticeably tidal. For magical control of the sea cf. 121 and comm., 166; Ovid *Met.* 7.154, 200-1; *PGM* XIII.871-6.

757 the laws ... been overturned: the Presocratic philosopher Heraclitus had identified god and law (DK22B114), and the Stoics identified their cosmic deity with law (see Pease on Cic. *N.D.* 1.36, 40), but the idea of laws governing the natural world is first prominent in Roman poetry, starting with Lucretius (5.58 *ualidas ... aeui ... leges*, 'the powerful laws of time'), then in Ovid (*Met.* 15.71 *qua sidera lege mearent*, 'by what law the stars move'; *Tr.* 1.8.5; *hal.* 1), Manilius, and later poetry (see *TLL* 7.2.1251.45-1252.9); and it is common in S.'s prose too (e.g. *Dial.* 4.27.2 *non enim nos causa mundo sumus hiemem aestatemque referendi: suas ista leges habent, quibus diuina exercentur*, 'we humans are not the reason for the universe bringing winter and summer in turn: they have their own laws, by which the divine world is controlled'; 1.1.2; *Nat.* 3.29.3, 7.12.4). The idea of breaking the laws of the universe is found elsewhere in S. at

Ag. 814 (Jupiter broke the law of the universe, *lege mundi* ... *rupta*, when he lengthened the night of Hercules' conception). M.'s magic breaks the laws of the universe, but so did the voyage of the Argo, see on 335 and 605-6.

758-9 and you, Bears ... forbidden sea: see on 404-5.

760 the summer earth has shivered: 'shivered' (*horruit*) is Markland's conjecture; the manuscripts read 'flowered' (*floruit*), which has been interpreted as meaning that flowers, which normally bloom in spring in the Mediterranean, are made to bloom in summer by M.'s magic. But some flowers bloom in summer too in the Mediterranean, so this is hardly satisfactory. With the conjecture her words mean that she has changed summer into winter and winter into summer. (See further Zwierlein [1986], 157-8.)

762 the Phasis ... to its source: on the Phasis see on 43. At 211 M. talks of the 'gentle meanders' of the river, here, by contrast, of its 'violent waters'. The contexts are important: at 211 she is giving a rather idealised account of her homeland; here the river's violence suggests its resistance, and its inferiority, to M.'s magical powers. In reality both descriptions are appropriate to different stretches of the river, which in antiquity was navigable as far as Sarapana (over 100 kilometres upstream), and above that was winding and strong-flowing (see Str. 11.2.17, C498, 11.3.4, C500; *RE* 19.1886-93). Reversing the course of rivers is one of the commonest attributes of witches (cf. e.g. Ap. Rh. 3.532; Pease on Verg. *A.* 4.489; Bömer on Ovid *Met.* 7.199-200; *PGM* I.120-5, quoted on 752-70), and one of the commonest adynata (see on 373-4), from Eur. *Med.* 410 onwards.

763 Hister: see on 585; again there is play on the etymology 'stopper'. **so many mouths**: the Danube was variously said to have five (Herod. 4.47), six (Plin. *Nat.* 4.79), or seven mouths, like the Nile (Strabo 7.3.15, C305; Mela 2.8). In some accounts of the return voyage of the Argo, the ship sailed up the Danube (see Ap. Rh. 4.282-96; Moreau [1994], 38-41).

766 the ancient forest's home: this use of *domus*, 'abode', 'home', of a forest, is found only in Senecan tragedy, here and at *Her. F.* 239 (see Fitch's comm.).

767 has lost its shade: i.e. has lost its leaves (for this use of *umbra* cf. *OLD* s.v. 3b).

768 Phoebus ... in mid course: the sun is made to stand still in the sky, prolonging the day; it abandons the day in the sense of abandoning its usual daily course. There is a pointed contrast between the sun, which normally keeps moving, but is made to stand still (768), and the Hyades, which are normally still (in relation to the other fixed stars), but are made to tremble (769). Cf. Apul. *Met.* 1.3 (in a list of things witches can do) *solem inhiberi*, 'stopping the sun'; Plaut. *Amph.* 276 (the extended night when Jupiter fathered Hercules) *ita statim stant signa, neque nox quoquam concedit die*, 'the constellations stand so still, and the night does not give way to day'; at S. *Phae.* 790-4 the Chorus mistakenly thinks that the moon has stopped because of magic. (Others have interpreted the line differently: (a) Costa, among others, thinks it describes the sun appearing at night, but *in medio stetit*, 'stopped in mid course', is not a natural way of describing that. (b) Zwierlein [1986], 159-64, argues that it refers to an eclipse, during which the fixed stars, like the Hyades, are visible. But an eclipse seems unlikely in this passage, since there is no mention of darkness; contrast the repeated references to dark in the parallels adduced by Zwierlein, e.g. *Her. F.* 939-44—note *tenebrae, obscuro, atrum*—, and Lucan 1.535-44—note *umbra, atra caligine*.)

769 **the Hyades**: see on 312. **waver, shaken by my chant**: after a series of main verbs in the past tense in lines 752-68 (although 762 *uertit* could strictly be either present or perfect), 'waver' is present tense, most likely a vivid historic present referring to the past. Others, however, think that M. is now talking about the present moment, and is causing the sun to halt or to be eclipsed, so that the Hyades are visible, as she speaks: Zwierlein (1986), 159-64, argues that she turns to the present moment at 768-9 (he takes 'has ... stopped' to be a true perfect), and others think she does so at 765. But there are no earlier linguistic clues to show she is turning her attention to the present moment, and there are no other references in what follows to the sun currently being eclipsed or stopped. See also below on 787, and on 874-8, where the Chorus is not aware of any eclipse or halt in the sun's motion.

770 **Phoebe**: see on 97-8.

771-86 M. continues her prayer to Phoebe/Hecate, describing the offerings she is making to the goddess, and at 785-6 she recognises the signs of her favour. The metre (see on 740-848) is the same as Horace uses in his first ten *Epodes*, including *Epode* 5 about witchcraft.

771 **with bloody hand**: the bloodstained hands suit M.'s magic, but in conventional religion, where everything must be pure, they would be ill-omened. For instance, Hector in Hom. *Il.* 6.263-8, coming bloodstained from the battlefield, refuses to sacrifice before he has washed; Aeneas at Verg. *A.* 2.717-20 similarly refuses to touch the statues of his household gods with bloodstained hands.

772 **nine serpents intertwine them**: snakes are used in magic (see on 684), but here we have the macabre idea of weaving nine of them into a garland (*nouena* singular = 'ninefold', see *OLD* s.v. *noueni* 2c); this may come from Ap. Rh. 3.1214-5 where Hecate's head is garlanded with 'terrible snakes and oak-branches'. The number three is frequent in magic and religion (see 840 below, Gow on Theocr. 2.43); for the significance of nine, see Gow on Theocr. 30.27; Wissowa (1912), 232 and n. 7; and on multiples of three generally, see Gow on Theocr. 17.82ff.; Green on Ausonius 15 (=16 in Loeb edition) 'The riddle of the number three'; for general background, *OCD*³ on 'numbers, sacred'.

773-4 **these limbs that ... kingdom tremble**: Typhoeus or Typhon (see on 409-10) was a monster who attacked Jupiter's position as ruler of the gods, and was eventually imprisoned beneath mount Etna. His appearance is variously described, but he always has numerous snakes' heads (often a hundred) growing from various regions of his partly-human body: in Hesiod (*Th.* 823-7) the heads grow from his shoulders, apparently in place of a human head, but later, in Apollodorus (1.6.3) the heads grow from his arms instead of fingers, and his lower body is formed of coiling snakes' bodies (see further Gantz [1993], 48-51; *LIMC* 8.1, 147-52, 8.2, 112-3). It is probably the latter picture that S. has in mind, the 'limbs' being snakes. The conceit that M. uses these monstrous limbs in her magic is suitably grandiose and subversive.

775-84 The next ten lines contain several echoes of the third choral ode, because the magical substances that M. lists are associated with various of the Argonauts, who, as the Chorus recalled, came to unhappy ends. The Chorus concluded the ode by praying for Jason's safety (668-9), but by using these substances M. is ensuring that Jason is punished. Again Althaea is a precedent for killing one's own children, cf. 644-6.

775-6 the blood ... which Nessus gave: see on 641.

777-8 The pyre on Oeta .. given to Hercules: see on 639-42.

779-80 You see the torch ... avenging Althaea: see on 644-6. **loving ... unloving:** see on
261. Ovid had described Althaea in similar terms: *incipit esse tamen melior germana
parente, / ... impietate pia est,* 'she begins to be a better sister than parent ... she is
loving through an unloving act' (*Met.* 8.475-7).

781-2 The Harpy ... from Zetes: on Calais and Zetes see on 231 and 634. They chased
away the Harpies, creatures with women's heads and birds' bodies, who had been
tormenting the blind prophet Phineus; see Ap. Rh. 2. 178-499; *OCD*³ on 'Harpyiae,
Harpies'. The name 'Harpy' was connected with the Greek verb *harpazo*, 'snatch'—
they tormented Phineus by snatching his food and defiling it before he could eat it (see
Ap. Rh. 2.188-9; Maltby [1991] on *Harpiae*).

783 a wounded Stymphalian bird: referring to one of Hercules' labours, the killing of the
Stymphalian birds, which lived beside Lake Stymphalus in Arcadia and terrorised the
surrounding area. According to some accounts the birds shot out their feathers like
arrows at attackers, which would make M.'s feathers more sinister (Hyg. *Fab.* 30.6;
Serv. *A.* 8.299; the same habit was attributed to the birds on the island of Ares in the
Black Sea, cf. Eur. *Phrixos* fr. 838 Nauck; Ap. Rh. 2.1036, 1088). (See Gantz [1993],
393-4; *LIMC* 5.1, 54-7, 5.2, 71-2.)

784 victim of the Lernaean arrows: Hercules shot the birds with his arrows, which he had
dipped in the poison of the Hydra of Lerna (see Stesichorus S15; Soph. *Trach.* 573-4;
above on 641).

785 Altars, you made a noise: probably the noise comes from the altar fires suddenly
blazing up (cf. 578), which was a good omen (see e.g. Verg. *Ecl.* 8.105-6; Mynors on
Verg. *G.* 4.384-5); cf. on 841-2. Or possibly the noise is made by the altars shaking, as
the tripods do in the next line; cf. Ovid *Met.* 9.782 *uisa dea est mouisse suas (et
mouerat) aras,* 'the goddess seemed to have shaken her altars (and she had)'; *Fast.* 3.47.
'Altars' may be poetic plural for singular (cf. 578, 808). On the Greek tragic stage there
was always an altar, as on the Roman Republican stage, and the presence of an altar is
assumed in other places in Senecan tragedy too. M. has already referred to altars in the
plural at 578, and later she lets some of her own blood drip on the altars (807-11); but
for problems posed by the altar(s) in the play, see on 797. (On stage altars see Arnott
[1962], 42-56; Beare [1964], 177; Sutton [1986], 19-20.)

785-6 I recognise that ... showed her favour: a tripod was a three-legged stand used to
support bowls or other objects in daily life and religious ceremonies; the shaking of a
tripod was a sign of the deity's presence. At Delphi it was a sign of Apollo's presence
and of his inspiration of the prophetess; here M.'s tripod is shaken by Apollo's sister
Phoebe/Hecate as a favourable sign. For the form *tripodas* see on 86.

787-842 Invocation of Hecate, and preparation of the poisoned gifts.

787 I see the swift chariot of Trivia: Trivia is another title of Hecate, and a translation of
Greek *Trioditis*, literally '(goddess) of the three ways (i.e. cross-roads, see on 6-7)',
because cross-roads were believed to be haunted by the dead (cf. S. I. Johnston, *ZPE* 88
[1991], 217-24). Are we to imagine that the moon is literally visible in the sky at this
point, or does M. have a private vision of the goddess herself? The description of
Trivia's appearance is appropriate both to the moon and to the goddess. But on the
ancient stage, where daylight and night-time had to be indicated by the words of actors,

it is hard to see how an actor could make a clear distinction here between seeing the moon and having a vision of the goddess. (On portrayal of darkness and night-time in ancient drama see H. M. Hine, *PLLS* 3 [1981], 263; Sutton [1986], 26-7; Tietze Larson [1994], 52 n. 67, 58.) See on 958-66 for a related problem regarding the appearance of the Furies and Apsyrtus' ghost; and on 768 and 874-8 on appearances of sun and moon.

788-92 not the one ... with a tighter rein: S. uses the conceit that Hecate/Diana drives one chariot at full moon, but another when attacked by witches. At full moon she drives 'all through the night', because the moon when full rises at sunset and sets at dawn, remaining visible throughout the night. The moon is 'lurid with mournful expression' and drives more slowly (that is the force of 'with a tighter rein'; cf. [Tib.] 3.7.91; S. *Ben.* 1.14.2) when threatened by Thessalian witches, because, in popular ancient belief, they drag down the moon (see on 674), causing an eclipse. For the moon being lurid or pale during an eclipse see *TLL* 7.2.1862.80-1863.3. On Thessaly and witchcraft, see on 720.

795 Dictynna: a name of the Cretan goddess Britomartis (see *OCD*³ s.v.), identified with Diana. (The name was connected with Greek *diktyon*, a net.)

795-6 let the precious bronzes ... to aid you: the clanging of bronze cymbals was supposed to counteract magic, and so was used to resist the power of witches over the moon, and to bring the moon back to normal during an eclipse (to counteract magic: Tib. 1.8.21-2; during eclipses: Livy 26.5.9; Plin. *Nat.* 2.54; Tac. *Ann.* 1.28; Plut. *Mor.* 944B; for general apotropaic uses, see Gow on Theocr. 2.36). In the Roman period Corinthian bronzes were especially prized (cf. Plin. *Nat.* 34.6-8; Smith on Petronius 50.2), but the description 'precious' has been regarded as anachronistic here in M.'s song. However, such standards of anachronism are doubtfully appropriate to Senecan tragedy, and there is sarcasm in M.'s allusion to the wealth of her enemies the Corinthians. For it is the costliness of M.'s gifts that will appeal to Creusa, and acquisitiveness will be her ruin (cf. 570-4 on the gold jewellery; 844 'precious gifts'; 881-2 Creon and Creusa have been trapped by gifts). Compare how the Chorus has characterised the Argonauts as plunderers of gold (613, 664-5). Euripides too stresses the fact that the gifts are made of gold (786, 961, 964-8, etc.), but, though there is a hint of Creusa's vanity at 1156-66, there is also recognition in the play of the heroic code of honour that requires exchange of costly gifts (see Kerrigan [1996], 95-7), a theme that is absent from S.'s play.

797-807 For you ... for you ...: see on 71-4.

797 turf: an altar improvised from turf; cf. Nisbet and Hubbard on Hor. *Carm.* 1.19.13; Gow on Theocr. 26.5. M. sets up turf altars in the open air at Ovid *Met.* 7.240-1 (one for Hecate, one for Iuventa or Youth). But it is not clear how a turf altar would be managed in a staged performance of S.'s play: on the Greek stage and the Roman Republican stage there was an altar (see on 785), but that would presumably be of a more permanent form; here we may imagine attendants setting up a turf altar some time after line 578, and probably after 739, since there is no mention of an altar in the Nurse's speech at 670-739. A further problem is that 578, on the most natural interpretation, refers to an altar inside the house, but it could refer to the noise of fire on an outside altar resounding through the house.

799-800 a torch snatched ... a funeral-pyre: a burning branch taken from a funeral pyre and used as a torch has sinister powers, and so is used by underworld deities: in Ovid (*Met.* 6.430) the Eumenides carry such torches, so does Megaera in S. *Her. F.* 102-3, cf.

983; and they are used in the necromancy scene in *Oed.* 550-1 (for such torches in other contexts cf. *Oed.* 874-5; Prop. 4.3.13-4).

802-3 a headband, worn in funereal fashion: the headband (*uitta*, fillet) was a standard part of female dress for girls and respectable women; it was worn in various religious contexts, by priests, prophets, and sacrificial victims, and was placed on statues, altars, and temples. For its use in a magical context see *PGM.* II.69-72 'And make of the sprig [of laurel, just described] ... a garland for yourself, weaving about it a binding consisting of white wool, bound at intervals with red wool, and let this hang down as far as the collarbone' (Betz [1992], 14); cf. Theocr. 2.2 (placed round a bowl); Verg. *Ecl.* 8.64 (on the altar). 'in funereal fashion' means it is the kind of headband used at funerals, to drape the corpse, the bier, or an altar (see Verg. *A.* 3.64 and Servius ad loc.; Prop. 3.6.30, where such a headband is used for magical purposes; Ovid *Ibis* 103; Festus 360 M.).

804-5 a sinister branch ... of the Styx: the Styx is one of the rivers of the underworld (see on 632-3, 742). The branch presumably comes from a tree associated with death, cypress or yew or wild fig (see e.g. Tarrant on *Thy.* 654; Mankin on Hor. *Epod.* 5.17-8). Trees were a standard feature of the underworld; see Hom. *Od.* 11.588-92 (the trees whose fruit tantalised Tantalus, see on 745); Verg. *A.* 6.282-4 (an elm), 473 (Dido runs off into a shady forest); S. *Her. F.* 689-90, 718.

806 like a Maenad: see on 382-4, 849.

807-11 I shall slash ... the sacred liquid: she cuts herself to draw blood, which flows onto the altar. Cutting oneself with a knife was associated with worshippers of Bellona, an old Roman goddess who by Augustan times had become identified with the Cappadocian goddess Ma and had acquired oriental characteristics; cf. Tib. 1.6.43-50; Lucan 1.565-6 (see *OCD* [3] on 'Bellona'; Wissowa [1912], 348-51).

810 your own dear blood: her own blood, but also, for the audience, a pointer to the shedding of her sons' blood.

811 the blow is struck: literally 'I, having been struck', *percussa*; Latin characteristically uses a past participle to describe the first of two actions in temporal sequence. The verb *percutio* can describe any kind of blow, but is also used specifically of killing sacrificial victims, so it continues the sacrificial imagery here (cf. *OLD* s.v. 2). Ancient stage props included 'stage knives' with retractable blades, and stage blood (Achilles Tatius 3.20.7; cf. Petron. 94.11-15, 108.10-1; Sutton [1986], 63-7; Artemidorus 4.2, p. 245 Pack, with Jones [1991], 189). Elsewhere in Senecan tragedy, Jocasta kills herself with a sword at *Oed.* 1038-9, and at *Tro.* 117-23 Hecuba draws blood from her arms and breasts as she beats herself in grief.

812-3 But if you complain ... I pray: a general request to the deity to spare (*parce*) or have mercy (*uenia*) is a common feature of ancient prayers (see Appel [1909], 121; Nisbet and Hubbard on Hor. *Carm.* 2.19.7), but this is more specific. Hecate is a dangerous goddess, and the magical papyri warn against lightly using rituals involving her: *PGM* IV.2639-40 'But perform this ritual in a holy manner, not frequently or lightly, especially to Selene [Greek name for the Moon]' (Betz [1992], 87); cf. IV.2504-5, 2569.

814 daughter of Perses: Hecate's father was Perses, the son of Crius, a Titan. (See West on Hes. *Th.* 409; Bömer on Ovid *Met.* 7.74.) In Ap. Rh. 3.467 M. uses the title 'daughter of Perses' in a prayer for Jason's safety, so if one here recalls that—and M. is talking about her frequent prayers to Hecate—there is irony in M. using the same title when bringing about Jason's ruin. (*Persei* is a Greek vocative of *Perseis*.)

814-5 invoking your bow: *arcus*, 'bows', is probably poetic plural for singular, referring to Hecate/Diana's bow and arrows; M. is not calling upon her in her aspect as huntress, but 'bow' could be metonymy or symbol for the goddess's power. However, Zwierlein (1986), 164, thinks it refers to the crescent moon, since *arcus* can refer to any crescent- or bow-shaped object, even though there is no parallel for it applied to the moon.

816 is always ... Jason: thus M. diverts any wrath the goddess may feel onto Jason; diverting divine anger and other evils onto one's enemies was a regular religious practice in antiquity, see Nisbet and Hubbard on Hor. *Carm.* 1.21.13.

817-32 M. completes the rituals aimed at poisoning the gifts. She describes a series of sources from which she has obtained destructive fire. The witch would normally keep a stock of herbs and other magical substances, but M.'s stock even includes different kinds of fire (cf. also 735). She has received fire of different sorts from Prometheus, Vulcan and Phaethon: S.'s M. has influential connections among the gods and heroes.

817-9 Now impregnate ... of her bones: see on 836-9.

819 creeping flame: the effect of the poison will be a cruel mockery of the love that a new bride should feel, because intense love was regularly described as a flame burning deep in the body, e.g. at Catul. 51.9-10 *tenuis sub artus / flamma demanat*, 'a slender flame creeps down within my limbs'; 100.7; Ovid *Rem.* 105 *interea tacitae serpunt in uiscera flammae*, 'meanwhile silent flames creep into the innards.' (See *TLL* 6.1.867.46-67; 7.1.295.32-65.) The 'creeping' (*serpens*) flame is like the snakes used by M. in 684-704 (*serpens* means 'snake' at 686, 702 and 704).

820 Enclosed in the yellow gold: the golden gifts for Creusa described at 572-4. Lines 817-9 have described the poisoning of the robe, and 820-32 refer to the golden jewellery.

821-4 by the one ... Prometheus: see on 709, where Prometheus has already, indirectly, supplied poisonous herbs, and now he supplies hidden, destructive fire. When Jupiter withheld fire from humankind, as a punishment for Prometheus deceiving him at a sacrifice, Prometheus stole it back; according to one version he concealed fire in a tube or stalk, hence he can teach M. to hide fire. The idea that M. was taught by him seems to be S.'s own. **entrails that reproduce themselves:** Vergil had already used metaphors of childbirth to describe the regrowth of the liver of Tityus, who suffered a similar punishment to Prometheus (Verg. *A.* 6.598-9 *fecundaque poenis / uiscera*, 'and entrails fertile in punishments', 600 *fibris ... renatis*, 'with lobes (of the liver) reborn'). **artfully, Prometheus:** the Greeks thought the name 'Prometheus' meant 'forethought' (in fact wrongly, see West on Hes. *Th.* 510), so the juxtaposition with 'artfully' is pointed.

824-5 also: *et* is postponed to second word in its clause, as is common in poetry from Vergil onwards. **Mulciber:** a title of Vulcan, god of fire. The name was linked to *mulcere*, 'to soften' (Maltby [1991] s.v.). **sulphur:** sulphur was commonly associated with fire, being used to make matches or fire-lighters (see Howell on Mart. 1.41.4; Courtney on Iuu. 5.47-8; *OLD* s.v. *sulpuratus* b). M. uses sulphur in the rejuvenation of Aeson at Ovid *Met.* 7.261, but there burning sulphur is used to purify the body.

826 lightning-flashes of living flame: the phrase *fulgura flammae*, 'lightning-flashes of flame', is found in Lucretius (1.725, 6.182), where *fulgura* retains the literal sense of 'lightning' (see West [1969], 7-9).

827 from my kinsman Phaethon: see on 32-6, 599-600. The Sun was father of Phaethon and grandfather of M.

828 from the middle of the Chimaera: the Chimaera was a monster that, in Homer's description (*Il.* 6.181-2) was 'in front a lion, behind a snake, and in the middle a chimaera [= goat], breathing out a dreadful force of gleaming fire'; cf. Hes. *Th.* 319-22 where she has three heads. The Homeric passage was sometimes interpreted to mean that the fire came from the goat section, as is assumed by S. here; cf. Ovid *Met.* 9.647-8 *Chimaera ... mediis in partibus ignem, / pectus et ora leae, caudam serpentis habebat,* 'The Chimaera had fire in the middle part, the breast and face of a lioness, the tail of a serpent.' For artistic representations see *LIMC* 3.1, 249-69, 3.2, 197-217.

829-30 flames snatched ... of the bull: i.e. flame from the fire-breathing bulls that Jason used to sow the dragon's teeth.

831 which I mixed with the bile of Medusa: Medusa, one of the Gorgons, was killed by Perseus. (See *OCD³* on 'Gorgo/Medusa'.)

834 seeds of flame: a phrase going back to Homer *Od.* 5.490; cf. Lucr. 6.160-1; Verg. *A.* 6.6-7; Ovid *Met.* 15.347-8 and Bömer.

835 let them elude the eye and permit touch: i.e. may the gifts not look fiery nor be hot to the touch.

836-9 The short messenger scene (879-90) gives no details of the death of Creusa or Creon, so these lines, where M. anticipates the effects of her poisons, function as a brief description of the death (see also 817-9). Contrast the much more detailed account by Euripides' messenger (*Med.* 1156-1203); for instance, compare S.'s 'let limbs melt and bones smoke' with Euripides: 'blood congealed with fire was dripping from the top of her head and, as the poison's jaws worked away unseen, the flesh melted away from her bones like resin from a pine-tree—a sight to stop the heart' (1198-1202, trans. Davie). S.'s M. expresses herself briefly and elegantly, with paired phrases in 835-7, and the conceit of the bride's burning hair eclipsing the wedding torches in 838-9.

839 new bride: *noua nupta* is a standard Latin phrase for 'bride' (see *OLD* s.v. *nupta* b; Horace applies the phrase to Creusa at *Epod.* 5.65-6, and Ovid at *Met.* 7.394; in Euripides, *Med.* 970, she is called νέαν γυναῖκα, 'new wife').

840 My prayers are being granted: for the phrase cf. Ovid *Epist.* 16.94 *multarum uotum sola tenere potes*, 'you alone can obtain what many women have prayed for' (*uotum* is there the thing prayed for); cf. *OLD* s.v. *teneo* 16b.

840-1 three times bold Hecate has barked: Hecate was sometimes believed to be in the form of a bitch (or a wolf or a mare); for her barking, see Tarrant on *Thy.* 675-6. Sometimes she was accompanied by dogs (Ap. Rh. 3.1216-7, Verg. *A.* 6.257-8). The number three is commonplace in magical contexts, see on 772, and especially appropriate for 'triple-formed' Hecate (see on 6-7).

841-2 and has shot out ... that brings grief: this may literally mean that flames have shot up from a torch carried by Hecate, or it may be a metaphorical description of the flame flaring up on Hecate's altar. Noises and altar flame are regular signals of divine favour, see on 785. *luctifera*, 'bringer of grief', literally 'grief-bringing', is a poetic compound, first found in S. (it is the manuscript reading at *Her. F.* 687).

843-8   At the conclusion of the act M. reverts to dialogue metre, summons her sons, and
sends them off with the poisoned gifts.

843   **The potent mixture**: literally 'The power'; the translation assumes this is a striking use
of abstract for concrete; cf. *Her. O.* 563 *Prolata uis est*, 'The power (of Nessus' blood,
cf. on 641) has been produced'; V. Fl. 7.460 *ille manu subit et uim corripit omnem*, 'he
(Jason) puts out his hand and seizes all the power (of the drugs M. has just offered
him).'   **summon my sons here**: to whom is this addressed? Probably to the Nurse,
who we can assume has remained on stage during M.'s long monologue; or else to an
anonymous attendant who is still indoors. In stage performance it need not take the
boys long to emerge from the palace, and until they arrive M. could, for example, be
occupied with placing the gifts in a box.

845   **Go, go**: the same urgent iteration is found three times in *Tro.* (191, 627, 1165); cf. on
117. **offspring of an ill-fated mother**: here 'ill-fated' (*infaustae*) primarily means
'unlucky, suffering ill fortune'; but it can also mean 'bringing ill fortune', which echoes
the sense it had at 706, and the ill-omened words of M. at 12 (see comm. there).

846-7   **appease your mistress and stepmother**: M. pretends that her children must try to
win Creusa's affection with the presents. In Euripides the children, who are meant to go
into exile with M., are to ask to be allowed to stay (969-72).

848   **enjoy a last embrace**: ambiguous—the children will think she means the final embrace
before her departure, but, for her and the audience, it may be the final one before the
sons' death. (On *ultimus*, 'last', in connection with funerals, see on 551-2.)

The Chorus's first words in 849-51 show that M. leaves the stage at this point, and
presumably the Nurse goes with her. It is not clear when they return. Zwierlein (1966),
91 and n. 11, 103 and n. 32, argues that in S. messengers are in dialogue with the
Chorus only when nobody else is on stage, which implies that M. and the Nurse cannot
be on stage at 879-90. This is certainly the Greek convention, and S. very likely follows
it here too, but we must not assume he was always consistent on such matters. At 891-4
the Nurse and M. clearly know the gist of what the Messenger has reported, so perhaps
they can be imagined entering and staying in the background, overhearing the
Messenger and Chorus.

FOURTH CHORAL ODE: 849-78

The final choral ode is brief compared with the preceding ones (for short final odes compare
Oed. 980-97 and *Phaed.* 1123-53, though in the latter play the third ode is also shorter, 959-
88). Thus it provides an interval for the boys to take the gifts to Creusa, but its brevity does
not delay for too long the news of the dreadful outcome that the audience will be expecting.
The Chorus describes M.'s frenetic behaviour, expresses fears about her intentions, and
voices hopes that she will leave as soon as possible, and that evening will come quickly. If
one tries to imagine the staging, it is not clear how the Chorus knows about M.'s behaviour,
or in other words, how much, if any, of the previous three acts it has spent on stage. The
Chorus presumably has not been present during the preceding magic scene, or it would know
more than it does of her intentions; although it could perhaps have appeared when the boys
were summoned at 843. Similarly it is unlikely to have listened to M. discussing her plans
with the Nurse at 380-430 or 560-78.

The Chorus's description of M.'s behaviour recalls the Nurse's description at 382-96, and details of this ode recall and contrast with the first ode (see the notes below). The Chorus's feelings have gradually changed: the first ode expressed joyful and optimistic hopes for the marriage; the second acknowledged that the Argo had transgressed nature's boundaries; the third acknowledged rather obliquely (without mentioning her name) the force of M.'s rage, and the punishment that many of the Argonauts had already suffered, and that now hung over Jason; the final ode openly expresses fears of what M. (named at 867) will do.

The opening sentence perhaps surprises with its reference to M.'s 'cruel love', for the previous act has lacked any talk of love. But the Chorus resumes and expands a theme that has recurred, usually briefly and sometimes obliquely, throughout the earlier part of the play: see 136, 139-42, 398, 416, 496. The Chorus, which in the previous ode recognised the violence of the woman 'robbed of her wedding-torches' (581), here recognises that love is central to M.'s rage. At 134-6 she contrasted anger and love, and at 137-42 we saw the two emotions pulling her in different directions. Now, in the Chorus's estimation, they pull together—at least in relation to Jason (for the Chorus cannot anticipate the conflict of anger and love for her children that will be prominent in the next act).

The metre is iambic, see Introduction §5.7.

[On this ode see also Fyfe (1983), 84-5; Davis (1993), 195-9.]

849 blood-stained Maenad: on M. as a Maenad see 383 and 806; 'blood-stained' is both metaphorical (it could be translated 'savage', see on 722) and literal, recalling M.'s shedding of her own blood at 808-11, and perhaps foreshadowing her murder of her sons. It may be recalled that in Euripides' *Bacchae* Agave, who led the Maenads and killed her son Pentheus, was stained with his blood (1163-4).

853-4 driven ... set firm: a paradoxical juxtaposition of passionate movement and immobility. Throughout this ode M. is associated with violent movement; contrast how in the first ode Creusa, though she was in the dance (93), was described with static similes (94-101).

854-5 tossing her head: Quintilian warns the orator against tossing the head, for *fanaticum est*, 'it's a mark of religious frenzy' (*Inst.* 11.3.71).

858-61 Her reddened cheeks ... no colouring for long: contrast 99-101 (and comm.), where the juxtaposition of rosy and white colouring in Creusa's complexion was a conventional sign of her beauty. Here we have sudden alternation between red and pale complexion, a sign of some sort of distress, and a symbol of the disruptive threat posed by M. Compare e.g. Ap. Rh. 3.297-8, describing the effect of 'Love the destroyer' on M.: 'and the colour of her soft cheeks alternated, now pale, now red, in her soul's anguish'; Ovid *Met.* 8.465-6 *saepe metu sceleris pallebant ora futuri, / saepe suum feruens oculis dabat ira ruborem*, 'often her [Althaea's, see on 644-6] face went pale from fear of the wickedness to come, often anger burning in her eyes produced redness'; Nisbet and Hubbard on Hor. *Carm.* 1.13.5.

862 She paces to and fro: the words resemble one of the fragments of Ovid's tragedy *Medea*, where presumably M. is speaking: *feror huc illuc, uae, plena deo*, 'I am driven this way and that, ah!, filled with the god' (fr. 2 Ribbeck). (But the combination *huc illuc ferre* is fairly common: cf. 221-2 above; *Dial.* 10.12.6; Ovid *Met.* 4.622-3 *(Perseus) nunc huc nunc illuc exemplo nubis aquosae / fertur*, 'he is carried now this way, now that, like a rain cloud', and Bömer's comm.)

863-5 as a tigress ... of the Ganges: M. is compared to a lioness in Euripides *Med* 187 (by
the Nurse) and 1342 (by Jason). In Ovid *Met*. 6.636-7 Procne drags away her son Itys
to kill him 'like a Ganges tigress (dragging) the unweaned offspring of a hind through
dark woods' (*ueluti Gangetica ceruae / lactentem fetum per siluas tigris opacas*). But
S. adds the detail that the tigress is 'bereft of her children' (like the lion in the simile in
Hom. *Il*. 18.318-22); this makes her resemble M., both because she has been sentenced
to exile without them (as the Chorus already knows), and, proleptically, because she is
going to kill them (as the audience knows). We may also recall that in the first ode
Jason was compared to Bacchus 'who puts yokes on tigers' (85), and reflect that, by
contrast, Jason has not yoked this tigress (cf. Davis [1993], 197).

868-9 have made common cause: a forensic metaphor—anger and love are fighting the
same court case. For the phrase cf. Cic. *Vat*. 33 *cum clarissimis uiris causam tuam esse
coniunctam*, 'that your case is linked with that of most eminent men', 41; *Ver*. 2.3.153.
Creon gave M. a chance to present her case (202), but wanted her to leave Jason to fight
his case alone (262); but now M. has gone beyond forensic argument.

870 Pelasgian: Greek; see on 127.

871 Colchian woman: *Colchis* is nominative singular feminine (*OLD* s.v. *Colchis*[2]; a Greek
noun, used e.g. at Eur. *Med*. 133).

873 the king's family: literally 'the kings'; this use of the plural of *rex* is found in Livy, see
OLD s.v. 6b; cf. 978, and above on 56-7 'the royal couple'.

874-8 Now, Phoebus, ... this frightful day: the Chorus hopes that night will fall quickly, so
that M. will have to leave Corinth. Ironically, the Chorus regards night as 'life-giving'
(*alma*) and day as 'frightful', although night is usually the setting for M.'s power; and it
prays to Phoebus, but he is M.'s ancestor (cf. 512, 28-34), so his loyalties are doubtful.
In the first choral ode at 71-4 Hesperus was to usher in the wedding, but here the
wedding has been pushed out of the Chorus's mind. (As the Chorus prays for night to
fall, it is clearly unaware of any eclipse having happened; see comm. on 768-9 for the
view that an eclipse has occurred there.) **life-giving**: it is normally day that is *alma*,
'kindly' or 'live-giving', from Vergil onwards, e.g. *Ecl*. 8.17; S. seems to be first to
apply the adjective to night, see Tarrant on *Ag*. 73-4; *Tro*. 438. The paradox is
increased if one recalls that the Romans derived *nox*, 'night', from *nocere*, 'to harm'
(see Maltby [1991] on *nox*). **drown this frightful day**: 'drown' because the sun sets,
and plunges his horses and chariot into the western ocean, in poetic descriptions such as
Ovid *Met*. 7.324-5 *ter iuga Phoebus equis in Hibero flumine mersis / dempserat*, 'three
times Phoebus had unyoked his horses that had been submerged in the river Ebro'; cf.
Tarrant on *Thy*. 777; *Phaed*. 679. The phrase 'drown (or submerge) the day' (*mergere
diem*), with its collocation of abstract and concrete, is first found in S.

ACT FIVE: 879-1027

The final act is in three sections: first the Messenger arrives and gives the Chorus the news of
the deaths of Creon and Creusa (879-90); then the Nurse advises M. to flee, but she delivers a
long monologue, during which she kills one of the sons (891-977); finally Jason arrives with
armed men, but is unable to prevent M. from killing the second son (978-1027). On the
question whether M. and the Nurse are on stage during the Messenger scene, see on 848.

879-90 This is one of the shortest Messenger scenes in ancient drama. Euripides, by contrast, has a long messenger scene (*Med.* 1121-1230), and S. has long messenger scenes in other plays (see Tarrant on *Thy.*, p. 180, on the development in S.'s handling of messengers). One may compare *Phoen.* 387-402: the manuscripts disagree whether the character who speaks those lines is a messenger or a servant, but whatever the label, the character gives a brief report from the battlefield, and then plays no further part. Here in *Med.* the audience can be assumed to know the basic story already, so the Messenger gives no details about the manner in which Creusa and Creon died, but he does briefly describe the spread of the fire throughout the palace, and the way that water feeds the flames. In contrast with Euripides' messenger scene, S.'s brevity and reticence are striking, and may be compared with the brevity of Ovid's coverage in *Met.* 7.394-7; we do not know what Ovid did in his *Medea*. On the other hand S. has concentrated on the lengthy description of M.'s magical preparations in the previous act (see particularly on 836-9), and will give M. a lengthy monologue in this act. In the present scene the rapid dialogue between Messenger and Chorus is characterised more by paradox and clever repartee than by narrative detail.

879 **The kingdom is in ruins**: literally 'The standing (or condition) of the kingdom has fallen', a paradoxical expression, and an echo of 286. Even though Creon there granted M.'s request, when she implored him 'by the condition of the kingdom', it has done the kingdom no good.

880 **Daughter and father lie in mingled ashes**: cf. Euripides *Med.* 1220 'they lie as corpses, the daughter and the aged father', which is the culmination of the Messenger's lengthy description of their deaths; so S.'s Messenger begins more or less where Euripides' Messenger left off.

882 **by gifts**: see on 795-6 for Creusa's susceptibility to costly gifts. Euripides' M. refuses gifts from Jason to ease her exile, because 'the gifts of a bad man confer no benefit' (616-8); compare the proverb that gifts from enemies are not really gifts (Soph. *Ajax* 665; cf. Verg. *A.* 2.49; Otto [1890], s.v. *donum*). But in S. the point is that gifts appeal to people like tyrants (because they are greedy and susceptible to flattery).

884 **What limit ... disaster?**: this could also be translated 'What is the nature of the disaster?', for *modus* can mean 'manner, method' as well as 'limit'; but questions with *quis modus?* most commonly mean 'what limit ...?', and in this context the Chorus already knows enough about the nature of the disaster to make 'what limit ...?' a more natural enquiry. (In S. see e.g. *Epist.* 2.6 *quis sit diuitiarum modus quaeris?*, 'you ask what limit should be put on wealth?'; 59.13 *... quis cibo debeat esse, quis potioni modus*, '... what limit should be put on food, what limit on drink.')

885-7 **Greedily fire ... for the city**: in Euripides the palace is not burnt down, although M. considers the idea at 378. The fire is mentioned briefly in Ovid *Met.* 7.395, *Ibis* 603-4; D. S. 4.54.5; Hyg. *Fab.* 25.3; V. Fl. 1.226; Apul. *Met.* 1.10; it could also have featured in Ovid's *Medea*. Could the fire have been represented realistically in stage performance? Suetonius (*Ner.* 11) records that Nero sponsored a performance of a comedy by Afranius called 'The Fire', *Incendium*, in which the actors were allowed to keep any furniture they rescued from the burning house; but such realism was doubtless exceptional. In Greek tragedy earthquakes occur during Euripides' *Bacchae* and *Hercules*, while at the end of the *Prometheus Vinctus* Prometheus and the chorus are carried down to Hades. But it is clear that though these events are described in the characters' words, they were not represented realistically; thus there is no subsequent reference to the effect of the earthquake in the Euripides plays (see Arnott [1962], 124-6). Likewise here there need not have been any attempt at realistic representation of the fire.

886 as if under orders: this implies that the fire spreads with unnatural swiftness, as though someone were spreading it deliberately. The use of *iussus* for inanimate things is poetic, cf. *TLL* 7.2.582.78-82.

887 people fear: impersonal passive *timetur*, literally 'it is feared' (*OLD* s.v. *timeo* 1b; Woodcock [1959], 43).

889 water feeds the flames: it was proverbial that fire and water do not mix, cf. Cic. *Phil.* 13.49; Otto (1890), s.v. *aqua* 1; for this adynaton (cf. on 373-4) in S. see *Thy.* 480, *Her. F.* 375, *Phaed.* 568. M. has again overcome the laws of nature (see on 28).

890 our means of defence: i.e. water.

891-2 Depart with all speed .. lands you choose: the exchange between the Messenger and Chorus is broken off suddenly, as the Nurse urges M. to escape (on their movements, see on 848). In any case, her sudden intervention curtails the Messenger's account of the disaster. Probably we should imagine that the Messenger now exits, and the Chorus too, for Jason's words at 978-9 imply that there is nobody around. The Nurse's warning to M. to escape is similar to the words of the Messenger as he arrives in Euripides (1122-3).

891 Depart ... from Pelops' home: this is a problematic expression which most likely means 'depart from the Peloponnese', i.e. southern Greece, which was named after Pelops (cf. *Her. F.* 1164-5 and Fitch's comm.). The problem is that 'Pelops' home' most naturally refers to Argos, where Pelops was king; but M. is being banished from Corinth. There have been other, less straightforward, explanations of the phrase: (a) It does refer to Corinth, because S. alludes to a rare and otherwise late tradition that Tantalus (Pelops' father) ruled in Corinth (see above on 745). (b) Corinth and Argos are only about 30 miles apart by road, in the north-east corner of the Peloponnese, so S. could have treated the Corinthian isthmus as virtually part of the territory of Pelops. There is perhaps a parallel in a tragic fragment, quoted by S. in *Epist.* 80.7, which seems to include the isthmus of Corinth in Pelops' kingdom: *en impero Argis, regna mihi liquit Pelops, / qua ponto ab Helles atque ab Ionio mari / urgetur Isthmos* ('See, I rule Argos; Pelops left me the kingdom where the Isthmus is menaced by the Hellespont [which must here stand for the Aegean] and by the Ionian sea [the sea to the west of Greece]').

893-977 M.'s speech, in which she debates whether to kill her children. It may be analysed as follows:

893-910   My revenge is only just beginning: I have grown in stature and ability and must find some form of vengeance to match.

911-5   My past crimes give me pleasure and valuable experience.

916-25   My children virtually belong to Creusa now; so they must die.

926-32   No, I must not think of killing my children.

933-44   They are tainted with their parents' guilt; no, they are innocent; but so was my brother. I am torn two ways by anger and love.

945-7a   My children, come and embrace me.

947b-51a I am losing them, so Jason must lose them too.

951b-66 The Furies and my brother seek punishment for his murder.
967-71a I kill this son to placate my brother.
971b-77 Jason is approaching; we shall go on the roof.

This is M.'s second longest speech in the play (the magic song is longest, 740-848), and the climax of her deliberations with herself. The changing vocatives chart the constant change of addressee. Down to 924a the speech is addressed to herself, or to her soul or emotions (the vocatives are 895 'soul', 914 'anguish', 916 'rage'); then at 924b-5 she addresses 'children, once mine', then reverts to her emotions (930 'madness', 937 'soul', 944 'anguish'); then in 945-7 she addresses her children, but reverts to talking of them in the third person at 949, and addresses 'anger' again at 953; at 958-70 she sees the Furies approaching and the ghost of her brother Apsyrtus, whom she addresses in 965-70a. At 970b-971a she kills one of her sons, then at 971b she hears Jason approaching with armed men, and moves up onto the roof, carrying the dead son and leading the surviving son at sword point, addressing the sons at 974b-5, and her soul at 976.

Certain actions are clearly implied by her words, other staging issues are less clear (see also on 958-66). The killing of the first son, and the exit for the roof, just mentioned, are implied clearly enough by the text. The question at what point her children are imagined coming on stage is more difficult, for the text is not explicit. Lines 924b-5 sound more like an address to children who are not present than an address to them on stage, for the vocative 'children, once mine', and the blunt injunction '*you* must pay the penalty for your father's crimes', would not naturally be spoken to the children face to face; and the surrounding context strengthens the view that this forms part of M.'s deliberations with herself. However, her words at 945f., 'Here, my dear offspring … come over here and throw your arms around me', do sound like a summons directly addressed to them. However, even here, M. ceases to address the children within a few lines and reverts to self-absorbed deliberations that could not reasonably be addressed directly to them. We could imagine either that the children emerge from indoors at 945f., or that they came out at the same time as M. and the Nurse, at 891. In either case, for most of the time they are on stage, M. ignores their presence. In Euripides there is a Tutor (*paedagogus*), who has a speaking part, in charge of the children, and a tutor is found portrayed in paintings of M. and the children before the murder (see the Roman wall-paintings in *LIMC* 6.2, 195 nos. 8 and 10); there could be a non-speaking tutor in a staging of S.'s play, or M.'s Nurse could look after them, perhaps exiting when M. goes up on the roof. But the Nurse is ignored throughout M.'s speech, and in the remainder of the play, so S. may not have thought clearly about her movements.

Scenes of perplexity and indecision are frequent in Senecan drama. A character urges himself or herself to action also at *Phaed.* 592-9, *Ag.* 131-44, *Tro.* 642-62, *Her. O.* 307-14; Thyestes' perplexity is briefly described at *Thy.* 419-22, 434-9. Such extremes of indecision are the antithesis of the imperturbability and serenity expected of the Stoic sage; see Tietze (1987).

The speech may fruitfully be compared with earlier speeches of mothers inciting themselves to infanticide.

(a) At the start of the corresponding speech in Euripides' play (1019-80) the children are already on stage with the Tutor, whom M. sends indoors at 1020. Much of the speech is directly addressed to the children. She talks ambiguously to them in words which they can understand to refer to their being parted from their mother, but which M., the Chorus and the audience know refer to their death. Her conflict is between carrying out her plan and taking the children with her into exile after all (1046-8), but she is swayed by the yearning to punish Jason, and by the thought that if she did leave the children behind they would probably be killed by the Corinthians anyway (1059-63). (The speech is thought by many scholars to be heavily interpolated [e.g. Diggle's Oxford Classical Text brackets 1056-1080 as an interpolation], but for present purposes it suffices to say that in S.'s day texts of the play would have had the entire speech as it is found in the manuscripts; it is included in papyri, and there were no ancient doubts about its genuineness. If modern scholars have detected inconsistencies that ancient scholars did not, that says something about the standards of dramatic consistency of S. and his contemporaries. Cf. on 19.)

(b) The longest surviving fragment from Neophron's *Medea* (fr. 2) is part of a speech in which M. addresses her soul, her children, her hand, and herself: 'Well then; what are you going to do, my heart? Ponder carefully before you go astray and turn what is dearest to you into what is most hateful. Where did you rush impulsively, you wretch? Restrain your wilfulness and your strength which is hated by the gods. Yet why am I uttering laments like these, seeing my soul left desolate and neglected by those who least ought to do so? Am I becoming *soft*, in spite of suffering such evils? You won't betray yourself in the face of these evils, will you, my heart? Alas, it's decided. Children, go from my sight. For already a murderous rage has possessed my strong heart. Oh, hands, hands, for what sort of deed are we arming ourselves? Alas, I am made wretched by my own daring, I who am going to eliminate my long suffering in a brief time.' (The text of the fragment can be found in Diggle's OCT of *Tragicorum Graecorum Fragmenta Selecta*. On the relative dates of Euripides and Neophron, see Introduction §3.2(c).)

(c) Ovid has several speeches by infanticides in the *Metamorphoses*. In his story of Procne, there is only a short speech as Procne decides to kill Itys in order to punish Tereus (6.631-5), but a much longer one as Althaea deliberates whether to bring about the death of her adult son Meleager in revenge for his killing of her brothers, a speech whose paradox and word-play anticipate S.'s (8.478-511; cf. the description of Althaea's behaviour at 465-74; see above on 644-6 for the story).

Although there are many points of contact between S. and his predecessors, there are also some unique features, in particular: (i) unlike her predecessors, S.'s M. is bent not just on revenge but also on achieving something spectacularly evil (see on 897-8); (ii) M. expresses her joy at the vengeance she achieves (see on 896); (iii) the vision of the Furies and the ghost of Apsyrtus has a crucial influence on M.'s decision to kill her sons, so that the murders are a form of self-punishment as well as a means of punishing Jason. (On the speech see Gill [1987].)

893   **Should I leave?**: for the construction see on 398-9.

894   **I am watching**: the verb suggests M. is a spectator, see on 993.

895   **my soul**: on address to the soul, which is frequent in this speech, see on 41. Euripides' M. addresses her heart at *Med.* 1242, and Neophron's M. does so in fr. 2.1, 9.

896   **you are enjoying**: M. also expresses joy over what she has done at 911-3, 991-2, 1016-7; cf. on 389-90.

897   **mad soul**: in the Latin there is just the adjective 'mad', without a noun, but the gender (masculine vocative *furiose*) shows that she is addressing her soul (895 *anime*), not herself. [The manuscripts have *furiosa*, feminine, which refers to M. herself; but she is still addressing her soul at 904 *uiolentus*, so the conjecture *furiose* creates consistency.]

897-8 if you are … Jason is unmarried: i.e. if you are satisfied merely with killing Jason's new wife. Latin *caelebs*, 'unmarried', can describe someone widowed or divorced as well as someone not yet married (see *OLD* s.v.). The turn of thought 'what I have done so far (dreadful though that is by normal standards) is not nearly enough' is found in S.'s other revenge play, *Thyestes*, where at 1052-68 Atreus regrets having missed opportunities for even viler forms of vengeance.

901 *pure* hands: M. speaks as though her behaviour up to now has been irreproachable; but there is also an allusion to her children who innocently carried the gifts to Creusa in their hands.

905 should be called love: see on 261. Compare *Thy.* 744-5 *hactenus si stat nefas, pius est*, 'if the evil stops there, he (Atreus) is *pius*', and Tarrant's comm. **Come on**: see on 562. **I shall make them recognise**: *faxo* is an archaic future form of *facio* (cf. *OLD* s.v. *facio* for some other instances in Augustan and later writers; it occurs only here in S.). Here it governs the subjunctive *sciant* without any connecting conjunction (parataxis, see on 189); cf. e.g. Ovid *Met.* 12.594-5 *faxo … sentiat*, 'I shall make him realise.'

907 the crimes … to oblige others: literally 'the crimes I have lent', without specifying for whose sake she has committed them; she is thinking of Jason.

909 the madness of a girl: cf. 49.

910 Now I *am* Medea: i.e. I have now reached my full potential, achieving what was promised at 171. **evils have increased my talent**: 'evils' (*malis*) can mean either her misfortunes, the evils she has suffered, or her crimes, the evils she has done—and probably it should be taken to mean both, for she has just been talking both about her previous crimes (904-7) and about her pain (907); cf. on 126.

911 I'm glad, I'm glad: see on 896. For the iteration, see on 13; the same verb is repeated again in 912 and 913 (see on 117); for the verb repeated elsewhere see *Ag.* 1011; Wills (1996), 105. (*iuuat* is impersonal, literally 'it is pleasing', or, more accurately, the infinitive phrases, *rapuisse fraternum caput* etc., are subjects; cf. *OLD* s.v. *iuuo* 5; Woodcock [1959], 168.) **tore off my brother's head**: Apsyrtus's, see on 132. For *rapere caput* in this sense cf. *Oed.* 1006-7; *Pers.* 1.100; *Sil.* 15.807.

912-3 his secret relic: 'relic' in the sense of a sacred object, referring to the golden fleece; see on 471 and 485-6.

913 the old man: Pelias, see on 133-4.

914 Look for your opportunity: literally 'seek material (for further crimes).'

916-7 your treacherous enemy: Jason, cf. 920.

917-9 My mind … to itself: for the idea that her mind has made some decision of which she is not yet fully conscious, cf. *Thy.* 267-70: *nescioquid animus maius et solito amplius / supraque fines moris humani tumet / instatque pigris manibus—haud quid sit scio, / sed grande quiddam est*, 'something greater and larger than the ordinary, and beyond the limits of human nature, is swelling in my soul and assailing my reluctant hands—I know not what it is, but it is something mighty'; M.'s final words in Ovid *Epist.* 12.212 *nescio quid certe mens mea maius agit*, 'certainly my mind is thinking of something greater' (see Heinze's comm.).

920-5 if only my enemy … your father's crimes: here for the first time M. begins to talk openly of harming her own children. The train of thought, which is elliptically expressed, is: 'if only Creusa had children by Jason (sc. then I could kill them; 920-921a); but my own children are effectively Creusa's children now (921b-922a); so they must pay the penalty for Jason's crimes (922b-5).' She does not yet spell out the penalty.

920 **his mistress**: a scornful reference to Creusa. Previously (462, 495) M. has angrily and ironically applied the word 'mistress' (*paelex*) to herself, adopting the perspective of Creusa. Now M.'s own feelings dominate.

921 **Yet whatever offspring *you* have by him** 'you' is here M. herself; i.e. her children by Jason, in effect, have become Creusa's children, because she must leave them behind in Corinth (cf. 508-12).

924 **children, once mine**: see on 893-977 for argument that the children are not on stage at this point.

928 **the wife in me ... reinstated**: 'in me' is not in the Latin, but added to make the translation clearer: 'the wife' and 'the mother' mean 'my feelings as a wife' and 'my maternal feelings.' Such phrases were used by Ovid; compare his description of Procne at *Met.* 6.629-30 *sed simul ex nimia matrem pietate labare / sensit, ab hoc iterum est ad uultus uersa sororis*, 'but as soon as she felt the mother in her wavering, through an excess of love (for her son), she again turned away from him to her sister's face'; cf. 8.463-4, 12.30; S. *Tro.* 626.

929-30 Should I spill ... my children: for the first time she talks specifically of killing the children, only to recoil from the idea in 930-2. (*egone ut ... fundam*: see on 398-9.)

930 **Ah, insane madness, better ...**: this echoes her words at 139-40 (literally 'better, ah, better, pain'); there she rejects the idea of killing Jason, and this may suggest here a false hope that she will draw back from killing the children (Edgeworth [1990], 155).

933-4 note the alliteration _maius scelus / Medea mater (see on 14 and 674-5).

934-5 if they are ... let them perish: i.e. if in effect they are *not* any longer my children (but Jason and Creusa's), then I need have no compunction about killing them; if, on the other hand, they *are* my children, they deserve to perish because of the guilt they inherit from me. S.'s uses terse parataxis (see on 189), literally 'let them die, they are not mine; let them perish, they are mine.' The tortuous logic and expression reveal M.'s attempt to distance herself from the children and her feelings for them, something that Euripides' M. does not attempt.

936 **so was my brother**: i.e. my brother Apsyrtus was innocent, but that did not prevent me from killing *him*.

938 **anger ... love**: here anger against Jason and love for her children pull in different directions; at 868-9 the Chorus spoke of love for Jason co-operating with anger against him.

939-43 An undecided tide ... my heart is surging: just as earlier her power was equal to that of the sea (121, 166, 755-6), so here her indecision is pictured in a sea-simile. *aestus* can mean 'heat, passion', but here it is translated 'tide', anticipating the sea-imagery; and after the simile ends, the imagery continues in 943 'is surging' (*fluctuatur*, picking up 941 'billows', *fluctus*). Ovid's Althaea undergoes similar agonies before causing her son's death (cf. on 644-6): *Met.* 8.470-3 *utque carina / quam uentus uentoque rapit contrarius aestus / uim geminam sentit paretque incerta duobus, / Thestias haud aliter dubiis adfectibus errat*, 'and just as a ship, when seized by a wind and by a tide opposing the wind, endures twin forces and indecisively obeys both, so the daughter of Thestius wanders with unstable emotions.' For an uncertain person compared to the sea cf. *Her. O.* 710-2, *Dial.* 10.2.3; for comparisons to a ship tossing at sea cf. *Ag.* 138-43, *Phaed.* 179-83; Tietze (1987), 138-9; Tietze Larson (1994), 29.

943-4 love: here 'love', three times repeated, is *pietas*, maternal affection (see on 261), whereas in 938 the word is *amor*, which can be both sexual love and affection for family and friends.

945-6 Here, my dear offspring: this is probably the only time in the speech that she directly addresses her sons; see on 893-977. **sole comfort:** cf. 538-9.

949 soon, soon: see on 13. **they:** her children, now spoken of in the third person, after the second person address of 945-7.

952-3 the ancient Erinys: the Erinyes (plural form of Erinys) were the Greek spirits of vengeance, who particularly punished crimes against relatives; they were also called Eumenides, and Furies in Latin. M. is now treating her anger and desire for revenge as externally, divinely motivated; cf. 958-71. **my reluctant hand:** the Erinys wants to use M.'s hand to kill her sons; cf. 969. **anger ... I follow:** Ovid's M. writes *quo feret ira, sequar* (*Epist.* 12.209), 'where anger takes me, I shall follow' (see Heinze's comm.).

954 the brood of Tantalus' arrogant daughter: the daughter of Tantalus is Niobe, who boasted that she had more children than the goddess Leto, and so Apollo and Artemis, Leto's children, killed all Niobe's children; she wept so much that she turned to stone. (See *OCD³* on 'Niobe'.) The comparison with Niobe could hint that the death of M.'s sons will be a punishment for her; this hint is developed in 958-71.

955-6 twice seven children: S. follows the version that Niobe had fourteen children (see *OCD³* loc. cit. for the variants). M. wishes that she had many children, so that the vengeance achieved by killing them would be even greater and sweeter. S. may have known that in a different, early version of the story, M. did have fourteen children (see Schol. Eur. *Med.* 264 and *Phoen.* 159).

957 my brother and my father: M.'s two sons will be enough to atone for the killing of her brother Apsyrtus and her betrayal of her father Aeetes.

958-66 M. sees the Furies (Greek Erinyes) approaching, with the ghost of her brother. This may be regarded as a fulfilment of her prayer to the Furies at 13-18, except that the result is unexpected, for the tables are turned: there she prayed for vengeance for herself and punishment for Creusa and family (and at 952-3 the Erinys is helping M. achieve her vengeance), but here the Furies are seeking to punish M. in order to avenge the murder of Apsyrtus. In Ap. Rh. 4.475-6 there is an Erinys at the murder of Apsyrtus, though in that account Jason does the killing; and at Ap. Rh. 3.703-4 M.'s sister Chalciope prays that, if she is betrayed by M., she may return as a Fury from Hades to pursue her. Whereas, for example, in Aeschylus the Furies pursue Orestes unremittingly, here the Furies appear to be easily satisfied by the death of one of her sons (but see on 963-4).

The passage poses two related questions:

(a) In a stage performance, would the Furies and ghost be played by mute actors, or just described by M.'s words, as a private vision or hallucination? In other Senecan plays a Fury and ghosts appear on stage as speaking characters (a Fury and Tantalus' ghost, *Thy.* 1-121; Thyestes' ghost, *Ag.* 1-56; see Tarrant on *Ag.* pp. 158-9 for precedents in Greek and Roman Republican tragedy; also Fitch on *Her. F.* 86ff.); but here the Furies and ghost do not speak, and to modern taste it might be more effective to rely on M.'s words to describe them, rather than have actors appear and rapidly leave; but we should not assume that ancient tastes were the same as ours (on private visions of Furies cf. *Her. F.* 982-6 and Fitch's comm.; *Ag.* 759-64 and Tarrant's comm.).

(b) Are the Furies and ghost, whether acted or described, to be regarded as objective supernatural realities or as hallucinations or figments of M.'s imagination? The Romans were familiar with the theory that visions of Furies were the product of a guilty conscience (see Nisbet on Cic. *Pis.* 46), and might have interpreted this passage in that way.

961-2 A huge serpent ... the whip is cracked: in the previous act, M. was in control of snakes, but here she is threatened by them. The Furies have snakes in their hair (see on 14), and carry whips (as at Ovid *Ibis* 183; Stat. *Theb.* 7.579; V. Fl. 8.20; Fronto *de orat.* 4; Apul. *Met.* 9.36); here, probably, they are using the snake as a whip, cf. Fitch on *Her. F.* 88 *uiperea saeuae uerbera incutiant manus*, 'let their cruel hands brandish viperous whips', and Tarrant on *Ag.* 760 and *Thy.* 96-7.

962-3 Whom is Megaera ... menacing brand?: Megaera is one of the Furies (traditionally the other two were Tisiphone and Allecto). The 'menacing brand' is her torch, used as a weapon to goad on her victims and agents (the same word *trabs* is used of Megaera's torch at *Her. F.* 103).

963-4 Whose shade ... dismembered: she sees the ghost of her mutilated brother approaching, but at first she cannot recognise him for certain. The fact that M. is pursued by her murdered brother might suggest to the audience that she may later be pursued by her murdered sons; but although in Eur. *Med.* 1389-90 Jason says 'May your children's Erinys and murderous Justice destroy you', there is no explicit statement of this sort in S.'s play. (See Edgeworth [1990] on this scene.)

965 we shall provide it—all of us shall: in tragedy the first person plural is regularly an equivalent for the first person singular, and can be translated by a singular (see e.g. 116 'I am ruined'; 394 'I recognise'). Here the verb 'we shall give' could initially appear to be singular in sense, but the unexpected addition of (literally) 'but all of us (sc. shall provide it)' shows she means a genuine plural, herself and the boys: in the next line and a half she urges the Furies to burn and mutilate herself; then in 967-71 she talks of killing her children to placate Apsyrtus. (Some have taken *omnes* to be accusative, with the meaning 'we shall provide the penalty, but a full one'; but this has less point.)

970 which has drawn its sword: there has been no earlier mention of M.'s sword; perhaps we are to imagine that she has had it in her hands since coming on stage at 891. In art she is portrayed holding a sheathed sword and pondering whether to kill the children, see *LIMC* 6.2, 195 nos. 8-11, 196 nos. 15-22.

970-1 with this victim I placate your shade: she kills one son as she speaks. The word 'shade', *manes*, is plural, and originally in Roman religion the *manes* were the undifferentiated spirits of the dead; the word came to be applied to the dead spirits of individuals in the late Republic, under the influence of Greek ideas of the afterlife (see *OCD*[3] on '*manes*'). 'victim', *uictima*, always has a religious flavour in Latin, meaning 'sacrificial victim', so her son is a placatory sacrifice. Murder is regularly construed as sacrifice in Senecan tragedy (see on 40; 66; 1005; 1020; Fitch on *Her. F.* 920-4; Tarrant on *Thy.* 687-90a; Putnam [1995]), and elsewhere in prose as well as poetry (see *OLD* s.v. *uictima* b).

971 What does that sudden noise mean?: again noise reveals the arrival of a character on stage (cf. on 177-8), here Jason accompanied by armed attendants.

972 seeking to destroy me: in Euripides the motive for Jason's arrival is different: he wants to prevent the Corinthians from punishing M. and her children for the death of Creon and Creusa (*Med.* 1293-1305; compare the early versions in which the Corinthians did kill the children, see Introduction §3.2(c)). Ovid in *Met.* 7.397 speaks of M. escaping Jason's forces, so his *Medea* may have had the same motif.

974-5 Her words indicate that she carries the corpse of the dead son and forces the living son to go ahead of her up the stairs onto the roof (see Introduction §6).

976 Come on, now: see on 562.

977 courage: see on 160 on the translation of *uirtus*. Here, perhaps, she shows more 'manliness' than Jason and his troops; or perhaps she is, perversely, appropriating moral virtue to herself, treating the killing of the son as a 'virtuous act', a proper and appropriate action in her situation (cf. Nussbaum [1994], 448; Nussbaum [1997], 225). See on 993.

978-1027 Jason comes on stage. Despite his appeals to M., she kills the second son and escapes in her serpent-drawn chariot, leaving the boys' corpses behind.

978 the king's family: see on 873.

980 Here, here: see on 13. **men bearing arms, brave band**: on the poetic compound 'bearing arms' see on 467-8. *armiferi* and *fortis ... cohors* are both vocative, standing in apposition; for the interlacing word-order, see Nisbet and Hubbard on Hor. *Carm.* 1.20.5; Tarrant on S. *Ag.* 800; Boyle on *Tro.* 15.

980-1 In a stage performance, Jason's arrival, and his four-line speech, including a summons to his armed men to join him, could allow M. time to get onto the roof. (In Plautus' *Amphitruo*, at 1008 the god Mercury says he will go up on the roof; there is then a speech of twelve lines by Amphitruo (1009-20), which gives Mercury time to get onto the roof and begin speaking from there at 1021.)

982-4 Now, now: see on 692. **I have regained ... virginity is restored**: this can be read either as hyperbole—she counts her vengeance as adequate compensation for all that she lost for the sake of Jason, even for the loss of her virginity (cf. on 49)—or more literally, as the crazed logic of madness, as though the years spent with Jason have literally been blotted out, and her virginity has been restored by her revenge, rather as Atreus in *Thy.* 1099 thinks that Thyestes' adultery with his wife has been undone (see Tarrant ad loc.). However one reads her words, one should remember that she is a specialist in the impossible. **sceptre**: see 203-19. **brother, father**: see on 44, 106, 118, 452-3. **is restored**: perhaps *redit* is perfect (as *rediere* is), a contracted form of *rediit* (cf. on 248), but it could be a genuine present.

986-7 Go, your wickedness ... your vengeance: i.e. she cannot do anything more wicked, but she can perform a further act of vengeance. 'Go', *uade*, means 'leave Corinth', 'you can leave Corinth now'; but then she corrects herself, as she remembers that her vengeance is incomplete. (Contrast the ironic use of *i*, 'go', see on 650-1.) **are on good form**: for this sense of *facio*, 'be effective, function successfully', see *OLD* s.v. 30; Zwierlein (1986), 168.

991 Great pleasure: see on 896.

992 see: *ecce*; this perhaps suggests that she first sees Jason at this point. She has certainly seen him by line 995, but she may have been aware of his presence throughout her speech. In any case in 982-94 M. addresses herself and not Jason.

993 **to have him watching me**: literally 'him as spectator'; compare comm. on 894, where M. is the spectator. The roof where M. stands is like a stage, with Jason and the others down below as audience; compare 1001 'as you watch.' Her craving for an audience has appeared earlier at 905-7 and 976-7.

993-4 **nothing ... achieved: every crime**: *facti* is partitive genitive with *nihil* (cf. *OLD* s.v. *nihil* 3), just as *sceleris* is with *quidquid* in 994 (*OLD* s.v. *quisquis* 2b; Woodcock [1959], 59). **was wasted**: *perit* is probably the contracted form of the perfect *periit* (see on 248), 'has gone to waste'; the historic present would have the same meaning, but would be less emphatic.

995 **from the steep-sloping roof**: literally 'from a precipitate part of the building.'

996 **Someone bring fire here**: so her own house is untouched by the fire that has destroyed the royal palace.

997-8 **Heap up ... a burial-mound**: i.e. if Jason sets fire to the building, it will become a funeral pyre for his sons. **funeral**: i.e. a funeral-pyre; perhaps abstract for concrete, but *funus* is used similarly at Prop. 2.13.34 *extincti funeris ... locum*, 'the site of a burnt-out funeral'; Suet. *Dom.* 15.3 *repentina tempestate deiecto funere*, 'when the funeral was destroyed by a sudden storm.'

1003 **that was not violated by my faithfulness**: he here protests that he was forced to marry Creusa, which is what M. herself said at 137-8; and Jason stressed his inescapable predicament in 431-7 and 516-29. At 437-8, on the other hand, he said 'It was not fear that defeated my good faith, but anxious parental love.' However, there is no absolute contradiction, though there is complexity: he did make the choice between M. or his children, and as a result broke faith with her; but he was forced into making the choice against his will by Acastus and Creon, so that coercion was the ultimate cause of his actions. (See Introduction §4.1.)

1005 **sacrifice**: see on 970-1.

1006 **there I shall plunge the steel**: the same expression was used at 126.

1007-8 **Go on now**: ironic, cf. 197, 650-1. **girls ... mothers**: see on 278-9.

1010 **it would not have sought any**: i.e. if my pain were so insignificant that it could be assuaged by killing just one son, it could have been assuaged without killing either.

1012-3 **If any pledge ... with the steel**: i.e. if I am pregnant, I shall destroy the foetus. M. wants to destroy every remaining link with Jason. For 'pledge' applied to children, see on 145. She uses the language of abortion; compare, in Ovid's protest at an abortion, *Am.* 2.14.27 *uestra quid effoditis subiectis uiscera telis*, 'why do you insert weapons and dig into your womb?'; Ovid goes on to compare abortion to M. or Procne murdering their own children.

1015 **at least ... drawn out**: here *donare* has the sense of *condonare*, 'to let (somebody, in the dative) off (something, in the accusative)', 'to spare (somebody something)', but here the dative is 'my tortures'; literally 'and at least spare my tortures any delay.' (It should not be translated 'give my tortures a respite', for *mora* does not have that sense.) *supplicis*: see on 743.

1016 **Relish**: see on 896. **do not hurry**: *ne propera*, see on 605-6.

1017 **the day is mine**: the Augustan epic poet Cornelius Severus made Roman troops on the eve of battle say *hic meus est ... dies*, 'this is my day' (meaning 'whatever happens in battle tomorrow, I can enjoy today'; Cornelius Severus fr. 11, ap. Sen. *Suas.* 2.12-13). S. gives the phrase a more striking application.

1020 to sacrifice to you: see on 970-1. The verb here used, *litare*, technically denotes a successful sacrifice. **your swollen eyes**: this is normally taken to mean 'swollen with weeping', but Zwierlein (1986), 169-70, points out that there is no other mention of Jason weeping, and he suggests the meaning is rather 'swollen with pride'; cf. 1007 'arrogant man', and *Thy.* 609 *ponite inflatos tumidosque uultus*, 'drop your puffed up, swollen expression', *Oct.* 109-10 *tumidos et truces ... / uultus tyranni*, 'the swollen and harsh expression of a tyrant'; *OLD* s.v. *tumidus* 5.

1022 in such a fashion: this has been interpreted as referring either (a) to the deaths she causes before leaving a place (as she killed Apsyrtus while fleeing Colchis, and Pelias before fleeing Thessaly), or (b) to her chariot (which she has already used to escape after the death of Pelias in Ovid *Met.* 7.350-6). She could well mean both. **A path to the heavens has opened up**: true both literally, because she can fly away in her chariot, and metaphorically, because she has successfully invaded the domain of the gods (in her own eyes at least, and perhaps in Jason's, see 1026-7).

1023-4 twin serpents ... to the yoke: the chariot was a familiar attribute of M. in literature (Eur. *Med.* 1321-2; Apollod. 1.9.28; Hor. *Epod.* 3.14; Ovid *Met.* 7.218-37, 350-6; Hyg. *Fab.* 27; Pacuvius below) and in art (*LIMC* 6.2, 198-202); in Euripides and elsewhere it is said to be the chariot of the sun, but in S. that is not specified. No serpents are mentioned in Euripides; they first appear in art (*LIMC* 6.1, 391 no. 35, from around 400 B.C.). In the Greek theatre M.'s chariot could appear at the end of Euripides' play, using the *mechane*, a sort of crane, so this could presumably have been handled on the Roman stage too; possibly Pacuvius *trag.* 397 Ribbeck, 242 Warmington, refers to a chariot on stage, but it could be a description of an event off-stage: *angues ingentes alites iuncti iugo*, 'two huge winged snakes, joined to the yoke.' This is the only place in Senecan tragedy where this piece of stage machinery is needed (on the Greek *mechane* see Arnott [1962], 72-8; S. refers to stage machinery, not necessarily used for tragedy, at *Epist.* 88.22). **scaly**: see on 685. **Now take your sons back, parent**: these words are sometimes taken to show that M. at this point throws the corpses down from the roof to the ground below; but she may leave them on the roof, and her words may just mean that Jason can have his sons back now that they are dead (so Sutton [1986], 50). Euripides' M., by contrast, takes the corpses away with her to give them proper burial and prevent them from being defiled or left unburied (1378-83), and there are various artistic representations showing M. escaping on her chariot with the corpses (see e.g. *LIMC* 6.2, 199 nos. 39-40, 200 nos. 46, 51, 201 nos. 58, 62-3). Possibly S. was the first to make M. leave the corpses behind. In S., M.'s action implicitly presents a further obstacle to Jason's pursuing her, even if he could: he must stop to bury the boys, just as Aeetes had to stop to collect the pieces of Apsyrtus' corpse for burial.

1025 winged chariot: i.e. drawn by winged serpents, see on 1023-4.

1026 Travel up above ... of the heavens: this translates Bothe's conjecture *sublime*, an adverb (see *OLD* s.v.), 'aloft, above'. E's reading, *sublimi*, is only possible either (a) on the assumption that it is a rare form of the genitive (instead of the normal *sublimis*), meaning 'travel through the high expanses of the lofty heavens', or (b) with the alteration of *aetheris* to ablative *aethere*, '... the high expanses in the lofty heavens.' As Zwierlein (1986), 170-2, says, a genitive further defining 'high expanses' is desirable. (The line is in manuscript *E* alone, because *A* omits the end of the play, from line 1009.)

1027 bear witness ... are no gods: the gods are the last word of the play, as they were the first word: M. appeals to them at the beginning, Jason denies their presence or their existence at the end. For further discussion, see Introduction §4.10. **wherever you go**: word order suggests this should be taken with 'there are no gods' (rather than 'bear witness'). In that case we might have expected the verb to be in the subjunctive, because subordinate clauses in indirect speech have their verbs in that mood. But the rule about the mood is not absolute (see K-S 2.542-4; H-Sz 547-8).

Abbreviations

The names of ancient authors and their works are generally abbreviated according to the conventions of Liddell and Scott's *Greek Lexicon* for Greek authors, and of the *Oxford Latin Dictionary* for Latin authors down to the second century A.D.; for later Latin authors the abbreviations of the *Thesaurus Linguae Latinae* are generally followed. The titles of journals are abbreviated according to the conventions of *L'Année Philologique*.

ap.   in, quoted by (an author or work; Latin *apud*)

ca.   about, around (of dates or numbers; Latin *circa*)

cf.   compare (Latin *confer*)

CHCL   E. J. Kenney, W. V. Clausen, edd., *The Cambridge History of Classical Literature*, Vol. 2, *Latin Literature* (Cambridge, 1982)

comm.   commentary

DK   H. Diels, W. Kranz, *Die Fragmente der Vorsokratiker*^{6} (Zurich, Berlin, 1951-2)

fr., frr.   fragment, fragments

H-Sz   J. B. Hofmann, A. Szantyr, *Lateinische Syntax und Stilistik*^{2} (Munich, 1972)

ibid.   in the same place, passage (Latin *ibidem*)

IG   *Inscriptiones Graecae* (1873-)

K-S   R. Kühner, C. Stegmann, *Ausführliche Grammatik der lateinischen Sprache*, II, *Satzlehre* (repr. Darmstadt, 1976)

LIMC   *Lexicon Iconographicum Mythologiae Classicae* (Zürich, 1981-)

loc. cit.   the passage cited (Latin *locus citatus*)

M.   Medea

Neue Pauly   *Der Neue Pauly: Enzyklopädie der Antike* (Stuttgart, 1996-)

no., nos.   number, numbers

OCD^3 *Oxford Classical Dictionary*, 3rd edition, ed. S. Hornblower, A. Spawforth (Oxford, 1996)

OCT   Oxford Classical Text

OLD   *Oxford Latin Dictionary*, ed. P. G. W. Glare (Oxford, 1982)

p., pp.   page, pages

PGM   *Papyri Graecae Magicae*, 2nd edition, ed. K. Preisendanz (Stuttgart, 1973-4); for the English translation see Betz (1992)

RE   *Real-Encyclopädie der classischen Altertumswissenschaft*, ed. Pauly, Wissowa, and others (Stuttgart, 1894-)

S.   Seneca

sc.   that is, namely (Latin *scilicet*)

Schol.   Scholia, ancient commentaries (on the author and passage that follows)

Suppl. Hell.   *Supplementum Hellenisticum*, ed. H. Lloyd-Jones and P. J. Parsons (Berlin, New York, 1983)

s.v.   under the heading or word (in an encyclopaedia or dictionary; Latin *sub voce*)

TLL   *Thesaurus Linguae Latinae* (Leipzig, 1900-)

trans.   translated, translator, translation

Bibliography

1. Editions of all Seneca's plays
Leo, F. (Berlin, 1878)
Zwierlein, O. (Oxford Classical Text, Oxford, 1986; corrected reprint, 1986)
Chaumartin, F.-R. (Budé edition, Paris, 1996-9)

2. Editions of individual plays
Agamemnon: Tarrant, R. J. (Cambridge, 1976)
Hercules Furens: Fitch, J. G. (Ithaca, London, 1987)
Medea: Costa, C. D. N. (Oxford, 1973)
Phaedra: Boyle, A. J. (Leeds, 1987)
Phaedra: Coffey, M., Mayer, R. (Cambridge, 1990)
Phoenissae: Frank, M. (Leiden, New York, Cologne, 1995)
Thyestes: Tarrant, R. J. (Atlanta, 1985)
Troades: Fantham, E. (Princeton, 1982)
Troades: Boyle, A. J. (Leeds, 1994)

3. English translations of *Medea*
Miller, F. J. (Loeb Edition of all the tragedies, Latin text with English translation; London, Cambridge, MA, 1917)
Ahl, F. (*Medea*; Ithaca, London, 1986)
Slavitt, D. R. (all the tragedies; Baltimore, London, 1992, 1995)

4. Other Works
Arnott, P. D. (1962): *Greek Scenic Conventions in the Fifth Century B.C.* (Oxford)
Appel, G. (1909): *De Romanorum precationibus (Religionsgeschichtliche Versuche und Vorarbeiten*, 7.2, Giessen)
Arcellaschi, A. (1990): *Médée dans le théâtre latin, d'Ennius à Sénèque* (Rome, Paris)
Axelson, B. (1933): *Senecastudien: kritische Bemerkungen zu Senecas Naturales Quaestiones (Lunds Universitets Årsskrift*, N. F. Avd. 1, Bd. 29, Nr. 3, Lund)
Axelson, B. (1967): *Korruptenkult: Studien zur Textkritik der unechten Seneca-Tragödie Hercules Oetaeus* (Lund)
Bain, D. (1981): *Masters, Servants and Orders in Greek Tragedy: some aspects of dramatic technique and convention (Publications of the Faculty of Arts of the University of Manchester*, 26, Manchester)
Bartsch, S. (1994): *Actors in the Audience: Theatricality and Doublespeak from Nero to Hadrian* (Cambridge, MA, London)
Beacham, R. C. (1992): *The Roman Theatre and its Audience* (Cambridge, MA)
Beare, W. (1964): *The Roman Stage*[3] (London)
Bers, V. (1997): *Speech in Speech: Studies in Incorporated* Oratio Recta *in Attic Drama and Oratory* (Lanham)
Betz, H. D., ed. (1992): *The Greek Magical Papyri in Translation including the Demotic Spells* (2nd edition, Chicago, London)
Billerbeck, M. (1988): *Senecas Tragödien: sprachliche und stilistische Untersuchungen (Mnemosyne Supplement*, 105, Leiden)

Biondi, G. G. (1984): *Il* nefas *argonautico:* Mythos *e* logos *nella* Medea *di Seneca* (Bologna)
Blundell, S. (1986): *The Origins of Civilization in Greek and Roman Thought* (London, Sydney)
Bonner, S. F. (1949): *Roman Declamation in the Late Republic and Early Empire* (Liverpool)
Bourgery, A. (1922): *Sénèque prosateur* (Paris)
Boyle, A. J., ed. (1983): *Seneca Tragicus: Ramus Essays on Senecan Drama* (Berwick, Victoria)
Boyle, A. J. (1988): 'Senecan Tragedy: Twelve Propositions', in A. J. Boyle, ed., *The Imperial Muse: Ramus Essays on Roman Literature of the Empire, To Juvenal through Ovid* (Berwick, Victoria), 78-101
Boyle, A. J. (1997): *Tragic Seneca: an essay in the theatrical tradition* (London, New York)
Braginton, M. V. (1933): *The Supernatural in Seneca's Tragedies* (Diss. Yale)
Braund, S. M., Gill, C., edd. (1997): *The Passions in Roman Thought and Literature* (Cambridge)
Bremmer, J. N. (1997): 'Why did Medea kill her brother Apsyrtus?', in Clauss & Johnston (1997), 83-100
Brunschwig, J., Nussbaum, M. C., edd. (1993): *Passions and Perceptions: Studies in Hellenistic Philosophy of Mind; Proceedings of the Fifth Symposium Hellenisticum* (Cambridge)
Burnett, A. P. (1998): *Revenge in Attic and Later Tragedy* (Berkeley, Los Angeles, London)
Canter, H. V. (1925): *Rhetorical Elements in the Tragedies of Seneca* (*University of Illinois Studies in Language and Literature*, 10, Urbana)
Capponi, F. (1979): *Ornithologia Latina* (Genova)
Carlsson, G. (1926): *Die Überlieferung der Seneca-Tragödien: eine textkritische Untersuchung* (*Lunds Universitets Årsskrift*, N.F. Avd. 1, Bd. 21, Nr. 5, Lund)
Casson, L. (1971): *Ships and Seamanship in the Ancient World* (Princeton)
Chaumartin, F. R. (1995): 'Observations critiques sur quelques passages des tragédies de Sénèque', *RPh* 69, 95-109
Clauss, J. J., Johnston, S. I., edd. (1997): *Medea: Essays on Medea in Myth, Literature, Philosophy, and Art* (Princeton)
Corti, L. (1998): *The Myth of Medea and the Murder of Children* (Westport, London)
Costa, C. D. N., ed. (1974): *Seneca* (London, Boston)
Davis, P. J. (1993): *Shifting Song: The Chorus in Seneca's Tragedies* (*Altertumswissenschaftliche Texte und Studien*, 26, Hildesheim, Zürich, New York)
Delatte, A. (1961): *Herbarius: recherches sur le cérémonial usité chez les anciens pour la cueillette des simples et des plantes magiques* (*Mémoires de l'Académie Royale de Belgique, Classe des Lettres*, 54.4, Brussels)
Delz, J. (1989a): review of Zwierlein (1986) and Zwierlein's OCT, *Gnomon* 61, 501-7
Delz, J. (1989b): 'Textkritisches zu den Tragödien Senecas, dem Hercules Oetaeus und der Octavia', *MH* 46, 52-62
Dench, E. (1995): *From Barbarians to New Men: Greek, Roman and Modern Perceptions of Peoples of the Central Apennines* (Oxford)
Dillon, J. M. (1997): 'Medea among the Philosophers', in Clauss & Johnston (1997), 211-18
Dingel, J. (1974): *Seneca und die Dichtung* (Heidelberg)
Edgeworth, R. J. (1990): 'The Eloquent Ghost: Absyrtus in Seneca's Medea', *Classica et Mediaevalia* 41, 151-61

Edwards, C. (1994): 'Beware of imitations: theatre and the subversion of imperial identity', in Elsner and Masters (1994), 83-97

Eliot, T. S. (1951): 'Seneca in Elizabethan Translation', in *Selected Essays* (London), 65-105

Elsner, J., Masters, J., edd. (1994): *Reflections of Nero: culture, history and repesentation* (London)

Faraone, C. A., Obbink, D., edd. (1991): *Magika Hiera: Ancient Greek Magic and Religion* (New York, Oxford)

Fitch, J. G. (1981): 'Sense-pauses and relative dating in Seneca, Sophocles and Shakespeare', *AJPh* 102, 289-307

Fitch, J. G. (1987): *Seneca's Anapaests: Metre, Colometry, Text and Artistry in the Anapaests of Seneca's Tragedies* (Atlanta)

Fyfe, H. (1983): 'An Analysis of Seneca's *Medea*', in Boyle (1983), 77-93

Gager, J. G. (1992): *Curse Tablets and Binding Spells from the Ancient World* (New York, Oxford)

Gantz, T. (1993): *Early Greek Myth: a Guide to Literary and Artistic Sources* (Baltimore, London)

Gill, C. (1987): 'Two Monologues of Self-Division: Euripides, *Medea* 1021-80 and Seneca, *Medea* 893-977', in M. Whitby, P. Hardie, M. Whitby, edd., *Homo Viator: Classical Essays for John Bramble* (Bristol, Oak Park), 25-37

Gill, C. (1997): 'Passion as madness in Roman poetry', in Braund and Gill (1997), 213-41

Graf, F. (1997a): 'Medea, the Enchantress from Afar: Remarks on a Well-Known Myth', in Clauss & Johnston (1997), 21-43

Graf, F. (1997b): *Magic in the Ancient World* (Cambridge, MA, London)

Griffin, M. T. (1976): *Seneca: A Philosopher in Politics* (Oxford)

Hardie, P. R. (1986): *Virgil's Aeneid: Cosmos and Imperium* (Oxford)

Heinze, T. (1997): *P. Ovidius Naso, Der XII. Heroidenbrief: Medea an Jason; mit einer Beilage: die Fragmente der Tragödie Medea* (*Mnemosyne Supplement*, 170, Leiden, New York, Cologne)

Henderson, J. (1983): 'Poetic Technique and Rhetorical Amplification: Seneca *Medea* 579-669', in Boyle (1983), 94-113

Henry, D., Henry, E. (1985): *The Mask of Power: Seneca's Tragedies and Imperial Rome* (Warminster, Chicago)

Henry, D., Walker, B. (1967): 'Loss of Identity: "Medea superest"? A Study of Seneca's *Medea*', *CPh* 62, 169-81

Hershkowitz, D. (1998): *The Madness of Epic: Reading Insanity from Homer to Statius* (Oxford)

Hickson, F. V. (1993): *Roman Prayer Language: Livy and the Aeneid of Vergil* (*Beiträge zur Altertumskunde*, 30, Stuttgart)

Hillen, M. (1989): *Studien zur Dichtersprache Senecas: Abundanz, explikativer Ablativ, Hypallage* (Berlin, New York)

Hine, H. M. (1989): 'Medea versus the Chorus: Seneca *Medea* 1-115', *Mnemosyne* 42, 413-9

Housman, A. E. (1972): *The Classical Papers of A. E. Housman*, ed. J. Diggle, F. R. D. Goodyear (Cambridge)

Hunter, R. L. (1993): *The* Argonautica *of Apollonius: Literary Studies* (Cambridge)

Inwood, B. (1993): 'Seneca and psychological dualism', in Brunschwig & Nussbaum (1993), 150-83

Johnson, W.R. (1988): 'Medea nunc sum: The Close of Seneca's Version', in P. Pucci, ed., *Language and the Tragic Hero: Essays on Greek Tragedy in Honor of G.M. Kirkwood* (Atlanta), 85-102

Jones, C. P. (1991): 'Dinner Theater', in W. J. Slater, ed., *Dining in a Classical Context* (Ann Arbor), 185-98

Jones, C. P. (1993): 'Greek Drama in the Roman Empire', in Scodel (1993), 39-52

Kerrigan, J. (1996): *Revenge Tragedy: Aeschylus to Armageddon* (Oxford)

Kershaw, A. (1994): '*En* in the Senecan dramatic corpus', *HSCP* 96, 241-50

Krafft, P. (1994): 'Notizen zu Senecas Medea', *RhM* 137, 330-45

Latte, K. (1967): *Römische Religionsgeschichte* (Munich)

Lawall, G. (1979): 'Seneca's *Medea*: The Elusive Triumph of Civilisation', in G. W. Bowersock, W. Burkert, M. C. J. Putnam, edd., *Arktouros: Hellenic Studies presented to Bernard M. W. Knox on the occasion of his 65th birthday* (Berlin, New York), 419-26

Lefèvre, E. (1981): 'A Cult without God, or the Unfreedom of Freedom in Seneca tragicus', *CJ* 77, 31-6

Lefèvre, E. (1995): 'Götter, Schicksal und Handlungsfreiheit in Senecas Tragödien', in B. Kühnert, V. Riedel, R. Gordesiani, edd., *Prinzipat und Kultur im 1. und 2. Jahrhundert* (Bonn), 164-85

McDonald, M. (1997): 'Medea as Politician and Diva: Riding the Dragon into the Future', in Clauss & Johnston (1997), 297-323

McGinn, C. (1997): *Ethics, Evil, and Fiction* (Oxford)

Maltby, R. (1991): *A Lexicon of Ancient Latin Etymologies* (Arca, Classical and Medieval Texts, Papers and Monographs, 25, Leeds)

Markus, D., Schwendner, G. W. (1997): 'Seneca's *Medea* in Egypt (663-704)', *ZPE* 117, 73-80

Masters, J. (1992): *Poetry and Civil War in Lucan's* Bellum Civile (Cambridge)

Mayer, R. G. (1978): 'Seneca, *Medea* 723', *CQ* 28, 241-2

Mayer, R. G. (1990): 'Doctus Seneca', *Mnemosyne* 43, 395-407

Mazzoli, G. (1970): *Seneca e la poesia* (Milan)

Meyer, M., Mirecki, P. (1995): *Ancient Magic and Ritual Power* (*Religions in the Graeco-Roman World*, 129, Leiden, New York, Cologne)

Moreau, A. (1994): *Le Mythe de Jason et Médée: le va-nu-pied et la sorcière* (Paris)

Nikolaidis, A. G. (1985): 'Some Observations on Ovid's Lost *Medea*', *Latomus* 44, 383-7

Nisbet, R. G. M. (1990): 'The Dating of Seneca's Tragedies with Special Reference to *Thyestes*', *PLILS* 6 (Leeds), 95-114

Nussbaum, M. C. (1990): *Love's Knowledge: Essays on Philosophy and Literature* (New York, Oxford)

Nussbaum, M. C. (1993): 'Poetry and the passions: two Stoic views', in Brunschwig and Nussbaum (1993), 97-149

Nussbaum, M. C. (1994): 'Serpents in the Soul: A Reading of Seneca's *Medea*', in M. C. Nussbaum, *The Therapy of Desire: Theory and Practice in Hellenistic Ethics* (Princeton), 439-83

Nussbaum, M. C. (1997): 'Serpents in the Soul: A Reading of Seneca's *Medea*', in Clauss & Johnston (1997), 219-49 [an abridged version of Nussbaum (1994)]

Ohlander, S. (1989): *Dramatic Suspense in Euripides' and Seneca's* Medea (New York, Bern, Frankfurt am Main, Paris)

Otto, A. (1890): *Die Sprichwörter und sprichwörtlichen Redensarten der Römer* (Leipzig; reprinted Hildesheim, 1962)

Pratt, N. T. (1983): *Seneca's Drama* (Chapel Hill, London)

Primmer, A. (1976): 'Die Vergleiche in Senecas Dramen', *GB* 5, 211-32

Pulleyn, S. (1997): *Prayer in Greek Religion* (Oxford)

Putnam, M. C. J. (1995): 'Virgil's Tragic Future: Senecan Drama and the *Aeneid*', in *Virgil's Aeneid: Interpretation and Influence* (Chapel Hill, London), 246-285

Robin, D. (1993): 'Film Theory and the Gendered Voice in Seneca', in N. S. Rabinowitz, A. Richlin, edd., *Feminist Theory and the Classics* (New York, London), 102-21

Romm, J. S. (1992): *The Edges of the Earth in Ancient Thought: Geography, Exploration and Fiction* (Princeton)

Rosenmeyer, T. G. (1989): *Senecan Drama and Stoic Cosmology* (Berkeley, Los Angeles, London)

Rosenmeyer, T. G. (1993): 'Seneca's *Oedipus* and Performance: The Manto Scene', in Scodel (1993), 235-44

Rusten, J. S. (1982): *Dionysius Scytobrachion (Papyrologica Coloniensia*, 10, Opladen)

Sandbach, F. H. (1975): *The Stoics* (London)

Schiesaro, A. (1994): 'Seneca's *Thyestes* and the morality of tragic *furor*', in Elsner and Masters (1994), 196-210

Schiesaro, A. (1997): 'Passion, reason and knowledge in Seneca's tragedies', in Braund & Gill (1997), 89-111

Schmidt, P. L. (1990): 'Nero und das Theater', in J. Blänsdorf, ed., *Theater und Gesellschaft im Imperium Romanum* (Tübingen), 149-63

Scodel, R., ed. (1993): *Theater and Society in the Classical World* (Ann Arbor)

Segal, C. (1982): '*Nomen sacrum*: Medea and other names in Senecan tragedy', *Maia* 34, 241-6

Segal, C. (1986): *Language and Desire in Seneca's* Phaedra (Princeton)

Share, D. (1998): *Seneca in English* (Harmondsworth)

Sharples, R. W. (1996): *Stoics, Epicureans and Sceptics: an introduction to Hellenistic philosophy* (London, New York)

Summers, W. C. (1910): *Select Letters of Seneca* (London)

Sutton, D. F. (1986): *Seneca on the Stage (Mnemosyne Supplement*, 96, Leiden)

Syme, R. (1987): 'Exotic names, notably in Seneca's tragedies', *AClass* 30, 49-64 = *Roman Papers* VI (Oxford, 1991), 269-86

Tarrant, R. J. (1978): 'Senecan Drama and its Antecedents', *HSCP* 82, 213-63

Tarrant, R. J. (1995): 'Greek and Roman in Seneca's Tragedies', *HSCP* 97, 215-30

Tietze, V. (1987): 'The Psychology of Uncertainty in Senecan Tragedy', *ICS* 12, 135-41

Tietze Larson, V. (1994): *The Role of Description in Senecan Tragedy (Studien zur klassischen Philologie*, 84, Frankfurt am Main)

Treggiari, S. (1991): *Roman Marriage*: Iusti Coniuges *from the Time of Cicero to the Time of Ulpian* (Oxford)

Watt, W. S. (1989): 'Notes on Seneca, Tragedies', *HSCP* 92, 329-47

Watt, W. S. (1996): 'Notes on Seneca's Tragedies and the *Octavia*', *MH* 53, 248-55

West, D. (1969): *The Imagery and Poetry of Lucretius* (Edinburgh)

Wilkinson, L. P. (1963): *Golden Latin Artistry* (Cambridge)

Wills, J. (1996): *Repetition in Latin Poetry: Figures of Allusion* (Oxford, New York)

Wissowa, G. (1912): *Religion und Kultus der Römer* (Munich)

Woodcock, E. C. (1959): *A New Latin Syntax* (London)

Zwierlein, O. (1966): *Die Rezitationsdramen Senecas* (*Beiträge zur klassischen Philologie* 20, Meisenheim am Glan)

Zwierlein, O. (1969): review of C. Giardina, *L. Annaei Senecae tragoediae*, in *Gnomon* 41, 759-69

Zwierlein, O. (1976): 'Versinterpolationen und Korruptelen in den Tragödien Senecas', *WJA* 2, 181-217

Zwierlein, O. (1977): 'Weiteres zum Seneca Tragicus (I)', *WJA* 3, 149-77

Zwierlein, O. (1978a): 'Die Tragik in den Medea-Dramen', *Literaturwissenschaftliches Jahrbuch* 19, 27-63

Zwierlein, O. (1978b): 'Weiteres zum Seneca Tragicus (II)', *WJA* 4, 143-60

Zwierlein, O. (1986): *Kritischer Kommentar zu den Tragödien Senecas* (*Abh. Akad. Mainz, Geistes- und Sozialwiss. Klasse, Einzelveröffentlichung*, 6, Stuttgart)

Zwierlein, O. (1987): 'Seneca, Medea 616-621', *Hermes* 115, 382-4

Index